EARLY CHRISTIANS IN DISARRAY

CONTEMPORARY LDS PERSPECTIVES ON THE CHRISTIAN APOSTASY

EARLY CHRISTIANS IN DISARRAY

CONTEMPORARY LDS PERSPECTIVES ON THE CHRISTIAN APOSTASY

Edited by Noel B. Reynolds

FOUNDATION FOR ANCIENT RESEARCH AND MORMON STUDIES

BRIGHAM YOUNG UNIVERSITY PRESS
PROVO, UTAH

Noel B. Reynolds (PhD, Harvard University) is Executive Director of the Institute for the Study and Preservation of Ancient Religious Texts at Brigham Young University.

Cover design by Diane Schultz

Cover art: *Disputa (Disputation over the Blessed Sacrament),* by Raphael. Scala / Art Resource, NY.

Frontispiece: *Disputa (Disputation over the Blessed Sacrament),* by Raphael. Scala / Art Resource, NY; and *The School of Athens,* by Raphael. Scala / Art Resource, NY.

Brigham Young University Press

Foundation for Ancient Research and Mormon Studies (FARMS)
P.O. Box 7113
University Station
Provo, Utah 84602

10 09 08 07 06 05   10 9 8 7 6 5 4 3 2 1

Library of Congress Cataloging-in-Publication Data

Early Christians in disarray : contemporary LDS perspectives on the Great Apostasy / edited by Noel B. Reynolds.
       p. cm.
  Includes bibliographical references and index.
  ISBN: 0-934893-02-0
  ISBN-13: 978-0-934893-02-2
  1. Great Apostasy (Mormon doctrine) I. Reynolds, Noel B. II. Title.

BX8643.G74E25 2005
230'.9332—dc22

                                                          2005012230

Contents

Acknowledgments

As every author and editor knows, books have their own stories. This book began with an informal faculty reading group which began meeting on a biweekly basis four years ago to read and reread the texts that have survived from the earliest centuries of Christian writing and teaching. I was both surprised and thrilled to see how many of my colleagues at Brigham Young University shared my feeling that a rethinking of early Christianity from the Latter-day Saint perspective was overdue, and that by reading through those texts together, we might be able to see important influences and developments that would help us understand better what actually happened in those first centuries to produce a Christian tradition that was so different from the original church and teachings established by Jesus.

After two years, we knew we had both information and insights that we wanted to share with the larger LDS community, and we organized a private conference to present papers and to get critical feedback from a wider range of our colleagues at BYU. Encouraged by the enthusiastic reception of that first effort, we undertook to produce the separately authored chapters that comprise this volume. I wish to express my deep appreciation to my fellow faculty members at Brigham Young University who participated in this process and contributed their thinking and their encouragement in the development of the papers that eventually found their way into the book.

Good critics are essential to progress in academic research and thinking, and the present volume has been significantly improved as it has been filtered and refiltered through a series of critical reviews. I am most grateful to a number of colleagues and anonymous peer reviewers who helped us revise and strengthen our presentations and arguments. They have also helped me to see why some chapters I had thought earlier to include would not fit that well with the present collection.

Even after all that, this book would not be completed today had it not been for the strong support and editorial management that Alison Coutts and her editorial and production staff brought to bear on it. I am particularly indebted to Alison, who compensated repeatedly for my inattention due to other, more urgent projects. Don Brugger helped in the early stages as staff editor. Jacob Rawlins did the typesetting. Shirley Ricks and Geniel Empey assisted in copyediting. Paula Hicken managed the sourcechecking and proofreading, assisted by Linda Sheffield, Sandra Thorne, David Solorzano, and Jennifer Messick. As director of research for FARMS, Jerry Bradford managed the peer-review process. To all of these I express my sincere thanks.

Noel B. Reynolds
Provo, Utah
May 2005

About the Authors

Richard E. Bennett (PhD, Wayne State University) is Professor of Church History and Doctrine at Brigham Young University.

Adam Bentley is an undergraduate at Brigham Young University studying philosophy.

Barry R. Bickmore (PhD, Virginia Polytechnic Institute) is Assistant Professor, Department of Geology, Brigham Young University.

Ryan Christensen is a PhD candidate in philosophy at Stanford University.

Eric R. Dursteler (PhD, Brown University) is Assistant Professor of History at Brigham Young University.

James E. Faulconer (PhD, Pennsylvania State University) is Professor of Philosophy at Brigham Young University.

John Gee (PhD, Yale University) is William (Bill) Gay Associate Research Professor of Egyptology at the Institute for the Study and Preservation of Ancient Religious Texts at Brigham Young University.

Daniel W. Graham (PhD, University of Texas) is A. O. Smoot Professor of Philosophy at Brigham Young University.

David L. Paulsen (PhD, University of Michigan) is Professor of Philosophy at Brigham Young University.

Noel B. Reynolds (PhD, Harvard University) is Executive Director of the Institute for the Study and Preservation of Ancient Religious Texts, Director of the Foundation for Ancient Research and Mormon Studies, and Professor of Political Science at Brigham Young University.

Amber J. Seidel is an MA candidate in Family Sociology at Eastern Michigan University.

James L. Siebach (PhD, University of Texas) is Assistant Professor of Philosophy at Brigham Young University.

John W. Welch (JD, Duke University) is the Robert K. Thomas Professor of Law at the J. Reuben Clark Law School, Brigham Young University, and Editor in Chief of *BYU Studies*.

Introduction

What Went Wrong
for the Early Christians?

Noel B. Reynolds

When Joseph Smith emerged from the grove in 1820, he had learned first hand from Jesus Christ himself that the Christian churches of his day were all wrong and that he was forbidden to join any of them. "Their creeds were an abomination in his sight," their "professors were all corrupt," and they were teaching "for doctrines the commandments of men, having a form of godliness," but denying "the power thereof" (Joseph Smith—History 1:19).

From that first vision onward, Joseph Smith, and the Latter-day Saints who believed his testimony, understood clearly that the "restoration of all things" was made necessary by the loss of the church established by Jesus Christ during his life upon the earth. These first generation Latter-day Saints were impressed by the rampant confusion and contradictions in the Christian world of their day and tended to see that confusion as sufficient evidence of an apostasy. Israel was scattered and lost. The restoration was necessary to gather Israel and to re-establish the true teachings and church of Jesus Christ in the world.

By the end of the nineteenth century, LDS scholars and leaders had entered a new phase in their understanding of the Christian apostasy by drawing on the findings of modern historians in an attempt to expand their understanding. Protestant historians, who focused on the failings of the Catholic tradition, provided seemingly endless evidences of apostasy in Christian history, justifying the Protestant Reformation in the process. They pointed to the obvious wickedness of late medieval popes and priests. They pointed to the sales of indulgences, a tactic to raise money for the church by selling forgiveness of sins in this world to prevent punishment in the next. Guided by these eighteenth and nineteenth century Protestant historians, LDS writers pushed the apostasy farther back in time by focusing on the sins of medieval European Christianity.

Over the last century there has been an outpouring of newly discovered manuscripts, written during the first Christian centuries, that enables us to get a much clearer picture of what the Christian experience was like in those early times. And as our knowledge of these times grows, the apostasy is again pushed back further, even into the first century. Hugh Nibley was the first LDS author to enter this third phase. Relying on the New Testament, the writings of the apostolic fathers, and the pre-1960 secondary literature that deals with this period, Nibley produced a list of forty "variations on a theme," that theme being that the primitive church would not last long or had already passed away. In this paper prominently published in *Church History*, he presented his extensive collections of references from the early manuscripts to argue persuasively that the earliest Christian leaders did not expect the church to endure and that many of them came even to lament the passing of the original.[1]

---

1. See Hugh W. Nibley, "The Passing of the Primitive Church," in *When the Lights Went Out: Three Studies on the Ancient Apostasy* (Provo, UT: FARMS, 2001), 1–47.

Though published in an international journal, Nibley's paper was destined to provide a watershed for LDS scholars, focusing their interest in the apostasy on the later decades of the very first century, from which almost no writings have survived.

In the 1960s, LDS historian Richard L. Bushman observed that LDS students of the apostasy had become too dependent on Protestant and often anti-Catholic writers and challenged us to look at the apostasy afresh. He said that while noting the various changes to the doctrines and to the ordinances is helpful, it is not enough for it does not address the heart or causes of the apostasy, rather focusing on its effects.[2] It is as if you were to approach the aftermath of a car wreck. You can conclude from the debris, the twisted metal frame, the shattered glass, the injured and dead bodies, that an accident has occurred. But you would not say that the broken and scattered parts, the injured and dead bodies, and the twisted frame caused the accident. Although evidence of the accident, they are only its results. Likewise, all the doctrinal changes, the subsequent corruption, the centuries of religious strife and schism may constitute good evidence that an apostasy occurred but may not be the causes of that apostasy.

As James Faulconer explains in "The Concept of Apostasy in the New Testament," the Greek term *apostasia*, as used in the New Testament, means rebellion. It was often used in classical Greek to indicate a military rebellion or coup in which traditional bonds of loyalty to a particular leadership are rejected. Thus, *apostasia* specifically refers to internal problems. Joseph Smith and Brigham Young both recognized this when they said that no force on this earth could destroy the church

---

2. Richard L. Bushman, review of Milton V. Backman, *American Religions and the Rise of Mormonism*, in *BYU Studies* 7/2 (1966): 161–64.

from without.[3] In so doing they were echoing the principle articulated by the angel who appeared to young Alma saying: "Alma, arise and stand forth, for why persecutest thou the church of God? For the Lord hath said: *This is my church*, and I will establish it; and nothing shall overthrow it, save it is the transgression of my people" (Mosiah 27:13).[4]

In the Old Testament, apostasy or rebellion against God consisted specifically in the breaking of covenants that men had made with Jehovah. The Lord warned Moses, "'You are going to rest with your fathers, and these people will soon prostitute themselves to the foreign gods of the land they are entering. They will forsake me and *break the covenant* I made with them. On that day I will become angry with them and forsake them'" (Deuteronomy 31:16 NIV). The Greek word used here is *apostasion*, meaning "little rebellion" or "little apostasy," and specifically indicates divorce, or breaking of the marriage covenant. The Lord repeatedly likened his covenant with Israel to the covenant of marriage, and apostasy from that covenant was likened to adultery. We might expect, therefore, that the demise of the early Christian church was also a result of internal developments—breaking of covenants—and not something imposed from the outside.

LDS scholars today conclude increasingly that the root causes of the apostasy were the abandonment or breaking of

---

3. *Journal of Discourses*, 7:145.

4. Captain Moroni appears to invoke this principle when he tells Zerahemnah that "never will the Lord suffer that we shall be destroyed except we should fall into transgression and deny our faith" (Alma 44:4). He later explained to the whole people, "Surely God shall not suffer that we, who are despised because we take upon us the name of Christ, shall be trodden down and destroyed, until we bring it upon us by our own transgressions" (Alma 46:18).

sacred covenants by the Christians themselves. The more we learn about the first decades after the passing of Christ, the more we can see internal rebellion against God's covenants and against his authorized servants—much like the rebellions against Moses in the wilderness, or against Joseph Smith in Kirtland in 1836. The rebels were members of Christ's church, sometimes leaders, who sought for earthly power, glory, and even justification for their own sins. The restoration scriptures give us some key insights: The first section of the Doctrine and Covenants says, "they have strayed from mine ordinances, and *have broken mine everlasting covenant;* They seek not the Lord to establish his righteousness, but every man walketh in his own way, and after the image of his own god, whose image is in the likeness of the world, and whose substance is that of an idol, which waxeth old and shall perish in Babylon, even Babylon the great, which shall fall" (Doctrine and Covenants 1:15–16).

Thus the Lord describes this apostasy as breaking covenants and straying from his ordinances. The Lord likewise says concerning his disciples during his earthly ministry, "My disciples, in days of old, sought occasion against one another and forgave not one another in their hearts; and for this evil they were afflicted and sorely chastened" (D&C 64:8). Thus, we see that apostasy involves breaking God's covenants, turning from him to idols and things of this world, and not repenting of our sins, which is of course the most fundamental thing we have covenanted to do.

The scriptures of the restoration make it clear that ordinances such as baptism, priesthood ordination, and marriage are all based in covenants between men and God. Those receiving the ordinance have made certain covenants with God to turn away from their sins and obey his commandments, and God in turn makes promises to them. The ordinance provides a public witness of these covenants.[5] What we had not previously realized is that when the second-century Christians redefined these ordinances as *sacraments*, they had already abandoned their covenantal understanding of the ordinances. There were significant efforts by some key thinkers in the Protestant Reformation to restore those covenantal understandings to the ordinances, but these all failed. Reinvented as sacraments, the ordinances were understood in traditional Christianity as the means by which God could bless a person with an infusion of divine grace, through the mediation of the priest. Once the covenantal understanding was lost, it made sense to bless everyone possible. So how could traditional Christianity deny baptism to infants if the recipient no longer was expected to be making a meaningful covenant in connection with that ordinance? A similar analysis applies to Christian sacraments such as last rites. This helps us understand what Nephi meant when he explained the apostasy by saying that "many covenants of the Lord have they taken away" (1 Nephi 13:26).

This volume of essays reports new research by several LDS scholars in different fields which we hope will be useful in helping Latter-day Saints understand the apostasy better. The authors identify several common myths and misconceptions that Latter-day Saints have about the apostasy and help us understand the falling away from Christ's church more accurately and completely. They argue that the Christian apostasy occurred sometime during the first century—or before

---

5. This is summarized simply by Alma at the waters of Mormon when he asks the new converts, "what have you against being baptized in the name of the Lord, as a witness before him that ye have entered into a covenant with him, that ye will serve him and keep his commandments, that he may pour out his Spirit more abundantly upon you?" (Mosiah 18:10).

AD 100. Traditional Christianity, as we know it, was not established until the Nicene Council in AD 325, or during the fourth
century. This volume is designed to support and encourage
further systematic research on this topic. It is not designed to
be a comprehensive or final treatment of any of these issues.
The goals of the authors and editor will be achieved if Latter-
day Saints find its contents helpful for understanding this important topic and if it provokes some of them to pursue these
and related questions with further research.

Myth #1: The apostasy happened because of outside persecution.

Both the Bible and the writings of early Christians extensively document internal divisions that were a major problem
within the first-century church. Paul's first epistle to the church
in Corinth (AD 55) lists several schismatic developments in the
Corinthian branch: "For it hath been declared unto me of you,
my brethren, by them which are of the house of Chloe, that
there are contentions among you. Now this I say, that every one
of you saith, I am of Paul; and I of Apollos; and I of Cephas;
and I of Christ. Is Christ divided? was Paul crucified for you?
or were ye baptized in the name of Paul?" (1 Corinthians
1:11–13). Paul marvels at how quickly the Galatian Saints
have "turned from the gospel" (Galatians 1:6–8). Paul's second epistle to the church in Corinth mentions false apostles
whom Paul describes as "ministers" of Satan (2 Corinthians
11:13–15). In his second epistle to Timothy (AD 65), Paul la-
ments that all Asia is "turned away" (2 Timothy 1:15). In his
letter to Gaius, John reports that in one unnamed branch of
the church, the leader Diotrophes, would have nothing to do
with John and his brethren. Not only did this local leader refuse to accept John's emissaries, but he opposed those who did

want to accept them and puts them "out of the church" (3 John 1:9–10). In the book of Revelation, John writes inspired letters to seven of the churches in Asia, calling them to repentance for the most egregious of sins (Revelation 2–3). Any stake president or bishop receiving one of these letters today would know that he and his members were way out of line and probably scheduled for church disciplinary action.

Virtually every epistle in the New Testament bears witness to divisions and rebellions in the church, though like most Christians, Latter-day Saints do not usually read the text with that in mind. We tend to see these as calls to repentance and assume that they were probably effective. But should we assume that they were effective? The apparent collapse of the church in the first century suggests that in the final analysis, they were not. When the second century opens, we are confronted with clear evidence of a growing variety of competing versions of Christianity, and the original structure of priesthood leadership has disappeared. All that remain are city leaders, still *known* as bishops, but *not called or supported* by a central structure under the direction of prophets or apostles. In his letters to the churches in Greece, Clement, bishop of Rome during the last few years of the first century, urged the saints to repent of their jealousies and divisiveness. Ignatius, a bishop in Antioch who was martyred around AD 115, warned of many of the same things.

These kinds of divisions and internal problems are not unknown to Latter-day Saints. Think of the Kirtland period and the rampant and recurring apostasy and opposition to Joseph Smith's leadership. In many ways, the early Christian church seems never to have transcended its "Kirtland period." The Latter-day restoration did transcend these early apostasies by the strength of its prophet and the loyal apostles that stood with him before and after his death. In early June of 2004, President Gordon B. Hinckley was in England and reminded his audience there how the restoration had been in deep trouble in Kirtland, and then again in Nauvoo. He then explained how the flood of faithful new converts from England was crucial in helping the church to survive those crises.[6] Since those difficult days, the church has benefited from higher and higher levels of unity and loyalty among its members, so that today we can hardly understand the challenges of internal strife that characterized much of our early church history.

But even today, new branches of the church with inexperienced members and leaders sometimes appear to recapitulate these earlier problems. It is not that unusual in that immature stage of development to see petty jealousies, small offenses, position seeking, and violation of the commandments threatening to wreck the church from within. But in spite of this, the unity and faithfulness of the church in this last dispensation has continued to grow. As the Prophet Joseph said, "No unhallowed hand can stop the work from progressing; persecutions may rage, mobs may combine, armies may assemble, calumny may defame, but the truth of God will go forth boldly, nobly, and independent, till it has penetrated every continent, visited every clime, swept every country, and sounded in every ear, till the purposes of God shall be accomplished, and the Great Jehovah shall say the work is done."[7] While Joseph recognized that all previous dispensations of the gospel had ended in apostasy, he had learned through revelations and visions that this last dispensation would succeed and would prepare a people

---

6. "Little Chapel's Keys Returned to Church" *LDS Church News,* 5 June 2004, 3.

7. *History of the Church,* 4:540.

who could welcome the Savior at his second coming and establish the foundation of his millennial reign.

Myth 2: The apostasy *was caused by* the hellenization of Christianity or the incorporation of Greek philosophy and culture into the teachings of the early church.

The world in which Jesus established his church was full of
pagan superstitions and excesses. But the educated and ruling
classes of the Roman empire—who had been thoroughly hellenized over the preceding few centuries—put their trust in the
teachings of the Greek philosophers who discouraged religious
superstition and challenged men to become virtuous by living
up to universally recognized standards of good human conduct. While the Christians found much that was admirable in
that stance, they could not accept the philosophers' rejection of
the gods or their claims to be able to make men good through
their own self-discipline alone. The Christians recognized that
without the atonement of Jesus Christ and the guiding and purifying effect of the Spirit in their lives, men could not become
truly good. Paul warned the saints: "See to it that no one takes
you captive through hollow and deceptive philosophy, which
depends on human tradition and the basic principles of this
world rather than on Christ" (Colossians 2:8, NIV). This, however, is the only explicit reference to philosophy in the New
Testament, suggesting that it was far from being Paul's major
concern with the first-century saints.

The main mistake in assuming that Greek philosophy was
a principal *cause* of the apostasy is that the chronology is off
by a whole century. The first Christian writer to know and use
philosophy extensively was Justin Martyr, who wrote in the
second quarter of the second century, by which time the apostles were long dead, the priesthood gone, and the ordinances

transformed. The apostasy was already in full swing. And even this first Christian philosopher was not encouraging the adoption of philosophical teachings in the church. Rather, he used his philosophical training principally to defend Christians before the ruling classes of Rome. He pointed out to them the virtues of Christians in terms that made them sound a lot like the Stoics and the Epicureans and that definitely distinguished Christian worship from the superstitious and orgiastic practices of the popular religions of the day.

At the end of the second and during the third century, however, in the city of Alexandria, Egypt, a new way of using Greek philosophy arose. Men like Clement of Alexandria, his star pupil Origen, and later Athanasius began to use elements of Greek philosophy to articulate and develop Christian doctrine. Clement wrote "Perchance, too, philosophy was given to the Greeks directly and primarily, till the Lord should call the Greeks. For this was a schoolmaster to bring 'the Hellenic mind,' as the [law of Moses brought] the Hebrews, 'to Christ.'"[8] Philosophy and reason were not deemed superior to revelation by Clement and Origen, but they did provide another fully reliable source of truth. For them, the Greek philosophical tradition was a rich resource for all who wanted to defend, establish, or develop Christian doctrine. The result of such efforts over the following centuries was a new Christianity that had been thoroughly hellenized.

Not all third-century Christians were comfortable with the fast-moving shift to philosophical discourse in Christian dialogue. Clement's contemporary Tertullian challenged this

---

8. Clement, *Miscellanies* 1.5 (alluding to Galatians 3:24), in *The Ante-Nicene Fathers* (hereafter *ANF*), ed. Alexander Roberts and James Donaldson (1885; reprint, Peabody MA: Hendrickson, 1994), 2:305.

new trend and asked, "What indeed has Athens to do with Jerusalem? What concord is there between the Academy and the Church? what between heretics and Christians . . . ? Away with all attempts to produce a mottled Christianity of Stoic, Platonic, and dialectic composition!"[9] Tertullian and some other writers and leaders saw the essential differences and antipathy between the Greek rhetorical style that seeks to uncover absolute, unchanging truths about the universe, and the Judaic-Christian tradition that believes in revelation and finds the grounds of truth and right in historical events of great religious significance.

But, already in apostasy, the third-century Christians were in deep trouble. Official persecutions were increasing. They were plagued by a rapidly multiplying diversity of Christian doctrines and sects—each claiming to be the true heir of Christ and the apostles. There was no central leadership to help them distinguish between the true and the false. They needed some universal standard and authority to which they could agree and by which they could divide true and false Christianity—the orthodox from the heretical. Threatened with the utter demise of Christianity, they turned to the well established and widely admired principles of Greek philosophy for a solution. Even Protestant historians, who used to criticize the hellenization of the early churches, now recognize that the Christian movement would have dwindled into an insignificant folk religion without the infusion of Greek thought.[10] Soon, the third-century Christian thinkers came to share Clement's appreciation for the work of Plato and his successors. They even went so far

---

9. Tertullian, *Prescription Against Heretics*, 7 (ANF 3:246).

10. Roger E. Olson, *The Story of Christian Theology: Twenty Centuries of Tradition and Reform* (Downers Grove, IL: InterVarsity, 1999), 39.

as to claim, echoing Origen, that God had sent the Greeks to prepare the systems of thought that would bring Christianity to its divinely intended completion. The fullness of Christian doctrine and understanding could only occur as the teachings of Christ and the apostles were united with the teachings of Plato and the other Greek philosophers. The Nicene Council of AD 325 and other later councils officially incorporated this approach and issued creeds that have been used to distinguish the orthodox from the heretical from that day to this. And this explains why the Christian world today is not willing to see the Latter-day Saints—or any other believers in Christ who refuse to accept the creeds of the councils—as Christians.

The most aggressive developments of Christian thought in the Greek mold during the fourth century took place in Asia Minor and the churches there. The great Cappadocian theologians, Basil of Caesarea, Gregory of Nyssa, and Gregory of Nazianzus, used their philosophical training—received to a significant extent in the schools of Athens—to refine and elaborate the meaning of the Nicene Creed and to formulate the orthodox Christian teaching that produced the final defeat of Arianism at the Council of Constantinople in AD 381. While many Christian writers have insisted that this newly established "orthodox theology" was always implicit in Christian teaching, more recent scholars are more inclined to acknowledge that it was an essential, if late invention that did succeed in pulling the splintered Christian movement together.

This new use of philosophy was accompanied by a subtle shift in Christian thinking. Consider the first-century declarations of John and Peter: "That which we have seen and heard declare we unto you, that ye also may have fellowship with us: and truly our fellowship is with the Father, and with his Son Jesus Christ" (1 John 1:3); "And we are witnesses of all things which he did both in the land of the Jews, and in Jerusalem; whom they slew and hanged on a tree: Him God raised up the third day, and shewed him openly; Not to all the people, but unto witnesses chosen before of God, even to us, who did eat and drink with him after he rose from the dead" (Acts 10:39–41).

These are declarations of fact, knowledge, and eye-witness accounts. They say that they have seen and heard, and they bear testimony. Compare these to the philosophical declarations that the church produced during the fifth century. The Athanasian creed reflects Augustine's theology and focuses on the definition of the nature of God: "the Son of God, is God and man; God, of the substance of the Father, begotten before the worlds; and man of the substance of his mother, born in the world; perfect God and perfect man, of a rational soul and human flesh subsisting."[11] Though the incorporation of Greek philosophy into Christianity was not an original cause of the apostasy, the apostate Christian churches generally reached out to embrace philosophy as a means of bringing common standards and rationality to Christian belief. It is widely recognized today by Christian historians that the apostate Christian churches saved the Christian tradition by so doing. But the Christian tradition that resulted was far different than the one established by Jesus Christ and his apostles in the first century. And this fact has also been repeatedly recognized by Christian scholars.[12]

---

11. "The Athanasian Creed," in Philip Schaff, *The Creeds of the Greek and Latin Churches* (New York: Harper, 1919), 2:68–69.

12. See, for example, David W. Bercot, *Will the Real Heretics Please Stand Up: A New Look at Today's Evangelical Church in the Light of Early Christianity*, 3rd ed. (Henderson, TX: Scroll, 1999), in which an evangelical Protestant lawyer reports years of research in the earliest Christian writings and bemoans how much Christian belief and practice have changed.

The essential partnership of Greek philosophy and the Christian church has been recognized and even celebrated in many ways. One of the most striking is the Signature Room in the Vatican Museum which boasts one of the most important works of Raphael and was painted in 1510–1511. The entire surface of the large room is covered with murals. The two largest murals face one another. One is the "Disputation over the Most Holy Sacrament" which depicts the Catholic Church on earth, the saints in heaven, the holy family, and the godhead— all focused on an empty sacrament table, with the disputants ranged on each end. The other is the "School of Athens," which depicts Plato and Aristotle in deep conversation in a classical peripatetic situation. Also portrayed are a number of other famous philosophers and scientists from ancient times engaged in conversations or reflections and distributed on the steps and porches. Raphael's juxtaposition of these sensational murals has evoked considerable scholarly commentary, but few viewers need help to recognize the endorsement of both revelation and reason as avenues to truth and the inclusion of the Hellenistic philosophy in the larger Christian tradition (see frontispiece).

Myth 3: The Roman Catholic Church specifically is the great and abominable church spoken of in Nephi's vision.

Given the dependence of the early LDS writers on Protestant historians, who were themselves often anti-Catholic in orientation, it is not surprising that Latter-day Saints tended to interpret Nephi's vision in this way.[13] The Protestant focus on the corruption in medieval Christianity naturally suggested

---

13. See the report of the vision in 1 Nephi 13:14–29; 14:3–17 and Nephi's elaborations and interpretations of the vision in 1 Nephi 22:13–15, 22–23; 2 Nephi 26:21–22; 28:3–32; 30:1–2.

the Catholic Church as the "church of the devil" described by Nephi in his vision. But if we look more closely at these scriptures, we will see that the church of the devil arose centuries before the Catholic Church was established with Rome as its acknowledged head, and we will see that it includes much more than just one such organization. There is much more to it.

In the vision, Nephi saw that the great and abominable church was formed in the first century when the record of the Jews went forth from the Jews to the Gentiles (1 Nephi 13:25–26), and that it was founded in opposition to the Church of God—which tells us that the two existed simultaneously (1 Nephi 13:5). Nephi saw further that the devil's church took away many parts of the gospel, including the covenants, as verse 26 tells us, and later took away many precious things out of the Bible (v. 28). In the first century, the Christian scriptures consisted of the Old Testament, available principally in a Greek translation called the Septuagint. And there was no canonical version of these pre-Christian texts until after the destruction of Jerusalem by the Romans in AD 70. A few years ago I had a personal experience that confirmed Nephi's account in a dramatic way. I was a guest of the director of the Vatican Library in Rome, and he brought out their fourth century copy of the complete Greek Bible for me to see—*Codex Vaticanus B*. The first page we looked at had numerous erasures, additions, and changes written right on the page in different inks and different hands I asked, pointing to some of these, "What is that?" The reply: "Oh, that's where they made corrections." Over the last two decades, many New Testament scholars have argued convincingly that the final versions of the gospels, and the epistles that were eventually canonized, took shape during a long period in which they were modified as necessary to support the emerging theological orthodoxy among the leaders of the Christian churches.[14] Nor did this process of change go unnoticed in those early centuries. In "The Corruption of Scripture in Early Christianity," John Gee cites convincing evidence from the early Christian writings that they believed the scriptures had been altered or twisted in many ways. Paul warned the Thessalonians that some people might try to stir them up with forged apostolic epistles. Peter said that many in his day were already "wresting" the scriptures, or distorting their true meaning (2 Peter 3:15–16). Ignatius of Antioch, a bishop who was martyred around AD 110, said that he could not write down all of the teachings of the apostles because they were too sacred. Justin Martyr, whom we mentioned before, accused Jewish leaders of deliberately removing passages from the Old Testament. During the second century, many bishops and writers in the church accused "heretics" of changing the scriptures. Tertullian of Carthage claimed that Marcion, a church leader in what is now Turkey, deliberately cut out pieces of the scriptures that he did not like, and Clement of Alexandria accused some people of rewriting parts of the Gospels. By the third century, the accusations of changes in the scriptures die down. However, we have virtually no texts predating the third century by which to measure the changes. Less than one percent of the surviving New Testament fragments can be dated before the third century, and those are mere fragments. We also have other writings, letters primarily, from the second century which quote

---

14. See, e.g., Bart D. Ehrman, *The Orthodox Corruption of Scripture: The Effect of Early Christological Controversies on the Text of the New Testament* (New York: Oxford University Press, 1993), and Ehrman, *Lost Scriptures: Books That Did Not Make It into the New Testament* (New York: Oxford University Press, 2003).

scriptures, and these quotations frequently differ from what we have in the New Testament today.

Nephi lists several identifying features of the church of the devil (1 Nephi 13:4–9). He says they will torture and slay the saints (v. 5). They will bind down the people with yokes of iron (v. 5), which recalls Joseph Smith's comparison of creeds to iron yokes (D&C 123:7–8). Nephi also tells us that this church was founded by the devil, followed materialistic pursuits, and sought worldly praise. He further tells us that there are only two churches, the church of God, and the church of the devil, which is the great and abominable church. It seems, then, that Nephi did not have a specific ecclesiastical organization in mind, but rather he was describing all organizations (for that is the original meaning of the word church, or *ekklesia*, in Greek) that sought worldly rewards and opposed the saints of God. It almost seems like the central, energizing, and coordinating headquarters of this church is in some invisible world.

In summing up the constituents of this evil church, Nephi later says, "For the time speedily shall come that all churches which are built up to get gain, and all those who are built up to get power over the flesh, and those who are built up to become popular in the eyes of the world, and those who seek the lusts of the flesh and the things of the world, and to do all manner of iniquity; yea, in fine, all those who belong to the kingdom of the devil are they who need fear, and tremble, and quake; they are those who must be brought low in the dust; they are those who must be consumed as stubble; and this is according to the words of the prophet" (1 Nephi 22:23). For notwithstanding the power of the devil and his church to blind the eyes and harden the hearts of the children of men through temptations and by taking away precious parts of the scriptures and the covenants (see 1 Nephi 12:17; 13:27), the Lord's work will triumph in the last days as he pours out his wrath on the great and abominable church (1 Nephi 14:7–15) and as he sends down protecting power like fire from heaven on his saints wherever they might be scattered and threatened in the nations of the earth (1 Nephi 14:14, 17). Finally, Jacob quotes the Lord God in making it perfectly clear that it is the conduct of individuals that makes them members of the church of the devil. "Wherefore, he that fighteth against Zion, both Jew and Gentile, both bond and free, both male and female, shall perish; for they are they who are the whore of all the earth; for they who are not for me are against me, saith our God" (2 Nephi 10:16).

Furthermore, as Nephi tells us later, many people throughout the ages preceding the restoration and the second coming would be true, humble followers of Christ who erred only because of their leaders (2 Nephi 28:14). We know further that the Spirit continued to strive with men and that some men were inspired. Nephi said of Columbus that he was inspired by God. Joseph Smith, when he read Foxe's *Book of the Martyrs* which records all those who have died for the faith from the early apostles to the Protestant movements, said that many of these people were true disciples who would receive salvation. President John Taylor said in 1873, "There were men in those dark ages who could commune with God, and who, by the power of faith, could draw aside the curtain of eternity and gaze upon the invisible world . . . have the ministering of angels, and unfold the future destinies of the world."[15] But none of these were called to restore Christ's church. That would wait until 1820. As the Prophet Joseph Smith revealed in these latter days, all those who died without knowing the gospel, who would have embraced it and lived it had they had the chance, will be heirs of the celestial kingdom (D&C 137:7).

---

15. *Journal of Discourses,* 16:197.

Summary of the Contents of This Book

This introductory chapter provides an overview of the topic as it has developed in recent years and summaries of the eight main chapters. These chapters represent a variety of different disciplinary approaches and even different interpretations of the apostasy itself. Some focus on scripture, others on recent scholarship. They all represent new thinking on Christian apostasy.

Part One of the volume introduces the conceptions of Christian apostasy that have dominated the writings of Latter-day Saints. Richard Bennett and Amber Seidel have surveyed the wide range of early Mormon preaching and missionary publications to ascertain how the Christian apostasy was understood and discussed in the first years of the restoration. While Joseph Smith's accounts of his first vision clearly indicate that he was personally concerned about the confusing and conflicting claims of the Protestant churches in his area, he was not prepared for the sweeping revelation that none of them was the true church of Christ. Like Joseph, the early members understood the apostasy largely in terms of the evident confusions and strife in the contemporary Christian world of their own immediate experience. But they also saw the scattering of Israel as evidence of God's rejection of his covenant peoples for their various apostasies, and the restoration, and the gathering it would inspire, as the divine remedy for it. The focus on the loss of priesthood authority and lost doctrines would develop much later.

Eric Dursteler's chapter examines the roots of the conceptions of the Christian apostasy accepted in the LDS community over the last century. He explains how the formative writings of B. H. Roberts, James E. Talmage, and Joseph Fielding Smith derived directly from the scholarship of nineteenth-century Protestant historians and eighteenth-century anti-clerical writings. Roberts set the pattern while drawing heavily on Johann Mosheim, who drew in turn on Swiss historian Jacob Burckhardt and his English counterpart, John Addington. This reliance on pro-Enlightenment and pro-Protestant writers produced a heavy emphasis in LDS accounts of the apostasy on the late medieval corruption of the Catholic Church—describing it as a time of severe spiritual darkness and intellectual and cultural backwardness. Dursteler then discusses the lack of support for this emphasis and portrayal in both the scriptures and in more recent academic research, thus signaling the need for twenty-first century Latter-day Saints to rethink the apostasy and its origins.

John Welch examines selected restoration scriptures as a means of reconstructing key elements of the prophetic views of the apostasy, providing a guide to our own further research on this topic. He finds in D&C 64:8 frequently overlooked evidence that the Christian apostasy may have occurred quite early due to unresolved conflicts between the disciples. His detailed analysis of 1 Nephi 13 shows that Jewish persecution of the disciples would contribute to their demise. He further identifies scriptural stages by which the great and abominable church would remove key doctrines and covenants and then alter the scriptures. Welch then turns his principal attention to the parable of the wheat and tares in D&C 86 as a prophecy of the apostasy. Welch concludes that this version of the parable, as revealed to Joseph Smith, is probably the original. In contrast with the softer versions in Matthew 13:24–30 and elsewhere, D&C 86 leaves no room to believe the early church would survive. Rather, it would be choked out by the tares and driven into the wilderness until there would be a new planting before the final harvest. Through all these scriptures, Welch notes, however, that in concord with 1 Nephi 13, there is no reason to conclude that there would be no saints, or righteous followers of Christ during the period of apostasy—only that the church as Christ's appointed institution would be lost.

James Faulconer discusses what the New Testament writers thought about the apostasy and what was meant by the term *apostasy* and related terminology during New Testament times. He argues that apostasy meant rebellion and was not the same as heresy or sin. Most specifically, apostasy—at least for the writers of the New Testament and their contemporaries—was the rejection of temple and priesthood. Apostasy arises from what one does or does not do, rather than what one believes or teaches. The concern with orthodoxy and heterodoxy comes only later, and thus is a symptom of the apostasy.

In Part Two, five scholars focus their investigations on different important features of apostate teachings or practices in the early Christian centuries. John Gee documents the evidence that many plain and precious things were taken away from the scriptures, as Nephi had foreseen (1 Nephi 13:28). While a great deal of scholarly attention has been focused in recent decades on the ways in which the New Testament writings were affected by theological politics in the third and fourth centuries,[16] as the Christian canon gradually took shape, Gee focuses on the second century to document the extensive changing of the inspired writings that was already in process. He points first to the widely repeated claims that Christians have made significant changes to those writings. And he also points out how many of the quotations from these writings in the first and second centuries do not match up with the New Testament that emerged a century later. Further, there are no surviving copies of their writings about scripture that can be

---

16. See, e.g., Ehrman, *Orthodox Corruption of Scripture*.

dated before the third century. The earlier copies, and any differences they might have preserved, have mostly disappeared.

Latter-day Saints will find in their own history numerous incidents that might illuminate the processes by which the inspired writings can be changed. Joseph Smith once publicly accused Oliver Cowdery of trying to revise his revelations.[17] James V. Strang forged documents justifying him in his quest for power in the church.[18] John C. Bennett and others, including modern polygamists, have pretended revelations to justify their conduct, including claimed letters of authorization from John Taylor or Wilford Woodruff.[19] More recently, Mark Hofmann forged many documents, including one that justified Joseph Smith III's claims to lead the church, which was then used extensively by the Reorganized Church of Jesus Christ of Latter Day Saints (now known as the Community of Christ). And even with the best of intentions, the scribes, copyists, and editors of the Book of Mormon over the last 173 years have both with and without intention introduced a significant number of changes into that text, many of which make a difference in how it would be translated into another language.[20]

Daniel Graham and James Siebach address the widespread misunderstanding that the apostasy was caused by the incorporation of Hellenistic (Greek) thought into the Christian church. Like Reynolds (see below), they see the hellenization of Christianity as a result of the apostasy, and not its cause. Their detailed account of the rise of Christian philosophical

---

17. *History of the Church,* 1:105.

18. See *Comprehensive History of the Church,* 2:429–30; *History of the Church,* 7:574.

19. See *History of the Church,* 5:42.

20. See Royal Skousen, *Analysis of Textual Variants of the Book of Mormon* (Provo, UT: FARMS, 2004).

thought shows in detail that it did not become a force in the church until the third century, at least a hundred years after the original church had splintered into dozens of different movements with widely differing teachings and organizations, none of which bore the unadulterated stamp of the original. In the process, these authors provide us with a valuable road map for understanding the Hellenistic transformations of Christianity in its first five centuries.

Joseph Smith's teaching that God has a body contradicts the teachings of all Christian churches today. David Paulsen draws from three of his previously published articles to show that in the first and second Christian centuries, both Jews and Christians generally believed that God was embodied. Philo was a lone exception in the Jewish community in Alexandria, as he promoted a Platonized Judaism. It was not until the end of the second century that Clement of Alexandria and his student Origen promoted the idea of an incorporeal God to the Christian community. Paulsen documents his conclusions by extensive quotations from early writers who candidly noted the common Jewish and Christian belief in an embodied God. Even as late as the fifth century, Augustine explained his initial revulsion toward Christianity as a reaction to this "vulgar" view. His conversion became possible when hellenized Christians helped him see how the emerging Christian theology supported the idea of an incorporeal deity.

As part of an ongoing interest in covenant, Noel Reynolds examines the second-century transformation of covenant-based ordinances into Christian sacraments as a principle cause of the apostasy, and thereby illuminates Nephi's statement that many of the covenants were taken away (1 Nephi 13:26). Once the emphasis on history as the source of religious truth lost its relevance (covenants take place in time and space and shape the moral world of all participants thereafter), the

Christians turned to Greek philosophy, which derived moral and intellectual structure from rational reflections on nature. Like the Jews and early Christians, Mormons take the historical approach of a covenant people. As Christianity abandoned this traditional emphasis on covenant, it needed stable grounding and imported Greek thought and culture by developing a new reliance on philosophical theology.

In addition to these chapters, we have included four appendixes that will provide a variety of reference materials for readers who may wish to pursue their study of the apostasy further. In the first appendix, Barry Bickmore lists and describes many of the Christian writers and writings that are important for an understanding of the apostasy. Adam Bentley assisted Bickmore in assembling the second appendix, which presents a concise survey of the Christian councils that shaped Christian teachings and practice over the centuries. This is followed in a third appendix with the evidences for apostasy in the first Christian decades that are found in the New Testament itself, as identified and explained by Reynolds. Finally Ryan Christensen provides us with a bibliographical essay that provides both descriptions and brief critiques of significant Latter-day Saint writings on the apostasy.

These chapters take a variety of different approaches. All, however, are committed to the reality of the apostasy and to its importance as a subject. The great apostasy was a profoundly formative event in sacred history, and an anomaly. When the Lord did not replace the apostles in ancient Palestine, he broke the pattern he had been following for thousands of years. Every previous dispensation came on the heels of one that preceded it, and faithful remnants from the last dispensation were always still alive when the new dispensation began. When Enoch was called as a prophet, Adam was still alive; when Abraham was called, Melchizedek was still alive; when Moses was called,

Jethro was still alive. Even though—or because—the world was in apostasy, the Lord revealed his gospel and renewed his means of salvation for a new generation of his children. Not so when the church rejected his apostles. The Lord removed the apostles from among them, severed the lines of revelation, and the purity of worship and doctrine did not long remain. Israel was finally and conclusively cut off from the Lord and scattered to the nations. But even this tragic development can be seen in retrospect as the means by which the Lord prepared the Gentile nations for their turn to be first.

This, then, is the great difference between the first Christian apostasy and the many other apostasies—it did not consist only in widespread rejection of God, but was accompanied by the disastrous loss of priesthood authority. Why was there an apostasy? How did it come about? What does it mean? What is the significance of new discoveries on the study of the apostasy? These are among the questions discussed in this book, and which we hope will be given new life with these essays.

Just as this book is not an official publication of The Church of Jesus Christ of Latter-day Saints, the explanations and explorations it contains are not intended to be official or final in any way. Some of the chapters included in this volume present snapshots of ongoing research. Others identify and recommend questions that will require further examination. The contents have generally been improved by dialogue among the various authors and other colleagues, and it is my hope that this volume will stimulate and support a new beginning to a much broader conversation.

Conclusion

The confusion and competition that Joseph Smith and his contemporaries observed in the Christian world continues to this day. A few years ago, spokesmen from a broad range of Christian churches met to lament this scandal of a divided Christian world and to assess the continuing barriers to unity. They recognized that the half-century of ecumenical efforts inspired by the organization of the World Council of Churches in 1948 and earlier reunification movements had failed, deteriorating into little more than local interfaith discussion groups and joint humanitarian efforts, most of which had been co-opted by the liberal wings of their churches. The mergers that have occurred in recent decades have been motivated more by declining membership and financial weakness than from reconciliations of differences in doctrines or practices. And we appear today to be on the brink of a new rash of divisions as mainline Protestant churches fail to resolve internal differences about the ordination of women or the status of homosexuals.

What is striking in this discussion, for a Latter-day Saint looking on, is the widespread agreement among conservative Christians of all stripes on the following two propositions: (1) there has long been a widespread apostasy from the true Christianity, and (2) the true church cannot be divided up; its doctrines are not disposable; and compromise between warring factions cannot lead to truth. Where they all disagree with each other is over the specific forms of apostasy, and over which churches are apostate, and which are not. The prospects of a united Christian world are so faint that one symposium participant mused, we will not likely make any progress until God sends us a solution from heaven. And then he noted ironically, if such divine aid were to come, it might be in just as unlikely and unrecognizable a form as a babe being born in a manger.[21]

---

21. See Robert P. George, "The Divisions We Must Sustain: Cultural Division and Christian Unity," in *Touchstone: A Journal of Mere Christianity* (July/August 2003): 51.

Studying the apostasy can help Latter-day Saints understand and appreciate the restoration even more. But there is also a lesson here that can benefit each one of us. As individuals, we must carefully keep our covenants, or we will lose the guidance of the Spirit and fall into apostasy ourselves. Further, we must teach this lesson to our children. Religious leaders usually understand that their movements are never more than one generation away from extinction. In each new generation, each individual member needs to be converted, to repent and make a covenant of obedience to the Father, and to grow in faithfulness in his service.

As contributing authors to this volume, we are grateful for the testimonies we have each received that the true church of Jesus Christ has been restored through the prophet Joseph Smith. As our understanding of the apostasy grows, so does our appreciation for the importance of the fact that both the Father and the Son, and then numerous angels came to him. By these means the long-lost priesthood of God has been restored. Lost scriptures have been translated and published. The kinds of historical inquiries and reflections presented in this book help make it clear that we are the most blessed of all peoples to live in a day when we can be led by a prophet, when the Church of Christ is solidly established throughout so much of the earth, when we have so many scriptures and revelations, and when we have temples in which the culminating ordinances of the plan of salvation can be administered. It is that testimony that drives our hope that others will discover the truth and importance of that restoration in their lives and for their eternal welfare.

Inheriting the "Great Apostasy": The Evolution of Latter-day Saint Views on the Middle Ages and the Renaissance

Eric R. Dursteler

The idea of a universal apostasy is one of the foundational elements of Mormonism. Indeed, it is often privileged with an uppercase *A* and designated as the "Great Apostasy." In this context the term refers specifically to what Latter-day Saints perceive as the "falling away"[1] from Christ's original church and his teachings in the centuries immediately following his crucifixion. It is no exaggeration to say that the concept of apostasy is one of the linchpins of the Latter-day Saint faith: without an apostasy there would have been no need for Joseph Smith or for a restoration. The great doctrinal commentator and Latter-day Saint apostle Bruce R. McConkie stated, "The apostasy is the first great sign

---

1. 2 Thessalonians 2:3. Kent P. Jackson has recently suggested that this phrase, derived from the Greek *apostasía*, should be rendered more dramatically as "rebellion," "mutiny," "revolt," or "revolution" (see his book *From Apostasy to Restoration* [Salt Lake City: Deseret Book, 1996], 9; also Todd Compton, "Apostasy," in *Encyclopedia of Mormonism*, 1:56–57).

of the times."[2] Among the Latter-day Saint faithful, the explanation and justification for this pivotal moment are historically based; indeed, as one acute observer has commented, "For Mormonism more than other religions, history evolves as part of the church's canon."[3]

The concept of a historical apostasy was most fully developed in the works of three influential Latter-day Saint doctrinal commentators and General Authorities—B. H. Roberts of the First Council of Seventy, apostle James E. Talmage, and apostle and future church president Joseph Fielding Smith—who wrote around the turn of the twentieth century. For each of these writers, the key moments of the apostasy were the first Christian centuries, when innumerable "plain and precious" truths were lost (1 Nephi 13:28). In their divine chronologies, however, the Middle Ages and Renaissance also play an important, if relatively brief, role in the historical evolution that led ineluctably to the restoration. All three writers point to the darkness of medieval times as the fullest expression of the effects of apostasy, in contrast to the light that the Renaissance revival of learning reflected into the world. The Renaissance set the stage for the Reformation, which, in turn, acted as a prelude to the restoration.

---

2. Bruce R. McConkie, *A New Witness for the Articles of Faith* (Salt Lake City: Deseret Book, 1985), 626.

3. Richard N. Ostling and Joan K. Ostling, *Mormon America: The Power and the Promise* (New York: HarperCollins, 1999), 247; see Edwin S. Gaustad, "History and Theology: The Mormon Connection," *Sunstone,* November-December 1980, 44–47. Historian Richard L. Bushman has noted, "Mormons have hung the course of western civilization since Christ" on the framework of the apostasy ("Faithful History," *Dialogue: A Journal of Mormon Thought* 4 [fall 1969]: 19). See also Jan Shipps, *Mormonism: The Story of a New Religious Tradition* (Urbana and Chicago: University of Illinois Press, 1985), 51, 73.

While this binary vision of the Middle Ages and the Renaissance was common in the intellectual world of the late nineteenth century, scholars have since come to see it as an obsolete and outmoded historical paradigm. Despite this transformation, the ideas of the aforementioned triumvirate of turn-of-the-century thinkers continue to influence Latter-day Saint views of history. This essay historically situates these influential commentators' viewpoints on the Middle Ages and Renaissance within their broader vision of the great apostasy. It also considers the enduring appeal of their views within the Latter-day Saint community. The question of the historicity of the Latter-day Saint view of apostasy or the specific events it purports to describe, while important and suggestive themes, are beyond the scope of this essay.

The Apostasy in Latter-day Saint Thought

During Mormonism's first sixty years, discussions of apostasy were very much a part of the faith's dialogue, but it was not until the last decade of the nineteenth century and the first decades of the twentieth century that more systematic and influential treatments of the apostasy appeared.[4] The most consequential were those of B. H. Roberts, James E. Talmage, and Joseph Fielding Smith, three of Mormonism's most influential doctrinal and theological thinkers. These writers all attempted to historicize the nature and progress of the great apostasy. Largely as a result of their writings, LDS theories of apostasy were codified in the first decades of the twentieth century as part of an extremely fertile theological era of definition and

---

4. See the somewhat confusing book by Janne M. Sjödahl, *The Reign of Antichrist or The Great "Falling Away"* (Salt Lake City: Deseret News, 1913); also George Reynolds and Janne M. Sjödahl, *Commentary on the Book of Mormon*, ed. Philip C. Reynolds (Salt Lake City: Deseret Book, 1955–61), 1:113–33; 3:376–82.

reconciliation with secular learning, described by Leonard J. Arrington as "the stage of creative adaptation."[5] These three scholars and church authorities of the second generation of Mormonism were most responsible for systematizing LDS theology. All wrote widely and perceptively on many of the doctrinal issues of the day.[6] While Smith and Roberts disagreed fiercely about evolution and other issues, Talmage often staked out something of a middle ground between them. In marked contrast, their historical theologies were virtually identical, particularly in how these men understood the place of the Middle Ages and Renaissance in the apostasy and the relation-

---

5. Leonard J. Arrington, "The Intellectual Tradition of Mormon Utah," *Proceedings of the Utah Academy of Sciences, Arts and Letters* 45, pt. 2 (1968): 358. See Thomas G. Alexander, "The Reconstruction of Mormon Doctrine: From Joseph Smith to Progressive Theology," *Sunstone*, July–August 1980, 28–32; and Alexander, *Mormonism in Transition: A History of the Latter-day Saints, 1890–1930* (Chicago: University of Illinois Press, 1986), 272–306.

6. In their number must be included John A. Widtsoe, another influential theologian-apostle (see Alexander, "The Reconstruction of Mormon Doctrine," 28). However, because he wrote little about the apostasy, I do not discuss him in this article. Most scholars emphasize the importance of the triumvirate of Roberts, Talmage, and Widtsoe in the development and definition of Latter-day Saint doctrines at the turn of the century but ignore Smith's importance. Perhaps this is because of his conservative rather than progressive doctrinal positions, or because of his opposition to the other three scholars over key theological issues. Arrington, in "Intellectual Tradition of Mormon Utah," 358–62, reports a survey of "some fifty prominent L.D.S. intellectuals" who ranked Roberts first, Talmage fifth, and Widtsoe sixth among the most influential Latter-day Saint intellectuals. Smith does not appear on the list of twelve.

ship of those periods to the restoration.[7] The church leadership and membership alike generally embraced the "priestly narratives" of Roberts, Talmage, and Smith as authoritative in their day; unquestionably, those works have provided the foundation for all subsequent discussions of the apostasy.[8] In many ways, this trio's conceptualizations still inform how Latter-day Saints think about the apostasy.

The Middle Ages and the Renaissance in Latter-day Saint Writings on the Apostasy

The first comprehensive treatment of the apostasy was that of B. H. Roberts, whom philosopher Sterling M. McMurrin has called "the intellectual leader of the Mormon people in the era of Mormonism's finest intellectual attainment."[9] In his *Outlines of Ecclesiastical History*, first published in 1893 as a Seventies

---

7. On the evolution dispute among Roberts, Talmage, and Smith, see Richard Sherlock, "'We Can See No Advantage to a Continuation of the Discussion': The Roberts/Smith/Talmage Affair," *Dialogue* 13 (1980): 63–78; D. Michael Quinn, *The Mormon Hierarchy: Extensions of Power* (Salt Lake City: Signature, 1997), 64; and Alexander, *Mormonism in Transition*, 286–88.

8. The quotation is from Shipps, *Mormonism*, 2.

9. Sterling M. McMurrin, "B. H. Roberts: Historian and Theologian," foreword to B. H. Roberts, *The Autobiography of B. H. Roberts*, ed. Gary James Bergera (Salt Lake City: Signature, 1990), viii. See Robert H. Malan, *B. H. Roberts, a Biography* (Salt Lake City: Deseret Book, 1966); Truman G. Madsen, *Defender of the Faith: The B. H. Roberts Story* (Salt Lake City: Bookcraft, 1980); and Quinn, *Mormon Hierarchy*, 686–88. For a critique of Roberts as a historian, see Davis Bitton, "B. H. Roberts as Historian," *Dialogue* 3/4 (1968): 25–44; for a less critical recent assessment, see Ronald W. Walker, David J. Whitaker, and James B. Allen, *Mormon History* (Urbana: University of Illinois Press, 2001), 34–37.

quorum manual, with five subsequent editions following over the next thirty years, Roberts developed a wide-ranging and all-encompassing view of the apostasy. He restated and amplified his ideas—though not substantially altering them—in a 1929 series of radio lectures published as *The Falling Away*.[10] Reflecting the view common since Joseph Smith's time, Roberts saw the apostasy primarily as the loss of priesthood authority—that is, the loss of divine sanction to act in the name of God in conducting such saving ordinances as sacrament, baptism, and temple sealings—and the end of continuing revelation. In these foundational works, however, Roberts attempted to historicize the theology of apostasy. He focused particularly on historical and doctrinal developments in late antiquity, changes in ordinances, the infiltration of pagan philosophies, the rise of the Mass, and variations from the original organization of Christ's church. For Roberts, the first three Christian centuries were the key period in the great apostasy. By the time of Constantine, the church that Christ had organized had ceased to exist. Roberts's ideas and approach, more than those of any other Latter-day Saint

---

10. See B. H. Roberts, *Outlines of Ecclesiastical History: A Text Book* (Salt Lake City: George Q. Cannon & Sons Co., 1893). I quote only from the first edition. See also his series of radio lectures published as *The "Falling Away," or The World's Loss of the Christian Religion and Church* (Salt Lake City: Deseret Book, 1931). Roberts also gave a brief overview of the apostasy in his introduction to *History of the Church of Jesus Christ of Latter-day Saints, Period 1* (Salt Lake City: Deseret News, 1902), 1:xlii–xcvi. *Outlines* has generally received less attention than Roberts's subsequent works, but he had a very high opinion of them (see *Autobiography of B. H. Roberts*, 220–21, 229). Davis Bitton, in "B. H. Roberts as Historian," classifies *Outlines* and *The "Falling Away"* not as history but as "works of polemic," "highly tendentious," and "historically naïve" (26).

scholar, effectively set the parameters and pattern for all subsequent discussions of the apostasy; indeed, his oeuvre provided the basic outlines of "a Mormon theology of history, nearly Augustinian in its vision."[11]

While Roberts's chief emphasis was on the first Christian centuries, he treated the Middle Ages and the Renaissance as important transitional moments in the lockstep evolution from apostasy to Reformation to restoration. In his discussion, Roberts concentrates on what he considered to be evidence of both the omnipotence and the depravity of the papacy as well as on the "state of morals" within the church.[12] Roberts also identifies a number of medieval events that he sees as preparing the ground for the all-important Reformation. He traces "the progress of popular liberty" to the rise of a "commercial class" around AD 1200 that financed the crusading movement in return for grants of "political privileges" from cash-strapped monarchs. This development, according to Roberts, led to the breakdown of the "Feudal Land Tenure System" and the ultimate weakening of the ecclesiastical stranglehold on European society. Despite these seemingly positive developments, however, Roberts's Middle Ages are painted overwhelmingly in murky, monochromatic tones. These are the Dark Ages, a backward bookmark between New Testament Christianity and the beginnings of its revival with Martin Luther. This period was, in his words, an "age of darkness," the "midnight period of our world." He exclaims: "A period of fifteen hundred years! In which a famine for the word of God existed; a period when men wandered from sea to sea, and ran to and fro to

---

11. Bitton, "B. H. Roberts as Historian," 42. See McMurrin, "B. H. Roberts: Historian and Theologian," xiii.

12. Roberts, *Outlines of Ecclesiastical History,* 210; also Roberts, *The Falling Away,* 90–128.

seek the word of the Lord, and found it not. How pitiful the picture of it!"[13]

In Roberts's theological chronology, this fifteen-hundred-year "Age of Darkness" was not only spiritual but also intellectual, blighting all aspects of European life: "The intellectual stupor of Europe had been as profound as spiritual darkness had been dense." Into this spiritual and intellectual obscurity, however, a ray of light began to break through with the "Revival of Learning" in the latter part of the fifteenth century, which set the stage for Luther's theses and eventually Joseph Smith's vision. Roberts points to a number of significant innovations in this period of awakening: the invention of gunpowder, the compass, paper, and printing; the discovery of the Cape route to India and Columbus's discovery of the Americas; innovations in art; and "a greater knowledge of antiquity" spread by Greek refugees fleeing the fall of Constantinople after 1453.[14] These are the key elements in Roberts's binary view of the Middle Ages and the Renaissance.

Although Roberts effectively set the parameters of what came to be the view of the apostasy most widely held in the Latter-day Saint community, the most recognizable and noted work on the topic is not his but rather Talmage's slender volume *The Great Apostasy*,[15] written in 1909, before his call as an apostle. Though in many ways quite derivative of Roberts's earlier *Outlines*, Talmage's book, intended "for use in the

---

13. Roberts, *The Falling Away*, 142, 145; see Roberts, *Outlines of Ecclesiastical History*, 231–32. Roberts borrows this picture of benighted wanderers from Amos 8:11–12.

14. See Roberts, *Outlines of Ecclesiastical History*, 229–30; and his *Falling Away*, 146–47.

15. James E. Talmage, *The Great Apostasy Considered in the Light of Scriptural and Secular History* (Salt Lake City: Deseret News, 1909).

Mutual Improvement Associations,"[16] is still in circulation and is regularly referenced today. Indeed, it often appears on approved reading lists for Latter-day Saint missionaries.[17] Like Roberts, Talmage emphasizes the nexus of apostasy and loss of priesthood authority; he devotes the bulk of his historical exegesis to the initial stages of apostasy in the early Christian church, emphasizing both external and internal causes. In his final chapter, "Results of the Apostasy—Its Sequel," however, he briefly surveys medieval oppositions to the church in Rome as a bridge to a discussion of the Reformation. When Talmage describes revolts against the "tyranny . . . [of] the thoroughly apostate and utterly corrupt . . . Church of Rome," he uses language reminiscent of Roberts's in describing the Middle Ages:

> The awakening of intellectual activity . . . began in the latter part of the fourteenth century. The period from the tenth century onward to the time of the awakening has come to be known as the dark ages—characterized by stagnation in the progress of the useful arts and sciences as well as of fine arts and letters, and by a general condition of illiteracy and ignorance among the masses.

This era of darkness was enlightened by "the revival of learning," which opened "the struggle for freedom from churchly tyranny."[18]

---

16. John R. Talmage, *The Talmage Story: Life of James E. Talmage—Educator, Scientist, Apostle* (Salt Lake City: Bookcraft, 1972), 171. See Quinn, *Mormon Hierarchy*, 703–5.

17. For an example of Talmage's reliance on prior authorities and the Victorian tendency to "borrow profusely" without attribution from the work of other scholars, see Malcolm R. Thorp, "James E. Talmage and the Tradition of Victorian Lives of Jesus," *Sunstone*, January 1988, 8–13. For a synopsis of Talmage's key arguments regarding the apostasy, see Compton, "Apostasy," 1:57–58.

18. Talmage, *The Great Apostasy*, 150.

In his widely respected *Jesus the Christ* of 1915, Talmage makes even more explicit the relationship of the Middle Ages and the Renaissance:

> Under the tyrannous repression . . . [of] the Roman church, civilization was retarded and for centuries was practically halted in its course. The period of retrogression is known in history as the Dark Ages. The fifteenth century witnessed the movement known as the Renaissance or Revival of Learning; there was a general and significantly rapid awakening among men, and a determined effort to shake off the stupor of indolence and ignorance was manifest throughout the civilized world. . . . [I]t was a development predetermined in the Mind of God to illumine the benighted minds of men in preparation for the restoration of the gospel of Jesus Christ.[19]

The lockstep linkage of the three Rs—Renaissance, Reformation, and Restoration—at the center of Roberts's depiction of the great apostasy is abundantly evident in Talmage's writings.

The influential writings of Roberts and Talmage culminated in the work of Joseph Fielding Smith, the third prominent Latter-day Saint theologian of the apostasy in the early twentieth century. Smith was a son of President Joseph F. Smith and a grandson of Hyrum Smith; he was ordained an apostle in 1910 at age thirty-three and was ordained and set apart as the tenth president of the church in 1970 at age ninety-three. Called a "soldier of truth" by his biographer grandson,[20] Smith was also one of the most important doctrinal thinkers

19. James E. Talmage, *Jesus the Christ* (Salt Lake City: The Deseret News, 1915), 749.

20. Joseph Fielding McConkie, "Joseph Fielding Smith," in *The Presidents of the Church*, ed. Leonard J. Arrington (Salt Lake City: Deseret Book, 1986), 321.

and probably the most influential conservative force of Mormonism's second century. He published more books and articles than any other Latter-day Saint president,[21] and President Heber J. Grant considered him "the best posted man on the scriptures of the General Authorities."[22]

Smith's views on the apostasy first appeared in his 1922 publication *Essentials in Church History.* His introduction includes a brief overview of the "falling away," which serves simply to set the stage for the real focus of his treatise: the restoration of all things by Joseph Smith and the subsequent history of the church he founded.[23] A decade later, Smith published a much more extensive study on the apostasy in *The Progress of Man* (1936). This rich treatise was commissioned by the board of the Genealogical Society of Utah, which, because of the "grave conditions" of the day, "thought it would be timely to have a course of study giving a brief outline of man's history on the earth." Smith's text was no ordinary universal history, however; it was "an outline history of man interpreted in the light of revelation. It tells of . . . [the] everlasting conflict between good and evil, light and darkness, freedom and oppression, [and] . . . the final and destined triumph of truth."[24] Smith's striking litany of binary oppositions foreshadows his treatment of the medieval apostasy.

Smith devotes more attention than Roberts or Talmage do to the Middle Ages and the Renaissance as they relate to

---

21. See Amelia S. McConkie and Mark L. McConkie, "Joseph Fielding Smith," in *Encyclopedia of Mormonism,* 3:1354.

22. Quoted in McConkie, "Joseph Fielding Smith," in *Presidents of the Church,* 329.

23. See Joseph Fielding Smith, *Essentials in Church History* (Salt Lake City: Deseret News Press, 1922), 6–21.

24. Joseph Fielding Smith, *The Progress of Man* (Salt Lake City: Genealogical Society of Utah, 1936), 1, 4.

the Latter-day Saint understanding of the apostasy. In his discussion, he links the Renaissance's revival of learning to Europe's increasing encounters with Islam and the rest of the world through the Crusades, Mediterranean trade, and the travels of Marco Polo. Despite Smith's greater detail, however, he does not depart significantly from the path outlined by Roberts and Talmage. Like both of them, he finds divine technological intervention in the invention of the compass, paper, gunpowder, and printing, though in each case he goes into greater detail than the other writers do. The Middle Ages for Smith, as for Roberts and Talmage, are the "dark ages [which] commenced with the fall of Rome and continued during the greater part of the next thousand years." It was an era characterized by a "condition of mental and spiritual stupor and stupidity."[25]

As with his precursors, Smith also saw the "Springtime of the Renaissance" beginning to stir in the dark medieval winter. For him this thaw began in the twelfth century, when "the world was like a great giant who gradually began to stir from a long drunken stupor." The real awakening, he believed, occurred during the Renaissance of the fourteenth century—the age of Petrarch, Giotto, and Boccaccio. Smith even appropriates Roberts's language in describing this era as "The Revival of Learning." He departs from his predecessors in generally avoiding their often virulent anti-Catholic stance (especially characteristic of Roberts), and he also suggests that, despite what he perceived as the terrible darkness of the medieval era, "the Spirit of the Lord was working among the people," preparing the way for "the day in which the fulness of freedom

---

25. Smith, *Progress of Man*, 192, 194, 201–5, 211–15.

and religious liberty was to be ushered in." This time of preparation, for Smith, was the Renaissance.[26]

Several key features of the Latter-day Saint view of the historical apostasy emerge from the writings of Roberts, Talmage, and Smith. All three emphasize that at its core the apostasy consisted of a loss of priesthood authority on the earth. All three devote most of their discussion to the early Christian centuries, which they see as the pivotal age of apostasy. In their often brief treatments of the Middle Ages and Renaissance, all three resort to the metaphor of light and dark. While their exact datings of the apostasy may vary slightly, in general the period from approximately AD 500 to 1500 is characterized as an undifferentiated mass and labeled the Dark Ages.[27] The Middle Ages, for these LDS observers, were an age of abject backwardness, of obscurity and apostasy. Roberts referred to this period as the "age of darkness," the "midnight period of our world." For Talmage, it was a "period of retrogression."[28] Other contemporary Latter-day Saint authors embraced this language as well. Hugh B. Brown, in a 1941 discourse revealingly entitled

---

26. References for the foregoing discussion are found in Smith, *Progress of Man,* 197–98, 200, 206. Because of his long life, Joseph Fielding Smith's views, while first expressed in *The Progress of Man* in 1936, reappeared over the next three decades in a number of the prolific author's other writings, including *Essentials in Church History* (Salt Lake City: Deseret News Press, 1922), *Seek Ye Earnestly* (Salt Lake City: Deseret Book, 1970), 315–31, and *Answers to Gospel Questions,* ed. Bruce R. McConkie (Salt Lake City: Deseret Book, 1960), 3:170–84.

27. See Shipps, *Mormonism,* 2.

28. Roberts, *The Falling Away,* 145–46; Roberts, *Outlines of Ecclesiastical History,* 229; and Talmage, *Jesus the Christ,* 749. For an earlier example of this widely shared view, see Parley P. Pratt, *Key to the Science of Theology,* 3rd ed. (Salt Lake City: Deseret News, 1874), 116.

"The Night of Darkness," terms this period "the Dark Ages, a time which has been designated as the midnight of time, . . . in which not only the artificial lamps of men burned low, but also the celestial lights of God's inspiration were extinguished."[29]

The darkness of the era was twofold in Latter-day Saint apostasy literature. On the one hand, there was the spiritual darkness of apostasy created by the absence of direct revelation and priesthood authority. The roots of this view can be traced back to Joseph Smith's accounts of his first vision, in which the spiritual darkness of his day was due to absent priesthood authority but was penetrated by the light of God and Christ breaking through to him in his moment of despair.[30] On the other hand, there is the innovation of Roberts, Talmage, and Smith that expands this metaphor of darkness beyond the purely spiritual realm. In their depictions, not only were the Dark Ages spiritually benighted, but the backwardness and degeneration of the spirit were accompanied by an absolute decline in Western civilization. For Talmage, "the dark ages . . . [were] characterized by stagnation in the progress of the useful arts and sciences as well as of fine arts and letters, and by a general condition of illiteracy and ignorance among the masses."[31] In "this period of retrogression" in Europe, "civilization was retarded and for centuries was practically halted in its course."[32] For Smith, it was an age characterized by intellectual and spiritual "stupor and stupidity."[33]

---

29. Hugh B. Brown, *Continuing the Quest* (Salt Lake City: Deseret Book, 1961), 385–86.

30. See Shipps, *Mormonism,* 2–3.

31. Talmage, *Great Apostasy,* 150.

32. Talmage, *Jesus the Christ,* 749.

33. Smith, *Progress of Man,* 194.

In contrast to the dark of the Middle Ages, these Latter-day Saint writers emphasize the light of the period immediately preceding the Reformation, the Renaissance, which is a privileged age in this holy history. For Talmage, the intellectual revival of the late fourteenth century was part of a general trend of rebellion against tyrannical ecclesiastical power. This "rapid awakening among men, and a determined effort to shake off the stupor of indolence and ignorance" was predetermined by God "to illumine the benighted minds of men in preparation for the restoration of the gospel of Jesus Christ."[34] For Roberts, "the intellectual stupor of Europe had been as profound as spiritual darkness had been dense. But with the close of the fifteenth century, literature, science and art seemed to spring into active life."[35] Similarly, Smith writes of the Renaissance that "the Lord never intended that man should be kept in ignorance [as existed in the Middle Ages]. The time had to come when the minds of men were to be freed from the chains that enslaved them."[36]

In sum, the historical narrative of the great apostasy generated by these Latter-day Saint thinkers during the pregnant doctrinal and intellectual atmosphere of the early twentieth century emphasized a generalized view of the period from AD 500 to 1500 as a time of spiritual and intellectual darkness in

34. Talmage, *Jesus the Christ*, 749; and Talmage, *Great Apostasy*, 150.

35. Roberts, *Outlines of Ecclesiastical History*, 229; and Roberts, *Falling Away*, 146.

36. Smith, *Progress of Man*, 197. Hugh B. Brown recycled this language of convergence and Roberts's line of argument almost word for word in a 1941 address (see Hugh B. Brown, "Divine Prophecy and World Events," *Deseret News*, Church Section, 5 April 1941, quoted in Brown, *Continuing the Quest*, 385–86, 389–90.

which all revelation and, indeed, progress of any sort disappeared. About 1500, the revolutionary changes associated with the Renaissance opened heaven's door a crack and allowed a beam of light to penetrate the gloom, thus setting the stage for the Reformation, which in turn blazed the trail for the restoration of all things by Joseph Smith. What I hope to show in the remainder of this paper is that the generally monochromatic discussion presented in LDS historical surveys of the medieval bridge between the great apostasy and the restoration is firmly planted in historical assumption of the nineteenth century and earlier. These ideas, while embraced in their day by many, perhaps even most, scholars, have largely been superseded by the scholarship of subsequent generations.

The Sources of Latter-day Saint Apostasy Literature

An examination of the citations of these three influential Latter-day Saint writers shows clearly that they relied chiefly on two types of sources in crafting their viewpoints: the highly polemical, popular, confessional, historical literature of the nineteenth century and the anticlerical literature of the eighteenth-century Enlightenment. While these authors often did not cite their sources, as was common in their day,[37] still a survey of their references is revealing. Roberts seems to have roamed most widely with his research, relying on a range of Protestant, Catholic, and Enlightenment authors.[38] His chief historical source was the Protestant theologian and historian Johann Lorenz

---

37. On the prevalence of this practice and the different definition of plagiarism in this period, see Thorp, "James E. Talmage and the Tradition of Victorian Lives of Jesus," 11. On modern citation practices, see Anthony Grafton, *The Footnote: A Curious History* (Cambridge, MA: Harvard University Press, 1997).

38. Because Roberts's books were preserved in the B. H. Roberts Memorial Library, part of the historical archives of the Church of

von Mosheim, especially his *Institutes of Ecclesiastical History, Ancient and Modern*. Roberts supplemented Mosheim with other important Protestant histories, as well as several Catholic sources, though these were used to support his ultimately anti-Catholic position. As Richard L. Bushman has rightly observed, Talmage's and Roberts's ideas were conceived "with the liberal assistance of Protestant scholars who were equally committed to belief in the apostasy of the Roman Church." He adds, "It would be interesting to know if . . . [they] have added anything to the findings of Protestant scholars."[39] Latter-day Saint apostasy literature also owed a great debt to the anti-Catholic polemics that dominated turn-of-the-century historical writing in Protestant America.[40]

Roberts, as well as Talmage and Smith, was influenced by Enlightenment and Romantic historians and trends. Latter-day Saint theologians, like many Romantic writers, tended to view history as drama, "the unfolding of a vast Providential plan," and generally shared the Romantic belief that a historian's task was "to arrange apparently disconnected events in their proper order."[41] Influential in a different way were the great Enlight-

---

Jesus Christ of Latter-day Saints, it is possible to get some sense of the range of his readings. For an illustrative selection of Roberts's library holdings, see John W. Welch, ed., *The Truth, the Way, the Life: An Elementary Treatise on Theology,* 2nd. ed. (Provo, UT: BYU Studies, 1996), 743–52.

39. Bushman, "Faithful History," 18–19. See Compton, "Apostasy," 1:57.

40. See Edward Muir, "The Italian Renaissance in America," *American Historical Review* 100 (October 1995): 1098.

41. David Levin, *History as Romantic Art* (Stanford, CA: Stanford University Press, 1959), 8–26, quoted in Bitton, "B. H. Roberts as Historian," 43. See J. B. Bullen, *The Myth of the Renaissance in Nineteenth-Century Writing* (Oxford: Clarendon, 1994), 11.

enment histories, in which it was common to see "nothing but barbarism, ignorance, superstition, violence, irrationality, and priestly tyranny" from the fall of Rome to the Renaissance, which those writers viewed as the birth of the rational, secular, modern era—that is, their own day. The Middle Ages, for them, provided the perfect irrational foil for their own, enlightened age. This *philosophe* history of progress posited the "dark centuries" of the Middle Ages as the gloomy backdrop against which the first stirring of modern progress, the light of Renaissance Italy, burst forth.[42] Or as Voltaire, in his *Essay on Universal History* famously described it, the Italians "began to shake off the barbarous rust, with which Europe had been covered since the decline of the Roman Empire."[43]

---

42. See Karl H. Dannenfeldt, ed., *The Renaissance: Basic Interpretations,* 2nd ed. (Lexington, MA: Heath, 1974), vii–viii. For a discussion of Enlightenment historical thought and the place it assigned the Middle Ages and Renaissance, see Wallace K. Ferguson, *The Renaissance in Historical Thought: Five Centuries of Interpretation* (New York: Houghton Mifflin, 1948), 78–112; also Paul F. Grendler, "The Renaissance in Historical Thought," in *Encyclopedia of the Renaissance,* ed. Paul F. Grendler (New York: Scribner's, 1999), 5:260–61.

43. Voltaire, *An Essay on Universal History and on the Manners and Spirit of Nations,* quoted in Denys Hay, *The Renaissance Debate* (New York: Holt, Rhinehart and Winston, 1965), 13. See Bullen, *Myth of the Renaissance,* 17–26. These anti-medieval, and often anti-Catholic, polemics were rooted in the thought of Italian humanist scholars intent on privileging their age by denigrating their medieval predecessors. On this topic, see Theodor E. Mommsen, "Petrarch's Conception of the 'Dark Ages,'" *Speculum* 17 (summer 1942): 226–42; Franco Simone, "La coscienza della rinascita negli umanisti," *La Rinascita* 2/10 (1939): 838–71, continued in vol. 3/11 (1940): 163–86; Paul Lehmann, "Mittelalter und Küchenlatein," *Historische Zeitschrift* 137/2 (1928): 197–213; Grendler, "Renaissance in

While the sources they cited tended toward outdated religious and philosophical works of a polemical nature, Roberts, Talmage, and Smith also relied to a degree on more recent general works, particularly those of a historical nature, to flesh out their understanding of the historical continuum of the apostasy. These included popular histories such as François Guizot's *History of Civilization in Europe* (1828) and general textbooks such as John J. Anderson's *A Manual of General History: Being an Outline History of the World from the Creation to the Present Time* and P. V. N. Myers' *Mediaeval and Modern History*, and *General History for Colleges and High Schools*. Treating the relationship between the Middle Ages and the Renaissance as an evolution from dark to light, so characteristic of Latter-day Saint apostasy literature, is evident in these texts. Anderson, for example, wrote: "The epoch at which Modern History commences is the dawn of intelligence that broke upon Europe in the latter part of the 15th [*sic*] century. . . . [T]he West, emerging from the night of mediaeval ignorance, began to glow with the first beams of an intellectual and social illumination."[44]

Roberts, Talmage, and Smith were apparently quite unaware of the burgeoning professional historical literature of their age, and indeed it would be unfair and unrealistic to expect them as generalists and nonprofessional historians to have been up-to-date on the latest historiographical developments of the day. However, elements of their thought suggest clearly that they were indirectly influenced by the work of one of the great nineteenth-century historians, Jacob Burckhardt, and by the less innovative

---

Historical Thought," 259–60; and Ferguson, *Renaissance in Historical Thought*, 1–28.

44. John J. Anderson, *A Manual of General History: Being an Outline History of the World from the Creation to the Present Time* (New York: Clark & Maynard, 1874), 231.

though widely influential English scholar John Addington Symonds. This link may seem at first glance rather tenuous: none of the authors makes direct reference to Burckhardt, and only Smith explicitly cites Symonds.[45] All three, however, appropriate directly both the concept and wording of the title of the second volume of Symonds's *Renaissance in Italy*, "The Revival of Learning," in their histories.[46] Yet it seems clear that Burckhardt's seminal vision of the Renaissance permeated the views of these three Latter-day Saint thinkers. Some evidence of this can be found in the sources that these authors relied upon, but their reliance on Burckhardt is even more evident in their way of conceptualizing the medieval and Renaissance periods in relationship to the "great apostasy."

An examination of the ideas of Burckhardt and Symonds clearly reveals Latter-day Saint apostasy literature's debt to their work. Burckhardt was one of the most respected and influential historians of the nineteenth century, and his great 1860 masterpiece, *The Civilization of the Renaissance in Italy*, was one of the most important historical monographs of that century.[47] With this work Burckhardt made his name. More

---

45. Smith, *Progress of Man*, 197.

46. John Addington Symonds, *Renaissance in Italy* (New York: Modern Library, 1935), 1:327. "The Revival of Learning" is the title of a section in Roberts's *Outlines* and in his *Falling Away*, as well as in Talmage's *Great Apostasy*. Smith, in his *Progress of Man*, composed an entire chapter under the same title.

47. Initially published in 1860 as *Die Cultur der Renaissance in Italien*, Burckhardt's *Civilization of the Renaissance in Italy* was first translated into English by S. G. C. Middlemore in 1878. I use the 1954 Modern Library edition of Middlemore's translation, *The Civilization of the Renaissance in Italy* (New York: Modern Library, 1954). On Burckhardt and the intellectual milieu of his time, see

importantly, he created a widely influential paradigm that must be dealt with by students of the Renaissance to this day. As Karl Brandi wrote, "Our conception of the Renaissance is Jacob Burckhardt's creation."[48] *The Civilization of the Renaissance in Italy* is a varied and rich work that has often suffered from overly reductive treatments, so a summary of its ideas is challenging. At its core, however, is a simple question, Whence modernity? Burckhardt felt compelled to find the roots of modernity, and in his greatest work he argued that he had traced them back to Renaissance Italy: "The Italian Renaissance must be called the leader of modern ages."[49]

To make his case for a dramatically changed Renaissance world, Burckhardt had to contrast it clearly with the Middle Ages. Thus he resorted to a language and metaphor that should ring familiar to readers of Latter-day Saint apostasy literature: "In the Middle Ages both sides of human consciousness . . . lay dreaming or half awake beneath a common veil. The veil

---

Lionel Gossman's important *Basel in the Age of Burckhardt: A Study in Unseasonable Ideas* (Chicago: University of Chicago Press, 2000), 201–95; Grendler "Renaissance in Historical Thought," 261–62; Peter G. Bietenholz, "Jakob Burckhardt," in *Encyclopedia of the Renaissance,* 5:288–91; and Hans Baron, "Burckhardt's 'Civilization of the Renaissance' a Century after Its Publication," *Renaissance News* 13 (fall 1960): 207–22.

48. Walter Goetz, ed., *Propyläen Weltgeschichte* (Berlin: Propyläen, 1931), 1:157, also quoted in Ferguson, *Renaissance in Historical Thought,* 179. As evidence of the continuing influence of Burckhardt's paradigm, see the recent lively forum discussion on the status of the Renaissance idea: *American Historical Review* 103 (February 1998): 51–124.

49. Burckhardt, *Civilization of the Renaissance in Italy,* 416. See Felix Gilbert, *History: Politics or Culture?* (Princeton: Princeton University Press, 1990), 61–62.

was woven of faith, illusion, and childish prepossession." This was true for all of Europe except in Italy, where "this veil first melted into air." Italian Renaissance culture freed itself "from the fantastic bonds of the Middle Ages" and witnessed the discovery of the individual.[50] The era was marked by a spirit of self-discovery, a recognition of human worth, and especially a dynamic outpouring of artistic activity by individualist geniuses, all of which emphasized the profound changes of nascent modernity and marked a sharp break with the past. In short, for Burckhardt the Renaissance represented the end of the Middle Ages and the beginning of the modern world.

Burckhardt's *Civilization of the Renaissance in Italy* made such a powerful, paradigmatic statement that few posited any competing interpretations. Instead, most scholars devoted themselves to supplementing and fleshing out elements of the master's vision.[51] For English-speaking readers, one voice rose above the others, that of John Addington Symonds, an English gentleman scholar and poet whose multivolume *Renaissance in Italy* (1875–86) developed a similarly broad and engaging portrait of the age. Symonds's vision of the Renaissance was not as conceptually sophisticated as Burckhardt's; indeed, he openly acknowledged his debt to the Swiss historian. However, while Burckhardt's reputation grew slowly in the English-speaking world, Symonds's "embarrassingly exuberant,"[52] if accessible, prose was much more widely read, and it was ultimately through him "that the Burckhardtian Renaissance

---

50. Burckhardt, *Civilization of the Renaissance in Italy*, 100, 132.

51. See Ferguson, *Renaissance in Historical Thought*, 290.

52. Anthony Molho, "The Italian Renaissance: Made in the USA," in *Imagined Histories: American Historians Interpret the Past*, Anthony Molho and Gordon S. Wood, eds. (Princeton: Princeton University Press, 1998), 265.

came to life in the minds of generations of students."[53] And it was Symonds's exaggerated emphasis on the light/dark metaphor to characterize the medieval/Renaissance dichotomy that came to permeate late-nineteenth-century views in the English-speaking world.

While Symonds was certainly a fine literary stylist, as a historian he was often derivative and tended toward exaggeration, hyperbole, and high drama.[54] In contrast to Burckhardt's more subdued and careful tone, Symonds characterized the Renaissance as "the most marvellous period that the world has ever known."[55] In his view, art, innovation, and knowledge all "had long lain neglected on the shores of the Dead Sea which we call the Middle Ages." In contrast to this bleak medieval landscape,

---

53. Ferguson, *Renaissance in Historical Thought,* 204–5. See J. R. Hale, *England and the Italian Renaissance* (London: Faber and Faber, 1954), 169–96; Philip Lee Ralph, *The Renaissance in Perspective* (New York: St. Martin's, 1973), 4–6; Bullen, *Myth of the Renaissance,* 15–16, 251–55; Grendler, "The Renaissance in Historical Thought," 5:262; and Paul F. Grendler, "John Addington Symonds," in *Encyclopedia of the Renaissance,* 5:292–93.

54. See Molho, "The Italian Renaissance: Made in the USA," 265; and Ferguson, *Renaissance in Historical Thought,* 204. The nuances of Burckhardt's view are evident in his defense of the Middle Ages from overzealous "enemies." He writes that one can "misjudge the Middle Ages, to be sure, but in the long run one could not despise the period. . . . [O]ur existence had its roots in it, even though modern culture was derived predominantly from antiquity. . . . The Middle Ages were the youth of today's world, and a *long* youth" (Jacob Burckhardt, *Judgments on History and Historians,* trans. Harry Zohn (Boston: Beacon Press, 1958), 25, 32; see 26–27, 61–62).

55. J. A. Symonds, *The Renaissance: An Essay read in the Theatre, Oxford, June 17, 1863* (Oxford: Hammans, 1863), 8–9, cited in Bullen, *Myth of the Renaissance,* 252.

the Renaissance brought "the emancipation of the reason for the modern world, and . . . shattered and destroyed . . . the thick veil . . . between the mind of man and the outer world, and flash[ed] the light of reality upon the darkened places of his own nature."[56] This passage suggests both the similarity of Symonds's interpretation to Burckhardt's and his expansion and exaggeration of it. In contrast to Burckhardt's ultimately negative view of his age,[57] Symonds sketched a historical trajectory that celebrated the triumphant march of progress, connecting the Renaissance to the Reformation and eventually to the English Revolution, all three acts in the "drama of liberty" so dear to the liberal, Protestant historiographical tradition of the nineteenth century.[58] In this drama, the Middle Ages were a time of intellectual backwardness and darkness, a world in which the individual was limited by the corporate tethers of community, guild, family, and especially church. The Renaissance that began in Italy flashed brilliant illumination into this dark, medieval world, waking (and creating) the independent, freethinking, modern individual.

The Apostasy in Recent Latter-day Saint Literature

This nineteenth-century view expressed most influentially by Burckhardt and Symonds, but shared and expanded by many others, should seem very familiar. In the Latter-day Saint apostasy literature, the treatment of this transitional era is clearly

---

56. Symonds, *Renaissance in Italy,* 1:4–5, 9.

57. See Gossman, *Basel in the Age of Burckhardt,* 226–49; and Peter Gay, *Style in History* (New York: Basic Books, 1974), 144–49.

58. See Symonds, *Renaissance in Italy,* 5–6; and Philip Benedict, "Between Whig Traditions and New Histories: American Historical Writing about Reformation and Early Modern Europe," in Molho and Wood, *Imagined Histories,* 299.

shaped by these views, which were generally widely accepted in nineteenth-century historiography. As Anthony Molho has persuasively demonstrated, American historians and the public in general from the late nineteenth through much of the twentieth century were fascinated by the Italian Renaissance. Americans saw their new land as the culmination of the historical process, the epitome of modernity. Thus they enthusiastically embraced Burckhardt's genealogy that traced the roots of the modern world—their roots—to the city-states of Renaissance Italy.[59] That Latter-day Saint authorities like Roberts, Talmage, and Smith should embrace this vision, then, is not at all surprising; their vision of the Middle Ages and Renaissance was in many ways entirely harmonious with the prevailing view of the contemporary historical community.

What is revealing is that, while scholars of the past century have increasingly distanced themselves from this Burckhardtian paradigm, Latter-day Saint treatments of the apostasy since the time of Roberts, Talmage, and Smith have retained much of their binary vision of the Middle Ages and Renaissance. The persistence of this view is most evident in the writings of Bruce R. McConkie, perhaps the best-known and most influential LDS doctrinal commentator of the last half of the twentieth century.[60] McConkie's rich and varied ideas span

---

59. See Anthony Molho, "Italian History in American Universities," in *Italia e Stati Uniti concordanze e dissonanze* (Rome: Il Veltro, 1981), 205–8; Molho, "American Historians and the Italian Renaissance: An Overview," *Schifanoia* 8 (1990): 15–16; and Molho, "The Italian Renaissance: Made in the USA," 263–94. See also Hajo Holborn, "Introduction," in Burckhardt, *Civilization of the Renaissance in Italy*, v–vi.

60. McConkie, a son-in-law of Joseph Fielding Smith, often cited Smith's works, including *The Progress of Man*, in developing his own

a wide body of work. He initially developed his views on the Middle Ages and the Renaissance in relation to the apostasy in the first edition (1958) of his ambitious and authoritative *Mormon Doctrine*,[61] but his most detailed exposition on the apostasy appears in his final work, *A New Witness for the Articles of Faith* (1985). In the context of a discussion of the eleventh article of faith, McConkie addresses the rise of religious freedom, the apostasy, and the Middle Ages as a critical prelude to the Reformation and the restoration in ultimately familiar terms. For him, the period from Constantine until 1500 was "The Black Millennium," in which "the world lay in darkness."

> It was a black and abysmal night; the stench of spiritual death poisoned the nostrils of men; and the jaws of hell gaped wide open to welcome the sensual sinners who loved darkness rather than light because their deeds were evil. In our more enlightened day, it is difficult to conceive of the depths to which government and religion and morality, both private and public, sank in what men universally describe as the dark ages. . . .
>
> [This was] such a decadent age that man, made in the image of God, was more like an animal than a divine being. Morality, culture, literacy, learning in general, even theological inquiry—all these were at a low ebb.[62]

---

views on the apostasy. He also regularly cited *Doctrines of Salvation*, 3 vols. (Salt Lake City: Bookcraft, 1954–56), a collection of Smith's sermons and writings that McConkie himself compiled. See Bruce R. McConkie, *Mormon Doctrine* (Salt Lake City: Bookcraft, 1958), 166, 646–47.

61. See especially McConkie's entries on "Apostasy," "Church of the Devil," "Dark Ages," and "Signs of the Times" in his *Mormon Doctrine*, 40–44, 129–31, 165–66, 645–48.

62. McConkie, *New Witness for the Articles of Faith*, 669–70.

In contrast to this gloomy medieval world is the Renaissance, "A Day of Awakening":

> The Black Millennium must end. A few hundred years thereafter, the gospel is to be restored. . . . Let the earth spin and the darkness pass, and a few rays of light will soon dawn in the eastern sky. . . . Then during the fourteenth and fifteenth centuries and the first part of the sixteenth, there came an awakening. It began in Italy, where the darkness was deepest, . . . and resulted in "achieving freedom from the intellectual bondage to which the individual man had been subjected by the theology and hierarchy of the Church. . . . The Renaissance insisted upon the rights of the life that now is, and dignified the total sphere for which man's intellect and his aesthetic and social tastes by nature fit him."[63]

Clearly, the vision of Roberts, Talmage, and Smith, but also of the nineteenth-century scholars, has survived intact. The Middle Ages are still the Dark Ages, their inflated span lasting from AD 500 to 1500. The spiritual retardation of this age is still accompanied by material and intellectual backwardness. And the Renaissance is still privileged as the turning point in this history, the staging ground for the Reformation and restoration. McConkie is not unique among Latter-day Saint writers and authorities in his continued embrace of this dichotomous view; indeed, even today many within the broader Latter-day

---

63. McConkie, *New Witness for the Articles of Faith*, 670–71. McConkie is quoting in part from David S. Schaff, *History of the Christian Church*, vol. 5, pt. 2, *The Middle Ages from Boniface VIII., 1294, to the Protestant Reformation, 1517* (New York: Charles Scribner's Sons, 1910), 559–60. Schaff, 555–60, cites Burckhardt and recommends him (and Symonds) as an important authority on the Renaissance. McConkie's reliance on Schaff, then, provides a direct connection in 1985 to Burckhardt's 1860 masterpiece.

Saint community probably still accept the image that Roberts, Talmage, and Smith created almost a century ago.[64]

The Middle Ages and the Renaissance in Twentieth-Century Historiography

Although the nineteenth-century view seems to have been remarkably durable in the LDS historical vision of the Middle Ages and Renaissance, it has been abandoned by the broader historical community as a problematic paradigm. The suggestive formulae of Burckhardt and his followers set the parameters for a fruitful and energetic debate that emerged after 1900 over what many saw as his teleological, oversimplified, and binary depiction of history. Trying to summarize the very rich historical literatures about medieval and Renaissance Europe that have evolved in the past century would be impractical. Still, a discussion of several dominant trends may illuminate the chasm that has arisen between Latter-day Saint scholars of the apostasy and the work of the larger historical community.[65]

---

64. Most recently, see Arnold K. Garr, "Preparing for the Restoration," *Ensign,* June 1999, 34–45. See also Alvin R. Dyer, *Who Am I?* (Salt Lake City: Deseret Book, 1966), 531–33; Alvin R. Dyer, *The Meaning of Truth,* rev. ed. (Salt Lake City: Deseret Book, 1973), 114–18; and Victor L. Ludlow, *Principles and Practices of the Restored Gospel* (Salt Lake City: Deseret Book, 1992), 515. During the height of the cold war, Latter-day Saint leaders often emphasized the explicit link between apostasy in the Dark Ages, the Renaissance revival, the Reformation, and the eventual rise of the United States. See Mark E. Petersen, *The Great Prologue* (Salt Lake City: Deseret Book, 1975), 1; and Ezra Taft Benson, *This Nation Shall Endure* (Salt Lake City: Deseret Book, 1977), 142–43.

65. For a recent general overview of many of the themes and important figures of Renaissance historiography, see the excellent *Encyclopedia of the Renaissance,* especially Grendler, "The Renais-

In the Burckhardt/Symonds portrait, the Middle Ages do not appear in a particularly sympathetic light; consequently, medieval scholars were among the earliest to challenge the description of their age as "one long, dreary epoch of stagnation, of insecurity, of lawless violence."[66] This "revolt of the medievalists" became increasingly vocal after 1900 when medieval studies underwent a dramatic expansion that produced a significantly altered understanding of this period, leading one eminent medievalist to observe that "no book written about the European Middle Ages before 1895 or so is still worth reading except for curiosity's sake."[67] While perhaps a bit hyperbolic, this statement is revealing for what it suggests about Latter-day Saint reliance on views that the broader historical community now considers obsolete and dismissive of this important era. Where Latter-day Saint authors often emphasize the backwardness and darkness of this age, medievalists since 1900 "have sought to reveal and celebrate the ideas and institutions of the high Middle Ages."[68]

Not only have medieval scholars emphasized the complexity and diversity of medieval civilization, but they have also insisted on its direct relationship to the developments that Burckhardt situated in the Renaissance. Essentially, this medievalist response has argued for continuity over radical change, for evolution over revolution. Johan Huizinga elegantly stated

---

sance in Historical Thought," 5:259–68, and "Interpretations of the Renaissance," 5:286–305.

66. Ferguson, *Renaissance in Historical Thought,* 329 passim.

67. Ferguson, *Renaissance in Historical Thought,* 329; Norman F. Cantor, *Inventing the Middle Ages* (New York: Quill, 1991), 44.

68. Cantor, *Inventing the Middle Ages,* 27. See Ferguson, *Renaissance in Historical Thought,* 330.

this position in his 1919 Dutch classic, *The Waning of the Middle Ages*,[69] and it was also at the heart of Charles Homer Haskins's influential 1927 work, *The Renaissance of the Twelfth Century*. Haskins argued that many of characteristics of the Renaissance—the revival of classical Latin literature, Greek science, and Greek philosophy—had medieval roots. He attacked the Burckhardtian paradigm head-on: "Do not the Middle Ages, that epoch of ignorance, stagnation, and gloom, stand in the sharpest contrast to the light and progress and freedom of the Italian Renaissance?" His response:

> The continuity of history rejects such sharp and violent contrasts between successive periods. . . . [M]odern research shows us the Middle Ages less dark and less static, the Renaissance less bright and less sudden, than was once supposed. The Middle Ages exhibit life and color and change, much eager search after knowledge and beauty, much creative accomplishment in art, in literature, in institutions.[70]

Huizinga and Haskins led the frontal assault on the Renaissance, but others joined them, defending the Middle Ages by drawing explicit links to modern institutions. Frederic William Maitland, for example, traced English common law and the jury system of trials—institutions still in use in the United States and Great Britain—to the thirteenth century. Joseph Strayer emphasized the construction of rational, centralized governmental institutions and the rise of national identities during the medieval period. More recently, scholars have traced "a continuous rising stream of rationality from the military advances of feudal technology and the organization

---

69. First translated into English as Johan Huizinga, *The Waning of the Middle Ages* (London: E. Arnold and Co., 1924).

70. Charles Homer Haskins, *The Renaissance of the Twelfth Century* (Cambridge: Harvard University Press, 1927), v–vi.

of urban commerce in the tenth century, through the classical recovery and dialectical capacity of the twelfth century, to the culminating anticipations of the scientific revolution in the fourteenth century."[71]

The work of the medievalists in the first half of the twentieth century was primarily devoted to demonstrating the continuity and relevance between medieval and modern times. Since the sixties, this "highly overdetermined . . . discourse of continuity and progress" has been replaced by a rich and more particularized field that does not lend itself to easy categorization. Recent scholarship, influenced by postmodernist, anthropological, and feminist theories, has "demodernized" and "defamiliarized" the Middle Ages, emphasizing their fundamental alterity. To be sure, these new interpretations have not gone unchallenged, but as Norman Cantor has recently observed, "The one conclusion that everyone can agree to is the great complexity of high medieval culture, society, government, law, economy, and religion."[72]

This refashioning of the Middle Ages as "other" has been mirrored within the community of Renaissance scholars who have challenged the position posited by their intellectual forefather, Jacob Burckhardt. While his views still inform debates within the field, it is probably safe to say that during the past century scholars have effectively revised the majority of Burckhardt's most evocative hypotheses. Burckhardt is generally no longer read to understand the history of the Renaissance, but rather as an important figure in the historiography of the idea.

---

71. Cantor, *Inventing the Middle Ages,* 369; see 66, 182, 251. See Gabrielle M. Spiegel, "In the Mirror's Eye: The Writing of Medieval History in America," in Molho and Wood, *Imagined Histories,* 243–47.

72. Cantor, *Inventing the Middle Ages,* 27. See Spiegel, "In the Mirror's Eye," 247–51.

For example, in contrast to Burckhardt's vision of the progressive secularization of Italian society—and indeed its irreligiousness—scholars have emphasized the complex and profound religiosity of the Renaissance. With the medievalists, they have convincingly shown that Burckhardt's revival of antiquity, evidenced in humanist thought, had deep medieval roots and that so-called medieval philosophies persevered in popularity throughout the fourteenth and fifteenth centuries and beyond.[73] The Renaissance state, which Burckhardt characterized famously as "a work of art," has been shown to have been a far cry from modern, centralized, rationalized, bureaucratic nation-states.[74] And finally, in the area of Burckhardt's most suggestive hypothesis—the rise of the individual—scholars have convincingly shown the importance of networks of relationships, patronage, and kin groups in the definition of self and in the construction of late medieval and early modern identities.[75]

---

73. Two scholars have been particularly influential in reworking Burckhardt's depiction of Renaissance humanism: Paul Oskar Kristeller and Charles Trinkaus. For a sense of Kristeller's work, see his *Renaissance Thought: The Classic, Scholastic and Humanistic Strains* (New York: Harper, 1961). See also Charles Trinkaus, *In Our Image and Likeness,* 2 vols. (Chicago: University of Chicago Press, 1970); and his *The Scope of Renaissance Humanism* (Ann Arbor, MI: University of Michigan Press, 1983).

74. On the Renaissance state see, among many important scholars, Giorgio Chittolini, *Formazione dello stato regionale e le istituzioni del contado* (Turin: Einaudi, 1979); and Chittolini, *Città, comunità e feudi negli stati dell–Italia centro-settentrionale (secoli XIV-XVI)* (Milan: Edizioni Unicopli 1996); also Julius Kirshner, ed., *The Origins of the State in Italy, 1300–1600* (Chicago: University of Chicago Press, 1995).

75. For example, see Jacques Heers, *Le clan familial au Moyen Age* (Paris: Presses Universitaires de France, 1974); Francis W. Kent,

Where Burckhardt and subsequent generations of scholars sought to trace and link the Renaissance to the modern world, the most recent generation of Renaissance scholars, paralleling similar trends among medievalists, have generally abandoned the search for modernity in fourteenth- and fifteenth-century Italy. Inspired by the work of anthropologists such as Clifford Geertz, Victor Turner, and Mary Douglas, they have sought to "defamiliarize . . . the Renaissance," emphasizing the alterity rather than the modernity of Renaissance Italy.[76] They describe the age as a "distant and alien reality," which must be penetrated and studied in much the same way as anthropologists studied the equally exotic Balinese or Berber cultures. The elaborate ritual life of the Renaissance, its criminality and violence, its witchcraft and superstitions are but a few of the areas of "alienness" or "pre-modernity" to which anthropologically inclined historians have turned their attention.[77] So complete, indeed, has been the refashioning of the Renaissance that the label itself has become a source of debate:

Household and Lineage in Renaissance Florence: The Family Life of the Capponi, Ginori, and Rucellai (Princeton: Princeton University Press, 1977); Anthony Molho, *Marriage Alliance in Late Medieval Florence* (Cambridge: Harvard University Press, 1994); and Stanley Chojnacki, *Women and Men in Renaissance Venice: Twelve Essays on Patrician Society* (Baltimore, MD: Johns Hopkins University Press, 2000).

76. Muir, "The Italian Renaissance in America," 1096. For a somewhat melancholy description of the waning of Renaissance studies, see William J. Bouwsma's 1978 presidential address to the American Historical Association, "Renaissance and the Drama of Western History."

77. Molho, "The Italian Renaissance: Made in the USA," 284. See also Anthony Molho, "Burckhardtian Legacies," *Medievalia et Humanistica*, n.s., 17 (1991): 133–39; Molho, "American Historians and the Italian Renaissance," 18–20; and Molho, "Italian History in American Universities," 220.

increasingly, the less ideologically pregnant label "early modern" has come into favor.

The century since Burckhardt published *The Civilization of the Renaissance in Italy* has seen a considerable change in the way the Renaissance is understood in its relationship to the Middle Ages. The Renaissance is no longer seen as the cradle of modernity, nor is it seen as separated by a chasm from the medieval world. Warren Hollister's assessment seems a fitting epitaph:

> A few generations ago the medieval centuries of European history were widely regarded as "The Dark Ages." Western man was thought to have dropped into a deep slumber at the fall of the Western Roman Empire in A.D. 476, awakening at length, like Rip Van Winkle, in the bright dawn of the Italian Renaissance. . . . It was . . . a millennium of darkness—a thousand years without a bath.
>
> Today this ungenerous point of view stands discredited, although it persists among the half-educated. Several generations of rigorous historical scholarship have demonstrated clearly that the medieval period was an epoch of immense vitality and profound creativity. The age that produced Thomas Aquinas and Dante, Notre Dame de Paris and Chartres, Parliament and the university, can hardly be described as "dark" or "barbaric."[78]

---

78. C. Warren Hollister, *Medieval Europe: A Short* History, 2nd ed. (New York: John Wiley and Sons, 1968), i. For a clever examination of the enduring misconceptions of the Middle Ages in modern culture, see Fred C. Robinson's presidential address to the Medieval Academy of America, "Medieval, the Middle Ages," *Speculum* 59 (October 1984): 745–56; also Mommsen, "Petrarch's Conception of the 'Dark Ages,'" 226–42.

Conclusions

What implications do these historiographical developments have for Latter-day Saint visions of the great apostasy,
the Middle Ages, and the Renaissance? It seems clear that
Roberts's views of Medieval darkness and Renaissance brilliance were formed in the bosom of nineteenth-century scholarship and religious polemics and that Talmage and Smith inherited his vision in large measure. Theirs is, as Davis Bitton
has written, a "conception of history . . . of the past century."[79]
Though diverse opinion certainly persists among students of
the Middle Ages and Renaissance, one would nonetheless be
hard-pressed to find any historian who would argue that the
Middle Ages were a period of political, technological, social,
or cultural backwardness, or that the Renaissance was the moment that brought light back into a dark world. Yet curiously,
this view has often persisted in LDS narratives of the "great
apostasy." Ideas clearly have remarkably long half-lives.

Despite the persistence of the turn-of-the-century paradigm of Roberts, Talmage, and Smith, recent years have seen
the stirring of a more expansive and balanced view of the
apostasy among some Latter-day Saint authorities and scholars. Though the familiar light/dark metaphor has not disappeared entirely, there have been some efforts to emphasize
the spiritual nature of the apostasy without embedding it in
an ahistorical picture of accompanying intellectual and moral
decline. The Latter-day Saint apostle M. Russell Ballard, for
example, has written that the darkness of the Middle Ages refers to the absence of "the light of the *fulness* of the gospel of
Jesus Christ, including the authority of His holy priesthood,"

---

79. Bitton, "B. H. Roberts as Historian," 43.

yet he also notes that good Christians lived during this time.[80] The apostle Dallin H. Oaks likewise affirmed that during the apostasy "men and women . . . kept the light of faith and learning alive" and that "we honor them as servants of God."[81] Indeed, despite his affinity with the work of Roberts, Talmage, and Smith, McConkie too acknowledged that "many good and noble souls lived during the dark ages, . . . and they received guidance from th[e] Spirit."[82]

While none of these recent entries can fairly be compared with the all-encompassing early historical narratives of apostasy, still they suggest perhaps the first stirrings of a change that may bridge the disjuncture between traditional Latter-day Saint and contemporary scholarly views of the Middle Ages and the Renaissance. These and some other recent works are moving away from necessitating and justifying the restoration by depicting the apostasy as an age of complete degradation, moral stupor, and intellectual stagnancy. Instead, the apostasy is depicted simply as an age in which priesthood authority did not exist, a view that may be closer in some ways to the views of apostasy in Mormonism's earliest days. By emphasizing the spiritual nature of the apostasy, Latter-day Saints may be able to acknowledge the historical complexity and richness of the Middle Ages and the Renaissance without challenging the need for God's calling of Joseph Smith to effect a restoration of priesthood authority. In this new picture there is no disjunc-

---

80. M. Russell Ballard, *Our Search for Happiness: An Invitation to Understand the Church of Jesus Christ of Latter-day Saints* (Salt Lake City: Deseret Book, 1993), 30–32.

81. Dallin H. Oaks, "Apostasy and Restoration," *Ensign,* May 1995, 84–87.

82. McConkie, *New Witness for the Articles of Faith,* 477. See also, Compton, "Apostasy," 1:58.

ture between the accepted historical understanding of the age and Latter-day Saint ideas on apostasy. If justification for such a reevaluation is necessary, historical precedent and inspiration for further research into other vintage views of apostasy can perhaps be found in apostle John Taylor's 1873 statement:

> I have a great many misgivings about the intelligence that men boast so much of in this enlightened day. There were men in those dark ages who could commune with God, and who, by the power of faith, could draw aside the curtain of eternity and gaze upon the invisible world[,] . . . have the ministering of angels, and unfold the future destinies of the world. If those were dark ages I pray God to give me a little darkness, and deliver me from the light and intelligence that prevail in our day.[83]

---

83. *Journal of Discourses* 16:197; see Compton, "Apostasy," 1:58.

This is an abbreviated version of an article that first appeared as "Inheriting the 'Great Apostasy': Medieval and Renaissance in Mormon Thought" in *Journal of Mormon History* 28 (Fall 2002): 23–59.

"A World in Darkness": Early Latter-day Saint Understanding of the Apostasy, 1830–1834

Richard E. Bennett and Amber J. Seidel

I was answered that I must join none of them, for they were all wrong; and the Personage who addressed me said that all their creeds were an abomination in his sight; that those professors were all corrupt; that: "they draw near to me with their lips, but their hearts are far from me, they teach for doctrines the commandments of men, having a form of godliness, but they deny the power thereof."

(Joseph Smith—History 1:19)

So wrote the Prophet Joseph Smith of his first vision experience that occurred early in the spring of 1820. Of the many transcendent truths the young boy prophet learned that fateful morning in the grove about the nature of God, about himself and his budding mission, we wish to comment on but one—namely, the apostasy: how he and his earliest associates regarded its causes, consequences, and possible implications.[1]

---

1. Perhaps still the best-known doctrinal study of the Latter-day Saint position of the apostasy is that by James E. Talmage, *The Great Apostasy: Considered in the Light of Scriptural and Secular*

Our first purpose will be to show that Joseph Smith's sense of an apostasy from the true Christian faith was ratified in the first vision; furthermore, that this understanding changed and developed during the early years of his prophetic training. Our second objective will be to examine how the doctrine of the apostasy was understood and taught by both leaders and missionaries within the first four years of the organization of the Church of Christ in 1830. Although this is a subjective rather than a quantitative study, we have concluded, after an extensive review of many of the contemporary sources, that early church views of the apostasy were very pronounced and multifaceted. In particular we note their teaching of the universality of the apostasy, of so great a corruption and contamination of the Christian church as to beg the imminent return of Christ, that more attention was given to the fallen state of Christianity than merely the loss of priesthood, and, finally,

---

History. (Salt Lake City: Deseret Book, 1909). While scores of missionary tracts, sermons, and conference addresses have addressed the doctrine of the apostasy, surprisingly little has been written in a formal academic way on the topic as understood and taught by early church leaders and missionaries. Two of the most ambitious studies of early Latter-day Saint missionary efforts are George S. Ellsworth's "A History of Mormon Missions in the United States and Canada, 1830–1860 (PhD diss., Berkeley, University of California, 1950) and Rex Thomas Price Jr.'s "The Mormon Missionary of the Nineteenth Century" (PhD diss., University of Wisconsin, 1991). While excellent for their information on missionary travels, habits of preaching, persecution, and style, neither work emphasizes the message of the missionaries to any great extent, although Price does discuss the importance of Zion and of gathering out of Babylon to Zion. Nor is the topic of central emphasis in any of the more notable biographies of the Prophet Joseph Smith.

that the apostasy extended to a scattering of an ancient covenant people as much as it was a retreat from theological truth.

The First Vision and the Apostasy

Joseph Smith's early sense of an apostasy stemmed from his deep distress with competing Christian faiths revivalistically warring one against another. Their divisions were, to him, far more than academic; they posed a very serious personal obstacle. Knowing which of the churches he should join was a matter of personal salvation. "He perceived that it was a question of infinite importance," said Orson Pratt "and that the salvation of his soul depended upon a correct understanding of the same. . . . To decide, without any positive and definite evidence, on which he could rely, upon a subject involving the future welfare of his soul, was revolting to his feelings."[2] Joseph Smith himself put it this way:

> When about fourteen years of age I began to reflect upon the importance of being prepared for a future state, and upon enquiring [about] the plan of salvation I found that there was a great clash in religious sentiment; if I went to one society they referred me to one plan, and another to another . . . considering that all could not be right . . . I determined to investigate the subject more fully.[3]

---

2. Milton V. Backman, Jr., *Joseph Smith's First Vision: The First Vision in Its Historical Context* (Salt Lake City: Bookcraft, 1971), 170–72. Orson Hyde's 1842 account of the first vision parallels that of Orson Pratt's in his reference to Joseph's concern "for a future state of existence" and "in what way to prepare himself" Backman, *Joseph Smith's First Vision*, 173–74. Spelling and punctuation have been normalized throughout.

3. Extract from the John Wentworth letter in Backman, *Joseph Smith's First Vision*, 168.

Such confusion explains his frustrations and his fears. "In the midst of this war or words and tumult of opinions," he later wrote, "I often said to myself: What is to be done? Who of all these parties are right; or, are they all wrong together? If any one of them be right, which is it, and how shall I know it?" (JS—H 1:10).

Unquestionably, nearby contemporary religious revivals had aggravated his soul. The more he listened and compared, the more his frustrations deepened, leading him into despair. He was clearly convinced that he, like so many others, had sinned and was in need of forgiveness. "I felt to mourn for my own sins and for the sins of the world," he later remarked. "Therefore I cried unto the Lord for mercy."[4] However, where was he to turn for a remission of his sins? "My mind became exceedingly distressed," he said in his first recorded account of the first vision, "for I became convicted of my sins and by searching the scriptures I found that mankind did not come unto the Lord but that they had apostatized from the true and living faith and there was no society or denomination that built upon the Gospel of Jesus Christ as recorded in the New Testament."[5] Put another way, the confusion in his mind begged to be settled before the confession of his heart.

To be sure, Joseph was not alone in seeking forgiveness. Almost every contemporary camp meeting and revival enjoined its listeners to seek the Lord in prayer. Not only in the so-called "Burned Over District" of upstate New York but also in scores of hamlets elsewhere in America and, indeed, in many other parts of the world, were other young men and women seeking for forgiveness of sin and for personal salvation. Wrote one Eliza Higgins of her 1818 experience:

4. Backman, *Joseph Smith's First Vision*, 156.
5. Backman, *Joseph Smith's First Vision*, 156.

I attended a Camp-meeting, resolved not to leave the ground until I was blessed with a change of heart. I thought if I perished, I would perish at the feet of sovereign mercy . . . after a sleepless night, I went early to one of these praying circles. For a while I *stood* as a critic and then went without an invitation and *knelt* as a *penitent*. . . I soon felt a firm belief that my Heavenly Father heard, and would answer to the joy of my heart.[6]

In June 1820, another young lad in Georgia "about thirteen or fourteen years old" told of how reading Ecclesiastes 12:1—"Remember now thy Creator in the days of thy youth"—brought him to seek forgiveness:

It came with such weight on his mind . . . that he was soon brought to see the wickedness of his heart, and how just it would be in God to cut him off in that state. But at length, after continuing in that state of distress and despondency for a long time, he said that as he was walking alone one evening he thought he would go and try for the last time to pray once more. But before he could find a suitable place, these words passed sweetly through his mind, "Come unto me, all ye that labor and are heavy laden, and I will give you rest." With these words he had a view of the Lord Jesus Christ, who satisfied the law for him.[7]

Yet another account, this one from England written in 1821, tells of another conversion story.

I opened the Bible . . . so intolerable was the burden of guilt under which I labored . . . that in the most fervent manner I was constrained to agonize with God in prayer. I continued

---

6. From a memoir of Miss Eliza Higgins, *Methodist Magazine* 5, May 1822, 290.

7. John Hamrick to A. Davis, 24 June 1820, *The American Baptist Magazine and Missionary Intelligencer* 3/1, January 1821, 37.

. . . for three days, when the Lord . . . graciously favored me with a sense of redemption, through the blood of Jesus, by forgiving all my sins. Being in the field, in the exercise of prayer, I heard, as it were, a voice, saying, "Ho! Every one that thirsteth, let him come and drink of the waters of life freely"; when by faith I beheld the Son of God evidently as crucified before me, was delivered of the burden of guilt, and was enabled to exclaim "Lord, I will praise thee." Thus was my darkness turned into light, and my mourning into joy, which was unspeakably great.[8]

Indeed, the religious literature of the day is replete with such accounts of men and women seeking and obtaining divine forgiveness, evidence of the remarkable effect of revivals among the people.

However, what Joseph Smith sought first was to know which church to join in order to submit himself to grace. The one issue could not be settled in his mind without addressing the other. In his official account, written in 1838, he wrote: "My object in going to inquire of the Lord was to know which of all the sects was right, that I might know which to join" (JS—H 1:18). The answer given him to "join none of them, for they were all wrong," would certainly address one of his concerns and that of many of his later followers, but in his earlier accounts, he seems to have stressed the more personal aspect of the vision. In his first recorded account of the vision, written in 1832, Joseph Smith emphasized this theme of atonement and personal forgiveness. "I saw the Lord," he said. "And he spake unto me saying 'Joseph my son thy sins are forgiven thee. Go thy way walk in my statutes and keep my commandments.

---

8. From a short biography of Mr. Stephen Butler and of his 1800 conversion experience, see *Methodist Magazine* 4, May 1821, 167.

Behold . . . I was crucified for the world that all those who believe in my name may have Eternal life.'"[9]

Orson Hyde, in his account of the first vision, alluded to the double meaning of this experience: he "received a promise that the true doctrine—the fulness of the gospel—should, at some future time, be made known to him; after which, the vision withdrew, leaving his mind in a state of calmness and peace indescribable."[10] Thus Joseph's theophany was both personal forgiveness and religious instruction.[11]

It would be grossly incorrect to argue that a sense of the apostasy began with Joseph Smith and the Latter-day Saints. For centuries, churches of the Reformation had been teaching that an apostasy had long ago occurred in the Christian world. The very essence of Calvinistic and Lutheran Protestantism had been to protest against corrupt, if not apostate, claims and beliefs that they believed had corrupted the Roman Catholic Church and to initiate essential reforms to purify and redeem the Christian

---

9. Backman, *Joseph Smith's First Vision*, 157.

10. Backman, *Joseph Smith's First Vision*, 175.

11. Elder Henry B. Eyring of the Quorum of the Twelve Apostles alluded to this truth when dedicating Avard T. Fairbank's sculpture of the Prophet Joseph Smith in the grove located in the Joseph Smith Building on the campus of Brigham Young University. Said Elder Eyring: "From studying the various accounts of the First Vision, we learn that young Joseph went into the grove not only to learn which church he should join but also to obtain forgiveness for his sins, something he seems not to have understood how to do. And in more that one account the Lord addressed the young truth seeker and said, 'Joseph, my son, thy sins are forgiven thee.'" Henry B. Eyring, unveiling ceremony of "The Vision," a statue by Avard T. Fairbanks, 17 October 1997, as inscripted in stone monument, first floor, Joseph Smith Building, Brigham Young University, Provo, Utah.

church. The following excerpt from the September 1820 issue of the American religious periodical, *Christian Disciple*, is but one of hundreds of examples of how many contemporary American Protestants, even the more liberal denominations, were then viewing the apostasy:

> Religion is not respected because it is not understood, because a low, earth-born rival has assumed the name and place of that principle whose origin is from heaven. . . . It is not necessary to consider the condition of Catholic countries where the monstrous corruptions which have been connected with Christianity, have left it scarcely any disciples, except among the lower and more ignorant classes of society. We may see enough of the disastrous consequences of error in Protestant countries, in our own neighborhood, among those whom we meet in the common intercourse of life. . . . The dark ages were the triumph and consummation of the errors and vices which were in the world when Christianity was introduced.[12]

Joseph Smith, therefore, was certainly not the author of the concept of an apostasy from the original Christian church.

Yet of all the many truths of the first vision, two stood out in his mind: first, that the resurrected Christ forgives sins upon the principle of repentance, and, second, that God affirmed the reality of a universal apostate world. In fact, the depth and decay of that apostasy were far greater than the young prophet could have ever realized for, as he himself later admitted, "at this time it had never entered into my heart that all were wrong."[13] In Joseph Smith's dawning understanding he learned that something terribly wrong had happened to original Christianity and that despite every good intention and reform, a "calamity" had overtaken the world.

---

12. *Christian Disciple* 11 (September/October 1820): 346, 358.
13. Backman, *Joseph Smith's First Vision*, 163.

Moroni and the Translation of the Book of Mormon

During the ensuing three years, Joseph once again fell into various transgressions and "foibles" of youth "which brought a wound upon [his] soul"[14] so much so that on the evening of 21 September 1823, he "betook [him]self to prayer and supplication to Almighty God for forgiveness" (JS—H 1:28–29).

In response, a light began to appear in his room "which continued to increase until the room was lighter than at noon-day" (JS—H 1:30) in which light the resurrected angel Moroni appeared. Inherent in Moroni's subsequent instructions concerning the coming forth of the Book of Mormon and the role Joseph Smith would play in that unfolding drama, was a renewed forgiveness of his sins and a reiteration of several gospel truths, the apostasy included.

Moroni's instructions and teachings from the Holy Bible, repeated in several consecutive visits that occupied the entire night and part of the following day, included many warnings and prophecies. He informed him that terrible consequences were inevitable because of the calamity of the apostasy, that "great judgments . . . were coming upon the earth, with great desolations by famine, sword, and pestilence; and that these grievous judgments would come on the earth in this generation" (JS—H 1:45).

In a remarkable series of letters published in the *Evening and the Morning Star* in 1834, Oliver Cowdery spoke freely of Joseph Smith's early visions. He said that Moroni quoted liberally from Isaiah about "a marvelous work and a wonder," and apparently expanded their view of the apostasy and its consequences. Moroni confirmed that according to:

---

14. Reproduced in Dean C. Jessee, ed., *Personal Writings of Joseph Smith,* rev. ed. (Salt Lake City: Deseret Book, 2002), 12.

his covenant which he made with his ancient saints, his people, the house of Israel, must come to a knowledge of the gospel, [and be] gathered in to rejoice in one fold under one Shepherd. . . . He then proceeded and gave a general account of the promises made to the fathers, and also gave a history of the aborigines of this country, and said they were literal descendants of Abraham. He represented them as once being an enlightened and intelligent people, possessing a correct knowledge of the gospel, and the plan of restoration and redemption.[15]

Yet despite this fall,

it will come to pass, that though the house of Israel has forsaken the Lord, and bowed down and [worshipped] other gods . . . and been cast out before the face of the world, they will know the voice of the Shepherd when he calls upon them this time.[16]

From Moroni, then, Joseph Smith learned that the apostasy encompassed more than the loss of a true Christian faith in the old world; it also included the dwindling of ancient covenant peoples, specifically the scattering of Israel, "in a cloudy and dark day" (D&C 109:61), and in such divergent and forbidden paths as to obscure their nobility, dignity and place as God's chosen people. And as with Ephraim and Manasseh, so, too, with Judah. Furthermore, Cowdery asserted that "calamity would fall upon that people," and that "the wrath of heaven

---

15. Letter IV from Oliver Cowdery to W.W. Phelps. First published in the *Evening and Morning Star,* 1834. Reproduced in Dean C. Jessee, ed., *The Papers of Joseph Smith, Autobiographical and Historical Writings* (Salt Lake City: Deseret Book, 1989), 1:52–53.

16. Oliver Cowdery to W. W. Phelps, in Jessee, *Papers of Joseph Smith,* 1:67, Letter VI.

[would] overtake them to their overthrow."[17] "In consequence of their rejecting the gospel, the Lord suffered them to be again scattered; their land to be wasted and their beautiful city to be trodden down of the Gentiles."[18]

The prophecies of Nephi as found in the early pages of the Book of Mormon refer often to the apostasy in words and images not easy to overlook. At the risk of equating Book of Mormon doctrine to their translator's understanding of them (not always nor necessarily the same), one is quickly made aware that the Book of Mormon says much about this catastrophe. While the term *apostasy* is not found in the Book of Mormon, it speaks often of "captivity," of perversion, of an "awful state of blindness" (1 Nephi 13:32) among the Gentiles, of a "great whore of all the earth" (see 1 Nephi 14), of "the mother of abominations" (see 1 Nephi 14) and of such "sinning" that "an exceedingly great many do stumble, yea, insomuch that Satan hath great power over them" (1 Nephi 13:29). Pending further study, it would appear that the Book of Mormon itself was a primer on the apostasy and likely was a major source of the unique Latter-day Saint view of the breadth and depth of the apostasy, especially when compared to contemporary interpretations.

The process of translating the Book of Mormon was itself a catalyst for further revelation. "No men in their sober senses, could translate and write the directions given to the Nephites," Cowdery wrote, "from the mouth of the Savior of the precise manner in which men should build up his church, and especially, when corruption had spread an uncertainty over all forms and systems practiced among men, without desiring"

---

17. Cowdery to Phelps, in Jessee, *Papers of Joseph Smith,* 1:39, Letter II.

18. Cowdery to Phelps, in Jessee, *Papers of Joseph Smith,* 1:59, Letter V.

baptism, or, as he defined it, "to answer 'a good conscience by the resurrection of Jesus Christ.'"[19] "After writing [translating] the account of the Savior's ministry to the remnant of the seed of Jacob," Oliver recalled: "it was easily to be seen, as the prophet [Moroni] said it would be, that darkness covered the earth and gross darkness the minds of the people. On reflecting further, it was easily to be seen that amid the great strife and noise concerning religion, none had authority from God to administer the ordinances of the gospel."[20]

What followed was the vision of John the Baptist and the restoration of the Aaronic Priesthood. Oliver summarized the effects as follows:

> What joy! what wonder! what amazement! While the world was racked and distracted—while millions were groping as the blind for the wall, and while all men were resting upon uncertainty, as a general mass, our eyes beheld, our ears heard, as in the "blaze of day."[21]

Later, in 1834, he put it this way:

> This gospel has been perverted and men have wandered in darkness. That commission given to the apostles at Jerusalem . . . has been hid from the world, because of evil, and the honest have been led by the designing, till there are none to be found who are practising the ordinances of the gospel, as they were anciently delivered.[22]

---

19. Cowdery to Phelps, in Jessee, *Papers of Joseph Smith,* 1:30, Letter I.

20. Letter I from Oliver Cowdery to W. W. Phelps, in Jessee, *Papers of Joseph Smith,* 1:30.

21. *Messenger and Advocate* 1 (October 1834), 14 (p. 59 of the PoGP).

22. Cowdery to Phelps, in Jessee, *Papers of Joseph Smith,* 1:59, Letter V.

Joseph Smith's later work in revising the Holy Bible also clarified their understanding further. "It will be seen by this that the most plain parts of the New Testament have been taken from it," wrote W. W. Phelps in June 1832, "by the Mother of Harlots . . . from the year A.D. 460 to 1400. This is a sufficient reason for the Lord to give command to have it translated anew."[23] Added Oliver Cowdery,

> I am ready to admit that men in previous generations have with polluted hands and corrupt hearts, taken from the sacred oracle, many precious items which were plain of comprehension, for the main purpose for building themselves up in the trifling things of this world.[24]

The very work of biblical translation gave rise to their argument that the sins of the apostasy were more than those of unfortunate omission and loss.

Even at this early date, Joseph Smith saw the apostasy in more than denominational or even solely religious terms. "The plain fact is this," he added later in January 1833,

> the light of the latter day glory begins to break forth through the dark atmosphere of sectarian wickedness and their iniquity [rolls] up into view and the nations of the Gentiles are like the waves of the sea casting up mire and dirt or all in commotion.[25]

While it would be totally unfair to argue that Joseph Smith saw wickedness in all the priests and teachers of the day, there is no question that sin, universal sin, was a characteristic of the apostasy which he saw as both rampant and tragic.

---

23. *Evening and Morning Star,* June 1832, 3.

24. Cowdery to Phelps, in Jessee, *Papers of Joseph Smith,* 1:72, Letter VII.

25. Joseph Smith to "Mr. Editor," 4 January 1833, as quoted in Jessee, *Personal Writings,* 296.

The apostasy had also corrupted secular knowledge. Joseph wrote:

> For some length of time, I have been carefully viewing the state of things as now appear throughout our Christian land and have looked at it with feelings of the most painful anxiety while upon the one hand beholding the manifest withdrawal of God's Holy Spirit and the veil of stupidity which seems to be drawn over the hearts of the people.[26]

Furthermore its contaminating effects had spread to nations and governments. "For not only the churches are dwindling away, but there are no conversions, or but very few, and this is not all, the governments of the earth are thrown into confusion and division and destruction."[27] Thus Joseph Smith's view of the apostasy had developed from a religious deterioration to include decay in secular learning, government, and authority.

And with this deterioration, the Prophet taught the urgency of declaring the restoration and the need for a gathering to Zion (Missouri) in expectation of the millennial return of Christ, if for no other reason than to blunt the wrath of Providence upon a world intent on the willful disregard of truth and disobedience to command. Joseph Smith was quick to argue that the restoration of Gospel truths and the reestablishment of the church did not signal the immediate end of the apostasy; rather its intensification.

> Some may pretend to say that the world in this age is fast increasing in righteousness; that the dark ages of superstition are held by only a few. . . But a moment's candid reflection

---

26. Jessee, *Personal Writings*, 295.

27. Jessee, *Personal Writings*, 296–97. This latter view, affecting the legitimacy of government, would come under close scrutiny.

... is sufficient for every candid man to draw a conclusion in his own mind whether this is the order of heaven or not.[28]

Who can look at the Christian world and see the apostasy therefore and not exclaim in the language of Isaiah, "the earth is defiled under the inhabitants thereof because they have transgressed the laws, changed the ordinances and broken the everlasting covenant?" The plain fact is this, the power of God begins to fall upon the Nations. . . . And now what remains to be done . . . in order [to] escape the judgments of God which are almost ready to burst upon the nations of the earth—Repent of all your sins and be baptized . . . that ye may receive the Holy Spirit of God.[29]

By way of review, then, after years of instruction Joseph and Oliver's understanding of a loss of truth had deepened to a sense of a great and global apostasy, that gross darkness blanketed the entire world and that the world lay in sin and captivity, that religious corruption had contaminated much of Christian communication and standards of behavior, that there had been a subtraction of priesthood legitimacy and authority, that the apostasy extended to the diminution and scattering of God's ancient covenant people Israel, and finally, if a less developed doctrine, that modern nations and governments acted without authority.

Proclaim the Word

Many of the earliest converts to the church could empathize with Joseph Smith's quest for religious truth. They, too, had explored the scriptures, compared the teachings in the New Testament with those of other faiths, and had sought a

---

28. Joseph Fielding Smith, comp., *Teachings of the Prophet Joseph Smith* (Salt Lake City: Deseret Book, 1965), 48–49.

29. Jessee, *Personal Writings*, 297.

forgiveness of sins. Joel Hills Johnson wrote in his diary, "When reading the New Testament I would often wonder why people did not baptize for the remission of sins."[30] Parley P. Pratt likewise said, "My mind was drawn out from time to time on the things of God and eternity. I felt deeply anxious to be saved from my sins, and to secure an interest in that world 'where the wicked cease from troubling, and the weary are at rest.'"[31] With the church still in its infancy, many of its newest converts sought to spread the word while at the same time gather to Zion. Jonathan Crosby, for instance, prayed that, "the Lord would rend the heavens and come down, and remove the darkness which covers the earth, and gross darkness the minds of the people."[32] Among the doctrines these earliest converts preached, the apostasy was prominent, if not paramount.[33] These included the loss of truth, resultant false religion, the absence of authority, and the scattering of Israel.

But can we answer particulars about such teachings? And can we be more specific about the time frame? In answer to this second question, it would appear that the apostasy was

---

30. Diary of Joel Hills Johnson, 1802–1882, 1:32, L. Tom Perry Special Collections Library, Harold B. Lee Library, Brigham Young University, Provo, Utah. Hereafter referred to as BYU Special Collections.

31. Scott Facer Proctor and Maurine Jensen Proctor, *Autobiography of Parley Pratt,* rev. ed. (Salt Lake City: Deseret Book, 2000), 24.

32. *Evening and Morning Star* 2/23, August 1834, 181. Letter from Jonathan Crosby Jr.

33. Of 16 missionaries who served in the period from 1830 to 1834, according to their diaries 75 percent taught various elements of the apostasy. These included Calvin Beebe, Jonathan Crosby Jr., Peter Dustin, William Draper, William Huntington, Joseph G. Hovey, Orson Hyde, Joel Hills Johnson, Wandle Mace, William E. McLellin, John Murdock, W. W. Phelps, Parley P. Pratt, Samuel H. Smith, Sylvester Smith, and Brigham Young.

understood and taught somewhat differently, or least with different emphasis, at various stages in early church history. In the very formative years of the church, from 1830 until the expulsion of the Saints from Independence, Missouri in late 1833 and their resultant sufferings in exile in Clay County, Missouri, in 1834, the literature—both printed and unpublished—emphasized the "gathering" to Zion and the earnest expectation of the second coming and millennial return of the Son of God. Indeed, the stress was on the wickedness of the surrounding world, the urgent need to come out of "Babylon" in advance of the "overflowing scourge" (D&C 45:31) God would soon send upon the earth. After 1834, there comes a subtle, yet distinctive change in tone and interpretation of the doctrine, a topic beyond the scope of this present study.[34]

Specifically then, for our present purposes, we wish to address the following four questions:

---

34. Preliminary studies indicate that the expulsion of the Saints from Independence, Missouri in late 1833 and their subsequent wintry exile in Clay County in 1834 may have rigidified or made more shrill Mormon comments about the world and its evil state. Note the following editorial comments, its tone and contents, after the persecutions of Jackson County: "The fact is established, that those who persecute are the children of 'that wicked one.' . . . Those who persecute this church . . . have forsaken his house, left the fold, and like wandering stars, filthy dreamers, or beasts of corruption, [are] abandoned to be taken and destroyed in their own wickedness." *Evening and Morning Star* 2/24, September 1834, 185. The enormous disappointment of their shattered dream of Zion can hardly be overstated. How much of their later views of the apostasy were really aimed at Missouri is hard to determine. Thus, for this study, our efforts are to try to ascertain how the Saints viewed the apostasy before their Missouri difficulties occurred.

• Did the early missionaries and church writers (1830 to mid-1834) teach the universality of the apostasy? What effect had it wrought upon other faiths and upon the lives of people all over the world? How pervasive and contaminating were its effects?

• Was the call to gather to Zion in part a result of the apostasy?

• In these early years, did they emphasize the loss of priesthood authority as a critical element and characteristic of the apostasy?

• Finally, did they teach the two apostasies, i.e., the scattering of Israel as well as the loss of the true Christian church?

That many missionaries inferred such negative consequences while teaching the happier news of the restored Gospel cannot be denied. The tone of their declarations is much more a positive than a negative declaration. Nevertheless we argue that in the angel of the restoration was the devil of the apostasy.

How Universal the Apostasy?

In a letter to an inquirer, Joseph Smith wrote that "the Gentiles have not continued in the goodness of God, but have departed from the faith that was once delivered to the Saints, and have broken the covenant in which their fathers were established."[35] To his way of thinking, the apostasy was the result of broken covenant. As stated in his revelation of 1 November 1831, the "Preface" to the Book of Commandments, the effects had been both universal and devastating,

> For they have strayed from mine ordinances, and have broken mine everlasting covenant; They seek not the Lord to establish his righteousness, but every man walketh in his own way, and after the image of his own god, whose image is in the likeness of the world, and whose substance is that

---

35. *Teachings of the Prophet Joseph Smith,* 15.

of an idol, which waxeth old and shall perish in Babylon, even Babylon the great, which shall fall. (D&C 1:15–16)

The early missionary force of the church spoke of the apostasy in very strident tones. They taught that it was a reality, long prophesied and now fulfilled, that the Christian world had lost its way, the results of which were spiritually and morally devastating. To minimize this fact is to misunderstand our history.

Joseph Smith's younger brother, Samuel, sometimes referred to as the "first missionary" of the restoration, fairly well echoed his brother's perspective in the following statement:

> I have written . . . to prove that the Gentiles have broken the everlasting covenant and that darkness has covered the earth since the days of the Apostles and to show the calamity that is coming upon them and to prove that while in this situation the Lord was to lift up a standard to the people which should . . . come forth to throw light into the minds of the people and to deliver them from the darkness that had happened unto them and to show the way of deliverance from the judgments that are coming upon the Gentiles.[36]

Wrote W. W. Phelps,

> The reformers of these last days, among those who call themselves reformers, are very near a ridiculous farce, possessing scarcely one feature of primitive Christianity, and savoring very much of Paul's apostasy, that is a form of godliness without the power. This seems to be the common failing of all the sects in Christendom, so called.[37]

Orson Hyde spoke in 1832 of "the blindness that had happened in consequence of the falling away from the faith that

---

36. Samuel H. Smith Journal, LDS Church Archives (written after 15 October 1832) np; typescript in BYU Special Collections, 22–23.

37. *Evening and Morning Star* 2/17, February 1834, 131.

was delivered to the Saints."[38] And Sylvester Smith, writing in May 1833 from his missionary labors in southern New York state added the following,

> I am sensible that the word will not grow and flourish upon the barren rocks of pride and unbelief, which is almost the only characteristic of the old churches. When I view the situation of the sectarians of the day, my heart cries, wo, wo, wo, to the scribes and pharisees, hypocrites, who build and garnish the sepulchers of the apostles! But alas! Their building upon the old covenant will not save them if they reject the new! Their crying out against the murderers of Christ and his apostles will not save them, while they stone those whom the Lord sends to warn them of the desolation which await the wicked.[39]

In 1834 William McLellin quoted from Jude 1:3 when he addressed a congregation "about an hour and a quarter on the situation or confusion of the world and on the faith once delivered to the saints."[40] Orson Hyde, referencing the same scripture but on another account, "show[ed] them the blindness that had happened in consequence of the falling away from the faith that was delivered to the Saints."[41]

Said W. W. Phelps in 1834,

> The world . . . was to wander far from God, and righteousness was so far to depart from the earth and the true principles of the religion of heaven to be so neglected, as to leave the world in a state of apostasy . . . Isaiah says in [60:2], "For

38. Samuel H. Smith Journal, 27 August 1832, 17.

39. *Evening and Morning Star* 2/14, July 1833, 109. Letter from a missionary serving in Chenago Point, New York.

40. Jan Shipps and John W. Welch, eds., *The Journals of William E. McLellin: 1831–1836* (Provo, UT: BYU Studies, 1994), 31 August 1834, 136.

41. Samuel H. Smith Journal, 27 August 1832, 17.

behold, the darkness shall cover the earth, and gross darkness the people." Any man who will read this ... will see ...
it was at this time that darkness was to cover the earth and
gross darkness the minds of the people.[42]

Orson Pratt, active in proselyting activity since late 1830,
summarized his teachings of the apostasy and of "the falling
away of the Church of Christ,"[43] and the fact that "there could
not but one church be correct"[44] in the following jubilant letter
he wrote to Oliver Cowdery:

> Who could have supposed five years ago that truth would
> have spread so rapid ... it moves in majesty and power, and
> continues its steady course, pulling down the strongholds of
> Babylon, and leaving her mighty towers, exposing the creeds,
> systems and inventions of men, exhibiting the extreme igno-
> rance, follies and errors of all sects, which causes their priests
> to rage and their mighty ones to tremble.[45]

Admitted Parley P. Pratt,

> At the commencement of 1830, I felt drawn out in an extra-
> ordinary manner to search the prophets, and to pray for an

---

42. *Evening and Morning Star* 2/22, June 1834, 162; and 2/23, July
1834, 169. Again from Phelps: "In consequence of the religious world
having lost the power of getting revelations for themselves they have
fallen into their present state of confusion, each partly manufactur-
ing duties for themselves. For instance, the Presbyterian, the Epis-
copalian, the Methodist, and the Catholic god with the god of some
other sects, requires them, (or at least they think he does) to sprinkle
their children, while the Baptist ... god is greatly offended with it"
(*Evening and Morning Star* 2/23, July 1834, 171).

43. Elden J. Watson, comp. and arr., *The Orson Pratt Journals* (Salt
Lake City: Watson, 1975), 13 March, 1835, 52, and 2 June 1835, 65.

44. Watson, *Orson Pratt Journals,* 23 August 1835, 70.

45. Watson, *Orson Pratt Journals,* letter of Orson Pratt to Oliver
Cowdery, 16 February 1835, 47.

understanding of the same. . . . I began to understand the things which were coming on the earth—the restoration of Israel, the coming of the Messiah, and the glory that should follow. I was so astonished at the darkness of myself and mankind on these subjects that I could exclaim with the prophet: surely *"darkness covers the earth, and gross darkness the minds of the people."*[46]

Nor was it only the Christian world that had so suffered. Oliver Cowdery, writing in 1834, clearly described it in universal terms:

No man in his sober senses, with the word of God in his hand, can reflect one moment upon these scenes without being filled with awe! In distant lands, now abandoned to darkness, where human beings bow down and worship the work of their own hands, and call for assistance upon a block of wood of their own carving, have also felt the *sting* of pestilence, the angel of death, and the calamity of war! . . . Century has slept after century: wickedness has borne its accustomed sway; the great deceiver has blinded and led captive his millions; truth has fled, virtue ceased, and righteousness failed from off the earth, and the boaster against God has raised his head in blasphemies, from age to age, and the end is not yet![47]

The perceived rise in criminal activity was also viewed as a result of the apostasy. Note the following editorial comments, presumably by Phelps, written in the summer of 1833,

The Lord has said, that he is holding his Spirit from the inhabitants of the earth, and when we see a robbery in one paper,

---

46. Proctor and Proctor, *Autobiography of Parley Pratt*, 33. Italics preserved from original.

47. *Evening and Morning Star* 2/24, September 1834, 185. From an "Address to the Patrons of the *Evening and Morning Star*," arguably written by Oliver Cowdery, then editor.

and a murder in another, yea, and all manner of crimes following each other, in quick succession, we are led to exclaim: "The Spirit of God has nearly done striving with man! Surely great things await this generation. . . . Notwithstanding man has been laboring for centuries, to preach the gospel to all nations, it has not been done; and the Lord has now commenced his strange act."[48]

Perhaps no one paints a more catastrophic picture of the omnipresent evil and ubiquitous wickedness in the world than Oliver Cowdery,

> Consider for a moment, brethren, the fulfillment of the words of the prophet: for we beheld that darkness covers the earth, and gross darkness the minds of the inhabitants thereof—that crimes of every description are increasing among men—vices of every enormity are practiced—the rising generation growing up in the fulness of pride and arrogance—the aged losing every sense of conviction, and seemingly banishing every thought of a day of retribution—intemperance, immorality, extravagance, pride, blindness of heart, idolatry, the loss of natural affection, the love of this world, and indifference toward the things of eternity increasing among those who profess a belief in the religion of heaven, and infidelity spreading itself in consequence of the same—man giving themselves up to commit acts of the foulest kind, and deeds of the blackest dye; lying, blaspheming, stealing, robbing, murdering, defaming, defrauding . . . forsaking the covenant of heaven, and denying the faith of Jesus Christ—and in the midst of all this, the day of the Lord fast approaching when none except those who have on the wedding garment shall be permitted to eat and drink in the presence of the Bridegroom, the Prince of Peace! . . . Who but those who can see the awful precipice

1834-35

---

48. *Evening and Morning Star* 2/14, July 1833, 107.

upon which the world of mankind stand in this generation, can labor in the vineyard of the Lord with a feeling sense of their deplorable situation? Some may presume to say that the world in this age is fast increasing in righteousness; the dark ages of superstition and blindness have passed over, when the faith of Christ was known and practiced only by a few, when ecclesiastical power held an almost universal control over Christendom. . . . But, a moment's candid reflection, . . . we think, is sufficient for every candid man to draw a conclusion.[49]

The apostasy, then, had thoroughly corrupted virtually all of the Christian world. And because of it "surely, gross darkness covers the earth, and wickedness greatly prevails among the people, and the truth makes them angry, for they are joined to their idols."[50] Seen as far more than a mere decayed institution, or loss of a validating priesthood, or even the absence of gospel truths, it had ushered in a time of sin and corruption, a terrible state of affairs which missionaries viewed as confirmation of that calamity.

Was the Gathering to Zion Taught as Evidence of the Apostasy?

The very earliest revelations of the restoration speak in no uncertain terms of the corruption in the world because of the apostasy. And because of it, the saints were to gather to

---

49. *Evening and Morning Star* 2/17, February 1834, 135. It is not absolutely certain that Oliver Cowdery wrote the above editorial. The conclusion is drawn from the fact that his name is given as editor of the *Star* once it was relocated to Ohio.

50. *Evening and Morning Star* 1/9, February 1833, 69. Letter from "Calvin and Peter," missionaries serving in Union, Missouri. Understood to be Brothers [Peter] Dustin and C. [Calvin] Beebe from a letter dated Cole County, Missouri, December 11, 1832, 1:8:63.

Zion (Missouri) to escape God's wrath. The one was the result of the other. The following is taken from a revelation dated September 1830:

> Wherefore the decree hath gone forth from the Father that they shall be gathered in unto one place upon the face of this land, to prepare their hearts and be prepared in all things against the day when tribulation and desolation are sent forth upon the wicked. For the hour is nigh and the day soon at hand when the earth is ripe; and all the proud and they that do wickedly shall be as stubble; and I will burn them up, saith the Lord of Hosts, that wickedness shall not be upon the earth. (D&C 29:8–9)

In a subsequent revelation, one month later, the fallen, "corrupted" state of the world is given as one key reason for the gathering.

> For verily, verily, I say unto you that ye are called to lift up your voices as with the sound of a trump, to declare my gospel unto a crooked and perverse generation. For behold, the field is white already to harvest; and it is the eleventh hour, and the last time that I shall call laborers into my vineyard. And my vineyard has become corrupted every whit; and there is none which doth good save it be a few; and they err in many instances because of priestcrafts, all having corrupt minds. . . . And even so will I gather mine elect from the four quarters of the earth, even as many as will believe in me, and hearken unto my voice. (D&C 33:2–4, 6)

And from yet another revelation of March 1831,

> Wherefore I, the Lord, have said, gather ye out from the eastern lands, assemble ye yourselves together ye elders of my church; go ye forth into the western countries, call upon the inhabitants to repent, and inasmuch as they do repent, build the churches unto me. . . . And it shall be called the New

> Jerusalem, a land of peace, a city of refuge, a place of safety
> for the saints of the Most High God. (D&C 45:64, 66)

This theme of gathering out of corruption unto safety, a refuge from the "desolating" "scourge" about to be poured upon the world (D&C 45:31), dominates much of the earliest literature of the church.[51] Even the Mormon apostate, Ezra Booth, writing in 1831 in the *Painesville Telegraph*, understood this point clear enough to say: "'The land of Missouri' . . . is also to be a city of Refuge, and a safe asylum when the storms of vengeance shall pour upon the earth."[52] In October 1832, Samuel H. Smith taught,

> of the situation in which the Apostolic churches were established . . . and then compared them with the churches at the present day and showed them that they had all gone out of the way and were involved in darkness and showed the means that God had provided for their deliverance from the confusion.[53]

A few months later, Seymour Brunson wrote from his missionary labors in Ohio: "O that the Lord would make bare his arm, and bring in that happy day, when Christ shall come in the clouds of heaven. The time is nigh, and the wickedness of the people is great. The fields are white already to harvest, and Babylon will soon realize her destruction."[54]

John F. Boynton, missionary and future apostle, wrote much the same sentiment in the form of a prayer

> O! That God would rend the heavens and come down to deliver his Saints; that the mountains might give way before

---

51. Price, "Mormon Missionary," 15, 21–23.

52. From an article in the *Painesville (Ohio) Telegraph,* 1 November 1831, 5.

53. Samuel H. Smith Journal, 28 October 1832, 25.

54. From a letter by Seymour Brunson, 6 May 1833. Published in *Evening and Morning Star* 2/13, June 1833, 100.

him; and flow down at his presence; that the kingdom of our Lord and Savior Jesus Christ might roll forth till it fills the whole earth! I long to see the time when the saints of the most high God shall take the kingdom, and possess it forever.[55]

The gathering was, therefore, a necessary act, not only to prepare for the second coming of Christ but also to leave behind the sinking vessel of a ruined world.

What of Authority?

We come now to the related question: was the loss of priesthood authority taught as a critical element of the apostasy in these early years? Considering the fact that a revelation given to the infant church on the day on which it was organized addressed this issue, one might conclude that this must have been a major point of discussion. After all, section 22 of the Doctrine and Covenants indicated to the earliest church members the need to be rebaptized, even though they had been baptized into other churches earlier.

> Behold, I say unto you that all old covenants have I caused to be done away in this thing; and this a new and an everlasting covenant, even that which was from the beginning. Wherefore, although a man should be baptized an hundred times it availeth him nothing, for you cannot enter in at the strait gate by the law of Moses, neither by your dead works. For it is because of your dead works that I have caused this last covenant and this church to be built up unto me, even as in days of old. Wherefore, enter ye in at the gate, as I have commanded. (D&C 22:1–4)

Phelps editorialized in 1833 on this subject:

> When the Savior came to the Jews, he called and chose twelve, ... gave them authority to build up his church; and they by

---

55. Letter of John F. Boynton, 20 January 1834, *Evening and Morning Star* 2/17, February 1834, 134.

theses of this book is: "nowhere near that long"

his authority, commissioned others, and so the gospel was preached. This state of order in the church of Christ, lasted for some time; perhaps till the Nicean Council, and from that time till the Book of Mormon came forth . . . there were many sects, that had a form, in some degree, of godliness, but none declared . . . that they were inspired by the Lord.[56]

Certain it is that they taught of the true church being upon the earth. From the preface to the Doctrine and Covenants, dated 1 September 1831:

And also those to whom these commandments were given, might have power to lay the foundation of this church, and to bring it forth out of obscurity and out of darkness, the only true and living church upon the face of the whole earth, with which I, the Lord, am well pleased, speaking unto the church collectively and not individually. (D&C 1:30)

Just three months later, one observer put it this way, speaking of church leaders: "These are the men sent forth, to promulgate a new revelation, and to usher in a new dispensation. . . . These are the leaders of the Church, and the only Church on earth the Lord beholds with approbation."[57]

This new knowledge came as quite a revelation to some of those who had been searching. Albeit writing years after the fact, Parley P. Pratt said of Hyrum Smith's early teachings,

He also unfolded to me the particulars of the discovery of the Book [of Mormon] . . . the rise of the Church of the Latter-day Saints, and the commission of his brother Joseph, and others, by revelation and the ministering of angels, by which the apostleship and *authority* had been again restored to the earth. After duly weighing the whole matter in my mind I

---

56. *Evening and Morning Star* 1/11, April 1833, 83.

57. *Painesville Telegraph*, 6 December 1831, 1. From a letter by Ezra Booth.

saw clearly that these things were true; and that myself and
the whole world were without baptism, and without the ministry and ordinances of God; and that the whole world had
been in this condition since the days that inspiration and
revelation had ceased.[58]

Pratt's words are poignant and informative but nevertheless autobiographical and certainly not contemporary to our
time. If the very earliest missionaries taught the loss of authority, it seems not to have been an area of particular emphasis or
even the distinguishing characteristic. More often they taught
the evil effects of the apostasy, the immediate need to come
out of the world, and to gather to Zion. Early Mormonism was
not presented as merely a denomination per se in contrast with
all other churches, but as the restoration of all things, the very
dispensation of the fullness of times, modern Israel preparing
for the millennial day.

The Scattering and Loss of Israel

But what of the scattering and loss of Israel? Did missionaries include in their teachings of a universal apostasy the scattering of the ancient tribes of Israel? Once again, the answer
was more often expressed in the positive declaration: that the
restoration was more than that of a New Testament Christian
church, that it marked the return of an ancient Old Testament
covenant people. Indeed, their new Zion would be the place for
the restoration of such people.

Wrote missionaries Eliel Strong and Eleazer Miller in early
1833:

We rejoice that the time has come, that the Lord has set
his hand again the second time to gather his elect. That he

---

58. Proctor and Proctor, *Autobiography of Parley Pratt,* 38; emphasis added.

has already set up the ensign and lifted the standard for the gathering of the nations; that the covenants and promises made to the fathers concerning the remnants of his people ... might be fulfilled. ...We long to see the time when we can see the tribes of Israel's remnants coming up to Zion with songs of everlasting joy ... when Jesus shall come in the clouds of heaven.[59]

Orson Pratt's journals are instructive in this matter. He often combined the apostasy of faith with the scattering of Israel as if they were two separate expressions of the same phenomenon, both evidenced in the Book of Mormon. Note the following: "Preached at Norwich upon the coming forth of the Book of Mormon," and "the prophecies that have been fulfilled in the scattering of Israel and apostasy of the gentiles."[60] On the 21st of June 1833, he preached "upon the scattering of Israel and the miracles that are to be wrought at their gathering."[61] Two days later, he spoke "upon the restoration of Israel and the blessings on Joseph."[62] His preachings were laced with references to Isaiah 29, Ezekiel 37, and Daniel 2, three of the most favorite scriptures used in the period from 1830 to 1833. To his view and that of several others, there would be two places of gathering: "the Jews to gather in unbelief [at Jerusalem]; the Saints at Mount Zion."[63] Orson Pratt in these very early years saw the church as part of modern Israel—the tribe of Joseph—called literally to gather to a new Zion upon the American continent.

---

59. Eliel Strong and Eleazer Miller to the editor, dated 19 March 1833. *Evening and Morning Star* 1/12, May 1833, 94–95.

60. Watson, *Orson Pratt Journals,* 7 August 1835, 68.

61. Watson, *Orson Pratt Journals,* 21 June 1833, 18. See also 20 and 22 February 1835, 48.

62. Watson, *Orson Pratt Journals,* 23 June 1833, 18

63. Watson, *Orson Pratt Journals,* 16 August 1833, 23. See also 19 January 1834, 31.

When approached by a Baptist minister claiming that there was no need for new revelation, Parley P. Pratt related,

> We asked him to open the New Testament and read to us a history and destiny of the American continent and its inhabitants, and the origin and lineage of the same; also, the history of the ten tribes of Israel, and where they now were. We also asked him to read to us from that book of his own commission and that of other ministers of this age to preach the gospel.[64]

Not only did Pratt pinpoint the lack of authority claimed by this minister, he also testified of the scattering and loss of Israel.

Before his baptism, William Draper emphasized this very point.

> After being in full Baptist membership for fifteen years, [I] began to be criticized for believing and teaching that the scriptures were to be understood in accordance to their obvious purpose, that the prophecies in the Bible were going to be fulfilled, and that the Israelites would be gathered. . . . [When I] heard Brigham Young preach [in 1833] . . . [I] recognized the truths that [I] had been searching for.[65]

The Book of Mormon was regarded as evidence of a scattered and lost Israel. Wrote Phelps,

> When darkness covered the earth, and gross darkness the people; when no man did walk in the old paths, nor did search out the everlasting gospel; when the church of Christ, and the gifts which he left in it, could not be found . . . , the Lord our Savior, saw it fit in his great goodness, endless mercy, and infinite wisdom, to send an angel and signify unto man, that

---

64. Proctor, *Autobiography of Parley Pratt*, 84–85.

65. "A Biographical Sketch of the Life and Travels and Birth and Parentage of William Draper who was the son of William Draper and Lydia Luthdrop Draper," 172, BYU Special Collections.

there was a sacred record to be unfolded in the eyes of all the nations, containing the fulness of the gospel. It was the [B]ook of Mormon.[66]

Conclusion

The purpose of this very exploratory study has been to show two things. First, that Joseph Smith's understanding of the apostasy played a key role in his quest for truth, and that it deepened as the years of his instruction intensified. Indeed, from his own account, it is clear that to Joseph Smith the first vision remained a divine affidavit of the apostasy. And from later periods of instruction and interpretation, his sense of a falling away only intensified. It was made manifest to him through visions, priesthood restorations, the Book of Mormon, and Biblical translations.

Second, we have attempted to show that early Latter-day Saint missionaries and writers in the period from 1830 to early 1834 taught various elements of the apostasy. To them, it was more than doctrine: it was historical fact, a tragedy that had compromised and contaminated the teachings of both the Christian and non-Christian world. The apostasy was a universal phenomenon, one that had negatively affected behavior as much as doctrine. Further, the apostasy had extended to the scattering of the tribes of Israel who were now to be restored in fulfillment of both Biblical and Book of Mormon prophecy. Because of it, the whole world lay in sin, necessitating the gathering to Zion, in part to escape a lost world in advance of the second coming of Christ.

In conclusion, we quote from Charles C. Rich,

How little do mankind realize their situation! How easy they are satisfied without knowing whether they are born

---

66. *Evening and Morning Star* 1/8, January 1833, 57.

of water and the Spirit or not! O that God would grant that they might humble themselves before him, that they might know the plan of Salvation.[67]

---

67. *Evening and Morning Star* 2/14, July 1833, 108. From a letter by Charles C. Rich, 25 May 1833, written in Pleasant Grove, Illinois.

This is a version of a paper published in *Window of Faith: Latter-day Saint Perspectives on World History,* comp. Roy A. Prete (Provo, UT: BYU Religious Studies Center, 2005). We wish to thank the BYU Religious Studies Center for permission to reproduce it here.

Modern Revelation: A Guide to Research about the Apostasy

John W. Welch

Whatever is taught about the apostasy should be checked against the four standard works. As researchers explore new approaches and digest primary historical source materials from the early years of the Christian era, the scriptures are an important guide, helping scholars to formulate promising questions for investigation and directing students in understanding the complex story of what has gone wrong (and also what has gone right) in the history of Christianity. According to scripture, especially the Book of Mormon and Doctrine and Covenants, what were the causes of the apostasy? What were its characteristics? What were its consequences? The answers to these scriptural questions are not simple. For that reason, stereotypes and oversimplifications are not particularly helpful, as a close reading of key passages will demonstrate. In order to understand what the scriptures say about the unfolding of the apostasy, this paper focuses, in particular, on what the relevant passages in 1 Nephi 13 and Doctrine and Covenants sections 64 and 86 teach about the apostasy.

Unforgiving Disciples: Doctrine and Covenants 64:8

One important question is this: Was the apostasy the result of internal problems or external pressures? In other words, did it occur because of the rise of false teachings or conflicts from within, or because of the untimely deaths of the apostles or persecutions from without? Certainly, many factors played a role in the difficulties faced by early Christianity, but one interesting passage in Doctrine and Covenants 64:8 discloses that a major problem that stood at the heart of the matter came from the failure of high-ranking church officials to forgive one another.

Given in September 1831, Doctrine and Covenants 64 is addressed to the elders of the newly established Zion, encouraging them, as is often quoted, exhorting them to be obedient and to "be not weary in well-doing" (v. 33), forbidding them to "get in debt to thine enemies" (v. 27), and requiring them "to forgive all men" (v. 10). Standing at the head of this crucial administrative revelation of the fledgling kingdom, however, is a sober disclosure that "there are those who have sought occasion against [the Prophet Joseph Smith] without cause" (v. 6); although he had indeed sinned, he had also confessed and had been forgiven by God (v. 7). The brethren, therefore, were told that they should not accuse him or any others who are willing to repent and confess their transgressions.

The seriousness of the problem of these young priesthood leaders seeking to find fault and to accuse one another is then driven home by a chilling revelation. The Lord had seen this once before among his young disciples in the Old World, and he had little desire to see it again: "My disciples, in days of old, sought occasion against one another and forgave not one another in their hearts; and for this evil they were afflicted and sorely chastened" (D&C 64:8). Although this passage is brief and cryptic, it may uncover an important insight: troubles that plagued the early Christian church seem attributable precisely to internal disharmony and aggressive confrontations among its leaders. Then, most problematical of all, they failed to forgive one another.

Such an insight can be used as a guide for research. Thorough examination of the New Testament and other early Christian records remains to be conducted to identify instances in which early leaders sought occasion against each other, but even a casual acquaintance with these texts produces promising prospects. For example, the early brethren scattered, one going one way, another going a different way. The inclination has been to see these missionaries going out on assignment in good faith to spread the word to their own corners of the world, but perhaps something more is going on here. Perhaps they split up because they were not getting along. Evidence of such tension is close to the surface in 1 Corinthians 1:12, "Now this I say, that every one of you saith, I am of Paul; and I of Apollos; and I of Cephas; and I of Christ." Concrete examples of disharmony can be sensed in the strong combative language used to describe the "no small dissension [*staseōs*] and disputation [*zētēseōs*]" that arose over the Gentile convert question (Acts 15:2), as well as in the disagreement between Barnabas and Paul over John Mark, where "the contention was so sharp [*paroxusmos*] between them, that they departed asunder one from the other" (Acts 15:39). The Greek words in these texts are strong words, strong enough to indicate not only verbal strife, discord, and controversy, but also provocation, irritation to the point of wrath, physical confrontation, and outright anger. While these contentions may have arisen over doctrinal debates and differences of theological opinion, the issue may have been or may have become more personal than intellectual. Polarization in a small, early religious movement can more easily occur at the personal level than at the institutional or theological level, because institutional group structures are still forming and the religion's theological discourse has not yet matured to the point of clearly articulated theoretical positions.

To be sure, Paul and others plead for unity again and again in their letters: "Is Christ divided?" (1 Corinthians 1:13); "be of one mind" (2 Corinthians 13:11); "endeavor to keep the unity of the Spirit in the bond of peace" (Ephesians 4:3); and "be ye all of one mind" (1 Peter 3:8). But for all these calls for unity, there are fewer admonitions for forgiveness: "forgiving one another, even as God for Christ's sake hath forgiven you" (Ephesians 4:32; some early manuscripts from as early as the second and third centuries even read "hath forgiven us"!). These passages seriously calling for unity take on a new and more urgent meaning when one understands that the early church was struggling to overcome grudges, petty jealousies, and hurt feelings. Thus, the instruction in the Epistle of James may reflect much more than simply good wisdom and common sense; it may reflect the existence of faultfinding, hard feelings, and the lack of forgiveness as a widespread condition throughout the church scattered abroad: "If ye have bitter envying and strife in your hearts, glory not [i.e., do not assume superiority over others] and lie not against the truth" (James 3:14).

At the core of the matter, therefore, the primary cause of the apostasy may not have been philosophy, secularization, political corruption, or persecution, as one generally tends to think or to hear mentioned. From a closer look at what this scripture says, it would appear that the trouble began because Christian disciples failed to keep the basic teachings of the Savior regarding humility, love, and forgiveness, and that God will deliver men from evil only to the extent that they forgive other people of their trespasses against them (Matthew 6:13–15).

A Closer Look at Nephi's Vision: 1 Nephi 13

The longest scriptural prophecy about the apostasy and the years between the first and the nineteenth centuries is found in Nephi's vision in 1 Nephi 13. Scholars seeking to understand the apostasy will benefit by using this text as a guide, step by step, in several important respects.

At the outset, the angel leading Nephi through his vision in 1 Nephi 11–14 (which was a repetition and interpretation of Lehi's vision in 1 Nephi 8 and 10; see 1 Nephi 14:29) makes it unmistakably clear that problems would ensue in the Old World after the death of the Messiah. Nephi saw "the multitudes of the earth, that they were gathered together to fight against the apostles of the Lamb" (1 Nephi 11:34), for this multitude was in the "large and spacious building" (1 Nephi 11:35). Nephi then beheld "the world and the wisdom thereof; yea behold the house of Israel" would gather together "to fight against the twelve" (1 Nephi 11:35). This prophecy seems to be completely fulfilled when persecution was immediately heaped by the Jewish potentates on Peter, John, Stephen, and others in Jerusalem; Christians in Damascus; and Paul in Pisidia, Thessalonika, Achaia, and elsewhere. The Christian "menace" seems to have brought Jewish factions together as never before; suddenly Pharisees and Sadducees in the Sanhedrin united against the Christians (Acts 5–7). As is often the case, nothing serves to draw squabbling sectarians together as does a new common enemy.

This revelation to Nephi draws attention of historians to the tensions and persecutions against Christians, not by Romans but by Jews, that occurred in the first three decades of

Christianity. These conflicts have been discussed to some extent by historians of the early church,[1] but the nature and possible consequences of these pressures in terms of the looming apostasy have not been fully examined by Latter-day Saints.

Indeed, Nephi did not see these immediate pressures on the Twelve as bringing down the church of Christ; rather he saw the fall of the great and spacious building, representing the pride of the house of Israel and of those who had initially fought against the apostles of the Lord (1 Nephi 11:36). This prophecy could then well relate to the destruction of Jerusalem in AD 70 at the conclusion of the Jewish War, which was similarly prophesied by Jesus himself (Mark 13:1–2; Luke 21:20–24). Such external pressures and oppositions the disciples would apparently be able to withstand.

Next, Nephi's vision turns attention to the posterity of Lehi in the New World during the years after the coming of the Messiah (1 Nephi 12). When the focus of Nephi's vision returns to the Old World, it has jumped ahead to just before the fifteenth century when the Christian world would reconnect with the remnant of Lehi's seed in the New World. At that time, Nephi beheld "many nations and kingdoms," presumably in Europe (1 Nephi 13:1), and by then "the formation of a great church" had occurred (1 Nephi 13:4). Nephi mentions

---

1. Consider the imprisonment of Peter and John, the stoning of Stephen, and the warrant for the arrest of Christians carried by Paul to Damascus. See further Bart D. Ehrman, *The New Testament: A Historical Introduction to the Early Christian Writings* (Oxford: Oxford University Press, 1997), 351–65, and also his *Lost Christianities: The Battles for Scripture and the Faiths We Never Knew* (New York: Oxford University Press, 2003). The harassment of Christians by Jews in its early years is discussed by W. H. C. Freund, *The Rise of Christianity* (Philadelphia: Fortress, 1984), 90–91, 101, 123, 144, 182.

very little about this church, except that it was unacceptable to God and it killed, tortured, bound, yoked, and brought into captivity "saints" and smaller church congregations (1 Nephi 13:5, 9). The mere fact that saints were still present in Europe at this time signals the truth that the Middle Ages could not have been entirely dark.[2]

Indeed, the Book of Mormon commits Latter-day Saints to the view that much of the gospel of Jesus Christ was preserved among the Gentiles. In particular, Nephi records that the spirit and power of God was still with some of the Gentiles (1 Nephi 13:12, 13, 16) and that they still had an important book, which may not have been complete, but still is said to be "of great worth" to the remnant of his peoples (1 Nephi 13:23). Nephi was assured that God would not leave the Gentiles in a "state of awful blindness" (1 Nephi 13:32) but that the Nephite record and other books would come forth precisely to establish the truth of the records of the prophets and apostles which the Gentiles still had and to make known "the plain and precious things which have been taken away" (1 Nephi 13:40). Although these records in the hands of the Gentiles will not be perfect, they will still be of great worth and will be amenable to corroboration.

At this point in Nephi's vision, the sequence of disclosures flashes back to the time when the words of the Bible first were spoken by the Savior. Most people who are generally familiar with Nephi's prophecy understand that the words of the Bible, as they originally "proceeded forth from the mouth of a Jew [the Lord]," originally came forth in purity (1 Nephi 13:24–25). What happened after that, however, needs to be followed carefully. Actually, Nephi's vision reveals here three important stages in the process of the apostasy.

---

2. Latter-day Saint scholars, however, have not searched the records of medieval Europe to find who those saints might have been.

First, things would be taken away, not from the texts or proto-texts of the Bible, but from the gospel itself. In the words of the angel, the first thing mentioned is that Gentiles would take "away *from the gospel* of the Lamb *many parts* which are plain and most precious" (1 Nephi 13:26). This stage possibly could have occurred more by altering the meaning or understanding of the concepts taught by the Lord than by changing the words themselves. For example, when people lost the part of the gospel that teaches about the premortal life of mankind, the words of Jesus regarding the man who was born blind in John 9 lost some of their meaning. When people lost the gospel concept of sacred covenants, the words of Jesus in his instruction to the disciples that they should not leave Jerusalem until they had been "endued with power from on high" (Luke 24:49) lost their potential for covenantal significance. When people forgot about holy ordinances, the instruction that they should not cast their "holy thing" before the dogs (Matthew 7:6) became baffling.[3] When people no longer understood the plan of salvation, the deeper meaning of various teachings, such as the parable of the Good Samaritan, would sooner or later pass them by.[4] This changing of understanding, the loss of many parts of the gospel, was a fundamental problem foreseen by Nephi. Many people would stumble because of those things "taken away *out of the gospel*" (1 Nephi 13:29, 32). Perhaps, we may add, in light of Doctrine and Covenants 64:8, discussed earlier, the disciples stumbled because they lost a proper understanding of the atonement, repentance, and forgiveness, which are all essential to the plan of

---

3. John W. Welch, *Illuminating the Sermon at the Temple and Sermon on the Mount* (Provo, UT: FARMS, 1999), 87–90.

4. John W. Welch, "The Parable of the Good Samaritan: A Type and Shadow of the Plan of Salvation," *BYU Studies* 38/2 (1999): 50–115, esp. 99–105.

redemption, the clear articulation of which does not appear to have survived long after the first century.

Second, the angel said that the Gentiles would take away "many *covenants* of the Lord" (1 Nephi 13:26). This step, too, could be taken without deleting any words from the Bible as such. The knowledge and benefit of the covenants of God could become lost simply by neglecting the performance of ordinances, or priesthood functions, or individual covenants as the Lord had taught. Changing and ultimately eliminating the covenant aspect of baptism— for example, by moving to infant baptism in place of the previous outward sign of adult repentance and covenantal admission into the fold of God—would be symptomatic of the loss of one such covenant. Diminishing the dimension of individual covenant renewal linked to the remembrance of the flesh and blood of the Savior in connection with the eucharist (which in some early Christian communities seems to have been turned into an *agape* feast) might be an indication of another. Evidences of temple covenants amidst early Christians have also been educed,[5] but these covenants also were lost. Latter-day Saint scholars would do well to focus on the consequences of the loss of these and other covenants in early Christianity. As has been shown by Hugh Nibley, baptism for the dead, the use of prayer circles, and the sacrament itself underwent transformation, if not elimination, in the early centuries. As is widely recognized, asceticism and celibacy enter Christianity at an early stage,[6] which distorted the meaning of the covenant of marriage and

---

5. See, for example, Hugh W. Nibley, *Mormonism and Early Christianity* (Salt Lake City: Deseret Book and FARMS, 1987). See also Welch, *Illuminating the Sermon at the Temple.*

6. See, for example, Carolyn Osiek and David L. Balch, *Families in the New Testament World* (Louisville, KY: Westminster Knox, 1997), 152–55.

many passages in the Bible. These losses were crucial. Without the covenants, the teachings of early Christianity are removed from their settings in a covenant-based religion and are given more general, diluted roles.

Moreover, Nephi's text identifies the cause of the loss of these covenants: people would take them away "that they might pervert the right ways of the Lord, that they might blind the eyes and harden the hearts of the children of men" (1 Nephi 13:27), that is, with the result that they would lead people into apostasy. When and under whose auspices the elimination of these covenants might have occurred remains a subject for serious investigatation; but, at some time and in some way, certain covenantal practices were dropped, turning aside from the straight and narrow path that the Lord had prescribed. The result of blinding the eyes and hardening the hearts recalls the words of Isaiah, as he described the condition of apostasy in Israel, "seeing many things, but thou observest not; opening the ears, but he heareth not, . . . for they would not walk in his ways, neither were they obedient unto his law, . . . yet he laid it not to heart" (Isaiah 42:20, 24, 25). These motivations and conditions would likely accompany the condition of people who were seeking cause one against the other and not forgiving one another in their hearts.

Third, and finally, Nephi beheld that there were "many plain and precious things taken away *from the book*" (1 Nephi 13:28). This third step apparently should be understood as a consequence of the two preceding steps, since verse 28 begins with "wherefore." Thus, the eventual physical loss of things from the actual texts of the Bible was perhaps less a cause than it was the result of the fact that first the gospel and second the covenants had been lost or taken away. Writings that no longer made sense, or no longer sounded right, or spoke of things no longer practiced would naturally fall into disfavor and out of use. As one can now see, significant losses of early Christian texts did in fact result. In some cases, entire books did not find their way into the canonical Bible,[7] leading Christian theologians and scholars to ask why certain books were excluded. Thomas Hoffman has written of the theoretical possibility "that a lost epistle of an apostle could still be accepted into the canon." He puzzled that the reasons "such books as the Shepherd of Hermas, the First Epistle of Clement, or the Epistle of Barnabas . . . were eventually dropped from the canon are not that clear."[8]

Whatever the process, the results are again clearly stated by Nephi. The loss of these plain and precious parts (1) of the gospel, (2) of the covenants, and (3) of the textual record would cause a loss of "plainness" so that, when the gospel would "go forth unto all the nations of the Gentiles," it would lack clarity, which would cause "many" to "stumble," giving Satan "great power over them" (1 Nephi 13:29). Perhaps their stumbling was related to their failure "to forgive all men" (D&C 64:10).

---

7. See Hugh W. Nibley, *Since Cumorah* (Salt Lake City: Deseret Book and FARMS, 1988), 26; Frank Moore Cross, "New Directions in Dead Sea Scroll Research II: Original Biblical Texts Reconstructed from Newly Found Fragments," *Bible Review* (summer and fall 1985): 12–35. For a list of known books missing from the New Testament, see John W. Welch and John F. Hall, *Charting the New Testament* (Provo, Utah: FARMS, 2002), chart 18–9.

8. Thomas Hoffman, "Inspiration, Normativeness, Canonicity, and the Unique Sacred Character of the Bible," *Catholic Biblical Quarterly* 44 (1982): 463.

Rereading the Parable of the Wheat and the Tares: Doctrine and Covenants 86

Matthew 13, sometimes labeled the "Parable Sermon," contains an important series of parables in which Jesus depicted many details of future events pertaining to the kingdom of God on Earth. In "the parable of the tares of the field" as it is called in Matthew 13:36, or "the parable of the wheat and of the tares" as it is called in Doctrine and Covenants 86:1, the Savior himself gives an important roadmap to the coming apostasy. He knows that trouble will come soon to his kingdom. It remains, however, for Latter-day Saint scholars to use this roadmap as a guide for understanding what was to come, how it was to come, and what the consequences would be.

Immediately after the parable of the sower at the beginning of Matthew 13 comes the parable of the tares in Matthew 13:24–30. According to this parable, the sower's "enemy" (Satan) comes into a recently planted wheat field and sows *zizania* seeds "in the sleeping of men" (*en de tōi katheudein tous anthrōpous*). The prediction of this disturbing development, although generally familiar to many people, is especially interesting to Latter-day Saints. While couched in the language of parable, in actuality it is a prophecy about the future of the church and contains significant disclosures about the coming apostasy in early Christianity. As Joseph Smith explained, the tares represent "the corruptions of the church" and that which binds them in bundles are "their creeds."[9] Elder Bruce R. McConkie has expounded: "In giving the parable of the wheat and the tares, Jesus was actually summarizing the doctrines of the apostasy, the restoration of the gospel in the latter-days, the growth and development of

---

9. *Teachings of the Prophet Joseph Smith,* sel. Joseph Fielding Smith (Salt Lake City: Deseret Book, 1976), 98, 101.

the latter-day kingdom, the millennial cleansing of the earth, the glorious advent of the Son of Man, and the ultimate celestial exaltation of the faithful."[10]

To understand the details of this prophecy about the apostasy, however, Latter-day Saints must carefully examine more than (1) the parable in KJV Matthew 13:24–30. In addition, we must consider (2) the explanation of the parable given by Jesus to his disciples according to KJV Matthew 13:37–43, (3) the Joseph Smith Translation emendations to the parable and explanation in Matthew 13, and (4) the version of the parable given by revelation to Joseph Smith on 6 December 1832, now found in section 86. On casual reading, these four texts appear to repeat generally the same information as if in quadruplicate.[11] On closer and more extended inspection, however, several important differences emerge. While these differences may reflect the fact that these texts were addressed to different audiences (the Matthean parable, to a general audience of Jews and early Christian converts; the Matthean explanation, to the Twelve Apostles; and the modern revelation, to readers in the last dispensation), the variations present two very different outlooks on the apostasy, as chart 1 (p. 114) with the following explication demonstrates.

---

10. Bruce R. McConkie, *Doctrinal New Testament Commentary* (Salt Lake City: Bookcraft, 1981), 1:297.

11. Most LDS commentators offer no particular analysis of the differences between these four texts. See James E. Talmage, *Jesus the Christ* (Salt Lake City: Deseret Book, 1915), 286–88; and Melvin R. Brooks, *Parables of the Kingdom* (Salt Lake City: Deseret Book, 1965), 28–32. Some note only the general contours of their differences. Roy W. Doxey, *The Latter-day Prophets and the Doctrine and Covenants* (Salt Lake City: Deseret Book, 1964), 3:127–28; and Richard O. Cowan, *The Doctrine and Covenants: Our Modern Scripture* (Salt Lake City: Bookcraft, 1984), 128.

Chart 1: Matthew 13 and Doctrine and Covenants 86

Matthew 13			D&C 86
Parable	**Explanation**	**JST Emendations***	**Parable**
a man [a sower] (24)	the Son of man (37)		apostles (2)
good seed (24)	children of the kingdom (38)		
field (24)	the world (*kosmos*) (38)		the world (2)
while men slept (25)			after they have slept (3)
enemy (25)	the devil (39)		great persecutor, apostate (3)
			whore, Babylon, her cup (3)
tare seeds (25)	children of the wicked *one* (38)	children of the wicked (49)	all nations who drink (3)
enemy went away (25)			
servants doubt sower (27)			Satan sits in hearts (3)
			tares choke the wheat (3)
			church driven out into the wilderness (3)
			blade is yet tender (4)

* Scott H. Faulring, Kent P. Jackson, and Robert J. Matthews, eds., *Joseph Smith's New Translation of the Bible: Original Manuscripts* (Provo, UT: BYU Religious Studies Center, 2004), 192–93, 267–68. The five emendations shown on this chart all appear in Manuscript 2 (John Whitmer, scribe); only the first three appear in Manuscript 1 (Sidney Rigdon, scribe).

	Matthew 13		D&C 86
Parable	**Explanation**	**JST Emendations***	**Parable**
both grow together (30)			both grow together (7)
harvest (30)	the end of the world (*aiōn*) (40)	destruction of the wicked before the Son of Man shall come (39–42)	last days, fully ripe (7)
reapers (30)	angels (41)	the messengers sent of heaven (40)	angels (5)
			crying, ready, waiting (5)
tares in bundles (30)	offensive things, iniquity (41)		
	people who do iniquity (*anomia*) (41)		
to be burned (30)	in a furnace of fire (42)	cast out among the wicked (43)	
then the wheat (30)		gather wheat first then tares bound in bundles to be burned (30)	gather wheat first then tares bound in bundles (7)
			field remains to be burned (7)
			right of priesthood remained (8–9)
	then the *righteous* (43)		continue in *goodness* (11)
	will shine forth, as *the sun* (43)		*a light* unto the Gentiles (11)
	in the kingdom (43)		been hid from the world (9)
	of their *father* (43)		in lineage of your *fathers* (8)

Several observations can be made regarding these four closely related texts and the apostasy. Although other commentators have compared and contrasted these accounts,[12] none has focused primarily and thoroughly on what these texts say specifically about the apostasy. The following examination moves in that direction by addressing several issues of scriptural interpretation.

Preliminarily, one may wonder, Which came first: Doctrine and Covenants 86 or JST Matthew 13? The relationship between the words in these two passages is intriguing but uncertain. Joseph Smith first worked on Matthew 13 sometime in the spring of 1832.[13] Doctrine and Covenants 86 was received on 6 December 1832. Although Joseph continued to work on his translation of the Bible after this time, he did not include the information contained in section 86 in the emendations to the text found in the Joseph Smith Translation.

Consideration of six differences between the wording of these four texts sheds light on how these texts relate to each other and which is more likely the original version of the parable given by Jesus during his Galilean ministry:

---

12. The most thorough is Danel W. Bachman, "Joseph Smith and the Parables of Matthew 13," in *A Symposium on the New Testament* (Salt Lake City: The Church of Jesus Christ of Latter-day Saints, 1980), 34–38.

13. Lyndon W. Cook, *The Revelations of the Prophet Joseph Smith* (Provo, UT: Seventy's Mission Bookstore, 1981), 179 and 317, comments that the initial draft of Matthew 13 JST was "sometime between 7 April and 19 June 1831" and that the passage was subsequently revised "to correspond with section 86" regarding the sequence of the harvest. The Prophet's comments on the parables in Matthew 13, which appeared in the *Messenger and Advocate* on November 19, 1835, mainly follow the version in the King James Bible, *Teachings of the Prophet Joseph Smith*, 97–98, 100–101.

1. *The "softer view" of the apostasy in Matthew 13.* Perhaps most significantly, the version of the parable found in the New Testament (which part of the parable was not modified in the Joseph Smith Translation) offers a "softer view" of the apostasy than does section 86. In the traditional text of the parable, the good seeds and the bad seeds grow together without any apparent difficulty for a long period of time. The tares are a serious nuisance in Matthew 13 but not a consequential problem.

Botanically speaking (and relevant to all versions of this parable), it is interesting that when tares sprout, they appear deceptively similar to wheat. Tares are practically indistinguishable from wheat, even after the head has begun to form. Not until the very end, when it finally becomes apparent that the weed has not produced kernels of wheat, is it possible to distinguish between the two without close inspection. Eventually, however, the heavy heads of wheat bend over and droop down, while the light and empty heads of the tares remain standing straight up. This may suggest the haughty pride of the tares, which stands in contrast to the humble bowing down of the wheat. This symbolism would usefully parallel and corroborate the visions of Lehi and Nephi in which the pride of the people in the great and spacious building was the source of their wickedness and the cause of their demise. But, other than the perennial problem of pride in the world and the need for church leaders to be patient in not trying to root out the tares too quickly, the situation presented in the familiar version of this parable does not appear to be grievous.

Even this soft view of the apostasy, however, may tell us something important. The problem would arise because people would not be able to distinguish in the early stages of Christianity between good "wheat" and useless "tares"; and perhaps, in response, some of the servants did not follow the master's instructions to wait but began precipitously pulling out the tares, and with them (unwittingly but inevitably) came the wheat. By reexamining the historical evidence with this perspective in mind, Latter-day Saint scholars and students may uncover overlooked evidence of these very problems and developments. For example, various teachings about the Godhead or the mode of baptism were propagated among early Christian denominations; in such cases, the problem was that none of them were correct, but since no one could distinguish or authoritatively declare which was right and which was wrong, eventually the correct doctrine faded into obscurity. At the same time, LDS scholars could then detect ways in which the restoration brought back keys of knowledge that would cure that basic problem by enabling people to distinguish wheat from tare.

2. *The "tougher view" of the apostasy in Doctrine and Covenants 86.* In the Doctrine and Covenants, however, it is obvious that the wheat and the tares do not coexist for very long. Soon, "the tares choke the wheat and drive the church into the wilderness" (D&C 86:3). In this text, the tares have the effect of crowding out the righteous elements within the church and driving away its true and living powers. While some LDS commentators have passed over the dire implications of this revelation without being fazed,[14] some others have recognized its tough consequences, especially in conjunction with Doctrine and Covenants 88:94,[15] which speaks of "that great church, the

---

14. E. Keith Howick, *The Parables of Jesus the Messiah* (Salt Lake City: Bookcraft, 1986), 31, makes no mention of the church being "choked" and even suggests that the operation of the parable "applies to the Church whenever it is in existence."

15. See, for example, Joseph Fielding McConkie and Craig J. Ostler, *Revelations of the Restoration* (Salt Lake City: Deseret Book, 2000), 620.

mother of abominations. . . . She is the tares of the earth; she is bound in bundles; her bands are made strong, no man can loose them; therefore, she is ready to be burned."

What can this point in section 86 tell us about the apostasy? Although a tare is a plant that looks very much like wheat, it lacks the essential kernel, the substance with which to produce a meaningful harvest for the master of the field. Once the wheat of the field has been choked out, although a few straggling stalks of wheat might still be found here and there in the world, the only effective cure is to replant the field with a new infusion of good seed.

The expectation that the church would suffer and would be forced into the wilderness is not without attestation elsewhere in the New Testament, as others have noted as well.[16] In Revelation 12:6, the Apostle John prophesied and expected that, after the child was caught up unto God and to his throne (that is, after the resurrection of Jesus), "the woman [the church] fled into the wilderness where she hath a place prepared of God," where she would remain under divine protection and preservation for an apocalyptic era. Accordingly, Doctrine and Covenants 33:5 speaks of the restored church as being "called forth out of the wilderness," reversing the development foreseen by John of old.

The essential element of this apostasy, according to this view, would appear to be the loss of the priesthood.[17] As section 86 explains, it was the priesthood that went into hiding: "The *priesthood* hath continued through the lineage of your

16. Sidney B. Sperry, *Doctrine and Covenants Compendium* (Salt Lake City: Bookcraft, 1960), 416; Doxey, *Latter-day Prophets and the Doctrine and Covenants,* 3:127–28; McConkie, *Doctrinal New Testament Commentary,* 1:297; Bachman, "Parables of Matthew 13," 37.

17. Discussed in Theodore M. Burton, "Salvation for the Dead: A Missionary Activity," *Ensign,* May 1975, 71.

fathers—For ye are lawful heirs, according to the flesh, and have been *hid from the world with Christ* in God—Therefore your life and the priesthood have remained, and must needs remain through you and your lineage until the restoration of all things spoken by the mouths of all the holy prophets since the world began" (D&C 86:8–10; emphasis added). Here, according to this modern revelation which appeared as the sixth revelation in the 1835 edition of the Doctrine and Covenants with the subtitle "On Priesthood,"[18] the priesthood was hidden from the world with Christ, in the same manner in which he himself had been taken up into the presence and protection of God in Revelation 12.

During the time when the priesthood was absent, of course, other characteristics of Christianity could well have remained, even under this tougher view of the apostasy. Several elements of true Christianity certainly did remain, such as many of its basic ethical teachings, its pious reverence and devotion to Christ's words, and its yearning for peace and heavenly salvation. Nevertheless, the loss of the priesthood, which was originally bestowed by Jesus upon his disciples, and the right to which continued down to the time of the restoration through the lineage of the fathers of those who would receive the priesthood in the last dispensation, was certainly the most monumental of losses.

3. *Who plants the good seed?* Whether the wheat would be strong enough and able to retain its place may relate to another difference between these two texts. In Matthew, the good seed is said to be planted by the Son of Man (Matthew 13:37). In the Doctrine and Covenants, the good seed is planted by the apostles: "the apostles were the sowers of the seed" (D&C 86:2).

---

18. *Doctrine and Covenants of the Church of the Latter Day Saints* (Kirtland, OH: F. G. Williams, 1835), 99.

This difference may be significant to our understanding of the apostasy in the following way: In Matthew (both in the KJV and the JST), the seed originally preached by Christ himself would have come with unmediated divine power and authority. Then, during Christ's lifetime and while men were asleep (or inattentive), the tares would be planted (Matthew 13:25). In this version, the sowing of the tares happens before the apostles die, for they (the servants) soon notice the tares growing and question the quality of the seeds the master had sown.

In the Doctrine and Covenants, however, the good seed was planted by the apostles, and it is only "after they have fallen asleep" (D&C 86:3) that Satan, who sits to reign, sows the tares that will choke the wheat and drive the church into the wilderness. The sleeping of the apostles "is generally interpreted by Latter-day Saints to mean after they were dead."[19] This offers a plausible reading of the parable, for the Greek text uses an articular infinitive, "in *the* sleeping of men" (*en de tōi katheudein tous anthrōpous*), which may refer to death. The English rendition of the KJV follows the Latin Vulgate, "cum autem dormirent homines," which is a construction invented by Jerome not parallel to the Greek. Section 86 does not include any reference to the servants awaking and finding the tares in the field, so it does not imply that the apostles would wake up and find the tares. Instead, according to this version, the word that will be crowded out and fail is the word as it was spread by various apostles, not the word as it came forth in its purity from the mouth of Jesus (compare 1 Nephi 13:24). Although the words of the apostles still would have been true enough for those with eyes to see and ears to hear, their delivery may not have been as strong or as clear as had been the original proclamation of

---

19. Bachman, "Parables of Matthew 13," 36.

the gospel by Jesus Christ, especially when those words were taken to the nations of the world in their various languages and cultures. In the Doctrine and Covenants, the tares were planted in earnest by the great persecutor of the church, the apostate, the whore, after the apostles were dead, not after just one night's sleep.

4. *When and how long do the wheat and tares grow together?* These two accounts also differ in terms of the duration over which they say that the wheat and tares will grow together. In the New Testament, which was written at a time when many disciples believed that the second coming of the Savior would happen within the first or second generation of Christianity, the parable leads readers to expect that the wheat and the tares will grow together continuously until the final judgment (Matthew 13:30), which need not have been understood in the days of Matthew as being a very long time away.

In section 86, however, the parable speaks of a new planting of wheat in the last days, when "the Lord is beginning to bring forth the word and the blade is springing up and is yet tender" (D&C 86:4). Thus, section 86 assumes that a second planting will occur at the time of the restoration.[20] Then, for a while, the new wheat will grow in the field (which at that time would have been full of well-established tares), will grow as the hosts of heaven wait for the final gathering and judgment.

Indeed, the overall emphasis in the two accounts is very different. In Matthew, the focus of attention in the parable is strictly on the final judgment, the separation of the wheat and the tares, the burning at the "end of this world" (Matthew 13:40), whereas

---

20. See Joseph Fielding Smith, "The Predicted Judgments," in *BYU Speeches of the Year, 1966–67* (Provo, UT, 1967), 4: "The sowing of the seed occurred twice"; Bachman, "Parables of Matthew 13," 37.

the JST and the Doctrine and Covenants are primarily interested in the separation of the wheat and the tares before the coming of the Son of man before the final burning, with greater emphasis on heavenly messengers, gathering, bundling, and preparation for the final judgment (D&C 86:7). Thus, JST Manuscript 2 removes the "furnace of fire" (Matthew 13:42) and says that those who work iniquity shall be separated "out among the wicked," before the offending world is burned.

5. *Who are the harvesters?* The various accounts also present different possibilities for the identity of the harvesters. In the Galilean account, the harvesters are unidentified. It is possible that the servants mentioned in Matthew 13:27 and 28 are not the same people as the reapers in Matthew 13:30. Teams of reapers would typically be brought in at harvest time to augment the normal work force available to a land owner.

In the revelations to Joseph Smith, however, the harvesters are again dealt with more strongly, being identified as overeager angels, begging the Lord day and night hoping to be sent out to reap the field (D&C 86:5),[21] while the Joseph Smith Translation identifies the reapers as "the angels, or the messengers sent of heaven" (Matthew 13:40 JST).[22] Because the Greek word for *angels* literally means "messengers," the JST may in fact be based on a good alternative translation of the term *aggelous* in Matthew 13:41. The implication in the JST is that these messengers will come with messages of warning and instruction before the overeager angels come for the actual harvest.

6. *Wheat before tares.* Indicative also is the difference in these two accounts between the order in which the wheat and

---

21. On their eagerness, see G. Homer Durham, comp., *Discourses of Wilford Woodruff* (Salt Lake City: Bookcraft, 1946), 251–52.

22. JST Manuscript 2. JST Manuscript 1 reads "and messengers of heaven."

the tares will be harvested. In the New Testament, the tares are cut first so that they can be bound into bundles and burned (Matthew 13:30), and then the reapers are told to gather the wheat into the man's barn. One must say, however, this seems an odd order in which to proceed. Going through a large field and cutting off the standing heads of the tares would be possible, but quite tedious. A more efficient way of harvesting, and thus a stronger natural order for the parable, would be for the wheat to be gathered, threshed, winnowed, and separated from the chaff (including the tares and its lighter-than-wheat grass seed), and then for all the chaff and the remaining stalks to be bound in bundles, leaving the stubble of the field to be burned.

In section 86, as well as in the Joseph Smith Translation, the latter order is in fact the sequence in which the harvest is prophesied to occur (D&C 86:7; Matthew 13:29 JST).[23] In these modern texts, it is expected that messengers will be sent from heaven and that a harvest or ingathering of wheat will first proceed throughout the world, after which it all becomes ripe for judgment.

With these six points in mind, one may then ask, Which, then, was the original version of this parable? Ultimately, Latter-day Saint interpreters of this parable are faced with a choice. Do these differences simply "illustrate the flexibility and levels of parable interpretation," as Bachman proposes;[24] or do they show a "double allusion or application," preferred by Robert Matthews;[25] or did the original version of this parable as given by Jesus look more like section 86 than like Matthew 13? Did

---

23. JST Manuscript only. As Bachman notes, the same order is followed in D&C 101:64–67. Bachman, "Parables of Matthew 13," 37.

24. Bachman, "Parables of Matthew 13," 36.

25. Robert J. Matthews, *The Parables of Jesus* (Provo, UT: BYU Press, 1969), 82.

Jesus prophesy only one planting of good seed, as in Matthew 13, or did he speak of two plantings as in section 86, one by his original apostles and another in the restoration? Or did Jesus possibly tell this parable on more than one occasion, speaking more softly about the apostasy when he addressed his public audiences and when he explained his general meaning to the disciples in the house, while spelling out the coming difficulties more drastically on other occasions to those who had ears to hear?

In whatever way these questions might be answered, for purposes of understanding the apostasy, section 86 is our strongest canonical guide. And in several ways, the version of the parable in section 86 may be preferable to, and actually makes better practical sense than does Matthew 13; for this reason this modern revelation might reflect a restoration of the original, making it an explanation[26] or "translation" in a strong sense, not merely an interpretation by the Prophet Joseph Smith.[27] Thus, the expectation advanced in section 86 might be relevant to what Jesus told some of his disciples would happen to the church after their deaths. This seems likely, for at least six reasons:

1. Doctrine and Covenants 86 allows readers to distinguish the plantings of wheat in the parable of the wheat and the tares (first by the apostles and then again in the restoration) from the plantings of seeds on four soils in the parable of the sower. In the

---

26. In his journal on 6 December 1832, Joseph Smith wrote that he spent the day "translating and received a revelation explaining the Parable [of] the wheat and the tears [*sic*] &c." Dean C. Jessee, ed., *The Papers of Joseph Smith* (Salt Lake City: Deseret Book, 1992), 5.

27. Joseph Fielding Smith assumed that we still lacked the original form of the parable: "If we had the parable just as He gave it, I am sure that this distinction [of the two sowings] would be in it." Smith "Predicted Judgments," 4.

parable of the sower, Jesus seems to speak of his own sowing of the seed. If both parables originally spoke of plantings by Jesus, then why do the stories go off in such different directions?

2. Doctrine and Covenants 86 clearly distinguishes between the initial servants and the reapers, and it places the harvesting of the wheat first. These points seem to reflect realistic agricultural practices and, therefore, would seem more likely to have been present in the original version of the parable. Moreover, Matthew 13 does not make particularly good agricultural sense by completely ignoring any consequences of the tares in the field. Patience is required, of course, but it has its costs.

3. According to section 86, two different eras are contemplated by the parable: the initial time of planting and the final season of harvesting. This duality may be reflected in the fact that the word for *world* shifts from *kosmos* in Matthew 13:38 to *aiōn* in Matthew 13:39, the first referring to a world set in order and the last pointing to an era or age. In other words, this difference in terminology allows for the understanding that the ordered world established in the field at the time of the first planting refers to a very different stage from the final conclusion of the overall era.[28]

4. Doctrine and Covenants 86 puts the sowing of the tares after the deaths of the apostles. It does not attribute any

---

28. The view of section 86 is also consonant with the fact that sowing a field with two kinds of seed was not only bad farming practice but also was prohibited by the law of Moses: "Thou shalt not sow thy field with mingled seed" (Leviticus 19:19); "thou shalt not sow thy vineyard with divers seeds: lest the fruit of thy seed which thou has sown, and the fruit of thy vineyard, be defiled" (Deuteronomy 22:9). Jesus's Jewish audience may have seen this element of defilement of the field by the evil enemy not only as an act of vandalism but as one of lawlessness and impurity.

negligence or inattentiveness to the Savior. Is it likely that Jesus would have told a story portraying such audacity by his enemy while he himself is still around but asleep on the job? As discussed above, the Greek in Matthew 13:25 points to something more than ordinary slumber.

5. Doctrine and Covenants 86 does not countenance any suggestion that the master was responsible for the presence of the tares in the field by planting poor seed; nor does it suggest that the initial servants had any doubts as to the goodness of the original seeds.

6. Doctrine and Covenants 86 speaks in terms similar to Revelation 12 regarding the apostasy, which adds yet another authentic ring. John may even have learned some of what he reports in Revelation 12 from the Savior's discussion of the parable of the tares.

From the Greek terminology in Matthew 13, it would have been more evident to original readers than it is to English readers that the parable contemplated an apostasy, for the Greek in Matthew 13 says that the reapers will come and rid the kingdom of *panta ta skandala kai tous poiountas tēn anomian*. These are strong words that invite further investigation. They say that there will be *things* in the field that are *skandala,* meaning "traps," "temptation to sin, enticement to apostasy, false belief," "that which gives offense or causes revulsion or opposition," or other desecrating or offensive things,[29] recalling "pervert" and "stumble" in 1 Nephi 13:27, 29. In addition, there will be people who do *anomia*. This word signals more than ordinary iniquity, describing complete lawlessness and

---

29. William F. Arndt and F. Wilbur Gingrich, *A Greek-English Lexicon of the New Testament and other Early Christian Literature* (Chicago: University of Chicago Press, 1957), 760.

apostasy. Workers of *anomia* are told to depart in Matthew 7:23; the man of *anomia* is the devil of the apostasy in the key scripture on this subject in 2 Thessalonians 2:3.

It also seems probable that some Christians living shortly after the deaths of the apostles would not have been comforted by the strong message of section 86. Some of those Christians, perhaps even Matthew himself, may have been tempted to modify the original story. They would have been saddened to hear the words "choke the wheat and drive the church into the wilderness" (D&C 86:3). As troubles mounted, they may have begun to wonder, "Didst thou not sow good seed?" and to look for someone else to blame. As they expected the end to come quickly, they could plausibly have foreshortened the time frame of the original parable. They also could have sought consolation in the idea that they should let the tares simply grow alongside the wheat, if they saw that they were losing the struggle to root out false teachings and false prophets in any event. If the stronger reading of the parable were the original, then this offers another example of a plain and precious part being taken from the gospel and then from the book.

In reshaping the parable to give a less drastic message, the early Christians may have found support in certain scriptures that speak of apostasy in the weaker, reversible sense. The strong version of the apostasy that stands behind the text in the Doctrine and Covenants and the weaker view of apostasy that is present in Matthew 13 reflect an ambivalence toward apostasy found elsewhere in scripture. This ambiguity may help to explain how these two readings of the parable of the wheat and the tares came into existence.

On the one hand, several passages in scripture view apostasy in a strong, disastrous sense. In these texts, apostasy is viewed as treason and rebellion against God, punishable by death, eradication, banishment, or destruction. For example, actually worshipping false gods constitutes the rejection of the true God. Thus, under Exodus 20 and Deuteronomy 13, worshipping idols or leading people into apostasy constitutes a capital offense. In the Book of Mormon, the people of the city of Ammonihah, who are put to death by the sword and whose city becomes a heap of defilement, and Korihor, who is convicted of blasphemy and apostasy and trampled to death by the people of Antionum, represent this kind of full-fledged, outright apostasy and rebellion.

On the other hand, apostasy is viewed in other passages as a curable lapse of faithfulness, from which it is possible to return through repentance and the termination of one's back-sliding. In the Old Testament, Israel is depicted in its apostasy as an unfaithful wife, even a whore, who is still loved by her lord and husband, but whose unfaithfulness causes pain and humiliation and will eventually result in divorce if the un-faithful wife does not mend her ways. The love of the husband is deep. He has written the name of his wife on the palms of his hands and will not forget her if she wishes to return. In the prophetic lawsuits of the Old Testament, a guilty verdict is an-nounced and judgments are proclaimed by the oracles of God against God's contract-breaking people, but the execution of the penalty is suspended in hopes that Israel will repent and return. In the Book of Mormon, both Alma the Younger and his son Corianton were covenant-breaking apostates who re-pented and became again acceptable to the Lord. Viewed in this way, apostasy is curable.

Accordingly, the parable of the wheat and the tares, as it was originally taught by the Savior and understood by his an-cient listeners, could well have declared the reality of power-ful consequences, while also leaving open the possibility of repentance. Thus understood, the version preserved in the New Testament overemphasized the optimistic view of apostasy that, in spite of the tares being sewn by the enemy in the field, the difficulties might not be so drastic. That trajectory of seeing the tares in an increasingly positive sense is, indeed, traceable from Clement of Alexandria, who saw the field as the entire world and the tares as alien Greek philosophy;[30] to Cyprian, who saw the field as the church and the tares as lapsed Christians within the church who reverted to sacrificing to heathen gods;[31] to Augustine, who interpreted the tares as the weaknesses found in each person, through which "the fruit of the wheat is increased."[32] Ultimately, Gregory of Nyssa, Jerome, and Cyril came to see the field only as the human heart and the tares as private evil thoughts or wicked desires.[33]

In this parable, however, Jesus clearly anticipated that a public apostasy would surely come. He made it clear that the apostasy would affect the entire field or world. No corner of the world was singled out as a protected area or one where the tares could be selectively uprooted. But at the same time, there was hope. At the appropriate time, harvesters would come with instructions and authorizations from the Master of the field, allowing the works of the last days to go forth.

---

30. Clement of Alexandria, *Stromata* 6.8; 7.15.

31. Cyprian, *Epistles* 50.3; see also 51.6; 51.25.

32. Augustine, *Psalms* 55.15.

33. Gregory of Nyssa, *On the Soul and the Resurrection;* Jerome, *Epistles* 130.7; 122.3; Cyril, *Catechetical Lecture 4, On the Ten Points of Doctrine,* 1. The increasing tendency of the later Fathers to see apostasy—and hence the meaning of the parable of the wheat and the tares—only in individual personal terms, rather than in collective institutional terms, is at least consistent with the decline in the institutional vulnerability of the church as a whole.

Other Passages on Apostasy in the Modern Scriptures

No other passages of scripture in modern revelation are as specific on this topic as are 1 Nephi 13 and Doctrine and Covenants 64 and 86. Nevertheless, Latter-day Saint students of the apostasy may find general guidance in other passages of modern revelation that are helpful in generating clues or giving background perspectives for studies of the apostasy. Several different models and teachings about apostasy can be found in the Book of Mormon. For example, Zenos's allegory of the olive tree depicts the problem of apostasy in ancient Israel in terms of decay and the production of bitter fruit; the remedy involved pruning, grafting, and eventually burning of the dead wood. Lehi's dream, which is closely related to Nephi's vision, sees the negative behaviors of apostasy as becoming ashamed, leaving the tree, going over to pride, wandering into unknown paths, and becoming lost in mists of darkness. The remedy is to hold to the rod, the word of God, and to stay on the straight and narrow path. Nephi's criticisms of Jerusalem laid the blame on the shepherds who misled the flock, and the cure was to depart and begin a new flock. In the Nephite prophetic view generally, the underlying problem is rejection of the divinity of the Savior and of his eternal sacrifice; scattering is the consequence of such apostasy.

Likewise, prophecies in the Book of Mormon about the conditions that would prevail in Joseph Smith's day might be combed for indication of the characteristics of the late period of the apostasy. Thus, in 2 Nephi 26:20–22, one reads of pride, stumbling, putting down of miracles, relying on one's own wisdom, seeking to get gain, grinding on the poor, contending, envying, and forming secret combinations; 2 Nephi 28:4 portrays members contending with each other, priests contending with each other, teaching with their learning and denying the Holy

Ghost. Statements by Jesus in 3 Nephi 16:13 indicate the need for the Gentiles to repent and return to Christ. Predictions by Moroni in Mormon 8 repeatedly say that the restoration "shall come in a day when" people shall say miracles are done away; the blood of saints will cry out because of secret combinations; the power of God shall be denied, churches defiled, and leaders proud and contentious; fires and tempests shall rage in strange lands; pollutions shall be found in the earth, such as murders, robbing, lying, deceit, adultery, and abominations; and forgiveness will be offered for money (Mormon 8:26, 27, 28, 29, 31, 32).

Thus, modern-day revelation provides not only prophetic insights into the nature and conditions of apostasy preceding the restoration but also speaks rather specifically on the causes and steps of apostasy in the early years after the mortal ministry of Christ. These guideposts of scripture promise to be of great worth in the search for further understanding of the history of Christianity.

The Concept of Apostasy in the New Testament

James E. Faulconer

We frequently speak of the "great apostasy," and we recognize that apostasy was a concern for early Christianity. Less often do we ask what the writers of the New Testament meant by the term *apostasy*. I suspect that we seldom ask what *we* mean by the word. It is a term we take for granted, but being clear about how apostasy was understood in the early church would help us be clear about what we mean when we speak of the apostasy in the first and second centuries AD, and it might help us understand better what constitutes apostasy in our own times. I will implicitly argue that understanding its New Testament meaning is important for an additional reason: understanding how early Christians understood apostasy will give us a better understanding of what it means to be a Christian. We will understand better what was essential to the early church and, therefore, also to the restoration by asking ourselves, "From what do we fall away when we apostatize?"

The Greek word from which we get the English word *apostasy* (*apostasia;* ἀποστασία) means literally "to stand away" or "to stand against," but those and "apostasy" are insufficiently nuanced translations. "Rebellion" is better.[1] The Book of Mormon seems also to think in these terms, as we see in 3 Nephi 6:18 ("they did wilfully rebel against God") and 4 Nephi 1:38 ("they who rejected the gospel . . . did wilfully rebel against the gospel of Christ"). We can understand apostasy in its widest sense as rebelling against God, and that meaning will be at the center of the following discussion of how early Christians understood apostasy: what characterizes rebellion against God?

Though we use the word *apostasy* regularly, the cognate Greek word *apostasia* occurs only twice in the New Testament, in 2 Thessalonians 2:3 and Acts 21:21. In the first of these, the King James Version translates *apostasia* as "falling away": Paul warns of a falling away that will come before the second coming. In the second, where the word is translated "forsake," James and the other elders in Jerusalem ask Paul to answer the charge that he teaches people to apostatize from the law of Moses. Nevertheless, though the Greek word we generally associate with apostasy is seldom used in the various texts of the New Testament, references to what we understand as apostasy are frequent. For example, in Mark 13:5, Jesus warns us not to be deceived (*planaō;* πλανάω) by false Christs; Romans 16:17 warns against those who would cause divisions (*dichostasia;*

---

1. "ἀποστασία," in Walter Bauer, William F. Arndt, F. Wilbur Gingrich, and Frederick W. Danker, *A Greek-English Lexicon of the New Testament and Other Early Christian Literature*, 3rd ed., rev. and aug. (Chicago: University of Chicago, 2000), 98. See also Stephen Robinson's discussion of this in "Early Christianity and 1 Nephi 13–14," in *The Book of Mormon: First Nephi: The Doctrinal Foundation*, ed. Monte S. Nyman and Charles D. Tate Jr. (Provo, UT: BYU Religious Studies Center, 1988), 177–92.

διχοστασία) and offenses (*skandalon;* σκάνδαλον) in the church; Paul tells us that we must not be moved away (*metakineō;* μετακινέω) from the hope of the gospel (Colossians 1:23); and he also tells us that if we do not care for our own, then we deny (*arneomai;* ἀρνέομαι) the faith (1 Timothy 5:8); Hebrews 6:6 speaks of those who fall away (*parapiptō;* παραπίπτω) after receiving the Holy Ghost; while Hebrews 3:12 warns its readers against departing (*aphistēmi;* ἀφίστημι) from the living God.

To understand better the background against which New Testament writers were using these words, we will look all too briefly at the Septuagint, a translation of the Old Testament into Greek from the third century BC and later. We can assume that as a Bible commonly used by early Christians, the Septuagint gives us a good look at how pre-Christian Jews as well as those of the early Christian era understood the Old Testament. In the Septuagint, the two most commonly used words for apostasy are *planaō* (eighty-four uses) and *aphistēmi* (one hundred forty-eight uses). In contrast, *apostasia* is used only five times.[2] Bauer, Arndt, and Gingrich give the meaning of *planaō* as "to mislead,"[3] but the *Theological Dictionary of the New Testament* argues that the word means specifically to instigate someone to idolatry.[4] *Aphistēmi* is used for both political rebellion (as

---

2. Two of these uses, Ezra 4:12 and 15, support the claim that the basic meaning of *apostasia* is "rebellion." In those two verses, the word is used to imply that the Jews who have returned to Jerusalem are in rebellion against Artaxerexes. See also 1 Maccabees 1:15, in the Apocrypha, which speaks of the rebellion of Mattathias and his followers as *apostasia*.

3. "πλανάω," in Bauer et al., *Greek-English Lexicon,* 665.

4. "πλανάω, πλανάομαι, ἀποπλανάω, ἀποπλανάομαι, πλάνη, πλάνος, πλανήτης, πλάνης," in Gerhard Kittel and Gerhard Friedrich, *New Testament Theological Dictionary,* trans. Geoffrey W. Bromiley (Grand Rapids, MI: Eerdmans, 1964), 6:233.

in Genesis 14:4 and 2 Chronicles 21:8) and religious rebellion (as in Deuteronomy 32:15 and Daniel 9:9). Obviously these meanings are closely linked, since to worship an idol is to rebel against God by refusing to recognize him.

Considering this background, we can see that what we call apostasy covers a range of things, including leaving the faith because of persecution, creating division in the body of the church (the New Testament meaning of *heresy*), losing faith because one continues to sin in various ways, teaching false doctrine, blaspheming, and denying the Holy Ghost, all of which can be summed up in the phrase "turning against God" or "departing from God" as in Hebrews 3:12: "Take heed, brethren, lest there be in any of you an evil heart of unbelief, in departing from [*aphistēmi*] the living God." Turning against God is the central problem in each of these instances. It follows that to charge someone with apostasy is not to say that they have committed any particular sin. It is to say that person has rebelled against God in some way or another. Heresy and sin are ways in which one can apostatize, but they are not the same as apostasy.[5] This means that one can have or

---

5. In an important sense, all sin is turning one's back on God. It is no coincidence that the same Hebrew root מסל (*msl*, meaning "to be unfaithful") is translated in 2 Chronicles 12:2 as ἁμαρτάνειν (*hamartanein*, "to sin") and in 2 Chronicles 30:7 as *aphistēmi* ("to depart from the way"). But there is a difference between turning one's back on God through sin, which we have all done, and explicitly rejecting him. For a discussion of sin and turning away from God, see James E. Faulconer, *Romans 1: Notes and Reflections* (Provo, UT: FARMS, 1999), 88. For an excellent discussion of the New Testament understanding of sin and its Jewish context, see Jonathan Klawans, "Ritual and Moral Impurity in the New Testament," in *Impurity and Sin in Ancient Judaism* (New York: Oxford University Press, 2000), 136–57.

sometimes even teach false beliefs without necessarily turning against Divinity. One can leave the church without apostatizing, as someone might do who has never had a testimony. One can lose one's faith without apostatizing, as happens to those whose faith is shallow and who do not receive sufficient spiritual nourishment.[6] Thus, in spite of the ways in which we can use the word *apostasy* to describe various things, strictly speaking neither heresy, leaving the church, nor losing one's faith are the same as apostasy—though it is impossible to apostatize without sinning since even if nothing else is involved, apostasy itself, rebellion against God, is a sin. In fact, one could say that rebellion is the fundamental sin. Perhaps the other things we think of as sins are best understood as *ways* of rebelling.

Given the Jewish context of early Christianity and their self-understanding as the fulfillment of Judaism rather than as an alternative to it—"Think not that I am come to destroy the law, or the prophets: I am not come to destroy, but to fulfil" (Matthew 5:17)—we can expect early Christians to have understood both faithfulness and apostasy in terms that we find in the Old Testament, where faithfulness to God and apostasy from him are often spoken of in terms of covenant. To be faithful is to keep covenant; to apostatize is to break covenant.[7] The word *apostasia* is part of this way of thinking. For example, in Joshua 22:22 of the Septuagint, we see the word

---

6. See the parable of the sower: Matthew 13:3–23 and parallels.

7. See, for example, Genesis 2:16–17; 8:16, 20–22; 9:1–17; 12:1–3; 15; 17:1–22; 22:16; 26:3; 28:13–15; 50:24; Exodus 6:4–8; 19:5–6; 34:28; Leviticus 26; Numbers 25:12–13; Deuteronomy 4:23, 31; 5:2–3; 7:8–9; 9:9; 29:1–15; Judges 2:1; 1 Kings 8:23; 1 Chronicles 16:15; Nehemiah 1:5; Psalms 89:34–35; 105:8–11; 106:45; 111:5, 9; Isaiah 54:10; 55:3; 56:4–7; 59:21; 61:8; Jeremiah 11:2–3; 22:9; 44:26–27; Ezekiel 16:59–63; and Micah 7:20.

apostasia used to describe what those do who become idolaters. Second Chronicles 29:19 says that King Ahaz destroyed all of the temple vessels "in his apostasy" (ἐν τῇ ἀποστασίᾳ). And Jeremiah 2:19 speaks of the *apostasia* of Israel, using *kakia* (κακία), meaning "evil doings," as a synonym for *apostasia*: Israel's apostasy, its evil doing, will teach it, will prove to it, that forsaking God is a bitter thing. Only the last of these is explicitly a reference to rebellion against God, but it is reasonable also to understand Israel's idol worship and their king's destruction of the temple as acts of rebellion against him.

Just as the Old Testament often speaks of entering covenant relation as marriage, it often uses the metaphor of divorce to speak of apostasy, and the Septuagint uses the word *apostasion* (ἀποστάσιον), with obviously the same root as *apostasia*, as the word for divorce (Isaiah 50:1; Jeremiah 3:8; Deuteronomy 24:1, 3). *Apostasion* means, generally, "the relinquishment of one's claim," which is why the word can be used for divorce.[8] Apostasy, rebellion against God, breaks covenant with God in the same way that divorce breaks covenant with a spouse: in both cases, I give up my claim on another and reject that person's claim on me.

Though it goes against our ordinary understanding, it is important to recognize that the covenant with God makes Israel holy, in other words, dedicated to him. Israel is holy because it is in covenant relation with God; it is not the case that he enters into covenant with Israel because it is holy. The history of Israel, from the time it left bondage in Egypt until the coming of Christ, should be sufficient evidence of that. As the book of Hosea illustrates (especially chapters 1–4), the Lord continues to strive with Israel, continues to choose her as his own, despite her inconstancy. If there is a divorce, then she is the one who seeks it. Israel may abandon God, but he will not abandon her. She is chosen,

---

8. "ἀποστάσιον," in Bauer et al., *Greek-English Lexicon*, 98.

covenanted—holy—even when she is unworthy. Speaking to the Israelites, the Lord made the same point in Deuteronomy:

> [The Lord] set his heart on you and chose you not because you were the most numerous of all peoples—for indeed you were the smallest of all—but because he loved you and meant to keep the oath which he swore to your ancestors: that was why he brought you out with his mighty hand and redeemed you from the place of slave-labour, from the power of Pharaoh king of Egypt. . . . *Hence*, you must keep and observe the commandments, laws and customs which I am laying down for you today. (Deuteronomy 7:7–11 New Jerusalem Bible; emphasis added)

Israel is a covenant people—lives in relation to God—and, therefore, must keep the law as the instantiation of that relation. The various commandments of the law are given *because* Israel is holy (chosen, or set apart), in other words, because Israel is a covenant people, not to make Israel holy, not to bring it into covenant relation. What is essential is the covenant, so rebelling against or disavowing that covenant—divorce—is apostasy.

One way to understand Exodus 19:5–6 is to see it as discussing the connection between covenant and priesthood service: "Now therefore, if ye will obey my voice indeed, and keep my covenant, then ye shall be a peculiar treasure unto me above all people: for all the earth is mine: And ye shall be unto me a kingdom of priests, and an holy nation." Just as the wife was the property of the husband, because Israel is covenanted to the Lord, it is the Lord's property ("peculiar treasure" = *sĕgūllâ*; סגלה: "possession, property"),[9] and he promises that he

---

9. See "סגלה," in Francis Brown, Samuel R. Driver, and Charles A. Briggs, *The New Brown, Driver, and Briggs Hebrew and English Lexicon of the Old Testament* (London: Oxford University Press, 1988;

will make it "a kingdom of priests and a holy nation." The root of the word translated "priest," *khn* (כהן), means "to set up or establish" and can mean "to stand." Thus, the word *priest, cohen* (כהן), "would probably denote the man standing before . . . and literally denotes one who stands serving God."[10] Though the priesthood was later limited to the tribe of Levi, we can understand Exodus 19:5–6 to suggest that the Lord intended that everyone be a priest, in other words, that all be prepared to stand in the presence of the Lord and serve him.[11] He gave the priesthood to Israel as part of making them a covenant people, and he gave them the law so that they could be ritually pure when they performed their priesthood service.

As the covenant people, Israel is in the presence of God, as the Ark and the Holy of Holies—God's dwellings among his people—demonstrate. Israel has God's priesthood because they have been made his, been brought into his presence. Similarly, because Israel has been brought into his presence, it must be obedient: one who is set apart for holy things must be pure, so the Lord has given Israel the law as a means for the nation to purify itself, but the law is not the essence of

---

hereafter *BDB*), 688. See also "סגל," in R. Laird Harris, Gleason L. Archer Jr., and Bruce K. Waltke, *Theological Wordbook of the Old Testament* (Chicago: Moody, 1980), 617.

10. Ernest Klein, *A Comprehensive Etymological Dictionary of the Hebrew Language for Readers of English* (New York: Macmillan, 1987), 271.

11. I am not the only one to understand Exodus 19:6 as foreseeing priesthood held by "all." That verse is an important justification for the Protestant doctrine of the priesthood of all believers. See John Calvin, *Institutes of the Christian Religion*, book 2, chapter 7, section 1. See also Philip Schaff, "§42. Clergy and Laity," in *History of the Christian Church* (Peabody, MA: Hendrickson, 1996), 2:123–30.

covenant: "Ye are the children of the Lord your God: ye shall not cut yourselves, nor make any baldness between your eyes for the dead. *For thou art an holy people* unto the Lord thy God, and the Lord hath chosen thee to be a peculiar people unto himself, above all the nations that are upon the earth" (Deuteronomy 14:1–2, emphasis added). The law is given *because* the Israelites are a people set apart, not to make them that people. That covenant brings Israel into the presence of God suggests it is a temple covenant, and the law is given so that Israel can be ritually clean as it serves God in the temple in ritual, sacrifice, and ordinance.[12]

Moses's call at the burning bush also shows that covenant was inseparable from ritual service in the presence of God: "And thou shalt say unto Pharaoh, Thus saith the Lord, Israel is my son, even my firstborn: And I say unto thee, Let my son go, that he may serve me" (Deuteronomy 4:22–23). Where the Masoretic Hebrew text uses the word *ʿābad* (עבד)—"to work" or "to serve as a slave,"[13] the Septuagint uses a narrower word, *latreuō* (λατρεύω). Originally, *latreuō* meant much the same

---

12. Doctrine and Covenant 84:19–23 agrees with this understanding of the purpose of covenant: "And this great priesthood administereth the gospel and holdeth the key of the mysteries of the kingdom, even the key of the knowledge of God. Therefore, *in the ordinances thereof, the power of godliness is manifest. And without the ordinances thereof, and the authority of the priesthood, the power of godliness is not manifest unto men in the flesh: For without this no man can see the face of God*, even the Father, and live. Now this Moses plainly taught to the children of Israel in the wilderness, and sought diligently to sanctify his people that they might behold the face of God" (emphasis added). Godliness requires priesthood and ordinances, which prepare us to stand before God.

13. "עבד," in *BDB*, 1104.

thing as ʿābad, namely work, service to another, or slavery.[14] However, particularly in this context, in the Septuagint it means "to serve in religious ritual, specifically in sacrifice."[15] Moses is commanded to tell Pharaoh that the Israelites are the children of God and that they are to serve God as priests, which Moses does in Exodus 5:1 and 3. Through Moses, we see that the promise to Abraham, "in thee shall all families of the earth be blessed" (Genesis 12:3; see Genesis 22:18), was a promise that his seed would stand before God as priests mediating for the rest of humanity.[16] To be chosen is to be chosen for a work, in this case the work of officiating in priesthood ordinances before God. Such service requires that Israel be ritually pure, so the Lord has given the law as a guide to ritual purity.[17]

---

14. See "λατρεύω," in H. G. Liddell and Robert Scott, *An Intermediate Greek-English Lexicon founded upon the Seventh Edition of Liddell and Scott's Greek-English Lexicon* (Oxford: Clarendon, 1889), 466.

15. See "λατρεύω, λατρεία," especially "λατρεύω and λατρεία in the LXX," in *New Testament Theological Dictionary*, 4:59. See also "λατρεύω," in Bauer et al., *Greek-English Lexicon*, 467.

16. Of course, this is not to deny that this also means that the earth would be blessed because the Messiah would come through Abraham's lineage. As the Great High Priest, Christ is the type of which every other priest is a shadow. I am grateful to James Olsen for pointing out that being set apart to serve is the meaning of the birthright tradition in which the son received a double portion: he received a double portion so that he could serve his siblings, so that he could be a blessing to them. Israel is the eldest son of the nations of the earth. If the purpose of the gospel is to allow us to inherit all that the Son has (see, for example, D&C 84:35–39; 132:20), that means that it is to prepare us to serve our fellows.

17. I ignore here the modifications of the law made after Israelites worshiped the golden calf at Sinai. Those modifications complicate the function of the law, but they do not change the point I am making.

It is reasonable to describe the Old Testament's understanding of apostasy as breaking the covenant that begins with Abraham and is brought to fruition through Moses. Those who break covenant with God—who divorce him—refuse to perform the acts of covenant, namely obedience and priesthood service. Such things as corruption of the priesthood, desecration of the temple, and idolatry are notable signs of apostasy because in them Israel explicitly turns its back on its covenant relation with God.

But what does this pre-Christian, Hebrew understanding of apostasy have to do with early Christianity? How can we understand apostasy in the New Testament as a rejection of covenant and, especially, how can we understand apostasy as the loss of a person's or a people's status as priests serving God in temple sacrifice and ordinance? Given the historical context in which Christianity came to the world, we should expect the Christian understanding of apostasy to be closely linked to the understanding of the Old Testament. However, we seldom speak of apostasy in those terms, and the usual way we think of the New Testament seems to have little to do with the restoration of a covenant people who can perform priesthood ordinances. I will argue that the concept of apostasy in the New Testament continues the Old Testament's understanding of apostasy as not only rebellion against God, but specifically rebellion that rejects priesthood service, a service that was, in early Christianity, best revealed in temple priesthood and ordinances.[18]

---

18. Though I think what I argue here is reasonable, I recognize that we know surprisingly little about early Christianity. An enormous amount of Christian literature from the first two centuries has been discovered in the past two hundred years, but our understanding of early Christianity has yet to be fully informed by those discoveries. See Wilfred Griggs, "Rediscovering Ancient Christianity," *BYU Studies* 3/4 (1999): 73–90.

Only recently have Bible scholars begun to notice the importance of the temple to early Christianity.[19] Nevertheless, the clues have been there all along. Consider, for example, one of the most obvious cases, namely Luke's account of the announcement of John the Baptist's birth (Luke 1:5–22, 59–79): While performing his priestly duties in the temple, burning incense, Zacharias saw an angel of the Lord standing on the right side of the incense altar. The angel told him that he and Elisabeth would have a son and that they should name him John. As a sign in response to Zacharias's skepticism, the angel told Zacharias that he would be unable to speak until the prophecy had come to pass. At the baby's circumcision, when asked what to name him, Zacharias wrote "John," and having done so, he was again able to speak. Rejoicing, Zacharias said, "Blessed be the Lord God of Israel; for he hath visited and redeemed his people, and hath raised up an horn of salvation for us in the house of his servant David; . . . to perform the mercy promised to our fathers, and to remember his holy covenant; the oath which he sware to our father Abraham, that he would grant unto us, that we being delivered out of the hand of our enemies might serve him without fear, in holiness and

---

19. For example, see Richard Neitzel Holzapfel and David Rolph Seely, *My Father's House: Temple Worship and Symbolism in the New Testament* (Salt Lake City: Bookcraft, 1994), and Margaret Barker, *On Earth as It Is in Heaven: Temple Symbolism in the New Testament* (Edinburgh: Clark, 1995). Some of the discussion of esoteric elements in early Christianity is also relevant. See, for example, Gedaliahu Guy Stroumsa, *Hidden Wisdom: Esoteric Traditions and the Roots of Christian Mysticism* (Leiden: Brill, 1996); also John W. Welch, *Illuminating the Sermon at the Temple and Sermon on the Mount: An Approach to 3 Nephi 11–18 and Matthew 5–7* (Provo, UT: FARMS, 1999).

righteousness before him, all the days of our life" (Luke 1:67–69, 72–75). As does the Septuagint version of Exodus 19:6, Luke uses the word for cultic, sacrificial service, *latreuō*,[20] in verse 74: "that we . . . might serve him without fear," and he puts that word in the mouth of one who has recently come from priestly service in the temple. Echoing the language of Exodus 19:5–6 and its mention of priests, Luke says that because Christ has come, Israel will once again be able to serve *before*—in other words, in the presence of [21]—God: "in holiness and righteousness before him, all the days of our life" (Luke 1:75). The language and the setting both point us toward temple service, presumably as a synecdoche for priesthood service in general.

It is significant that Luke begins his account of Christ's life with this story: the prophetic announcement of the Savior's birth begins with events in the temple, and it is made by a temple priest who has recently officiated in the temple; that priest's prophecy tells us that the Savior will come to restore his holy covenant with Israel and that by doing so he will make it possible for Israel to serve in the temple once again. Luke's story begins in the temple and its beginning points us to the temple as one end of the story he will tell.[22] In addition, Zacharias's message suggests that at the time of the Savior's coming, Israel was no longer able to serve properly in the temple. By putting Christ's birth in a temple context, Luke gives us a reason for Christ's coming: to restore the covenant, and the sign of

---

20. Of course, *latrueuō* also has other meanings, but few of those other meanings fit the context as clearly as does "priestly service."

21. The Greek word translated "before" is *enōpion* (ἐνώπιον): "in the presence of" or "in the sight of" ("ἐνώπιον," in Bauer et al., *Greek-English Lexicon*, 270–71).

22. Luke's story also ends in the temple: "And [they] were continually in the temple, praising and blessing God" (Luke 24:53).

that restoration will be the restoration of the priesthood service, denoted for Zacharias by temple service. Christ came to
apostate Judaism, not because it did not hold correct beliefs (it
may or may not have) and not because it did not obey the law
(its attempt to live that law scrupulously were at the center of
the controversy between the Pharisees and Jesus). If we understand Zacharias's message in the context of Jesus's disputes
with the Pharisees, we see that Christ came to restore covenant. Throughout the Gospels, we see that, for the Pharisees,
the two signs of covenant, the law and priesthood service, had
been reduced to one, law-keeping. Thus, to emphasize temple
worship is to underscore the reinstitution of the covenant and
the priesthood.

To understand why Zacharias's message was important,
first consider the teachings of the Old Testament concerning the temple and the coming of the Messiah. Then consider
briefly the history of Judah during the two or three hundred
years prior to Christ's birth.[23] It is clear that the temple was
significant as the abode of God. It was understood as the
place from which he rules and judges the earth (see, for example, Micah 1:2 and Habakkuk 2:20). Given that, it would
be difficult to imagine a messianic reign that did not include
a purification and restoration of the temple. But besides an
argument that the temple *ought* to have been central to messianic expectations among the pre-Christian Jews, we have
texts that demonstrate those expectations.

A number of Old Testament scriptures speak of the Messiah
and make it plain that he will restore not only the kingdom of

---

23. For an excellent book on the background and history of the
New Testament, see Frank F. Bruce, *New Testament History* (Garden
City, NJ: Anchor, 1972).

Israel, but also the temple. For example, Haggai 2:6–7 and 22–23 make it clear that Haggai's prophecy is not only about the return of Israel from Babylon, but is also eschatological, concerned with the coming of the Messiah. Thus, as did pre-Christian, post-exilic Jews, we can read Haggai's discussion of the restoration of the temple and of the Lord coming to his temple (for example Haggai 1:8) not only as a prophecy about the return from Babylon, but also as a description of what the Jews expected to happen with the coming of the Messiah. Similarly, the prophecy in Isaiah 44:28 could be read in two ways: "[I am the Lord] that saith of Cyrus, He is my shepherd, and shall perform all my pleasure: even saying to Jerusalem, Thou shalt be built; and to the Temple, Thy foundation shall be laid." But perhaps no scripture could be read as a messianic prophecy of the Temple more than Zechariah 6:12–13: "Behold the man whose name is The Branch; and he shall grow up out of his place, and he shall build the temple of the Lord: Even he shall build the temple of the Lord; and he shall bear the glory, and shall sit and rule upon his throne; and he shall be a priest upon his throne: and the counsel of peace shall be between them both." Passages such as these show that, for those waiting for the Messiah in Zecharias's time, the expectation was that he would be a priest-king who would build (or restore) the temple just as he would institute (or restore) the kingdom of Israel.

We see a similar expectation in *The Testament of the Twelve Patriarchs*, specifically in the *Testament of Levi* 17–18. Though the textual history of the *Testament of Levi* is, as one commentary says, "Byzantine,"[24] and though chapters 17 and 18 show redaction by a Christian editor or interpolater, those chapters

---

24. Harm W. Hollander and Marinus de Jonge, *The Testaments of the Twelve Patriarchs: A Commentary* (Leiden: Brill, 1985), 2.

also reflect pre-Christian ideas and messianic understandings.[25] In 17:8 through 18:1, the *Testament of Levi* describes an apostasy, and it describes that apostasy as a corruption of the priesthood. Then, in 18:2–3 it describes the restoration of the priesthood in a new priest-king. Even if the verses in question are Christian rather than pre-Christian, they show two things: first, that apostasy was understood to involve the corruption of the priesthood and, second, that the Messiah was understood as a priest-king who would restore the priesthood. In fact, these passages support my claim more strongly if they are Christian rather than pre-Christian, for in that case they show not just that the figure of the temple and the priesthood were important during the intertestamental period, but that they were probably a part of Christian understanding as well. If these passages are the result of Christian redaction, they show that the concern for what is represented by the temple and priesthood, namely covenant, was indeed a part of Christian and not only pre-Christian thinking.

Beginning at least at the return from Babylon, Judah's history and the resulting divisions in Judah—a result of problems centered on the temple and its priesthood—prepared the Jews to see the Messiah as bringing a restoration of temple worship. There had been considerable debate as to who could participate in rebuilding the temple (see, for example, Ezra 5) and various subsequent events, such as the exile of Onias III, the purchase of the priesthood by Jason and Menelaus, and the eventual self-appointment of the Hasmoneans resulted in serious questions and divisions over the legitimacy of the high priest. One of those divisions was that of the Pharisees, or separatists, who seem to have fought against the hellenization of Israel by appealing to

---

25. Robert A. Kugler, *The Testaments of the Twelve Patriarchs* (Sheffield: Academic, 2001), 47–52.

the oral tradition and the law, but went along with Hasmonean priestly rule while awaiting the return of a legitimate High Priest. Another was the party of the Sadducees (Zadokites) who seem to have supported the Hasmonean high priest, focused on the temple rather than the law, and rejected the oral tradition.

Against this background, Zacharias's prophecy stands out radically, for it is a rejection of both the priestly families with which the Sadducees were associated and the powerful Pharisees who opposed them. Couched in terms of temple service, because that was the language of priesthood and covenant with which he was familiar, Zacharias's message is that, as Messiah, Jesus has come to restore priesthood service to its proper place in religious life as the service in which covenant is established and re-established. Presumably he will do that by purifying the priesthood. Zacharias's prophecy also suggests that Jesus has come to put the written law in its proper place in relation to the covenant represented by the temple—as a work of purifying preparation—and it suggests no need for the oral law of the Pharisees. The confrontation with the Pharisees holds a prominent place in the New Testament, and scriptures such as Matthew 12:1–13 and Mark 2:23–28 illustrate well this difficulty. Zacharias's prophecy must be understood within that context.

The message that Christ has come to restore covenant is not only found at the beginning of Luke. It is also implicit in Matthew's references to him by the messianic title, Son of David,[26] a title that seems to have been a standard title for the Messiah at the time of Christ's birth.[27] Presumably, among

---

26. The relevant New Testament references are Matthew 1:1; 12:23; 20:15; 21:9, 15; 22:42; Mark 12:35; and Luke 3:31.

27. See, for example, the use of the title in the first-century BC work, *Psalms of Solomon* 17, and the scriptural references to the Davidic king in Isaiah 11:10; Jeremiah 23:5–6; 30:8–9; 33:15–16; Haggai 2:23; Zechariah 3:8–10; and Amos 9:11.

other reasons, the title was appropriate to the Messiah because Solomon was the shadow of the Messiah (the type), so the promises made to Solomon applied also to the Messiah: "I will set up thy seed after thee, which shall proceed out of thy bowels, and I will establish his kingdom. *He shall build an house for my name, and I will stablish the throne of his kingdom for ever.* I will be his father, and he shall be my son. . . . And thine house and thy kingdom shall be established for ever before thee: thy throne shall be established for ever" (2 Samuel 7:12–16, emphasis added). I take it that the central part of the promise is the sentence I have italicized: the Son of David will build a temple for God, and God will make him king forever. By referring to Jesus as the Son of David, Matthew reminds his readers that the Messiah, as king, will restore the kingdom of Israel *and*, as priest, he will restore the temple and its priesthood service.

In this context, Matthew's account of the cleansing of the temple takes on a fuller significance. Unlike Mark, Matthew has juxtaposed the triumphal entrance into Jerusalem and the cleansing of the temple, putting no other event between them. Matthew wants us to see the connection between these two events: As Jesus rides into Jerusalem, the crowds acknowledge him as the Son of David: "Hosanna to the Son of David: Blessed is he that cometh in the name of the Lord; Hosanna in the highest" (Matthew 21:9). Then Jesus goes to the temple, casting out the money changers and overturning the tables of those who sell doves (vv. 12–13).[28] The chief priests and the scribes are not happy with what has happened: "And when the

---

28. The healing of the blind and lame in the temple after its cleansing (Matthew 21:14) is fraught with messianic symbolism, but not directly relevant to the question at hand.

chief priests and scribes saw the wonderful things that he did, and the children crying in the temple, and saying, Hosanna to the Son of David; they were sore displeased" (v. 15). Putting this story in the historical context of the controversy over the temple, we can understand at least part of their displeasure to be evinced by the people's proclamation of Jesus as the Son of David, the builder of the temple—a proclamation to which he conformed by cleansing the temple.

John places the cleansing of the temple earlier in Christ's ministry than do Matthew and Mark, and he doesn't connect it to the triumphal entry (John 2:13–17). Nevertheless, some of the same themes can be seen in his account. The first thing to notice about John's version of this event is the ambiguity of his phrase "my Father's house." Of course, Jesus is referring to his Heavenly Father. But we may be able to read this as a reference to his father, David, appropriating to himself the position of Solomon, the son of David, as the king and the builder of the temple. Notice also the disciples' response to the cleansing. They quote Psalm 69:9, "The zeal of thine house hath eaten me up," putting the cleansing in a messianic context.[29] Zechariah had prophesied that the messianic time would include the cleansing of the temple (Zechariah 14:21), and the disciples witness the fulfillment of that prophecy. As each of the other three Gospels teaches, one sign that Jesus is the Messiah is that he comes to cleanse and restore the temple, and he does so as its builder, the Son of David. For the Gospel writers, the language of the temple was the language in which to speak of the restoration of God's covenant with Israel and of priesthood service.

Though less apparent, the connection of Christ to the temple is also an important part of Paul's teaching. For example, in

---

29. Psalm 69 is the most frequently quoted psalm in the New Testament, invariably as a messianic text.

Romans 1:3, Paul uses a variation of the messianic and temple-builder title, "Son of David," and given his education (Acts 22:3), the connotations of that title could not have escaped him. I believe that priesthood service is also central to Paul's understanding of salvation. In the first eight chapters of his letter to the Romans, Paul seeks to put the law into perspective, and by doing so to counter the Pharisaic tendencies that he finds in the church, tendencies presumably brought in by converts from Judaism. He argues:

(1) No law can be sufficient to save us, agreeing with John: "If we say that we have no sin, we deceive ourselves, and the truth is not in us" (1 John 1:8).

(2) This means that we cannot be pure without grace (which, when we have received it, obligates us to keep God's law).

(3) By grace we have the Holy Spirit, which makes possible a life that is not possible by mere obedience.

(4) Those with the Holy Spirit will be made the children of God.

Particularly in Romans 8, Paul explains how we come into the presence of God: the Law cannot purify us from sin, but we can be pure through Jesus Christ if we live by the Spirit (Romans 8:3–5), and—using a different familial metaphor than the Old Testament metaphor of marriage—if we are led by the Spirit, then we are the children of God (Romans 8:14).[30] Presumably, if we are the children of God, we stand in his presence and serve him with authority, for to become a child

---

30. We must distinguish between being children of the Father because we are his spiritual offspring and becoming the children of God by becoming inheritors of his kingdom. Like the Prodigal Son, we are children who have given up our inheritance and, so, must become children once again.

of God is no longer to be his slave.[31] It is to serve him as a child, as an heir. (Paul often speaks of his service to God in cultic terms, using the same verb that Zacharias uses, *latreuō* .)[32] As Deuteronomy 14:1–2 has already told us, to be a child of God is to be related to him by covenant: "Ye are the children of the Lord your God: . . . For thou art an holy people unto the Lord thy God, and the Lord hath chosen thee to be a peculiar people unto himself."[33] For Paul, as for those in ancient Israel, the service of a covenant people, the children of God, is priesthood service. Though not as obvious in most of Paul's letters, temple service is the appropriate figure for all priesthood service: the point of true religion is to make us children and priests of the Father; true religion is to be in covenant relation with God, a relation manifest in priesthood worship.

Though there is not room here to do the analysis, one need not read the book of Hebrews very closely to see the centrality of priesthood and the temple in it as well: Hebrews specifically uses language of the temple and temple service to explain that the covenant God made with Israel has been renewed in Jesus Christ so that, finally, the promises of that covenant can be fulfilled. Unlike most LDS scholars, most non-LDS scholars take Hebrews to be a late document.[34] Even if they are right,

---

31. See my discussion of the metaphor of slavery in the book of Romans in *Romans 1*, 6–9.

32. See Acts 24:14; 26:7; 27:23; 2 Timothy 1:3; Romans 1:9, 25; Philippians 3:3; and Hebrews 8:5; 9:9, 14; 10:2; 12:28; and 13:10.

33. That Israel is the son of God or that the Israelites are the sons of God is something we find in many scriptures, for example, Exodus 4:22; Deuteronomy 14:1; 32:5–6, 18–19; Jeremiah 3:4; 31:19–20; Isaiah 43:6; 45:11; 63:16; 64:7; Ezekiel 16:20; Hosea 2:1–4; and Malachi 2:10.

34. Since 1 Clement refers to Hebrews in many places and it was written in AD 95, Hebrews had to be written before AD 95. Most

the temple theme runs from the earliest New Testament texts to the latest. However, whatever the date of Hebrews, it is clear from its message that the importance of the covenant manifest through priesthood service is not something unique to Luke. The language of the temple and of temple service are central to New Testament Christian self-understanding.

Thus, though there are many ways of apostatizing, in the New Testament as well as in the Old, we cannot untangle the New Testament understanding of apostasy from turning one's back on God in covenant-breaking, and we cannot untangle covenant-breaking from refusing to stand as a priest before him to act in priesthood service. Paul helps us understand that the priesthood is, once again, offered not only to the Levites, but to all of Israel. And he teaches us that membership in Israel is no longer confined to those who are literal descendants of Jacob, though the inclusiveness of membership does not undo the promises made to Abraham, Isaac, and Jacob (see Romans 11). Neither do these changes affect the fundamental purpose of covenant, to bring us into God's presence. That purpose is enacted in priesthood service, particularly in the temple.

---

scholars agree that it could not have been written before AD 60, the approximate date to which most Latter-day Saint scholars would assign it. See "Hebrews, Epistle to the," for more information, in David Noel Freedman, ed., *Anchor Bible Dictionary* (New York: Doubleday, 1992), 3:97. For an example of 1 Clement's reference to Hebrews, see chapter 19: "Wherefore, having so many great and glorious examples set before us, let us turn again to the practice of that peace which from the beginning was the mark set before us," which is almost certainly a paraphrase of Hebrews 12:1: "Wherefore seeing we also are compassed about with so great a cloud of witnesses, let us lay aside every weight, and the sin which doth so easily beset us, and let us run with patience the race that is set before us."

As noted in the beginning, any number of things can lead someone into apostasy: affliction and persecution (Matthew 13:21; 24:10); lawlessness (Matthew 24:12); the difficulty of Christ's teachings (John 6:66); a lack of spiritual discernment (Acts 28:26–27); blasphemy (1 Timothy 1:19); worldly empty chatter (2 Timothy 2:16); love of the present age (2 Timothy 4:10); as well as deception by false prophets and teachers, desire for followers, lust, resentment of authority, and promises of freedom from restraint (2 Peter 2:1–22). But these cannot be understood apart from also understanding apostasy as rejecting the requirement that we stand before God in priesthood service. This distinguishes Christianity as a religion from what we might describe as a merely Christian *ethos*. One could live according to the principles of Christianity, its law, if you will, without believing in God. In principle, one could even live according to those principles and believe in God and have one's mind attuned to spiritual things without being a Christian. In other words, one can be ethical or even spiritual without being godly—without being covenanted. In the end, however, the Father requires godliness of us, not merely ethics and not only spirituality.[35] To be ungodly is not to be apostate; insofar as we remain human we are, in a certain sense, ungodly. To *reject* godliness and its requirements is to be apostate, and in neither the Old nor the New Testament, can godliness, life in

---

35. I am indebted to Rabbi Noson Gurary for helping me see this distinction between spirituality and godliness. He said that to be spiritual is to live a certain kind of life. To be godly is to live a certain life because one loves God (personal communication, 18 June 2002). Though I use his distinction, I do not use the word *godly* exactly as he does. I take godly life to be life in covenant which, of course, is also a life in which one loves God. But it is also a life in which one serves God, and priesthood service is at the heart of service to God.

covenant relation with God, be understood apart from priesthood service.

Where, then, does heresy, false doctrine, fit? How is it related to apostasy? As early as the time of Tertullian (c. AD 160– c. AD 225), the concern for heresy and false teaching is obvious,[36] though as Wilfred Griggs points out, "No argument can be presented and defended which shows that doctrinal or ecclesiastical unity in the Christian church definitely was of great concern in the first and early second century Egypt."[37] One can reasonably suppose that if orthodoxy was of no great concern in Egypt in the first century and into the second, it was probably of no great concern in other regions either. On the other hand, the concern for orthodoxy did not arise only after the New Testament era. For if it did, then scriptures such as 2 Peter 2:1 would make no sense: "There shall be false teachers among you, who privily shall bring in damnable heresies, even denying the Lord that bought them, and bring upon themselves swift destruction."[38] Thus, though there was concern over false doctrine in New Testament times, I do not believe that false doctrine is at the heart of New Testament thinking about apostasy.

Notice that when Jesus speaks of false teachers and prophets, he speaks of those who teach others to break commandments rather than those who have unusual or false doctrines: "Whosoever therefore shall break one of these least

---

36. See, for example, Tertullian, *The Prescription Against Heretics* 4 and 7.

37. C. Wilfred Griggs, "The Emergence of Orthodoxy and Heresy in Egyptian Christianity," in *Early Egyptian Christianity: From Its Origins to 451 CE* (Leiden: Brill, 1990), 46.

38. However, 2 Peter is perhaps the latest text of the New Testament and, therefore, may reflect a concern for false teachings that arises only relatively late.

commandments, and shall teach men so, he shall be called the least in the kingdom of heaven" (Matthew 5:19).[39] Of course, teaching someone to sin is teaching them a false doctrine. But the problem is not a problem of belief so much as it is a problem of action. Notice also that the word translated *heresy* in 2 Peter 2:1, *hairesis* (αἵρεσις), is also translated *sect* or *faction* (see Acts 5:17; 15:5; 24:5; 24:14; 26:5; 28:22; 1 Corinthians 11:19; and Galatians 5:20). In the New Testament, a heresy is not a false belief. It is something that creates a division or faction in the church, and, of course, a false teaching can do that. But the creation of division is apostasy, not necessarily holding the beliefs that occasion those divisions.

Paul's first letter to the Corinthians gives an important reason for why divisions are a problem. In 1 Corinthians 1:11–12, we see that the Corinthian saints had created divisions among themselves, perhaps claiming different persons as their leaders. When Paul responds directly to this problem in the second part of chapter 11, he does so by pointing out that these factions in the church have made it impossible for the saints to

---

39. When the Lord speaks to Joseph Smith, he speaks in a similar way: "They teach for doctrines the *commandments* [not the teachings] of men, having a form of godliness, but *they deny the power thereof*" (Joseph Smith—History 1:19, emphasis added). Notice how often the New Testament identifies doctrines with commandments rather than with beliefs. See, for example, Matthew 15:1–9 and Mark 7:5–9; as well as Colossians 2:20–21. This also seems to be the spirit of the Lord's remark "he that is not against us is on our part" (Mark 9:40; see also Luke 9:50). We can also see this focus on practices rather than beliefs in Doctrine and Covenants 19:31: "And of tenets thou shalt not talk, but thou shalt declare repentance and faith on the Savior, and remission of sins by baptism, and by fire, yea, even the Holy Ghost."

partake of the Sacrament of the Lord's Supper. They partake, but what they eat and drink is no longer the sacrament: division in the church makes priesthood service impossible. Thus, teaching people to break the commandments and creating divisions in the church are condemned because they make service in the presence of God, service as one of God's children and priests, impossible.

We see a similar concern in the use of *apostasia* in 2 Thessalonians 2:3. The man of sin who will reveal himself before the coming of the Lord does not explicitly teach false doctrine. He rebels against God, setting himself above him (compare Daniel 11:36–37), and he gets others to do the same. True, the man of sin lies (2 Thessalonians 2:9) and causes many to believe a lie (vs. 11), and those who believe his lies are damned (v. 12). But the context shows that these lies are not merely false beliefs. Instead, they are lies that try to convince another to do evil. Presumably those who believe they should do evil will do evil; their acts condemn them. We see this in verse 12 where, in his summative description of those who follow the man of sin, Paul tells us that they take pleasure in *adikia* (ἀδικία). The basic meaning of that word is "unjust acts," and it can be translated as "lawlessness" or, as in Acts 8:23, as "iniquity." These people take pleasure in or choose (*eudokeō*; εὐδοκέω)[40] injustice and lawlessness. In other words, they rebel against God. In doing so, they reject the desire for truth (2 Thessalonians 2:10), which in this context is not so much a desire for true beliefs as it is a desire for God's righteousness.[41] Paul is not merely prophesying that people will have false beliefs. Instead, he is

---

40. "εὐδοκέω," Bauer et al., *Greek-English Lexicon*, 319.

41. Compare this use of *truth* (*aletheia*; ἀλήθεια) with the Hebrew use of *ʾĕmet* (אמת) in passages such as Psalm 15:2; 86:11; Ezekiel 18:8–9. See "ἀλήθεια," in Kittel and Friedrich, *New Testament*

prophesying that they will rebel against God and choose to act wickedly (and, of course, holding false beliefs is often part of acting wickedly).

The problem of false belief arose as a primary difficulty, a difficulty *in itself*, only as Christianity began to deal with the response of the broader community in which Christians founds themselves, especially when they were faced with the fact that Christ's incarnation was a stumbling block to both the Jews and the Greeks (meaning those of Greek culture, including the Romans; see 1 Corinthians 1:23). As Christianity spread, the incarnation became increasingly difficult, for the claim that God is incarnate made no sense to *any* of those outside of Christianity.[42] For most Greeks, what was most real was what was intelligible. They believed that the body got in the way of intellecting the intelligible; for the Greeks, however one was to understand salvation, it was a matter of turning from the sensible world to the intelligible, and the body, being

---

Theological Dictionary, 1:232–47. Note also the way in which this compares philosophy and true religion: philosophy is the desire for true beliefs; true religion is the desire for the righteousness of the Father. Presumably those who receive the Father's righteousness will also have true beliefs, but those who reach their quest for true beliefs will not necessarily become righteous by doing so.

42. For an excellent discussion of the problem of incarnation for those outside of Christianity in the first and second centuries and the importance of the body to Christian belief, see Michel Henry, *Incarnation: Une philosophie de la chair* (Paris: Seuil, 2000), 9–32. Francis Ferrier, *What Is Incarnation?* trans. Edward Sillem (New York: Hawthorne, 1962), gives a good, general overview of the Catholic understanding of the incarnation and how that understanding developed historically. The entries for "Gnosticism" and "Incarnation" in the *Anchor Bible Dictionary* also have good information about this problem for early Christianity.

part of the sensible world, made that turn more difficult, if not impossible. Partly under the influence of Greek philosophy, Jewish intellectuals thought of God as absolutely transcending the world.[43] Thus, for Greeks and Jews, the central tenet of Christianity, that God had come to the earth in a human body, suffered, died, and was resurrected to return to his Father, was sheer foolishness at best: an affront to human intelligence for the Greeks, blasphemy for the Jews.[44]

In response, some Christians, primarily those in a constellation of groups that we label broadly *Gnostics*, tried to weaken the belief in Christ's embodiment. Some argued, for example, that he did not really have a body but only seemed to. Two things resulted from this response to intellectual opposition: schism and the need to defend Christian beliefs not only to those outside the church, but against those within the church— and those two were inseparable. The need to defend Christian beliefs was a response to the need to avoid schism, the need to preserve the unity of the church. That need for unity gave rise to the emphasis on doctrinal teachings and the emphasis

43. For a representative case, consider this from Philo of Alexandria (c. 20 BC–AD 50): In an imagined conversation between Moses and God, Philo has God say "I myself am invisible and only appreciable by the intellect. And what I call appreciable only by the intellect are not those which are already comprehended by the mind, but those which, even if they could be so comprehended, are still such that the outward senses could not at all attain to them, but only the very purest intellect. . . . Do not, then, ever expect to be able to comprehend me nor any one of my powers, in respect of our essence." *On the Special Laws*, in Philo, *The Works of Philo: Complete and Unabridged* (Peabody, MA: Hendrickson, 1996, 1993), I. 46–49.

44. I suspect that this Greek way of thinking about the body, combined with a paucity of clear references to resurrection in the Old Testament, was behind the Sadducee's rejection of resurrection.

Romans destroyed the temple in order to break the Jewish resistance to Roman Law. This forced both Jewish and Christian theology to re-define itself to find relevance in the absence of temple worship.

on false belief as apostasy. Combined with the absence of the temple after AD 70 (a theological as well as a functional problem for Christians as much as for Jews), this need to prevent schism and to defend the church meant that apostasy gradually came to be understood differently than it had been. Rather than a sign of apostasy, holding false beliefs came to be central to its concept as Christianity gradually allegorized its understanding of covenant, the temple, and priesthood service.[45]

In sum, the essential element in the Old Testament understanding of apostasy and therefore also in the New Testament, was that to be apostate was to turn against God's covenant and that entailed the refusal to stand before him in priesthood service. After the exile and as a result of political difficulties and the corruption of the temple priesthood, many Jews, specifically those who identified themselves as Pharisees, began to understand apostasy as law-breaking, forgetting that worship for Israel is enacted in the temple through covenanted priesthood service, and replacing that worship with obedience to the law. For the Pharisees, all impurity, whether ritual or moral, became moral impurity, sin. Christ's confrontations with the Pharisees and Paul's preaching were directed at that change in the understanding of what covenant and worship require. Christ restored the covenant, manifest in the kingdom and its priesthood, and symbolically restored the temple. A bright thread running through the various ways of understanding apostasy in the New Testament is that inherited from the Old Testament: to apostatize is to refuse to be in covenant with God. This refusal of covenant is, at the same time, a refusal of the priesthood service

Covenant <=> temple

Gospel is Temple Centric

Gospel is Covenant Centric

---

45. The disconnection of the covenant from priesthood ordinance is complete only with the Reformation and only with some of those who descend from the Reformation.

Traditional Christianity has no concept of Covenant and no concept of temple in which the covenant is enacted, as well as a refusal to understand that the purity necessary for priesthood service comes not by obedience to the law (in other words, not from us), but by the Holy Spirit (in other words, from God). With the problem of schism in the church and the need to explain Christianity to Greeks and Jews in times of pending and actual persecution, Christians gradually moved away from the biblical understanding of apostasy as the rejection of covenant and focused instead on apostasy as false belief. Belief rather than covenant manifest in obedience and priesthood service became central. In spite of that understandable shift in emphasis and understanding, it is a change from the New Testament's understanding. We cannot understand what apostasy means for New Testament Christians without understanding that it included the loss of the temple and, so, of the priesthood, for ultimately the rebellion of apostasy involves severing one's covenant relation to God, a relation manifest through the priesthood, through standing in the presence of God.

The Corruption of Scripture in Early Christianity

John Gee

Latter-day Saints are familiar with the concept of the corruption of scripture coming from a passage in the Book of Mormon that discusses the removal "from the gospel of the Lamb many parts which are plain and most precious" (1 Nephi 13:26). Latter-day Saint discussions of the removal of plain and precious things from scripture can benefit from clarity of the processes of removal and their historical setting. One early discussion by W. W. Phelps in 1832, for example, claims that "It will be seen . . . that the most plain parts of the New Testament, have been taken from it by the Mother of Harlots . . . from the year A.D. 460 to 1400."[1] While the image of medieval monks making changes to the text of scripture might be true in certain isolated instances, the changes came long before. We neither need to nor should look later than the second century for these changes. By the early second century, Christianity had

---

1. W. W. Phelps, *Evening and Morning Star* 1 (June 1832): 3.

fragmented into dozens of splinter groups[2] with each group charging that the other possessed both forged and corrupted texts.[3] I shall limit this discussion to documenting changes and corruptions of scripture during the second century under three headings: (1) Christian groups of the second century accuse each other of corrupting scripture, providing both the class of errors and the motives for such changes. (2) No substantial biblical manuscript antedates these charges of

---

2. Tertullian, *Scorpiace* 1.1 in *The Ante-Nicene Fathers* (hereafter *ANF*), ed. Alexander Roberts and James Donaldson (1885; reprint, Peabody MA: Hendrickson, 1994), 3:633–64; Irenaeus, *Contra Haereses* 1.28.1, 29.1 (*ANF* 1:353) describes them as popping up "like mushrooms"; more poignantly, Mārūtā, the bishop of Maipherqaṭ says that there was only one ear of wheat left in all the tares, see Mārūtā, *Against the Canons from the Synod of 318*, 5, in Arthur Vööbus, *The Canons Ascribed to Mārūtā of Maipherqaṭ and Related Sources*, 2 vols., CSCO vol. 439–40 (Louvain: Peeters, 1982), 1:22. See also Henry Chadwick, *The Early Church* (Harmondsworth, Middlesex: Penguin, 1967), 34; W. H. C. Frend, *The Rise of Christianity* (Philadelphia: Fortress, 1984), 201–3; Elaine Pagels, *The Gnostic Gospels* (New York: Random House, 1979), 7–8.

3. Acts 20:30 (Paul prophesying the coming corruption of the teachings; cf. Kent P. Jackson, "'Watch and Remember': The New Testament and the Great Apostasy," in John M. Lundquist and Stephen D. Ricks, eds., *By Study and Also By Faith*, [Salt Lake City: Deseret Book and FARMS, 1990], 1:85); 2 Peter 3:15–16 (showing the process starting in apostolic times); Justin Martyr, *Dialogus cum Tryphone* 1.73 (accusing the Jews); Irenaeus, *Contra Haereses* 1.7.3, 8.1, 9.4, 18.1, 19.1, 20.1–2, 22.1–2, 26.2, 27.2, 4; 5.30.1 (*ANF* 1:558–59) (accusing various groups); 3.2.1 (*ANF* 1:415) (for the counter charges); Tertullian, *De Baptismo* 1.17 (*ANF* 3:677) (discussing well-intentioned but nonetheless misguided tampering with Paul); Tertullian, *Contra Marcionem* 14.2.2–5 (*ANF* 3:347) (charging Marcion with corrupting Luke); Tertullian, *De*

corruption. (3) Those scriptural passages that are quoted by Christian authors at the beginning of the second century are different from those preserved in the scriptural canon.

A wide variety of types of changes will be discussed here under the heading of corruption that can be distinguished in theory but often elide in practice. Textual corruption is the deliberate or unintentional changing of the text, either through the expansion, deletion, or alteration of the passages. Corruption can also occur through faulty interpretation (either exegesis or translation), and manipulation of the canon (which books are considered scripture).

Accusations of Corruption

Though the number of Christian authors from the first two centuries of Christianity is limited, a close look at the few Christian authors of the first and second centuries shows that they were aware of changes in scripture.

Praescriptione Haereticorum 16–19, 38–40 (*ANF* 3:251–52, 261–63) (the charges run both ways); Mārūtā, *Against the Canons from the Synod of 318*, 5, in Vööbus, *Canons Ascribed to Mārūtā of Maipherqaṭ*, 1:22–23, 25–26 (with a long list of groups); Mārūtā, *The Seventy Three Canons* 1, in Vööbus, *Canons Ascribed to Mārūtā of Maipherqaṭ*, 1:57–58, cf. 135; *The Apocalypse of Peter* VII, 76, 24–78, 31 (no specific sect specified); *Apocalypse of Adam* V, 77, 18–82, 25 lists fourteen different views of Christ, thirteen of which—including the "orthodox" one—are labeled as being in error; see also *New Testament Abstracts* 1 (May, 1956): 31–34; Pagels, *Gnostic Gospels*, 20–21. Though from the fourth century, Epiphanius, *Panarion* 30.13.1, 14.1; 42.9.1–2 accuses the second century figures Ebion, Cerinthus, Carpocrates, and Marcion of corrupting the text of the Gospel of Matthew; Epiphanius, however, is not necessarily a reliable source. See *The Panarion of Epiphanius of Salamis*, trans. Frank Williams (Leiden: Brill, 1987), 1:129–30, 278–79.

Peter noted that one of the processes of corruption, misinterpretation, had started in apostolic times: "And account that the longsuffering of our Lord is salvation; even as our beloved brother Paul also according to the wisdom given unto him hath written unto you; As also in all his epistles, speaking in them of these things; in which are some things hard to be understood, which they that are unlearned and unstable wrest, as they do also the other scriptures, unto their own destruction" (2 Peter 3:15–16).

The most sacred teachings of Jesus were not committed to writing (3 John 1:13–14) but reserved for a close few.[4] Indicative of this are the fifty-three parables of Jesus preserved in the Gospels, of which only three have interpretations, all of the interpretations being given behind closed doors to a small, select group.[5] Those so privileged to receive this hidden treasure of knowledge prized it most highly[6] but shared it with few if any others.[7] The situation is most poignantly explained by one of John's disciples, Ignatius of Antioch (d. ca. 110)[8] as he was lead off to his death:

---

4. Matthew 13:11–16; 19:11; Mark 4:2, 33; Luke 18:34; 22:67; John 3:12; 6:60–61; 8:43; 10:27; 16:12, 18, 25; Acts 10:41. See also William J. Hamblin, "Aspects of an Early Christian Initiation Ritual," in Lundquist and Ricks, eds., *By Study and Also By Faith,* 1:204–7.

5. This was noted in ancient times in the *Apocryphon of James* I, 8, 4–10 listing some previously unknown parables as well.

6. Tertullian, *De Praescriptione Haereticorum* 1.20–22 (*ANF* 3:252–53).

7. 1 Corinthians 3:1–2; 2 Corinthians 12:4; Colossians 1:26; Hebrews 5:11; 2 John 1:12. See also Pagels, *Gnostic Gospels,* 17–18; Hamblin, "Early Christian Initiation Ritual," 208–10.

8. *Ignatius the Martyr,* in J. B. Lightfoot, ed. and trans., *The Apostolic Fathers,* 2nd ed. (Peabody, MA: Hendrickson, 1989), 2.1:29–30.

Could I not write you the celestial matters? I fear, however, lest I might set harm before you, since you are but babes; so pardon me, lest, if you are unable to make room, you be suffocated; for although I am bound and am able to comprehend the celestial matters and the angelic orders and the principle revelations,[9] seen and unseen, nonetheless I am not yet a disciple.[10]

Oral communication, or lack thereof, however, is only part of the problem; even the written texts could be corrupted.

Justin Martyr, a Christian philosopher who lived in the middle of the second century,[11] levels the following accusation against the Jews: "From the ninety-fifth (ninety-sixth) Psalm they have taken away this short saying of the words of David:

---

9. Greek *tas systaseis tas archontikas*. Unless specified, all translations are the author's own. Though Ignatius does use the word *systasis* in other senses (see Ignatius, *To the Romans*, 5; see *ANF* 1:75–76), here it seems to be used in a more technical sense of oracular inquiry, the equivalent of the Demotic *ph̭-nt̬r*; see Janet H. Johnson, "Louvre E 3229: A Demotic Magical Text," *Enchoria* 7 (1977): 90–91; Robert K. Ritner, "Gleanings from Magical Texts," *Enchoria* 14 (1986): 95; Robert K. Ritner, *The Mechanics of Ancient Egyptian Magical Practice*, SAOC 54 (Chicago: Oriental Institute, 1993), 214–20.

10. Ignatius, *To the Trallians* 5 (see *ANF* 1:68). This list of characteristics of the secret teachings makes its way into the magic tradition eventually to end up in an English fairy tale as the content of the magician's "one big book bound in black calf and clasped with iron, and with iron corners;" see "The Master and his Pupil," in Joseph Jacobs, comp., *English Fairy Tales*, 3rd ed. rev. (London: Nutt; 1898, reprint New York: Schocken Books, 1967), 74–77. These matters are also the principle subject of the books of 1 Jeu and 2 Jeu as well as much of the Jewish Hekalot literature.

11. For more information, see Johannes Quasten, *Patrology* (Utrecht-Brussels: Spectrum, 1950), 1:196–219.

'From the wood.' For when the passage said, 'Tell ye among the nations, the Lord hath reigned from the wood,' they have left, 'Tell ye among the nations, the Lord hath reigned.'" Justin's antagonist, Trypho downplays the accusation by saying, "Whether [or not] the rulers of the people have erased any portion of the Scriptures, as you affirm, God knows; but it seems incredible."[12]

A work attributed to Clement of Alexandria (ca. 150–215), head of the catechetical school at Alexandria,[13] describes the corruption of the Gospel of Mark by Carpocrates:

> Now then, Mark during Peter's stay in Rome wrote down the acts of the Lord, nevertheless not telling all, nor even hinting at the sacred ones (*tas mystikas*), but selecting those which he thought most useful for the growth of the investigators' faith. When Peter was martyred, Mark came to Alexandria; polishing both his own and Peter's notes, from which by transferring into his first book those things appropriate for those progressing in the testimony (*gnōsis*), he compiled a more spiritual gospel for the use of those being perfected (*tōn teleioumenōn*). In no way, however, did he betray those things not discussed, nor did he write down the initiatory teaching (*hierophantikēn didaskalian*)[14] of

---

12. Justin Martyr, *Dialogus cum Tryphone* 73 (*ANF* 1:235, brackets in original).

13. For a biography and discussion of his writings, see Quasten, *Patrology*, 2:5–36.

14. For a discussion of other ways this phrase has been taken, see Werner Jaeger's comments in Morton Smith, *Clement of Alexandria and a Secret Gospel of Mark* (Cambridge, MA: Harvard University Press, 1973), 38; John W. Welch, *The Sermon at the Temple and the Sermon on the Mount* (Salt Lake City: Deseret Book and FARMS, 1990), 59; and the response of Todd Compton, review of Welch, *Sermon at the Temple and the Sermon on the Mount*, in *Review of Books*

the Lord. But adding to the previously written acts yet others, he still added certain sayings thereto, the explanation of which would be capable of initiating (*mystagōgēsein*) their hearers into the holy of holies (*adyton*) of the truth veiled seven times. Wherefore he prepared it thus—neither corruptly nor unprecautiously—so I deem it. And when he died he left his compilation at the church which is in Alexandria, where it is kept very safe and secure to this day, being read only to those who are initiated into the great mysteries (*tous myoumenous ta megala mystēria*).

But Carpocrates who was taught by the defiled demons who continually plot destruction for the children of men, having even used the arts of deception, thus enslaved a certain elder of the church in Alexandria so that he prepared a copy of the secret gospel (*tou mystikou euangeliou*). And he explained it according to his own blasphemous and carnal thought. But still he defiled it by mixing into the immaculate and holy words the most abominable lies. From this tincture he extracted the Carpocratian doctrine.[15]

Ironically, it is not known whether this text itself is authentic or an ancient, medieval, or modern forgery.[16]

The bishop of Lyon at the end of the second century, Irenaeus,[17] claims that the Valentinians changed the scriptures

in the *Book of Mormon* 3 (1991): 322; Hamblin, "Early Christian Initiation Ritual," 209.

15. Clement of Alexandria, *Letter to Theodore*, 1.15–2.10, in Smith, *Clement of Alexandria and a Secret Gospel of Mark*, 448–51, plates I–II; cf. Hamblin, "Early Christian Initiation Ritual," 210–11.

16. When I originally wrote this article, I considered it genuine. When the manuscript repository that supposedly possessed the work denied its existence, I began to have my doubts about its authenticity. At the present I simply do not know whether it is authentic or not.

17. For a biography and discussion of his work, see Quasten, *Patrology*, 1:287–313.

"by transferring passages, and dressing them up anew, and making one thing out of another."[18] Irenaeus notes that among some biblical manuscripts circulating in his day, the number of the beast in Revelation was not 666 but 616.[19] (Manuscript variations, like this one cited by Irenaeus, can come either inadvertently or intentionally, but reveals a type of corruption nonetheless.) Irenaeus reveals that accusations of corruption of scripture were also applied to the orthodox church as well, for the so-called heretics "turn round and accuse these same Scriptures, as if they were not correct."[20]

Tertullian was a lawyer who lived at the end of the second century.[21] He was a prolific author and the first Christian father to write in Latin. Tertullian wrote against many of the Christian sects in his day and eventually switched from what we today call the "orthodox" Christian sect to the Montanist Christian sect because the Montanists still believed in continuing revelation, whereas the other Christian sects did not. He claimed there was "proof of the Gospel . . . having become meanwhile adulterated."[22] Tertullian notes that a Christian sect of his day "does not receive certain Scriptures; and whichever of them it does receive, it perverts by means of additions and diminutions, for the accomplishment of it[s] own purpose; and such as it does receive, it receives not in their entirety; but even when it does receive any up to a certain point as entire, it nevertheless perverts even these by the contrivance of diverse interpretations."[23] One of the sects that Tertullian deals with is

---

18. Irenaeus, *Contra Haereses* 1.8.1, (*ANF* 1:326).

19. Irenaeus, *Contra Haereses* 5.30.1, (*ANF* 1:558–59).

20. Irenaeus, *Contra Haereses* 3.2.1 (*ANF* 1:415).

21. For a biography and discussion of his works, see Quasten, *Patrology*, 2:246–340.

22. Tertullian, *Contra Marcionem* 4.2 (*ANF* 3:347).

23. Tertullian, *De Praescriptione Haereticorum* 17 (*ANF* 3:251).

that of Marcion, a Christian leader in the early second century who accepted Paul and a modified form of Luke, but rejected all other Christian scriptures. Tertullian specifically claims that "Marcion expressly and openly used the knife, not the pen, since he made such an excision of the Scriptures as suited his own subject-matter,"[24] and that "Marcion seems to have singled out Luke for his mutilating process."[25] Another sect that Tertullian writes about is the Valentinians, named after Valentinus, a mid-second century Christian leader who almost became bishop of Rome. Tertullian also claims that although Valentinus "seems to use the entire volume, he has none the less laid violent hands on the truth only with a more cunning mind and skill than Marcion,"[26] for although he "abstained from such excision, because he did not invent Scriptures to square with his own subject-matter, but adapted his matter to the Scriptures; and yet he took away more, and added more, by removing the proper meaning of every particular word, and adding fantastic arrangements of things which have no real existence."[27] Tertullian discusses "writings which wrongly go under Paul's name" but instead were composed by a presbyter in Asia.[28] Each of these leaders, Marcion, Valentinus, and other like them, had his own Christian sect. Tertullian acknowledges that these other sects "go so far as to say that adulterations of the Scriptures, and false expositions thereof, are rather introduced by ourselves [meaning Tertullian's sect, the one that later became orthodox], inasmuch as they, no less than we maintain that truth is on their side."[29]

---

24. Tertullian, *De Praescriptione Haereticorum* 38 (*ANF* 3:262).
25. Tertullian, *Contra Marcionem* 4.2 (*ANF* 3:347).
26. Tertullian, *De Praescriptione Haereticorum* 38 (*ANF* 3:262).
27. Tertullian, *De Praescriptione Haereticorum* 38 (*ANF* 3:262).
28. Tertullian, *De Baptismo* 1.17 (*ANF* 3:677).
29. Tertullian, *De Praescriptione Haereticorum* 18 (*ANF* 3:251).

At this distant time in history, the evidence that might prove or disprove individual allegations has long been unavailable. What we can note is that in the second century, there were a variety of accusations of corrupting scripture made against every party, including the sect that eventually became the "orthodox" or "Catholic" one. *universal or "Commonly accepted"*

Methods of Corruption

We learn about some of the types of changes made in the Christian texts because, ironically, they are clearly enumerated by the very people responsible for preserving them. For example Rufinus (fourth century) says of the earlier Christian texts he is copying:

> Wherever, therefore, we have found in his [in this case Origen's] books anything contrary to that which was piously established by him about the Trinity in other places, either we have *omitted* it as corrupt and interpolated, or edited it according to that pattern that we often find asserted by himself. If, however, speaking to the trained and learned, he writes obscurely because he desires to briefly pass over something, we, to make the passage plainer, have *added* those things that we have read on the same subject openly in his other books. . . . All who shall copy or read this . . . shall neither add anything to this writing, nor remove anything, nor insert anything, nor change anything.[30]

---

30. Rufinus, preface to Origen, *Peri Archon*, 2–4, in *Patrologia Graeca,* ed. J.-P. Migne (Paris: Garnier, 1857–86), 11:113–14 (author's translation; hereafter *PG*); cf. *Origen On First Principles,* trans. G. W. Butterworth (Gloucester, MA: Peter Smith, 1973), lxiii–lxiv. This particular work of Origen's is preserved only through Rufinus's Latin translation and a few fragments quoted by Greek authors. Rufinus's unreliable translations of this and other works were known both to his contemporaries and to modern scholars as "'vitiated and

＊ early "copyrite" symbol.

In this Rufinus simultaneously and almost hypocritically pleads that others not do to him what he has done to them. Rufinus is explicitly following the example of his predecessors, specifically the example of Macarius:

> who when he translated over seventy works of Origen, which are called homilies and also several of his writings on the apostle into Latin in which are found several offensive passages, therefore he *removed or cleaned up all of these* when he translated, so that a Latin reader would find nothing in them that disagrees with *our* belief. *This, therefore, we follow* even if we are not so eloquent, nevertheless as much as we can, by the same rules, watching to be sure not to reveal those passages in the books of Origen that disagree and contradict with himself.[31]

Rufinus provides us with a convenient list of types of textual corruption: Omission or deletion, addition, and alteration.

Removal is the easiest textual corruption to introduce and the most frequent form of scribal error. Justin Martyr accuses the Jews of removing small phrases from the scriptures that were significant for Christian understanding and interpretation of Old Testament passages as prophecies of Christ.[32] Tertullian makes the same accusation against Marcion: he made "such an excision of the Scriptures" that he used "the knife, not the pen."[33] From a modern vantage point, it is difficult if not impossible to tell whether any particular omission in a scriptural

---

confused'" if not "very hasty and careless" since "he frequently paraphrases and misinterprets his original." Quasten, *Patrology*, 3:172, 240, 315; see 1:61, 170; 2:37, 49–50, 58, 146; 3:341, 533.

31. Rufinus, preface to Origen, *Peri Archon*, 2, in *PG* 11:112–13, emphasis added (author's translation).

32. Justin Martyr, *Dialogus cum Tryphone* 73 (*ANF* 1:235).

33. Tertullian, *De Praescriptione Haereticorum* 38 (*ANF* 3:262).

passage is the work of an intentional, potentially malicious, editor or the work of a careless, all too human, scribe. Scribal omissions, called haplography, occur frequently. Those that are caused by identical sequences of letters at the beginning (homoeoarchteon) or the end of words (homoeoteleuton) are at least understandable, but most omissions by scribes have no such apparent explanation. The second century authors, however, make specific accusations of deliberate malicious deletion of specific portions of the text.

Addition is also a textual corruption, though less frequent than deletion. Scribal additions can result in simply repeating a portion of a text twice (dittography), supplying material from familiar turns of phrase (a form of harmonization), or sometimes from a slip of the eye that may or may not be caught. Intelligible additions of nonduplicate material are more likely to be the result of editorial work. Unfortunately for the modern scholar, when two groups of manuscripts differ in the inclusion of material, it is difficult and sometimes impossible to discern whether one group omits material or the other group adds it. The most extensive form of addition is when not just a passage but an entire work has been created. Tertullian, for example, discusses entire forged "writings which wrongly go under Paul's name" and which circulated in his day.[34] Another method of forging was simply to circulate something anonymously. Tertullian makes the accusation that Marcion "ascribes no author to his Gospel, as if it could not be allowed him to affix a title to that from which it was no crime (in his eyes) to subvert the very body."[35]

Alteration of the text can include both addition or omission but sometimes it is the simple substitution of one word

---

34. Tertullian, *De Baptismo* 17 (*ANF* 3:677).
35. Tertullian, *Contra Marcionem* 4.2 (*ANF* 3:347).

for another. Comparison of manuscripts shows that this was a common phenomenon. Is it deliberate editorial work or accidental on the part of the ancient scribe? It is interesting that although an examination of the manuscripts reveals this as a common phenomenon, the second century authors do not seem to isolate this as a problem. (Perhaps they thought that the essential message was more important than the exact wording and thus they did not think that it was a problem.)

Deleting,[36] altering, and even adding to works have been problems in antiquity,[37] in the Renaissance,[38] and even in the

---

36. See Rufinus's preface to pseudo-Clement, *Recognitiones* (*ANF* 8:75, and n. 3). "The most common scribal error (I think) is haplography, that is, reading two identical sequences of letters as one and omitting whatever intervenes." P. Kyle McCarter Jr., *Textual Criticism: Recovering the Text of the Hebrew Bible* (Philadelphia: Fortress, 1986), 17.

37. An excellent introduction to the problems involved may be found in Hugh Nibley, "The Way of the Church," in *Mormonism and Early Christianity* (Salt Lake City: Deseret Book and FARMS, 1987), 209–63. An awareness of the problems of textual tampering appears very early in human history; see, for example, Ur-Nammu (2112–2095 BC), the first king of the Ur III Dyansty: *lú mu-sar-ra-ba šu bí-íb-ùr-a ᵈBìl-ga-mes-e nam a-ba-da-ku₅-e* "may Gilgamesh curse whosoever alters this inscription;" Urnammu 41, in Ilmari Kärki, *Die Königsinschriften der dritten Dynastie von Ur* (Helsinki: Finnish Oriental Society, 1986), 26; similar imprecations spanning the length of Babylonian history may be found in Hermann Hunger, *Babylonische und assyrische Kolophone* (Kevelaer: Butzon & Bercker, 1968); for the spread of this curse formula into Hittite culture at the beginning of its written history, see O. R. Gurney, *The Hittites* (London: Penguin, 1990), 141.

38. See A. E. Housman, *M. Manilii Astronomicon*, 2nd ed. (Cambridge: Cambridge University Press, 1937), 1:xiv-xxii; for an estimate of Renaissance and previous Byzantine textual work, see Alexander

present day.[39] But other types of corruptions also affect the text, including presuppositional, grammatical, and lexical reinterpretations.

Presuppositional reinterpretation occurs when the basic assumptions with which the text is read are changed. For example, Irenaeus accuses Valentinus of acting in a fashion similar to some modern biblical critics and dividing "the prophecies [into different classes], maintaining that one portion was uttered by the mother, a second by her seed, and a third by the Demiurge. In like manner, they hold that Jesus uttered some things under the influence of the Saviour, others under that of the mother, and others still under that of the Demiurge."[40] The Valentinians believed, in line with the best Neo-Platonic thinking of their day, that God did not create the world, but rather a junior god who created a more junior god, and so on until one of these junior gods created a devil, called the Demiurge, who created the world.

Hugh McDonald, "Textual Criticism," *Oxford Classical Dictionary*, 2nd ed. (Oxford: Clarendon, 1970), 1049.

39. On the modern rewriting of Polybius, see Robert K. Ritner, "Implicit Models of Cross-Cultural Interaction: A Question of Noses, Soap, and Prejudice," in Janet H. Johnson, ed., *Life in a Multi-Cultural Society: Egypt from Cambyses to Constantine and Beyond* (Chicago: Oriental Institute, 1992), 287–88. This central point in Ritner's argument, was itself omitted in the original published version and the errata sheet must be checked. Another egregious example of rewriting the sources is Morton Smith's *Jesus the Magician* (San Francisco: Harper and Row, 1978). On page 53, Smith claims to take Pliny the Younger's *Epistulae* X.96 "as it is usually taken, at face value" and then proceeds to introduce magical spells, demons, and cannibalism into a text which actually lacks all of these elements.

40. Irenaeus, *Contra Haereses* 1.7.3 (*ANF* 1:326).

They gather their views from other sources than the Scriptures; and to use a common proverb, they strive to weave ropes of sand, while they endeavour to adapt with an air of probability to their own peculiar assertions the parables of the Lord, the sayings of the prophets, and the words of the apostles, in order that their scheme may not seem altogether without support. In doing so, however, they disregard the order and the connection of the Scriptures, and so far as in them lies, dismember and destroy the truth. By transferring passages, and dressing them up anew, and making one thing out of another, they succeed in deluding many through their wicked art in adapting the oracles of the Lord to their opinions.[41]

Another type of presuppositional reinterpretation is the process by which the texts are reinterpreted in a nonliteral or allegorical framework.[42] Allegorical interpretation had been a well-known way of reinterpreting texts in Egypt,[43] and became a popular way of reinterpreting texts among Alexandrian

parable interpretation

---

41. Irenaeus, *Contra Haereses* 1.8.1 (*ANF* 1:326).

42. See Richard Lloyd Anderson, *Understanding Paul* (Salt Lake City: Deseret Book, 1983), 376–77; Layton, *Gnostic Scriptures*, 317. For an exhaustive analysis of the switch in interpretation in one passage of scripture, see Thomas W. Mackay, "Early Christian Millenarianist Interpretation of the Two Witnesses in John's Apocalypse 11:3–13," in Lundquist and Ricks, eds., *By Study and Also By Faith*, 1:222–331. For the use of the allegorical approach in Rabbinic Judaism, see Jacob Neusner, "The Case of Leviticus Rabbah," in Lundquist and Ricks, eds., *By Study and Also By Faith*, 1:366–70. For a historical discussion of allegory, see C. S. Lewis, *The Allegory of Love: A Study in Medieval Tradition* (Oxford: Oxford University Press, 1936), 44–111.

43. J. Gwyn Griffiths, "Allegory in Greece and Egypt," *Journal of Egyptian Archaeology* 53 (1967): 79–102.

intellectuals: Pagans like Theagenes, Anaxagoras, Metrodorus, and Stoics allegorized Homer;[44] Philo allegorized the Old Testament, and some Egyptian sects of Christianity did the same with Christianity. In combating this trend, Irenaeus along with the leaders of the catechetical school in Alexandria, Clement of Alexandria and Origen, brought the method into mainstream Christianity.

Grammatical reinterpretation exploits ambiguities in Greek (and later Latin) to fashion understandings of the text that significantly differ from previous understandings. Origen provides a good example of such grammatical reinterpretation in his interpretation of the beatitude in Matthew 5:8:

> If the question is put to us why it was said, 'Blessed are the pure in heart, for they shall see God', I answer that in my opinion our argument will be much more firmly established by this passage. For what else is 'to see God in the heart' but to understand and know him in the mind, just as we have explained above? For the names of the organs of sense are often applied to the soul, so that we speak of seeing with the eyes of the heart, that is, of drawing some intellectual conclusion by means of the faculty of intelligence.[45]

Origen has moved the modifying phrase *tē kardia* "in the heart" from modifying the adjacent *katharoi* "pure" to the distant *opsontai* "they shall see," and by so doing has denied the explicit promise of the scripture.[46]

---

44. Griffiths, "Allegory in Greece and Egypt," 79.

45. Origen, *On First Principles* 1.1.9, in Origen, *On First Principles*, trans. Butterworth, 14.

46. This is no mere isolated interpretation by Origen, see also Origen, *On First Principles* 2.11.7, in Origen, *On First Principles*, trans. Butterworth, 154.

Lexical reinterpretation is the changing of the meanings of words, such as occurred during the second sophistic period.[47] Between the time of writing the New Testament and the end of the second century, the meanings of several of the words changed. Examples include the change of the principle meanings of *pistis* from "collateral, guarantee" to "belief;"[48] of *pisteuein* from "to trust, rely on; entrust, commit, put up collateral" to "to believe;"[49] of *homologein* from "to agree to terms, accept an agreement, enter into a legal contract, promise" to "to confess;"[50] of *mystērion* from "(initation) rite" to "secret."[51] Such changes in language are common in all languages and in all periods, some deliberate and some not. The Christians, like the Jews before them, used the Greek language in an idiosyncratic way that seemed strange to non-Christians around them. For example, both Christians and Jews used the term *ouranoi* "heavens", the plural of *ouranos* "sky", as a term for the dwelling place of God, even though Greeks never used the term in the plural.[52] In the second century, however, various

---

47. In general, this topic has not received adequate treatment. Preliminary steps in this direction are Hugh Nibley, "Evangelium Quadraginta Dierum," in *When the Lights Went Out* (Provo, UT: FARMS, 2001), 75–76 n 61; Welch, *The Sermon at the Temple and the Sermon on the Mount*, 88. For analysis of some of the dynamics involved, see Hugh Nibley, "Victoriosa Loquacitas: The Rise of Rhetoric and the Decline of Everything Else," in *The Ancient State* (Salt Lake City: Deseret Book and FARMS, 1991), 243–86.

48. H. G. Liddell, R. Scott, H. S. Jones, *A Greek-English Lexicon*, 9th ed. (Oxford: Clarendon, 1940; hereafter *LSJ*), 1408.

49. *LSJ* 1407–8.

50. *LSJ* 1226.

51. *LSJ* 1156.

52. *LSJ* 1273. The distinction between singular and plural in the Greek does not usually appear in the King James Version.

sects of Christianity began to redefine terminology to mean something different.[53] Irenaeus claims that the Valentinians adopted pagan fables "changing . . . the names of the things referred to" to fit into Christian scripture.[54] Because the New Testament is usually read with meanings of the second sophistic period and later—meanings which have often changed—the understanding of the text has sometimes been drastically changed. This can be seen in the interpretation of a passage from Paul's epistle to the Romans:

The word is nigh thee, even in thy mouth, and in thy heart: that is, the word of **faith**, which we preach; That if thou shalt **confess** with thy mouth the Lord Jesus, and shalt **believe** in thine heart that God hath raised him from the dead, thou shalt be saved. For with the heart man **believeth** unto righteousness; and with the mouth **confession is made** unto salvation. For the scripture saith, Whosoever believeth on him shall not

"The word is next to you through your mouth and through your heart." That is the word of **collateral** that we announce, that if you will **make an agreement** by means of your mouth that Jesus is Lord and **put up collateral** by means of your heart that God raised him from the dead, you will be saved; for by means of the heart **is collateral put up** toward righteousness, and by means of the mouth **are terms agreed upon** toward

---

53. James Allen provides an interesting argument that the Egyptian pharaoh Akhenaten did the same thing, and that his Amarna revolution was not so much monotheistic as naturalistic and ultimately atheistic. See James P. Allen, "The Natural Philosophy of Akhenaten," in *Religion and Philosophy in Ancient Egypt*, ed. William Kelly Simpson (New Haven: Yale Egyptological Seminar, 1989), 89–101.

54. Irenaeus, *Contra Haereses* 2.14.1 (*ANF* 1:376).

be ashamed. For there is no difference between the Jew and the Greek: for the same Lord over all is rich unto all that **call upon** him. For whosoever shall **call upon** the name of the Lord shall be saved.

salvation; for the scripture says: "Every one who relies on him will not be disgraced;" because there is no discrimination of Jew or of Greek, for he himself is the Lord of all, generous towards all who **invoke** him; for "whosoever shall **invoke** the name of the Lord shall be rescued."

How then shall they **call on** him in whom they have not **believed**? and how shall they **believe** in him of whom they have not **heard**? and how shall they **hear** without a preacher? And how shall they preach, except they be sent? (Romans 10:8–15, KJV, emphasis added)

How therefore shall they **invoke** him with whom they have no **agreement**? How shall they **make an agreement** with him whom they have not **obeyed**? How shall they **obey** without one proclaiming? How shall they proclaim if they have not been commissioned? (Romans 10:8–15, author's translation, emphasis added)

How the words in a text are understood can make an enormous difference.

All of the methods of changing the text that we have just discussed occur in the second century. The result is that there were many different interpretations of scriptures and scriptural events among the Christian communities. An indicative example of the variety of interpretations can be seen in the *Apocalypse of Adam,* a text that dates no later than the fourth century, where it enumerates fourteen different views of the events leading to the baptism of Jesus, of which we sample five:

The third kingdom says about him that he came into being from a virgin mother. He was cast out of his city, he and his mother. He was received in a desert place. He nourished himself there. He came and he received glory and power. And in this way he arrived at the water.

. . .

The sixth kingdom says about him that a [. . .] to this world which is below in order to gather flowers. She became pregnant from the desire of the flowers. She bore him in that place. The angels of the garden nourished him. He received glory and power in that place. And in this way he arrived at the water.

. . .

The tenth kingdom says about him that his god loved a cloud of lust. He begot him by his hand, and he cast from this drop upon that nearby cloud and begot him. He received glory and power in that place. And in this way he arrived at the water.

. . .

The thirteenth kingdom says about him that every birth of their ruler [is] a word. And this word received an appointment in that place. He received glory and power. And in this way he arrived at the water so that the desire of these powers might be mingled.

But the indomitable generation says about him that God chose him from all the Eons. He caused a knowledge of the undefiled truth to exist in him. He said that [that great] heavenly light came from a strange air from the great Eon. And [he caused] that generation of those men whom he chose for himself to give light, so that they light this whole world. Then that seed, all those who will receive his name upon the water, shall oppose that power.[55]

---

55. *Apocalypse of Adam* V, 77, 27–83, 7 (author's translation).

The variety of interpretations set forth in this work begin from different assumptions and result in completely different views of the Savior.

Motivations for Manipulating the Text

What motives did second century individuals and groups have to change scripture? Clement, the bishop of Rome, wrote his epistle at the beginning of the second century at the request of leaders in Corinth to settle a dispute they were having. Clement accuses individuals at Corinth of "pride and sedition" and as setting themselves up as "leaders" and usurping the authority that was not theirs.[56] Irenaeus cites the Corinthians to whom Clement directed his letter as precursors of Valentinus and Marcion.[57] Toward the end of the second century, a text attributed to Clement of Alexandria notes that the Carpocratians changed scripture to sanction their own homosexual and other immoral practices.[58] Irenaeus claims that the Valentinians "endeavour to adapt with an air of probability to their own peculiar assertions the parables of the Lord, the sayings of the prophets, and the words of the apostles, in order that their scheme may not seem altogether without support."[59] Irenaeus further claims that the Valentinians wanted to "bring together the things which have been said by all those who were ignorant of God, and who are termed philosophers" and have their Christian teachings match the intellectual traditions of

---

56. 1 Clement 14 (*ANF* 1:8; 9:233; for original text see Oscar von Gebhardt, Adolf von Harnack, Theodor Zahn, *Patrum Apostolicorum Opera* [Leipzig: Heinrichs, 1906], 8–9).

57. Irenaeus, *Contra Haereses*, 3. chaps. 3–4 (*ANF* 1:416–17).

58. Clement of Alexandria, *Letter to Theodore*, in Smith, *Clement of Alexandria and a Secret Gospel of Mark*, 448–53, plates I–III.

59. Irenaeus, *Contra Haereses* 1.8.1 (*ANF* 1:326).

the Roman world;[60] they wanted intellectual respectability. Another example is the author of *The Sophia of Jesus Christ* who took the philosophical writings of Eugnostos and put them, mostly word for word, into the mouth of the risen Jesus.[61] Tertullian says that "writings which wrongly go under Paul's name" were forged by a presbyter in Asia to give "a license for women's teaching and baptizing."[62] Changes in the texts and the motivations to alter the text of scriptures both canonical and noncanonical,[63] in general, match those Nephi gave "After the book hath gone forth through the hands of the great and abominable church, that there are many plain and precious things taken away from the book" (1 Nephi 13:28). "Behold the gold, and the silver and the silks, and the scarlets, and the fine-twined linen, and the precious clothing, and the harlots, are the desires of this great and abominable church" (1 Nephi 13:8). While not all second century Christians were consumed by these desires, some clearly were.[64]

---

60. Irenaeus, *Contra Haereses*, 2.14.1–6 (*ANF* 1:376–78).

61. See the edition of Douglas M. Parrott, *Nag Hammadi Codices III, 3–4 and V,1* (Leiden: Brill, 1991). It is interesting that whoever compiled Nag Hammadi Codex III recognized this because he copied the texts back to back in the volume.

62. Tertullian, *De Baptismo* 1.17 (*ANF* 3:677).

63. Also Tertullian, *De Praescriptione Haereticorum* 1.38–40 (*ANF* 3:261–62); other categories and examples given in Stephen D. Robinson, "Lying for God," in *Apocryphal Writings and the Latter-day Saints*, ed. C. Wilford Griggs (Provo, UT: BYU Religious Studies Center, 1986), 144–46.

64. 1 Clement 44:1 (*ANF* 1:17; 9:282); Hegesippus, quoted in Eusebius, *Historiae Ecclesiasticae* 3.32.7, in *The Nicene and Post-Nicene Fathers*, series 2, ed. Philip Schaff (reprint, Peabody, MA: Hendrickson, 1994), 1:164; *Second Treatise of the Great Seth* VII, 59, 19–61, 24.

Manuscript Evidence

The accusations of the second century writers might be shown to be mistaken if only one could show that the scriptural texts have not become corrupted during the time period specified. Unfortunately, the nature of the manuscript evidence does not allow us to determine such a proposition. While thousands of Greek biblical manuscripts have survived, each fragment that contains any portion of the Bible counts the same as one that includes the entire Bible. Most of these manuscripts are cursive manuscripts, later manuscripts written in the cursive business handwriting rather than the earlier manuscripts which were written in a clear literary hand (called uncial) that has more of the appearance of a printed book. If we consider only those of the New Testament, we have about 341 uncial manuscripts (which are generally earlier than the cursive manuscripts).[65] Of these, about ten percent date before the time of Constantine, and only one dates to the second century. This second century manuscript (P52 = Rylands 458) is about the size of a postage stamp and contains only ten complete words. (Peter Thiede's redating of the Magdalen College fragments to the first century[66] would be wonderful if true, but his arguments have been demonstrated wrong.)[67] Ninety-nine

---

The urge to usurp authority might have been the cause of the anonymous accusations attested in Pliny the Younger, *Epistulae* 10.96.5.

65. The information in this section was compiled from Kurt Aland et al., *Novum Testamentum Graecae*, 26th ed., 7th corrected printing (Stuttgart: Deutsche Bibelgesellschaft, 1983), 684–702.

66. Carsten Peter Thiede, "Papyrus Magdalen Greek 17 (Gregory-Aland P64) A Reappraisal," *Zeitschrift für Papyrologie und Epigraphik* 105 (1995): 13–20.

67. Klaus Wachtel, "P64/67: Fragmente des Matthäusevangeliums aus dem 1. Jahrhundert?" *Zeitschrift für Papyrologie und Epigraphik* 107

point seven percent of Greek uncial New Testament manu-scripts come after the time period when accusations of textual corruption are rampant. If we included the cursive manu-scripts as well, the percentage of second century manuscripts would become even smaller. So only ten complete words of the New Testament are attested in manuscript form *during* the time of textual corruption, and not a single one is attested *before* that time.

If we assemble all the manuscripts from the second and third centuries and note just those chapters where even a part of a verse is attested, we find that entire books are missing, including 1–2 Timothy, 1–2 Peter, 2–3 John, and Jude. Of the twenty-eight chapters in the Gospel of Matthew, there is no manuscript containing even a single verse of sixteen of these chapters before the end of the third century (see table 3). Reconstruction of a pre-second century text is simply not pos-sible unless one makes the *a priori* assumption that there are no changes, which is a circular argument. So the biblical man-uscripts themselves cannot test the second century accusations of textual corruption.

So one is left with no definitive way to show from manu-scripts what the scriptural text looked like at the beginning of the second century and thus to show whether the text was corrupted or not. Occasional passages show that the text was already corrupt when the manuscript tradition appeared. Consider the text of Matthew 19:9 where Jesus identifies who commits adultery in the case of divorce and remarriage. The passage is not preserved before the fourth century when there

---

(1995): 73–80. Thiede appears to have been something of an imposter posing as an expert; Harald Vocke, "Papyrus Magdalen 17—weitere Argumente gegen die Frühdatierung des angeblichen Jesus-Papyrus," *Zeitschrift für Papyrologie und Epigraphik* 113 (1996): 153–57.

are three major variant traditions,[68] one of which reads: "whosoever divorces his wife except by reason of sexual immorality makes her commit adultery and whosoever marries the divorced woman commits adultery;"[69] another reads: "whosoever divorces his wife except for adultery and marries another commits adultery;"[70] a third reads "whosoever divorces his wife except for adultery and marries another commits adultery himself and whosoever marries the divorced woman commits adultery."[71] Here, between the variants, we have Jesus making opposite rulings about who is guilty in case of divorce. We have no way of knowing which of the textual readings, if any, is correct, but we know that at least two cannot be. We cannot appeal to the earliest text because all the variants are attested in the fourth century when the earliest manuscripts appear. The matter discussed in this passage is a very practical one with significant implications for Christian practice, one where the text is significantly corrupted, and the manuscripts reflect various biases.

While we are looking at the biases of our sources, we should also consider geographical bias in the biblical manuscript record. Not all climates preserve manuscripts equally well. The earliest manuscripts come from Egypt which has the most suitable climate for preservation of manuscripts. But this does not mean that the manuscripts from Egypt are necessarily superior to those of other locations. Paul's letters, for example, were directed to churches in Ephesus, Corinth, and Thessalonike, not

---

68. I have used only the fourth century manuscripts. Others manuscripts back various readings and other variants are attested for this passage.

69. Following Codex Vaticanus (fourth century).

70. Following Codex Sinaiticus (fourth century).

71. Following P25 = P. Bertlin. 16388 (fourth century).

to the Egyptian backwater of Oxyrhynchus.[72] Yet that same Oxyrhynchite backwater has provided 36 New Testament papyri manuscripts (just over a third of the papyri corpus, all of which comes from Egypt).[73] Egypt has never been considered in the mainstream of what became normative Western Christianity, and yet the manuscripts from this location dominate current editions of the Greek New Testament and most recent translations.

The Scriptures of the Early Second Century

If biblical manuscripts cannot give us a view of the biblical text before the accusations of corruption in the second century, early second century quotations of scripture may provide a somewhat restricted view of the state of scripture before those charges.

The scriptures that the Christians had at the beginning of the second century were different from those that they had at the end of the second century at both the level of the canon and the level of the text. By the end of the second century, Christian quotations of scriptures were closer to those we have at present. Tertullian, writing at the end of the second century, cites every book in the New Testament except Philemon. Irenaeus, also writing at the end of the second century, cites every book in the current New Testament except the tiny books of Philemon, 3 John, and Jude. Irenaeus also cites a few apocryphal books as authoritative. (Even in the third century the canon of scripture was still in flux, the Chester Beatty codex contained a copy of

---

72. See Roger S. Bagnall, *Egypt in Late Antiquity* (Princeton: Princeton University Press, 1993), 138–42.

73. See the lists in Aland et al., *Novum Testamentum Graece*, 684–89, and Orsolina Montevecchi, *La Papirologia*, 2nd ed. (Milan: Vita e Pensiero, 1998), 309–21.

the first book of Enoch in the New Testament as well as a homily on the Passion by Melito, bishop of Sardis.)[74]

Accordingly Christian writers at the beginning of the second century had a different set of authoritative writings than their counterparts at the end of the second century. Clement of Rome is generally seen as the earliest of the Christian authors after the New Testament. Clement quotes from many books of the Old Testament (Genesis, Exodus, Numbers, Deuteronomy, Joshua, 1 Samuel, 2 Chronicles, Esther, Job, Psalms, Proverbs, Isaiah, Jeremiah, Ezekiel, Daniel, Malachi), and the New Testament books of Matthew, Mark, Luke, Romans, 1 Corinthians, Hebrews, and 1 Peter. But Clement also quotes from the apocryphal books of the Wisdom of Solomon and Judith. Furthermore, Clement quotes from other scriptural passages, passages that are not known from any writings. We will list these in roughly the order they might have been found in our current Bibles if they contained them. For example, Clement quotes Moses as saying: "I am smoke from a vessel,"[75] a quotation that is not found in any known biblical or apocryphal work.[76] Clement further cites a passage from Psalm 28:[77] "Thou shalt raise me up and I shall acknowledge thee."[78] This reading of the psalm, however, is not attested in any extant manuscript. Clement also quotes from a passage attributed to Ezekiel[79] but not in our text, "Repent, O

---

74. See Campbell Bonner, *The Last Chapters of Enoch in Greek* (London: Christophers, 1937), 1–12.

75. 1 Clement 17:6 (*ANF* 1:9–10; 9:234).

76. See *The Epistle of S. Clement* 17 (Lightfoot, *Apostolic Fathers*, 1.2:64–65).

77. See *The Epistle of S. Clement* 17 (Lightfoot, *Apostolic Fathers*, 1.2:89).

78. 1 Clement 26:2 (*ANF* 1:12; 9:237).

79. See *The Epistle of S. Clement* 17 (Lightfoot, *Apostolic Fathers*, 1.2:39–41).

house of Israel, from your sins from the earth to heaven, and though they be red like scarlet and black as ashes, and you turn to me with your whole soul and say: Father, hearken to us as to the holy people."[80] Clement quotes the following passage as scripture, although its source is currently unknown,[81] "Wretched are the double-minded, who doubt in their soul, who say: This we have heard against our fathers and behold, we have grown old and none of them have happened even to us. O fools, compare yourselves to a tree—take the vine—first it sheds the leaf, then the bud comes, then the leaf, then the blossom, and after that the sour grape, then comes forth the ripened grape."[82] Finally, Clement cites as scripture "Cleave to the saints, for those who cleave to them shall be sanctified,"[83] though this is not found an any current body of scripture:[84]

The homily known as 2 Clement, a second century letter which may or may not have been written by the same Clement of Rome, also contains variations in quotations of the scriptures. Consider the following passage which comes from a gospel but is not found in any of the gospels known to us: "Ye shall be as sheep in the midst of wolves. And Peter answering, said to him: What if the wolves should scatter the sheep? Jesus saith to Peter: The sheep shall not fear the wolves after they kill them; ye also shall not fear those who shall kill you and cannot do anything against you, but ye shall fear him who hath power after your death to cast soul and body into the hell of

---

80. 1 Clement 8:3 (*ANF* 1:7; 9:231).

81. See *The Epistle of S. Clement* 17 (Lightfoot, *Apostolic Fathers*, 1.2:80–81).

82. 1 Clement 23:3–4 (*ANF* 1:11; 9:236).

83. 1 Clement 46:2 (*ANF* 1:17–18; 9:243).

84. "This quotation is no where [*sic*] found in the Old Testament." Lightfoot, *Apostolic Fathers*, 1.2:139–40.

fire."[85] The sentiments are generally found in gospels but not as they are here. Second Clement attributes the following saying to Jesus also: "If ye are gathered to me in my bosom and do not my commandments, I shall cast you out and shall say to you: Depart from me, workers of iniquity; I know not whence ye are."[86] Of course, this passage resembles the Sermon on the Mount, but if the passage is from Matthew, it is a different form of Matthew than what we now have.

The epistle of Barnabas purports to be written by Barnabas, normally presumed to be Paul's missionary companion, to his sons and daughters in the gospel. Most scholars date the epistle to the early second century rather than the first century. The epistle of Barnabas is largely a pastiche of scriptural quotations; he simply strings one scripture after another. Barnabas cites Genesis, Exodus, Leviticus, Numbers, Deuteronomy, Psalms, Proverbs, Isaiah, Jeremiah, Ezekiel, Daniel, Zachariah, *4 Ezra,* Sirach, Matthew, Romans, *1 Enoch,* and the *Didache,* although editors routinely note that the citations of these passages differ from the later standard text. Among these quotations is the following attributed to the prophets but not found in the scriptures: "And they shall eat from the goat offered by fasting on behalf of the sinners. . . . And the priests only shall eat the innards, unwashed with vinegar"[87] Barnabas quotes from Enoch: "The final offense has arrived, about which is written, as Enoch says. For therefore the Lord cuts off the times and days, so that his beloved might hurry and come to his inheritance."[88] The epistle also includes the following as part of the law of Moses referring to the scapegoat rite: "And all you shall

---

85. 2 Clement 5:2–4 (*ANF* 7:518–19; 9:252).

86. 2 Clement 4:5 (*ANF* 7:518; 9:252).

87. Barnabas 7:4 (*ANF* 1:41).

88. Barnabas 4:3 (*ANF* 1:138).

spit and pierce it, and encircle its head with scarlet wool, and let it be driven into the wilderness."[89] Leviticus, however, does not contain this rite. The epistle of Barnabas also includes the following as part of the words of the prophets, but which we do not find in our scriptures: "The parable of the Lord, who shall understand it except the wise and learned who also loves his lord?"[90] The epistle attributes this quotation to the prophets but it is also absent from our scriptures: "And when shall these things come to pass? Saith the Lord: When the tree shall bend and arise, and when blood shall flow from the wood."[91] And this is attributed to the Lord but not found in the scriptures: "Behold, I make the last as the first."[92]

In all of these instances, Christian authors quote from scriptures that either are not in the current canon or have been substantially altered; even when quoting from scriptures that we presently have, the quotations do not match the surviving manuscripts. The standard explanation is that these passages found in writers of the beginning of the second century but not elsewhere "are sometimes loosely and inaccurately cited from memory. . . . Indeed they are so unlike anything to be found in the known books of the Bible that despairing critics are reduced to supposing that Clement has taken them from some lost apocryphal source."[93] While one can assume that quotations that do not match the current text are made from memory—and it certainly is a possibility—it is an assumption; one could equally assume that there have been changes to the

89. Barnabas 7:8 (*ANF* 1:141).

90. Barnabas 6:10 (*ANF* 1:140).

91. Barnabas 12:1 (*ANF* 1:144).

92. Barnabas 6:13 (*ANF* 1:140–41).

93. Maxwell Staniforth, trans., *Early Christian Writings: The Apostolic Fathers* (New York: Dorset, 1986), 22.

text in the intervening period. When an early second century author quotes scripture, it is often unlike anything to be found in the books of the Bible as we know them. We know them, however, from manuscripts that date after the second century authors noted widespread charges of textual corruption. These two facts together can equally well be taken as evidence that the charges of textual corruption are correct.

Conclusions

In viewing the state of Christian scripture in the second century, we have not, generally, had to rely on scholarly interpretation or writers later than the early third century to detect a large shift in the concept and content of scripture in the second century. The books that were considered scripture, and some of the content of those books, changed from the beginning to the end of the century. During the second century various fragmentary groups of Christians accused other groups of having changed the texts to fit their own ideas. These changes took the form of deletions, some additions, and the redefining of the text. What the angel told Nephi is largely supported by what remains of early Christian literature. To the second century, if not before, we may trace the corruption of scripture and the loss of the plain and precious things, and it is worth noting that none of the extant Greek manuscripts dates before that time period. We cannot look to scholarship to restore the plain and precious portions of the text that were lost. If it is not revealed again we shall never have it.

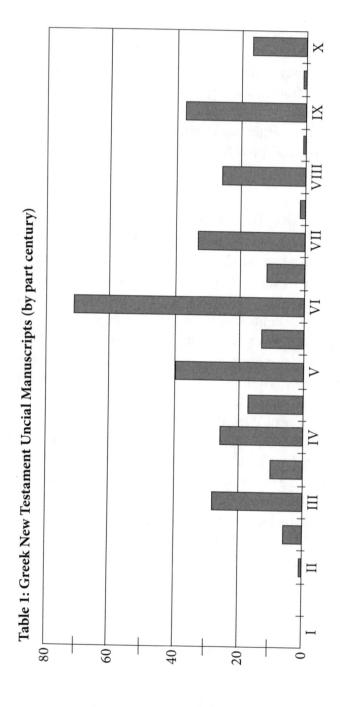

Table 1: Greek New Testament Uncial Manuscripts (by part century)

Table 2: Portions of the Pre-Constantine New Testament Attested in Manuscripts

The manuscripts are placed paleographically by century and the attested verses in each chapter are given in parentheses. Sections marked with an asterisk (*) do not have a lacuna for the missing verses in the chapter, the manuscript is continuous but does not have the verses.

	II	II or III	III	III or IV
Matt. 1			p1 (1–9, 12, 14–20)	
2			p70 (13–16, 22–23)	
3		p64+67 (9, 15)	p70 (1)	
4				
5		p64+67 (20–22, 25–28)		
6				
7				
8				
9				
10				0171 (17–23, 25–32)
11			p70 (26–27)	
12			p70 (4–5)	
13				
14				
15				
16				
17				
18				
19				
20			p45 (24–32)	
21			p45 (13–19)	
22				
23		p77 (30–39)		

	II	II or III	III	III or IV
Matt. 24			p70 (3–6, 12–15)	
25			p45 (41–46)	
			p53 (29–40)	
26		p64+67 (7–8, 10, 14–15, 22–23, 31–33)	p45 (1–39)	p37 (19–52)
27				
28				
Mark 1				
2				
3				
4			p45 (36–40)	
5			p45 (15–26, 38–43)	
6			p45 (1–3, 16–25, 36–50)	
7			p45 (3–15, 25–37)	
8			p45 (1, 10–26, 34–38)	
9			p45 (1–9, 18–31)	
10				
11			p45 (27–33)	
12			p45 (1, 5–8, 13–19, 24–28)	
13				
14				
15				
16				
Luke 1			p4 (58–59, 62–80)	
2			p4 (1, 6–7)	
3			p4 (8–38) p75 (18–22, 33–38)	
4			p4 (1–2, 29–32, 34–35) p75 (1–2, 34–44)	
5			p4 (3–8) p75 (1–10, 37–39)	

	II	II or III	III	III or IV
Luke 6			p45 (31–41, 45–49)	
			p75 (1–4, 10–49)	
7			p45 (1–7) p75 (1–32, 35–39, 41–43, 46–50)	
8			p75 (1–56)	
9			p45 (26–41, 45–62) p75 (1–2, 4–62)	
10			p45 (1, 6–22, 26–42) p75 (1–42)	
11			p45 (1, 6–25, 28–46, 50–54) p75 (1–54)	
12			p45 (1–12, 18–37, 42–59) p75 (1–59)	
13			p45 (1, 6–24, 29–35) p75 (1–35)	
14			p45 (1–10, 17–33) p75 (1–35)	
15			p75 (1–32)	
16			p75 (1–31)	
17			p75 (1–15, 19–37)	
18			p75 (1–18)	
19				
20				
21				
22			p69 (41, 45–48, 58–61) p75 (4–71)	0171 (44–56, 61–64)
23			p75 (1–56)	
24			p75 (1–53)	
John 1		p66 (1–6, 11)	p5 (23–31, 33–40) p75 (1–51)	
2			p75 (1–25)	0162 (11–22)
3			p75 (1–36) p80 (34)	

	II	II or III	III	III or IV
John 4			p75 (1–54)	
5			p75 (1–47)	
6		p66 (35–71)	p28 (8–12, 17–22) p75 (1–71)	
7		p66 (1–52)*	p75 (1–52)*	
8		p66 (12–59)*	p39 (14–22) p75 (12–59)*	
9		p66 (1–41)	p75 (1–41)	
10		p66 (1–42)	p45 (7–25, 30–42) p75 (1–42)	
11		p66 (1–57)	p45 (1–10, 18–36, 42–57) p75 (1–45, 48–57)	
12		p66 (1–50)	p75 (3–50)	
13		p66 (1–38)	p75 (1, 8–9)	
14		p66 (1–26, 29–30)	p75 (8–30)	
15		p66 (2–26)	p22 (25–27) p75 (7–8)	
16		p66 (2–4, 6–7, 10–33)	p5 (14–30) p22 (1–2, 21–32)	
17		p66 (1–26)		
18	p52 (31–33, 37–38) p66 (1–40)			
19		p66 (1–42)		
20		p66 (1–20, 22–23, 25–31)	p5 (11–17, 19–20, 22–25)	
21		p66 (1–9)		
Acts 1				
2				
3				
4			p45 (27–36)	
5		0189 (3–21)	p45 (10–21, 30–39)	
6			p45 (7–15)	
7			p45 (1–2, 10–21, 32–41, 52–60)	

	II	II or III	III	III or IV
Acts 8			p45 (1, 14–25, 34–40)	
9			p45 (1–6, 16–27, 35–43) p53 (33–43)	
10			p45 (1–2, 10–23, 31–41) p53 (1)	
11			p45 (2–14, 24–30)	
12			p45 (1–5, 13–22)	
13			p45 (6–16, 25–26, 46–52)	
14			p45 (1–3, 15–23)	
15			p45 (2–7, 19–27, 38–41)	
16			p45 (1–4, 15–21, 32–40)	
17			p45 (9–17)	
18				p38 (27–28)
19				p38 (1–6, 12–16)
20				
21				
22				
23			p48 (11–17, 23–29)	
24				
25				
26			p29 (7–8, 20)	
27				
28				
Rom. 1			p40 (24–27, 31–32)	
2			p40 (1–3)	
3			p40 (21–31)	
4			p40 (1–8) 0220 (23–25)	
5		p46 (17–21)	0220 (1–3, 8–13)	

	II	II or III	III	III or IV
Rom. 6		p46 (1–3, 5–14)	p40 (4–5, 16)	
7				
8		p46 (15–25, 27–35, 37–39)	p27 (12–22, 24–27, 33–39)	
9		p46 (1–32)	p27 (1–3, 5–9) p40 (16–17, 27)	
10		p46 (1–21)		
11		p46 (1–22, 24–33, 35–36)		
12		p46 (1–21)		
13		p46 (1–14)		
14		p46 (1–23)		
15		p46 (1–9, 11–33)		
16		p46 (1–22)		
1 Cor. 1		p46 (1–31)		
2		p46 (1–16)		
3		p46 (1–23)		
4		p46 (1–21)		
5		p46 (1–13)		
6		p46 (1–20)		
7		p46 (1–40)	p15 (18–40)	
8		p46 (1–13)	p15 (1–4)	
9		p46 (1–2, 4–27)		
10		p46 (1–33)		
11		p46 (1–34)		
12		p46 (1–31)		
13		p46 (1–13)		
14		p46 (1–14, 16–40)		
15		p46 (1–15, 17–58)		
16		p46 (1–22)		
2 Cor. 1		p46 (1–24)		
2		p46 (1–17)		
3		p46 (1–18)		

	II	II or III	III	III or IV
2 Cor. 4		p46 (1–18)		
5		p46 (1–21)		
6		p46 (1–18)		
7		p46 (1–16)		
8		p46 (1–24)		
9		p46 (1–15)		
10		p46 (1–18)		
11		p46 (1–10, 12–21, 23–33)		
12		p46 (1–21)		
13		p46 (1–13)		
Gal. 1		p46 (1–8, 10–24)		
2		p46 (1–9, 12–21)		
3		p46 (2–29)		
4		p46 (2–18, 20–31)		
5		p46 (1–17, 20–26)		
6		p46 (1–8, 10–18)		
Eph. 1		p46 (1–23)		p92 (11–13, 19–21)
2		p46 (1–7, 10–22)		
3		p46 (1–21)		
4		p46 (1–32)	p49 (16–29, 31–32)	
5		p46 (1–6, 8–33)	p49 (1–13)	
6		p46 (1–6, 8–18, 20–24)		
Philip. 1		p46 (1, 5–15, 17–28, 30)		
2		p46 (1–12, 14–27, 29–30)		
3		p46 (1–8, 10–21)		p16 (10–17)
4		p46 (2–12, 14–23)		p16 (2–8)
Col. 1		p46 (1–2, 5–13, 16–24, 27–29)		
2		p46 (1–19, 23)		

	II	II or III	III	III or IV
Col. 3		p46 (1–11, 13–24)		
4		p46 (3–12, 16–18)		
1 Thes. 1		p46 (1, 9–10)	p65 (3–10)	
2		p46 (1–3)	p65 (1, 6–13)	
3				
4			p30 (12–13, 16–17)	
5		p46 (5–9, 23–28)	p30 (3, 8–10, 12–18, 25–28)	
2 Thes. 1			p30 (1–2)	p92 (4–5, 11–12)
2				
3				
1 Tim. 1				
2				
3				
4				
5				
6				
2 Tim. 1				
2				
3				
4				
Titus 1				
2				
3				
Philem. 1			p87 (13–15, 24–25)	
Heb. 1		p46 (1–14)	p12 (1)	
2		p46 (1–18)		p13 (14–18)
3		p46 (1–19)		p13 (1–19)
4		p46 (1–16)		p13 (1–16)
5		p46 (1–14)		p13 (1–5)
6		p46 (1–20)		
7		p46 (1–28)		

	II	II or III	III	III or IV
Heb. 8		p46 (1–13)		
9		p46 (1–16, 18–28)		
10		p46 (1–20, 22–30, 32–39)		p13 (8–22, 29–39)
11		p46 (1–40)		p13 (1–13, 28–40)
12		p46 (1–29)		p13 (1–17)
13		p46 (1–25)		
James 1			p23 (10–12, 15–18)	
2			p20 (19–26)	
3			p20 (1–9)	
4				
5				
1 Pet. 1				p72 (1–25)
2				p72 (1–25)
3				p72 (1–22)
4				p72 (1–19)
5				p72 (1–14)
2 Pet. 1				p72 (1–21)
2				p72 (1–22)
3				p72 (1–18)
1 Jn. 1				
2				
3				
4			p9 (11–12, 14–17)	
5				
2 Jn. 1				
3 Jn. 1				
Jude 1				p72 (1–25) p78 (4–5, 7–8)
Rev. 1				p18 (4–7)
2				
3				

	II	II or III	III	III or IV
Rev. 4				
5				
6				
7				
8				
9			p47 (10–21)	
10			p47 (1–11)	
11			p47 (1–3, 5–19)	
12			p47 (1–18)	
13			p47 (1–18)	
14			p47 (1–20)	
15			p47 (1–8)	
16			p47 (1–15, 17–21)	
17			p47 (1–2)	
18				
19				
20				
21				
22				

THE INTRODUCTION OF PHILOSOPHY
INTO EARLY CHRISTIANITY

Daniel W. Graham and James L. Siebach

The Jews require a sign, and the Greeks seek after wisdom: but we preach Christ crucified, unto the Jews a stumbling-block, and unto the Greeks foolishness; but unto them which are called, both Jews and Greeks, Christ the power of God, and the wisdom of God. Because the foolishness of God is wiser than men; and the weakness of God is stronger than men.... But God hath chosen the foolish things of the world to confound the wise. (1 Corinthians 1:22–25, 27)

Paul, the best-educated and most worldly wise of the apostles, warned against the seductions of philosophy: "Beware lest any man spoil you through philosophy and vain deceit, after the tradition of men, after the rudiments of the world, and not after Christ" (Colossians 2:8). Yet three centuries later, philosophy had entered into Christianity so completely that one could not be considered a Christian without espousing a philosophical position.[1] How did philosophy come to dominate the

---

1. By philosophy we mean two things: first, the systematic effort to make enquiries into and answer questions about the ultimate

Christian religion? In this paper we shall examine the complex interaction between philosophy and early Christian thought, identifying three stages of development, and the influence, for good and ill, that Greek philosophy had on early Christianity.

Philosophy as a Tool of Self-Defense

Although there may have been splinter groups of early Christianity who based their false doctrines on philosophical theories, there is little evidence that the early Christians as a whole concerned themselves with philosophy. Letters of the apostles, and the apostolic fathers who had known the apostles stay close to the teachings of the gospels and avoid philosophical theories. As Paul noted to the Corinthians, God had chosen the foolish things of the world, rather than the wise and learned, as his followers. If Paul's converts did not include many intellectuals, neither did those of Peter and John, unlearned fishermen from rural Galilee. The new faith spread rapidly, especially in the urban areas of the Roman Empire, but it spread largely among the common people, while the rich and powerful took no notice of it unless conflicts with the Jews caused riots or public disturbances.[2]

---

nature of reality, the nature of knowledge, the nature of the good, and like questions, *by reason alone*; second, the doctrines of the philosophical schools such as stoicism and platonism bequeathed to the intellectual tradition.

2. For a useful introduction into the cultural and social propagation of the gospel, as well as the nature of early Christian communities, see Wayne A. Meeks, Allen R. Hilton, and H. Gregory Snyder, *In Search of the Early Christians: Selected Essays* (New Haven, CT: Yale University Press, 2002), and Wayne A. Meeks, *The First Urban Christians: The Social World of the Apostle Paul* (New Haven, CT: Yale University Press, 1983).

Christianity was, however, regarded as an illegal association, with adherents to be punished if they were made known. Hence persecution hung over the heads of the faithful, and sometimes Christians were called to renounce their faith or die.[3] In the early second century, martyrs such as Ignatius and Polycarp went to their deaths gladly.[4] But by the mid-second century some Christians began to see it as their duty not to wait in silence for the sword of persecution to fall, but to stand up and defend the faith in public forums. Justin Martyr had studied in several philosophical schools before converting to Christianity. Recognizing similarities between the teachings of the philosophers and the doctrines of Christianity, he determined to use his education to defend the faith against false charges. For instance, Christians were commonly charged with atheism:

> And we confess that we are atheists, [as we are accused of being,] so far as gods of this sort are concerned, but not with respect to the most true God, the Father of righteousness and temperance and the other virtues, who is free from all impurity. But both Him, and the Son (who came forth from

---

3. For a collection of ancient texts and translations documenting persecutions of the Christians, see Herbert Musurillo, comp. *The Acts of the Christian Martyrs* (Oxford: Clarendon, 1972). For a discussion of Christian persecutions, see W. H. C. Frend, *Martyrdom and Persecution in the Early Church: A Study of a Conflict from the Maccabees to Donatus* (Oxford: Blackwell, 1965), 572–604.

4. Ignatius discouraged the Roman Christians from using their influence to prevent his martyrdom. "Let me be given to the wild beasts, for by their means I can attain to God." See Henry S. Bettenson, ed., *The Early Christian Fathers: A Selection from the Writings of the Fathers from St. Clement of Rome to St. Athanasius* (London: Oxford University Press, 1969), 45.

Him and taught us these things, and the host of the other good angels who follow and are made like to Him), and the prophetic Spirit, we worship and adore, knowing them in reason and truth, and declaring without grudging to every one who wishes to learn, as we have been taught.[5]

Justin spoke up for Christian beliefs in an effort to dispel misconceptions and slanders against the faith.

But he also takes the offensive against pagan worship:

And neither do we honour with many sacrifices and garlands of flowers such deities as men have formed and set in shrines and called gods; since we see that these are soulless and dead, and have not the form of God (for we do not consider that God has such a form as some say that they imitate to His honour), but have the names and forms of those wicked demons which have appeared. For why need we tell you who already know, into what forms the craftsmen, carving and cutting, casting and hammering, fashion the materials? And often out of vessels of dishonour, by merely changing the form, and making an image of the requisite shape, they make what they call a god; which we consider not only senseless, but to be even insulting to God, who, having ineffable glory and form, thus gets His name attached to things that are corruptible, and require constant service.[6]

The criticisms of idol worship are reminiscent of statements from both Old and New Testaments. But there is an additional

---

5. Justin Martyr, *First Apology*, 1.6 (*ANF* 1:164). For its easy accessibility, we have taken translations of the early church fathers from *The Ante-Nicene Fathers*, ed. Alexander Roberts and James Donaldson (1885; reprint, Peabody, MA: Hendrickson, 1994, hereafter *ANF*). All citations are to this work, save where otherwise noted.

6. Justin Martyr, *First Apology* 1.9 (ANF 1:165).

dimension to his criticisms in that he knows that his educated readers would agree with him. For Greek philosophers had similar worries about popular worship and believed in a deity that could not be properly represented in images.[7] Justin also shows how the coming of Christ fulfilled ancient Hebrew prophecies, using his defense as an opportunity to preach to the pagan world.

Tertullian, a lawyer from north Africa, uses his legal training to question the unfair way Christians were treated in the courts:

> If . . . it is certain that we are the most wicked of men, why do you treat us so differently from our fellows, that is, from other criminals, it being only fair that the same crime should get the same treatment? When the charges made against us are made against others, they are permitted to make use both of their own lips and of hired pleaders to show their innocence. They have full opportunity of answer and debate; in fact, it is against the law to condemn anybody undefended and unheard. Christians alone are forbidden to say anything in exculpation of themselves, in defence of the truth, to help the judge to a righteous decision; all that is cared about is having what the public hatred demands—the confession of the name, not examination of the charge.[8]

Like Justin, Tertullian shows that Christians were not atheists but had a higher conception of God than the pagans, and had good reasons for rejecting the pagan's gods.

The same period that saw the rise of the Christian apologists also saw the appearance of leaders who sought to combat

---

7. As early as the sixth century BC, Xenophanes had attacked, from a philosophical point of view, corporeal representations of the gods. See Jonathan Barnes, *Early Greek Philosophy* (New York: Penguin, 1987), 93–99.

8. Tertullian, *Apology* 1.2 (*ANF* 3:18).

heresies. Many of these heresies grew out of an application to Christian doctrine of Greek philosophical theories. According to Hippolytus, "their [the heretics] doctrines have derived their origin from the wisdom of the Greeks, from the conclusions of those who have formed systems of philosophy."[9] As bishops anxious to refute heresies that troubled some Christians, Irenaeus and Hippolytus wrote long expositions of heretical views, tracing them to Greek philosophical positions. "It does not follow," argues Irenaeus, "because men are endowed with greater and less degrees of intelligence, that they should therefore change the subject-matter (of the faith) itself, and should conceive of some other God besides Him who is the Framer, Maker, and Preserver of this universe (as if He were not sufficient for them), or of another Christ, or another Only-begotten."[10] Some skill in philosophy was required to expose the false doctrines of philosophical heresies, but philosophy was not required to understand the doctrines of the Christian church, nor to appreciate the nuances of Christian theology.

Indeed, the church fathers of the late second century felt the challenge of Greek philosophy keenly. If it were introduced carelessly into Christian doctrine, it could produce confusions and heresies; it also offered an understanding of the world that conflicted with the Christian understanding. In the second century no single school had emerged as the chief philosophy, so at least there was not a single, pervasive contrary position. But everywhere there was a temptation to accept foreign points of view into Christianity. Realizing the threat philosophy posed, Tertullian argued that Christians should have nothing to do with Greek philosophy:

---

9. Hippolytus, *The Refutation of All Heresies*, proemium (*ANF* 5:10).

10. Irenaeus, *Against Heresies* 1.10.3 (*ANF* 1:331).

What indeed has Athens to do with Jerusalem? What concord is there between the Academy and the Church? what
between heretics and Christians? Our instruction comes
from "the porch of Solomon," who had himself taught that
"the Lord should be sought in simplicity of heart." Away
with all attempts to produce a mottled Christianity of Stoic,
Platonic, and dialectic composition! We want no curious
disputation after possessing Christ Jesus, no inquisition after enjoying the gospel! With our faith, we desire no further
belief. For this is our palmary faith, that there is nothing
which we ought to believe besides.[11]

The scriptures provide all the knowledge necessary both for
salvation and for ordinary understanding. Anything the world
can offer is either better said in the scriptures, or not worth
saying at all.

Although Justin recognized some good in Greek thought
and culture, he also saw Greek thought and practice as being
corrupted by demons who were wrongly worshipped as gods.[12]
And he argued that whatever valuable doctrines the Greeks possessed did not originate with them. For Moses was earlier than
all the Greek sages and philosophers, and similarities between
their teachings and those of Moses show that they borrowed
whatever truth they have from him. Thus Greek philosophy
amounts to plagiarism from the Hebrews. Why not, then, come
to the source of all wisdom, and accept the Christian revelation from God?[13] Here Justin's complaint is not new, but comes
from the Jewish thinker Aristobulus, continued by Philo of
Alexandria. If the argument is right, the greater antiquity and

---

11. Tertullian, *Prescription against Heretics* 1.7 (*ANF* 3:246).

12. Justin Martyr, *Apology* 1.14 (*ANF* 1:167).

13. Justin Martyr, *Hortatory Address to the Greeks* 9–15 (*ANF* 1:277–79).

authority of Judeo-Christian belief allows the Christian to assert its superiority. The one area in which the classical Greeks feel inferior is in the relative tardiness of their own culture; here the Christians can score a point for their own tradition. Justin also points out that the Greek philosophers contradict each other, and even Plato contradicts himself, whereas the Christian teachers are consistent with each other.[14] Thus Greek philosophy does not present a united front or a unified position, but merely a set of conflicting opinions.

Tertullian's attack on philosophy is quite right from one point of view: Greek philosophy has nothing to add to Christian doctrine by way of new content. Yet his position presents a practical problem: the science of the Roman Empire was built on a foundation of Greek philosophy, and science had made important advances, including the recognition that the earth is spherical; it correctly explained the moon's light, the cause of eclipses, some meteorological phenomena, etc. If the Christian renounced Greek philosophy, he would have to renounce all secular learning as well. Was that practical, or beneficial? In any case, one does not have to read far into Tertullian to find that, despite his public scorn for Greek learning, he has already imbibed a great deal of it and incorporated it into his own thought. He is not himself in a position to show us how to adhere to a Christianity pure of Greek intrusions.

Justin's argument for Greek plagiarism is untenable in light of our present historical knowledge, though perhaps it was not far-fetched given the crude state of world history and the history of ideas in antiquity. He was on the right track in pointing out the plurality and mutual incompatibility of Greek theories, though that point was destined to be obscured as Middle and Neoplatonism rose to prominence in the first through the third

---

14. Justin Martyr, *Hortatory Address* 5–8 (*ANF* 1:275–76).

centuries, claiming to be able to harmonize the theories of Plato and Aristotle, as well as those of Pythagoras and others. In any case, the apologists of the early second century were interested in philosophy only as a starting point for a conversation in which they could defend the faith and exhort pagans to repent and accept the Christian revelation; or as a background against which they could expose the fallacies of false doctrine. If apologists were more indebted to philosophy than they realized, they were at least not consciously advocating an important role for philosophy in the Christian church. For them the Greek intellectual tradition provided only a medium for communication with the wider world and for criticism of failings endemic to the intellectual tradition.

Philosophy as the Handmaid of Theology

From the end of the second century to the middle of the third century, a new attitude toward Greek learning arose in Alexandria, Egypt. At the Catechetical School, the first Christian university, Clement of Alexandria (d. 215) and Origen (d. 254) saw in Greek philosophy an opportunity for an expanded Christian understanding. In the eight books of his *Miscellanies*, Clement began by defending his use of philosophy. He pointed out the positive function philosophy had for Greek culture:

> Accordingly, before the advent of the Lord, philosophy was necessary to the Greeks for righteousness. And now it becomes conducive to piety; being a kind of preparatory training (*propaideia*) to those who attain to faith through demonstration. . . . For God is the cause of all good things; but of some primarily, as of the Old and the New Testament; and of others by consequence, as philosophy. Perchance, too, philosophy was given to the Greeks directly and primarily, till the Lord should call the Greeks. For this was a schoolmaster to bring "the Hellenic mind," as the law, the

Hebrews, "to Christ." Philosophy, therefore, was a preparation, paving the way for him who is perfected in Christ.[15]

This may seem to a modern reader unwarranted enthusiasm for an alien intellectual tradition. But we should note here that Greek philosophy, especially the Socratic tradition, had made ethics the central feature of the intellectual life and had anticipated many of the most advanced teachings of Christian revelation: it was never right to do wrong; we should do no harm to anyone, not even our enemies; God is not jealous, but desires all to be as much like him as possible; the soul is damaged by doing evil and benefited by doing good.[16] Indeed, it was Greek philosophy that criticized and corrected the stories of Greek mythology, according to which the gods did wrongs to each other and to mortals.[17] Furthermore, at least from the time of Socrates, philosophers looked on philosophy, the love of wisdom, as not simply a pastime or even an occupation, but as a way of life to be practiced at all times, in the way a devout Christian saw his religion. Thus Greek philosophy, not Greek religion, offered the closest parallel in classical antiquity to the Judeo-Christian conception of religion as an all-inclusive way of life informed by ethical doctrines and an exalted conception of deity.

Philosophy aims at wisdom; "Wisdom is therefore queen of philosophy, as philosophy is of preparatory culture."[18] Using Abraham's life as an allegory, Clement interprets Sarah as wisdom, which without secular culture, represented by Hagar, is barren. [19] Thus philosophy is understood as the handmaid of

---

15. Clement of Alexandria, *Miscellanies* 1.5 (*ANF* 2:305).

16. See Plato's *Republic* 613 B–C; *Theaetetus* 176 B, *Laws* 716 C–D.

17. Barnes, *Early Greek Philosophy*, 95.

18. Clement, *Miscellanies* 1.5 (*ANF* 2:306).

19. Clement, *Miscellanies* 1.5 (*ANF* 2:306).

theology. If this interpretation seems forced to modern readers, we can still appreciate Clement's general insight: as the law of Moses was a schoolmaster to bring the Hebrews to Christ, so philosophy was a schoolmaster to bring the Greeks to Christ. For philosophy taught a higher appreciation of God and an ethical attitude toward man, opening the door to an appreciation of the gospel.

But what precisely is the true philosophy?

> The way of truth is . . . one. But into it, as into a perennial river, streams flow from all sides."[20] There is no one school of philosophy that has a monopoly of truth, for God has distributed his wisdom randomly: "The Greek preparatory culture, therefore, with philosophy itself, is shown to have come down from God to men, not with a definite direction, but in the way in which showers fall down on the good land, and on the dunghill, and on the houses. . . . And philosophy—I do not mean the Stoic, or the Platonic, or the Epicurean, or the Aristotelian, but whatever has been well said by each of those sects, which teach righteousness along with a science pervaded by piety,—this eclectic whole I call philosophy.[21]

Thus Clement sees what he calls philosophy not as a monolithic whole with a single doctrine to teach and a single unified theory but as the sum total of all the insights achieved by the Greek thinkers. No single school has attained to a full knowledge of the truth, and consequently the learned Christian must use an understanding of revelation as a touchstone for evaluating Greek learning. There is, to be sure, much wisdom in Greek culture, but it is mixed with errors and confusions. The Christian must be an eclectic, picking and choosing what is valuable in the garden of ideas offered by secular culture.

---

20. Clement, *Miscellanies* 1.5 (*ANF* 2:305).
21. Clement, *Miscellanies* 1.7 (*ANF* 2:308).

Indeed, Clement's whole approach is to survey secular learning in search of insights which can be assimilated to a Christian view of the world. The Christian view is the standard of understanding; Greek theories are to be examined and individual points selected, but not taken over as a whole, certainly not uncritically absorbed.

Clement's student and successor in the Catechetical School, Origen, continued in the path of combining Christian faith with a study of secular knowledge. But unlike Clement, Origen sought to make a systematic study of Christian beliefs. "Since many . . . of those who profess to believe in Christ differ from each other, not only in small and trifling matters, but also on subjects of the highest importance, as, e.g., regarding God, or the Lord Jesus Christ, or the Holy Spirit; and not only regarding these, but also regarding others which are created existences, viz., the powers and the holy virtues; it seems on that account necessary first of all to fix a definite limit and to lay down an unmistakable rule regarding each one of these, and then to pass to the investigation of other points."[22] This might seem an obvious thing to do: in a time when there were disputations about doctrine, to use our understanding of scriptures to explain and lay out the doctrines clearly so as to avoid false doctrines and misunderstandings. In fact, no one had yet attempted to make a systematic exposition of Christian doctrines. At most learned Christians had assembled collections of heresies and refuted them. But this is a negative enterprise, and, moreover, inherently frustrating, since there would be no end of new heresies as long as there was no clear statement of doctrine to start from. If one could define clearly the doctrines of the Christian church, one might forestall confusions and false teachings.

---

22. Origen, *First Principles*, proemium 2 (*ANF* 4:239).

Origen undertakes this project, producing a treatise on Christian principles in four books. The work is a systematic theological study, the first of its kind in the Judeo-Christian world. For no one before Origen had set out the beliefs of the Jews or Christians in the form of a treatise covering the major doctrines systematically. The genre is evidently Greek in origin: to set out the principles of a body of knowledge in a systematic way is the goal of scientific exposition. It was invented by Aristotle as part of his program of organizing knowledge into departmental studies, each founded on the principles peculiar to it. Before Aristotle the Pre-Socratics mostly expounded their theories in the form of a cosmology and cosmogony in which the present order of the world was seen to arise from a primeval chaos by the action of physical principles. Plato wrote dialogues in which theories were presented dramatically as discussions on theoretical topics. Aristotle first articulated a strict scientific conception of knowledge as a deductive system of propositions deriving from first principles. Although the ideal of presenting all knowledge as a series of deductions eluded him, he did expound his theories subject by subject, science by science, in each case giving an informal justification of his theories. The theological treatise of Origen is a kind of scientific discussion of the nature of God, following the pattern set by Aristotle.

It is important to note that Origen does not look to Greek philosophical theories to understand Christian doctrines. He wishes only to use the format of the scientific treatise as the vehicle for expounding Christian doctrine. If he sometimes is influenced by philosophical theories, such as Plato's view that souls exist prior to their birth into mortality, he also has scriptural reasons for accepting that view. In particular his view of the Godhead does not draw on Greek models of deity. Origen holds that the Son makes "the willing in himself just what it was in the Father, so that . . . the will of the Son is inseparable from the will of the Father, so that there are no longer two wills but one. And this unity of will is the reason for the saying of the Son 'I and my Father are one [John 10:30].'"[23] Thus "they are two separate persons, but one in unity and concord of mind and in identity of will."[24] And Origen expressly resists the Greek tendency to make God impassible or incapable of emotion:

> [Jesus] came down to earth in pity for human kind, he endured our passions and sufferings before he suffered the cross, and he deigned to assume our flesh. . . . What is that passion which he suffered for us? It is the passion of love. The Father himself and the God of the whole universe is "long-suffering, full of mercy and pity" [Psalm 86:15]. Must he not then, in some sense, be exposed to suffering? . . . The Father himself is not impassible. If he is besought he shows pity and compassion; he feels, in some sort, the passion of love.[25]

Origen is not trying to make the Father and the Son sound like the ineffable One and the eternal Logos of the Platonists. He is trying to put into the language of philosophy the traits of God he finds in the Bible.

Clement and Origen see Greek learning as providing genuine insights but not as constituting a body of truth independent of the scriptures and revelation. We should learn what the world has to teach us of worldly knowledge but depend on revelation for our understanding of God and his ways. We may use

---

23. Origen, *Commentary on John* 13.13, in Bettenson, *Early Christian Fathers*.

24. Origen, *Against Celsus* 8.12.

25. Origen, *Sermon on Ezekiel*, in Bettenson, *Early Christian Fathers*, 186–87.

rational methods to organize the teachings of the scriptures, and we may profitably evaluate them by the use of reason. But we do not need to adhere to any school of Greek philosophy to understand Christian doctrine; on the contrary, we should use Christian doctrine to evaluate philosophical theories.

Philosophy as a Foundation for Doctrine

> What, after all, is Plato but Moses in Attic Greek?
> Numenius of Apamea[26]

For reasons enumerated above, many early Christian thinkers (though not all) were suspicious of Greek philosophy. Nevertheless, subsequent thinkers recognized it was incumbent upon them to respond to philosophical criticism and confrontation. A failure to reply surrendered the field to those who would quickly destroy a young Christian community and certainly thwart fledgling evangelism. When Christianity began to enjoy greater tolerance and growth, many theological questions and problems arose, problems which New Testament texts appeared unable or unconcerned to resolve. Fourth- and fifth-century Christian attitudes toward philosophical enquiry varied from those earlier centuries—*pace* Justin Martyr, who taught philosophy in Rome in the second century. Those who considered human reason and its activity, i.e. philosophical thought, one of God's gifts, quickly used that gift to clarify and formulate doctrine, in spite of historical disapproval. Indeed, it is remarkable that after four centuries, Christian doctrine, which began nearly exclusive of philosophical thought, should become so completely infused with it. By the end of the fourth century, "Compared with other religions of its time and place [Christianity] was far more successful in organizing its beliefs

---

26. Quoted in Clement, *Stromata*, 1.150.4.

into a coherent system. In doing this it borrowed largely from philosophy, and especially from Platonism."[27]

How was philosophical thought baptized? Biblical texts are not philosophical documents in the usual sense. The New Testament grows, culturally, from Judaism, not Greek philosophy, though traces of philosophical thinking appear to have influenced certain passages. The New Testament does not seek to resolve metaphysical issues. It does not provide the reader with a new physics which would explain the cosmos and its operations. It does not give a systematic defense of a new ethics nor discuss new forms of logic.

The New Testament is, among other things, a narrative which sets forth basic historical events surrounding Jesus of Nazareth and his followers. It sets forth a new covenant between God and all who would be saved. As such, it is not a systematic theological document. It does not seek even to set forth all the dogma nor to settle all the possible theological or ecclesiological problems which appear in a well-established church. The texts cannot, of themselves, bear such demands. It is not even generally the purpose of the New Testament to accomplish these narrow theological purposes, although Paul is anxious to assert certain essential theological dogmas, for example the nature of faith and justification. One consequence is that Christian thinkers, if they wished to address such problems, turned to other authorities, particularly rational thought and the Greek philosophical tradition, to formulate and ground doctrine. They discovered that, ultimately, Christianity could be itself a kind of philosophy, and with other philosophies could be synthesized.

---

27. Christopher Stead, *Philosophy in Christian Antiquity* (New York: Cambridge University Press, 1994), 79.

From the third century onward, many Christian thinkers believed the question of God's nature to be one such theological enquiry which the New Testament did not elucidate sufficiently. The gospels and epistles, read simply and straightforwardly, did not thoroughly expound the relationship between the Father and the Son and the Holy Spirit, and so could not satisfactorily be used by Christians to defend themselves from philosophical critics who wondered whether Christians were not a throwback to earlier polytheisms. Indeed, the New Testament's depiction of God's nature was not sufficiently precise or thorough to resolve conflicts even among Christian sects themselves. Early Christian authorities expended much effort attempting to eradicate heretics from the church who conceived of and worshipped God in unorthodox ways. Indeed, it was not until the fourth century that the church even attempted to formulate a "universal"—i.e., binding upon all members of the church—doctrine of God's nature, at Nicea in 325. And that Nicean formulation itself came about as a result of a conference called by Constantine, who, as emperor of the new Byzantine Empire, worried that theological strife, bordering on open warfare among Christians, was about to tear apart the empire itself. This first ecumenical, worldwide council brought together nearly all the known bishops of fourth century Christianity to Nicea. They gathered and debated two proposals concerning the nature of God. They resolved the issue by vote. The substance of the debate was philosophical argument designed to resolve questions such as: What does reason tell us about God's nature? How can we interpret scripture in such a manner that it coheres with what reason tells us God must be like? The bishops concluded that while Jesus is the Son of God, and is himself God, as John says, the concept *Son* cannot imply a subordinate or a second distinct nature from God the Father, in this case. Subordination and essential individuation imply polytheism, a charge Christian thinkers were anxious to refute. The resolution, the doctrine of the Trinity, was the result of importing and applying to God concepts from the Greek philosophical tradition, terms such as *hypostasis* and *ousia,* terms and concepts completely foreign to scripture.

The details of the Nicean disputation are less important than the manner in which the participants resolved their problems. Theologians had no reluctance to analyze rationally a theological problem about which the scriptures were insufficiently informative. They turned for help to a philosophical tradition which their predecessors had suspected and shunned, in large measure, and they used these concepts as the ground of their doctrine. By the fifth century, theologians had few qualms at all about employing not only reason but the Greek philosophical tradition to resolve theological difficulties and to establish doctrine.

Augustine says, in *The City of God,* that philosophical schools are to be distinguished primarily by their different conceptions of the supreme or highest good.[28] Among these schools, the conception nearest to Christianity was Platonism, he believed. Indeed, Augustine thought that Plato's conception of the Good as absolute reality, and the descriptions given of this Good provided by Plato's later followers, for example Plotinus, was simply a description of God as Christians understood him, and Christians should understand God in Platonic terms, even if they did not employ Platonic vocabulary. Behind the biblical vocabulary is a Platonic meaning. Augustine reaffirmed the lofty status of Platonists in *True Religion* 7, when he says "If these men

---

28. Augustine, *City of God* 19.1, in *Nicene and Post-Nicene Fathers,* first series, ed. Philip Schaff (Peabody, MA: Hendrickson, 1994), 2:397–99. According to this criterion, Augustine says that Varro, a near contemporary, identified 288 different philosophical schools.

[Platonists] could have had this life over again with us. . . . They would have become Christians, with the change of a few words and statements."[29]

No Christian thinker exemplifies more clearly the new attitude toward philosophy, and no philosopher synthesizes his own theology with Platonism, more deftly than Augustine. While recounting his search for spiritual direction, shortly before his conversion, he sought out the advice of Simplicianus, a mature believer. "I went to Simplicianus, the spiritual father of Ambrose who was now a bishop. . . . I told him how I had drifted from error to error, and when I mentioned that I had read some of the books of the Platonists . . . Simplicianus said that he was glad. . . . *In the Platonists, he said, God and his Word are constantly implied.*"[30] While one cannot be certain if Augustine and Simplicianus were referring to Plato's dialogues themselves, or to Plotinus and other Neoplatonist writings, nevertheless, what is remarkable is Simplicianus's readiness to reread Platonic texts so harmoniously with Christian doctrine. Simplicianus referred, when making the claim that the Platonic texts constantly imply God and his Word, to Plotinus's distinction among the three hypostases, or ultimately realities: the One, the Logos, or offspring of the One, and the World Soul. Simplicianus also refers to Plato's doctrine of the Good, the greatest reality, and to the forms or essences of things, the presentation of which is found particularly in *The Republic*. Plato's traditional metaphysics centered on an ultimate reality, goodness itself, whose features Simplicianus takes to be those of God. Thus, as noted above, the Christian God is thought of and described in terms of Plato's

---

29. See note 10 in Augustine, *City of God* 8.5, ed. David Knowles (Harmondsworth: Penguin, 1972), 304.

30. Augustine, *Confessions* 8.2, trans. R. S. Pine-Coffin (Harmondsworth: Penguin, 1961), 159, emphasis added.

metaphysics. Christian doctrine, then, can be roughly synthesized with Platonism and vice versa since both are committed foremost to the same ultimately real principle.

Not only do readers such as Augustine and Simplicianus find Christian doctrine in Platonism, they find Platonism in Christian doctrine. Shortly before his conversion, Augustine describes the experience of discovering, in Platonic books, the central doctrines of John's prologue, as well as teachings found in Paul's epistles to the Romans and Philippians. Augustine summarizes the content of the books by weaving them with scriptural quotations, illustrating the identity of their content. This passage, though lengthy, shows how compatible—"the sense was the same"—Augustine understood the two philosophies to be.

> So you, [Lord], made use of a man . . . to procure me some of the books of the Platonists, translated from Greek into Latin. In them I read—not, of course, word for word, *though the sense was the same* and it was supported by all kinds of different arguments—that at the beginning of time when the Word already was; and God had the Word abiding with him, and the Word was God. He abode, at the beginning of time, with God. . . . In him there was life, and that life was the light of men. And the light shines in darkness, a darkness which was not able to master it. I read too that the soul of man, although it bears witness of the light, is not the Light. But the Word, who is himself God, is the true Light, which enlightens every soul born into the world. He, through whom the world was made, was in the world, and the world treated him as a stranger. . . .
>
> In the same books I also read of the Word, God, that his birth came not from human stock, not from nature's will or man's but from God. . . .
>
> Though the words were different and the meaning was expressed in various ways, I also learned from these books

that God the Son, being himself, like the Father, of divine nature, did not see, in the rank of Godhead, a prize to be coveted. . . .

The books also tell us that your only-begotten Son abides for ever in eternity with you; that before all time began, he was; that he is above all time and suffers no change; that of his plenty our souls receive their part and hence derive their blessings; and that by partaking of the Wisdom which abides in them they are renewed, and this is the source of their wisdom.[31]

It appears that all the truths of John's prologue Augustine had already discovered in Platonism. To be sure, he does not find the Platonist writings sufficient for salvation. Crucially, they omit the doctrine and necessity of the incarnation and atonement. But what Augustine does find is that the Platonist books elucidate the nature of God, the relationship between God the Father and God the Son, and God's relationship to the human soul.

Augustine can read Platonists in this synthetic way, because he already inhabits a theological community which reads scripture through a Platonic lens, and reads Platonic texts through a scriptural lens. The two texts are read in light of each other with the effect that the metaphysics of the Neoplatonists fills a theological void left by scripture, which is not itself concerned to resolve such theological/ontological questions as the nature of God satisfactorily to philosopher/theologians. (Remarkably, the scriptural terms *Father* and *Son,* which biblical writers thought adequate, appear not to be so to Augustine nor to his contemporaries.)

The same generous sentiment appears in *The City of God* where Augustine points out that there are no other philosophers

---

31. Augustine, *Confessions* 7.9, trans. Pine-Coffin, 144–45, emphasis added.

that come nearer to Christianity than the Platonists, because "Plato says that the wise man is the man who imitates, knows, and loves God, and that participation in this God brings man happiness."[32]

Behind this praise is a specific view of the soul's aspirations and purpose: the Christian seeks to live a virtuous life understood as imitating God, followed by enlightenment, that is, a mystical vision, followed by union with God. This project Plotinus calls an "ecstatic" union with the One. Descriptions of this achievement appear in Plotinus's *Enneads* 1.6–7, and, in its Christian incarnation, twice in Augustine's *Confessions*. Augustine recounts his theological conversion—his coming to know the truth of Christianity, as opposed to living according to its stringent ethical requirements—in thoroughly Plotinian terms. What is crucial to the account is the trajectory. Illumination begins with virtuous living. Virtuous living separates, detaches one from the transience of the world and its vices, the world of becoming. Virtue's freedom moves the intellect to understand itself, toward self-knowledge, to turn inward and see its own unchanging virtue. The intellect moves from self-knowledge to the forms, essences of things, and beyond those to the ultimate reality itself: pure being, the Good, or God.

> By the Platonic books I was admonished to return into myself. With you as my guide I entered into my innermost citadel, and was given power to do so because you had become my helper (Ps. 29:11). I entered and with my soul's eye, such as it was, saw above that same eye of my soul the immutable light higher than my mind—not the light of every day, obvious to anyone, nor a larger version of the same kind which would, as it were, have given out a much brighter light and filled everything with its magnitude. It

---

32. Augustine, *City of God* 8.5, 304.

was not that light, but a different thing, utterly different from all our kinds of light. It transcended my mind, not in the way that oil floats on water, nor as heaven is above earth. It was superior because it made me, and I was inferior because I was made by it. The person who knows the truth knows it, and he who knows it knows eternity. Love knows it. . . . When I first came to know you, you raised me up to make me see that what I saw is Being, and that I who saw am not yet Being. And you gave a shock to the weakness of my sight by the strong radiance of your rays, and I trembled with love and awe. And I found myself far from you "in the region of dissimilarity". . . .

And you cried from far away: "Now, I am who I am" (Exod 3:14). . . . I would have found it easier to doubt whether I was myself alive than that there is no truth. . . .

I was caught up to you by your beauty. . . .

I found the unchangeable and authentic eternity of truth to transcend my mutable mind. And so step by step I ascended from bodies to the soul which perceives through the body, and from there to its inward force. . . . From there again I ascended to the power of reasoning to which is to be attributed the power of judging the deliverances of the bodily senses. This power . . . withdrew itself . . . so as to discover the light by which it was flooded. . . . So in the flash of a trembling glance it attained to that which is. At that moment I was your "invisible nature understood through the things which are made" (Rom. 1:20).[33]

---

33. Augustine, *Confessions* 7.10–12, 17, trans. Henry Chadwick (New York: Oxford University Press, 1991), 123–24, 27. Later in the *Confessions* 9.10, Augustine describes a second vision received during a conversation with his mother. The description employs the same vocabulary and the vision has the same trajectory: from created becoming to final being.

Of interest in these passages is the fact that Augustine's vision begins with reading Platonic texts and ends with a description of the Good, derived from St. Paul's Romans. Paul and Plato have in mind the same being, in Augustine's view, and so one may easily employ either description. The source of this conversional structure is Plotinus's *On Beauty, Ennead* 1.6.7–9.

> So we must ascend again to the good, which every soul desires. Anyone who has seen it knows what I mean when I say that it is beautiful. It is desired as good, and the desire for it is directed to good, and the attainment of it is for those who go up to the higher world and are converted . . . until, passing in the ascent all that is alien to the God, one sees with one's self alone That alone, simple, single and pure, from which all depends and to which all look and are and live and think: for it is cause of life and mind and being. . . . He who has seen it glories in its beauty and is full of wonder and delight. . . .
>
> How can one see the "inconceivable beauty" which stays within in the holy sanctuary and does not come out where the profane may see it? Let him who can, follow and come within, and leave outside the sight of his eyes and not turn back to the bodily splendours which he saw before. . . . "Let us fly to our dear country." . . . Our country from which we came is there, our Father is there. . . . And what does this inner sight see? . . . Go back into yourself and look; and if you do not yet see yourself beautiful, then . . . you too must cut away excess and straighten the crooked and clear the dark and make it bright, and never stop "working on your statue" till the divine glory of virtue shines out of you, till you see "self-mastery enthroned upon its holy seat." If you have become this, and see it . . . [you are] yourself, nothing but true light . . . then you have become sight. . . . No eye ever saw the sun without becoming sun-like, nor can a soul see beauty without becoming beautiful. You must become

first all godlike and all beautiful if you intend to see God and beauty. First the soul will come in its ascent to intellect and there will know the Forms, all beautiful, and will affirm that these, the Ideas, are beauty. . . . That which is beyond this we call the nature of the Good, which holds beauty as a screen before it. . . . That which is beyond, the "spring and origin" of beauty; or one will place the Good and the primal beauty on the same level.[34]

The depth of Augustine's commitment to Plato's theory of forms appears clearly in his work entitled *Eighty-Three Different Questions*.[35] There he points out that though Plato first used the term *ideas*, certainly others before Plato knew the forms, labeling them with different terms. Others must have known the forms, Augustine says since there were wise men before Plato, and to be wise is to understand the forms.[36] Augustine continues to discuss the nature of the forms, or ideas, modifying Plato's metaphysics by locating the ideas in the mind of God. Augustine defines the forms as "certain original and principal forms of things, i.e., reasons, fixed and unchangeable, which are not themselves formed and, being thus eternal and existing always in the same state, are contained in the Divine Intelligence. And though they themselves neither come into being nor pass away, nevertheless, everything which

---

34. Plotinus, *Enneads* 1.6.6–7, trans. A. H. Armstrong, Paul Henry, Hans-Rudolf Schwyzer (Cambridge, MA: Harvard University Press, 1966), 253–63.

35. Augustine kept track of various philosophical and theological questions which arose shortly after his conversion. He recorded the questions and his responses and published them as a book. Augustine, *Eighty-Three Different Questions* (Washington, DC: Catholic University of America, 1982) [Question 46], 79–81.

36. Augustine, *Eighty-Three Different Questions*, 80.

can come into being and pass away and everything which does come into being and pass away is said to be formed in accord with these ideas."[37]

God has made these forms accessible and contemplatible only to rational souls, and indeed, this contemplation is the very purpose of the soul, that is its excellence, and it does so because God has given the soul an inner countenance or intelligible capacity. But a soul does not know these forms simply by its rationality. Rather, the soul must cultivate virtue, particularly the Christian virtues of holiness and purity. It follows then, that the wisest of people are Christians, since they are made holy and pure by God's grace.

Furthermore, Augustine says, no Christian trained and devout in true religion would ever dare to deny that all things which are "fixed in their own order by a certain particular nature so as to exist, are produced by God as their cause? And that by that cause all things which live do live? And that the universal soundness of things and the very order whereby those things which change do repeat with a certain regularity their journeys through time are fixed and governed by the laws of the most high God?"[38]

In other words, no Christian would deny that God has created the world and everything in it by use of a rational plan, and that creation is, by means of the individual forms, unique to each thing. Thus, there is a form for a horse separate from that form for man. These forms, Augustine says, exist in no other place "but in the very mind of the Creator. For it would be sacrilegious to suppose that he was looking at something placed outside himself when he created" anything.[39] And since

---

37. Augustine, *Eighty-Three Different Questions*, 80.

38. Augustine, *Eighty-Three Different Questions*, 80.

39. Augustine, *Eighty-Three Different Questions*, 81.

the forms are in the mind of God, they must be eternal and unchangeable, since the divine mind can contain nothing except what is so. Because these ideas are eternal and unchangeable, Plato can call them true. And "it is by participation in these that whatever is exists in whatever manner it does exist."[40]

Here Augustine has appropriated Plato's theory of forms, but amplified it further to cohere with the biblical description of God as creator. Thus, the creation story of Genesis covers a Platonic explanation of the world's being. He also employs Plato's familiar doctrine of participation, so prominent in *Republic*, and criticized in the *Parmenides*. Echoing *Republic* 613, *Laws* 716, and *Theaetetus* 176, Augustine concludes his discussion by pointing out that the rational soul is the most excellent thing created by God, because it is most godlike when it is pure. This godlike transformation of the soul by purity takes place among those who cling to God in love, because God imbues that soul with light, intelligible light. The soul is illumined by intelligible light, perceived by its highest part, in which lies its virtue, that is, with its intelligence. And this illumination, Augustine says, is full blessedness, that is, true happiness.[41]

Of related significance to the passage above is Augustine's Platonic gloss of John 18:34, where Jesus says "My kingdom is not of this world." At issue in Augustine's discussion in *De Ordine (On Order)*, is whether or not anyone should ever strive to become a philosopher. Augustine's reply begins by employing Plato's distinction between the visible and intelligible

---

40. Augustine, *Eighty-Three Different Questions*, 81.

41. Augustine, *Eighty-Three Different Questions*, 81. Augustine here alludes to Plato's *Alcibiades I*, in which Socrates says that the portion of the soul which understands, the seat of knowledge and thought, most resembles God, and by gazing on the divine, at the content of one's knowledge, one comes to know the divine.

worlds (*Republic* 510–511). Augustine says that the true philosophers are those who seek to know the intelligible world (the world of mathematical objects, forms, and the good), since that is the realm of God. That the intelligible world is God's world is demonstrated by the fact that God says his world is not of this (i.e., visible, material) world. "But there is another world," says Augustine, "utterly remote from these eyes of ours, a world which the intellect of a few sound men beholds. This, Christ Himself indicates clearly enough. He does not say: 'My kingdom is not of the world'; He says: 'My kingdom is not of *this* world.'" The conclusion is that the true philosopher is, by definition, a lover of wisdom, that is, a lover of the intelligible realm which is God's kingdom.[42] Of particular interest in the passages above is the manner in which Augustine employs Platonic metaphysics, not only to interpret scripture, but to understand "things as they are," to which things scripture points us. Thus, what Jesus says is to be understood in light of Plato's account of reality. Jesus's description of his kingdom as otherworldly, points us toward Plato's description of the intelligible realm and the manner in which it is known.

The purpose of this discussion has been to show how Greek philosophy, particularly Platonism, though suspect among earlier church fathers, becomes, by the time of Augustine, perfectly compatible in its essential elements with much of Christian understanding of the world, God, and human life. Indeed, by the time of Augustine and as a result of Augustinian thinking, Greek philosophy and rational analysis has become the foundation of Christian doctrine.

---

42. Augustine, *Divine Providence and the Problem of Evil* [translator's title; original *De Ordine*], in *Writings of Saint Augustine*, trans. Robert P. Russell (New York: Cima, 1948), 271.

While we have, for constraints of space, limited our discussion to Latin, Western Christianity, there is an extremely important account yet to be given of Christianity and philosophy in the Eastern, Greek church. In the late fourth and early fifth centuries, Gregory of Nyssa, Basil the Great, his brother, Macrina, their sister, and Gregory Nazianzus, among others, engaged in a very important discussion on the status and importance of classical learning, as well as Christian attitudes toward reason. They all, at times and places, argued about the dangers posed to Christianity by classical learning and "worldly philosophy." These Cappadocians finally agreed that true philosophy could lead to a knowledge of God, and that reason properly employed was a legitimate instrument both in defending and establishing Christian doctrine. In this respect it is fair to say that the fusion of philosophy and Christian theology in the East not only paralleled, but, in important ways, served as a model and impetus for the theological practices in the Latin West.[43]

The Hellenization of Christianity

What began as a Jewish religion founded on revelation and faith became an appendage of classical civilization. It became hellenized and was transformed in the process. It was inevitable that Christianity, as it entered the Hellenic culture of the Roman Empire, should be hellenized in some measure. Religious terms and concepts from Hebrew and Aramaic were rendered into Greek, and then Latin. Missionaries would have

---

43. See the very important and valuable discussion in Jaroslav Pelikan, *Christianity and Classical Culture: The Metamorphosis of Natural Theology in the Christian Encounter with Hellenism* (New Haven, CT: Yale University Press). Pages 169–87 are of particular relevance.

to reach Greeks through their language, culture, and values. The apostle Paul, who was equally trained in Greek and Hebrew learning, knew how to be "all things to all men" (1 Corinthians 9:20–22). Though he deeply distrusted the wisdom of the Greeks, he used his knowledge of Greek culture to communicate with Gentiles. He used classical rhetoric in his defense before Agrippa (Acts 26:1–29). He quoted a Greek poet in his speech to the council of the Areopagus in Athens (Acts 17:28). Paul's sometime traveling companion and fellow missionary Luke used Greek literary conventions in his Gospel to appeal to a Greek audience.[44] In the earliest days of Christian expansion outside of Judea, Christian missionaries were communicating in terms the Greeks could understand.

Despite the ability of some Christian leaders to communicate in Greek using the resources of Greek culture, the content of early Christian writings remained close in character to that of Hebrew writings. It is only in the mid-second century that Christians began to use Greek forums and genres to communicate publicly with the pagan world. They did so at first only to make their case to the secular world and to refute heresies which had some philosophical inspiration. Although in retrospect we can see some philosophical ideas creeping into Christian thought, the authors of apologies did not consciously embrace the theories of Greek philosophy and typically understood any wisdom found among the Greeks to be a borrowing from the Hebrews.

At the end of the second century and in the third century, leaders of the Catechetical School in Alexandria took a more positive view of philosophy. According to Clement, God had inspired the pagans with wisdom, which was to be found randomly in all

---

44. See, John A. Darr, *On Character Building: The Reader and Rhetoric of Characterization in Luke-Acts* (Louisville, KY: Knox, 1992).

the philosophical schools. He sent philosophy to the Greeks as a schoolmaster to bring them to Christ, as he had provided the Hebrews with the law of Moses. Advanced concepts of deity and of ethical responsibility had prepared the Greeks for the good news of the gospel. Thus philosophy was a way into Christianity. There was no need to borrow or advocate the theories of philosophers, but their insights could be appreciated, and a common ground for conversation could be established. Origen employed the model of scientific exposition to develop a systematic Christian theology. Avoiding Greek philosophical theories, he expounded Christian doctrines held by faith in the form of a scientific exposition.

Christian intellectuals of the fourth century, pressed by ever more aggressive and philosophically sophisticated heresies, finally accepted a philosophical definition of faith at the Council of Nicea. By the fifth century, it is clear that philosophical thinking, as well as the content of the Greek philosophical tradition, particularly Platonism, had not only become accepted but widely employed as a means for understanding scripture and establishing Christian doctrine. So compatible are the two "philosophies" that Augustine can state the purpose of philosophy as the knowledge of God and the soul, God's creation. He can also say that Platonists, with the change of a few words and statements, would be Christians. Not only Augustine, but Ambrose, Simplicianus, and others could summarize Platonism by quoting the prologue of John's Gospel, so completely infused had the two worldviews become.

What effect did Greek philosophy have on the development of Christianity? The disappearance of the apostles by the early second century made it inevitable that the authority of the priesthood could not continue. When the few bishops and priesthood leaders appointed by John, the last apostle, died out, there was no more authority on the earth. Although some false doctrines inspired by philosophy seem to have appeared in the first century, most Christians and their leaders seem to have been innocent of philosophical training and interests, and it is doubtful that the false doctrines were a sufficient cause of the apostasy. Philosophy came into Christianity gradually, first as offering a forum for discussion of Christian beliefs and a venue to defend the faith against slanders and misrepresentations. Later, it offered a common ground for discussion of shared beliefs, and a method for systematically organizing Christian beliefs. Finally it offered to fill the gap left by the loss of continuing revelation. When debates broke out about church doctrine, based on sophisticated philosophical conceptions that went far beyond the simple message of the scriptures, the church needed an authoritative method of adjudicating the issues. Originally the apostles could go to God in prayer and receive revelation to resolve the difficulty. Now that they were gone, and the immediate connection to God was cut; the church needed a reliable procedure for resolving conflicts. The Council of Nicea set a precedent: a worldwide council of bishops—local leaders—could provide the authority, and philosophy could provide the method. Doctrines would be defined ever-more narrowly in ever-more sophisticated terms. Faith would be determined by philosophical theology. Church leaders would henceforth have to be conversant in philosophical theology, which presupposed a knowledge of Greek philosophy. When disputes about doctrines arose, they would be settled by philosophical debates and political machinations, not by revelations to inspired leaders.

In the end, the church founded by the son of a carpenter and spread throughout the world by fishermen, a tax-collector, and a well-educated tent-maker, became a vast bureaucracy patronized by the imperial government and staffed by trained theologians and rhetoricians who saw themselves as heirs of both the apostles and the Roman pontifices. The adoption of Greek philosophy in Christianity was more an effect than a cause of the apostasy. But it did in the end irresistibly change the character of Christianity. Grafted onto the trunk of Greek philosophy, the Christian faith became a branch of Hellenism, while Hellenism became Christianized. The result was medieval or Byzantine Christianity, which would survive the barbarian invasions to emerge victorious as the cultural foundation of medieval Europe. It was of utmost importance for the future of the world that some form of Christianity should survive the desperate times that marked the fall of the Roman Empire; but the form that did survive was not identical to primitive Christianity in faith, ordinances, authority, or doctrine.

Divine Embodiment: The Earliest Christian Understanding of God

David L. Paulsen

It is the first principle of the Gospel to know for a certainty the Character of God, and to know that we may converse with him as one man converses with another . . . and . . . if you were to see him today, you would see him like a man in form—like yourselves in all the person, image, and very form as a man.[1]

So the Prophet Joseph Smith taught the Latter-day Saints assembled in a grove in Nauvoo, Illinois, on 7 April 1844. Joseph's understanding of God as a supremely perfect, embodied person, humanlike in form, departed radically from the traditional Christian understanding as typified by the Westminster Confession of Faith: "There is but one only, living, and true God: who is infinite in Being and perfection, a most pure Spirit, invisible, without body, parts, or passions."[2]

---

1. *Teachings of the Prophet Joseph Smith,* sel. Joseph Fielding Smith (Salt Lake City: Deseret Book, 1976), 345. This section is drawn from Joseph's famous address commonly called the "King Follett Discourse," given on 7 April 1844.

2. The Westminster Confession of Faith (1646), chapter II; Philip Schaff, ed., *The Creeds of Christendom,* 6th ed. (Grand Rapids, MI: Baker Books, 1996), 3:606.

While creedal god-concepts like those found in the Westminster Confession were largely the product of rational theologizing, Joseph's understanding was not derived in this way. Nor was it the outcome of a careful exegesis of relevant biblical texts. Rather, according to Joseph, it was based on God's own self-disclosures. God's initial self-disclosure to Joseph, known now as the first vision, occurred in 1820 in a grove of trees near Joseph's home in Palmyra, New York. On that occasion, God the Father and Jesus Christ appeared to Joseph as gloriously embodied persons and gave him instructions relating to their latter-day work.

Joseph's vision was tradition-shattering in many ways. In an age when Christians claimed that public revelation had forever ceased, it marked a reopening of the heavens—a resumption of direct revelation from God to man. And with the first vision and the many revelations that followed came Joseph Smith's creed-contradicting understanding of God: God is a supremely perfect divine person, humanlike in form, with whom man may converse as one man converses with another. Reflecting on this divine self-disclosure and others with which the Lord privileged him, Joseph once exclaimed: "Could you gaze into heaven five minutes, you would know more than you would by reading all that ever was written on the subject."[3]

Though God's self-disclosures to Joseph radically contradicted the established Christian creeds, it is critical to note that Joseph never claimed that what he learned about God's nature was "new" truth, hidden by God until the nineteenth century. To the contrary, Joseph testified that his view was a restoration of the biblical and primitive Judeo-Christian understanding of God, an understanding that was lost because of

---

3. *Teachings of the Prophet Joseph Smith,* 324.

a "falling away"—an apostasy—from the truths once held by the earliest Christians.[4]

My study of the relevant evidence convinces me that Joseph is correct: biblical writings and the documents of formative Judaism and primitive Christianity consistently portray God as an embodied person, humanlike in form. In this paper, I detail this evidence, showing that the later Christian loss of the knowledge that God is embodied resulted from the attempt of early Christian apologists to reconcile their beliefs with their dominantly Greek culture.

Primitive Christian Belief in an Embodied Deity

Some of the evidence I cite for primitive Christian belief in an embodied deity is indirect and circumstantial, but when all the evidence is considered cumulatively, it seems quite convincing. Ironically, a considerable amount of this evidence is drawn from the writings of two of the most uncompromising incorporealists, Origen and Augustine. Given their strong opposition to the doctrine of divine embodiment, the evidence they provide is particularly persuasive.

First and Second Centuries

That the earliest Christians believed God to be embodied is admitted by the noted church historian Adolph Harnack, though he buries this admission in two footnotes in his seven-volume work, *History of Dogma*. Writing about first-century believers, he explains:

---

4. See Donald Q. Cannon, Larry E. Dahl, and John W. Welch, "The Restoration of Major Doctrines through Joseph Smith: The Godhead, Mankind, and the Creation," *Ensign,* January 1989, 27–33.

God was naturally conceived and represented as corporeal by uncultured Christians, though not by these alone, as the later controversies prove (*e.g.,* Orig. contra Melito; see also Tertull. De anima). In the case of the cultured, the idea of a corporeality of God may be traced back to Stoic influences; in the case of the uncultured, popular ideas co-operated with the sayings of the Old Testament literally understood, and the impression of the Apocalyptic images.[5]

He further concedes, "In the second century . . . realistic eschatological ideas no doubt continued to foster in wide circles the popular idea that God had a form and a kind of corporeal existence."[6]

Harnack identifies several possible sources of primitive[7] Christian belief in an embodied deity including popular religious ideas, Stoic metaphysics, and literally construed Old Testament scripture. It is common knowledge that ordinary persons, including the early Greeks,[8] have always (as Harnack suggests) naturally conceived God (or the gods) to be embodied. Further, Harnack proposes that Christians influenced by Stoic views could have reached the same conclusion on meta-

---

5. Adolph Harnack, *History of Dogma* (New York: Dover, 1961), 1:180 n 1.

6. Harnack, *History of Dogma,* 2:255 n 5.

7. The primitive period of the Christian Church is usually understood to last from the apostolic years to the middle of the second century. See J. N. D. Kelly, *Early Christian Doctrines,* 5th ed., rev. (London: Adams and Charles Black, 1977), 31–35.

8. See Gilbert Murray, *Five Stages of Greek Religion* (Garden City, NY: Doubleday, 1955), 9–10. For an excellent study of the popular Greek understanding of the gods, see Martin P. Nilsson, *Greek Folk Religion* (Philadelphia: University of Pennsylvania Press, 1972).

physical grounds. From the Stoic beliefs that only matter is real and that God is real, it follows that God is a material being.[9]

The Hebrew Bible

Whatever the impact of popular belief and Stoic metaphysics on the primitive Christian understanding of God, perhaps a more significant influence was the Hebrew Bible. J. N. D. Kelly informs us, "from the apostolic age to the middle of the second century . . . there was as yet no officially sanctioned New Testament canon."[10] Indeed, "for the first hundred years, at least, of its history the Church's Scriptures, in the precise sense of the word, consisted exclusively of the Old Testament."[11] And as Harnack reminds us, the Old Testament literally construed describes God in decidedly anthropomorphic terms. For example, Edmond Cherbonnier has shown that the God of biblical revelation, in contrast with the deity of Platonist metaphysics, was personal, not abstract; invisible as a matter of choice, not inherently; everlasting or enduring through time, not timeless; and ethically constant, not metaphysically immutable. He concludes that in many respects, the God of the Bible

---

9. Stoicism, "founded by Zeno of Citium, c. 300 BC . . . was mostly a closely knit system of logic, metaphysics and ethics. . . . From the theological point of view, however, what was most remarkable about it was its pantheistic materialism. The Stoics reacted vigorously against the Platonic differentiation of a transcendent, intelligible world not perceptible by the senses from the ordinary world of sensible experience. Whatever exists, they argued, must be body, and the universe as a whole must be through and through material. . . . Thus Stoicism was a monism teaching that God or Logos is a finer matter immanent in the material universe." Kelly, *Early Christian Doctrines*, 17–18.

10. Kelly, *Early Christian Doctrines*, 31.

11. Kelly, *Early Christian Doctrines*, 52.

has more in common with the gods of the Greek and Roman pantheon than with Plato's idea of ultimate Being or Aristotle's Unmoved Mover.[12]

More to the point, many biblical passages straightforwardly describe God as embodied. For instance, Genesis 1:26 records, "And God said, Let us make man in our own image, after our likeness."[13] Even more explicit are the many references to God's body parts, such as "I [Jacob] have seen God face to face" (Genesis 32:30); "they saw the God of Israel: and there was under his feet . . ." (Exodus 24:10); "the Lord spake unto Moses face to face" (Exodus 33:11); and "I will take away mine hand, and thou shalt see my back parts: but my face shall not be seen" (Exodus 33:23).[14] It is hard to imagine a being with a face, feet, hands, and back parts but without a body.

---

12. See Edmond La Beaume Cherbonnier, "The Logic of Biblical Anthropomorphism," *Harvard Theological Review* 55 (1962): 187; and Cherbonnier, "In Defense of Anthropomorphism," in *Reflections on Mormonism: Judeo-Christian Parallels,* ed. Truman G. Madsen (Provo, UT: BYU Religious Studies Center, 1978), 155–73. Cherbonnier provides a clear description of the anthropomorphic God of the biblical record, particularly in contrast with later mystical or Platonist views of deity.

13. Umberto Cassuto explains that "there is no doubt that the original signification of this expression in the Canaanite tongue was, judging by Babylonian usage, corporeal, in accordance with the anthropomorphic conception of the godhead among the peoples of the ancient East." Umberto Cassuto, *A Commentary on the Book of Genesis* (Jerusalem: Magnes, 1961), 1:56.

14. It has been a traditional Jewish belief that God is anthropomorphic (or better, humans theomorphic), and with some notable exceptions, late antique Jews rejected the metaphysics which demanded he be otherwise. I would not wish to minimize the great diversity of Jewish belief. Certainly there have been and are Jew-

God also appears embodied in New Testament accounts of divine appearances. For instance, Acts 7:56 tells of Stephen seeing the Son of Man standing on the right hand of God.[15] And Hebrews 1:3 informs us that Jesus Christ, a gloriously embodied being, humanlike in form, is in "the brightness of [the Father's] glory, and the express image of his person." On the basis of scriptures such as these, early Christians no doubt simply took it for granted that God has a body in form like man's. But this does not mean they thought of God as similar to man in all respects. Unlike man, for example, God is holy, as in Hosea 11:9: "For I am God, and not man; the Holy One in the midst of thee." Cherbonnier acknowledges that a considerable variety exists in scripture and that this and similar passages do point away from an overly simple anthropomorphism. However, passages that distinguish God from man do not indicate that the later biblical prophets gave up the ideas that God has a body and that man's body was created in his image. To the contrary, Cherbonnier claims that modern scholarship, "by restoring these passages to their context and so recovering their original meaning, reverses such an interpretation."[16]

Only after divine embodiment was rejected on philosophical (primarily Platonist) grounds was the image of God identified

---

ish theologians who are committed incorporealists, but there has never been, in any event, a general and unambiguous rejection of the anthropomorphism that characterizes so much of the Torah and classical Jewish literature. See Jacob Neusner, *The Incarnation of God: The Character of Divinity in Formative Judaism* (Philadelphia: Fortress, 1988).

15. Consider also the postascension appearances of the resurrected Christ to Saul on the road to Damascus (Acts 9:3–7), to John the Beloved on the Isle of Patmos (Revelation 1:10–18), and to many others who saw the resurrected Lord (1 Corinthians 15:5–8).

16. Cherbonnier, "Biblical Anthropormorphism," 188.

with the soul or the rational aspect of the soul. Once Platonism took hold of Christianity, biblical passages referring to God's body or bodily parts were explicitly given figurative interpretations. While the philosophical critique of anthropomorphic conceptions of deity has its roots in ancient Greece and while there is evidence that anthropomorphism was an issue for the translators of the Septuagint,[17] Philo Judaeus (20 BC–AD 40), a Jewish Platonist educated in Alexandria, appears to be the first thinker who applied allegorical interpretations to the anthropomorphic passages in the Old Testament. Although Philo's views were not generally accepted by his mainstream Jewish contemporaries, Albinus, a second-century non-Christian and Middle-Platonist, did follow Philo's lead and, in turn, greatly influenced Origen and later Christian thinkers.[18]

First Century Judaism

Aside from direct revelation as a source for the primitive Christian belief that God is embodied, Harnack fails to mention another, no doubt powerful, influence—the understanding of God within the first-century Jewish communities out of which Christianity first emerged. According to J. N. D. Kelly,

---

17. See B. H. Roberts, *The Truth, The Way, The Life: An Elementary Treatise on Theology*, ed. John W. Welch (Provo, UT: BYU Studies, 1994), 173 n. 1; and Harry M. Orlinsky, "Introductory Essay: On Anthropomorphisms and Anthropopathisms in the Septuagint and Targum," in Bernard M. Zlotowitz, *The Septuagint Translation of the Hebrew Terms in Relation to God in the Book of Jeremiah* (New York: KTAV, 1981), xv–xxiv.

18. For an insightful examination of the reasons why the later church fathers rejected the primitive view of a corporeal deity, see Grace M. Jantzen, "Theological Tradition and Divine Incorporeality," in *God's World, God's Body* (London: Darton, Longman, and Todd, 1984), 21–35.

Judaism was the cradle in which Christianity was nurtured, the source to which it was uniquely indebted. It left a deep imprint, as is generally agreed, on the Church's liturgy and ministry, and an even deeper one on its teaching. In evaluating this impact, we must take account both of Palestinian Judaism and of the hellenized version current at Alexandria. The former can be dealt with quite briefly, for the heyday of its influence falls outside this book in the apostolic age, when it moulded the thought of all New Testament writers. Yet, in spite of the early rupture between Christians and Jews, it would be a grave error to dismiss it as a negligible force in our period. Until the middle of the second century, when Hellenistic ideas began to come to the fore, Christian theology was taking shape in predominantly Judaistic moulds, and the categories of thought used by almost all Christian writers before the Apologists were largely Jewish. [19]

---

19. Kelly, "Early Christian Doctrines," 6. Jacob Neusner has cautioned against the presumption that this "Judaistic mould" was all of one piece. He asks: "Can we identify one Judaism in the first centuries BCE and CE? Only if we can treat as a single cogent statement everything all Jews wrote. That requires us to harmonize the Essene writings of the Dead Sea, Philo, the Mishnah, the variety of scriptures collected in our century as the Apocrypha and Pseudepigrapha of the Old Testament, not to mention the Gospels! This is to say, viewed as statements of systems, the writings attest to diverse religious systems, and, in the setting of which we speak, to diverse Judaisms. There was no one orthodoxy, no Orthodox Judaism. There were various Judaisms." Jacob Neusner, "Judaism and Christianity in the First Century: How Shall We Perceive Their Relationships?" in *A Tribute to Geza Vermes: Essays on Jewish and Christian Literature and History*, ed. Philip R. Davies and Richard T. White (Sheffield, England: Sheffield Academic Press, 1990), 256. Nevertheless, E. P. Sanders argues that there was, at least, within first-century Palestinian Judaism, a common theological core underlying all this rich diversity of

Those early Christian categories, based as they were upon a literal reading of the Hebrew scriptures, were unabashedly anthropomorphic.[20] For instance, James Drummond admits that even as the Jews advanced theologically to a higher conception of God, "we can hardly doubt that the mass of the people would be satisfied with [the scriptures'] literal meaning, and that their idea of God was the purest anthropomorphism."[21] Similarly, George Foot Moore claims that Palestinian Judaism was "innocent . . . of an 'abstract' or 'transcendent'—or any other sort of a philosophical—idea of God."[22] Indeed, he asserts, "the philosophical horror of 'anthropomorphisms' which Philo . . . entertained was unknown to the Palestinian schools. They endeavored to think of God worthily and to speak of him reverently; but their criterion was the Scripture and the instinct of piety, not an alien metaphysics."[23]

Thoroughly influencing the basic concepts of formative Judaism was, indeed, the understanding of God's "incarnation,"

thought and practice. *Judaism: Practice and Belief, 63 BCE to 66 CE* (London: SCM, 1992), 241–78.

20. "Jewish anthropomorphism seems to have been notorious in the first centuries c.e." Gedaliahu G. Stroumsa, "Form(s) of God: Some Notes on Meṭaṭron and Christ," *Harvard Theological Review* 76 (1983): 269–88, at 271.

21. James Drummond, *Philo Judaeus; or, The Jewish-Alexandrian Philosophy in Its Development and Completion* (London: Williams and Norgate, 1888), 1:135.

22. George Foot Moore, *Judaism in the First Centuries of the Christian Era: The Age of the Tannaim* (Cambridge: Harvard University Press, 1927), 1:421. For a recent treatment of this topic see Elliot R. Wolfson, *Through a Speculum That Shines: Vision and Imagination in Medieval Jewish Mysticism* (Princeton: Princeton University Press, 1994), 13–51.

23. Moore, *Judaism in the First Centuries,* 1:438.

which Jacob Neusner describes as "a commonplace for Judaisms from the formation of Scripture forward."[24] By incarnation, Neusner means "the representation of God in the flesh, as corporeal, consubstantial in emotion and virtue with human beings, and sharing in the modes and means of action carried out by mortals, . . . doing deeds that women and men do in the way in which they do them."[25] So powerful and natural was Judaism's "rich legacy of anthropomorphism"[26] that Rabbi Hoshaiah could tell a story about the time when God came to create man and how the ministering angels mistook Adam for God: "What did the Holy One, blessed be He, do? He caused sleep to fall upon him, and so all knew that he was [but mortal] man."[27] Of course, in this portrayal of divinity the purpose was never to confuse God with man but rather to teach an understanding "that draws humanity upward and does not bring God downward."[28]

Nowhere is this Jewish anthropomorphism more evident than in the teachings of several classical rabbis. For instance, in his recently published study, Alon Goshen Gottstein claims:

> In all of rabbinic literature [covering both the tannaitic (70–
> 200 A.D.) and amoraic (220–500 A.D.) periods] there is not a

---

24. Neusner, *Incarnation of God*, 4.

25. Neusner, *Incarnation of God*, 12, 17, emphasis deleted.

26. Neusner, *Incarnation of God*, 6.

27. *Midrash Rabbah* Genesis 8:10, quoted in Neusner, *Incarnation of God*, 3.

28. Neusner, *Incarnation of God*, 3. The tractate *Shi'ur Qomah* (*The Measure of the Body*) describes God's body in huge proportions. See *Encyclopaedia Judaica*, 14:1418, s.v. "Shi'ur Komah." A widely acknowledged source for studies of Jewish anthropomorphism, this tractate is from the period of the Tannaim and is associated with Kabbalah, but its concepts are known in rabbinic midrashim.

single statement that categorically denies that God has body or form.

In my understanding, the question of whether the rabbis believed in a God who has form is one that needs little discussion. . . . Instead of asking, "Does God have a body?" we should inquire, "What kind of body does God have?"[29]

Gottstein further contends: "The bodily meaning is the only meaning of *zelem* [image] in rabbinic literature. This suggestion is borne out in all tannaitic and amoraic sources."[30]

---

29. Alon Goshen Gottstein, "The Body as Image of God in Rabbinic Literature," *Harvard Theological Review* 87 (1994): 172. See also Arthur Marmorstein, *The Old Rabbinic Doctrine of God* (1937; reprint, New York: Ktav, 1968), which deals with the literal versus allegorical interpretation of scripture in rabbinic tradition. Marmorstein suggests that the allegorical interpretations among the rabbis were moving away from anthropomorphic conceptions of God.

30. Gottstein, "Body as Image of God," 174, emphasis in original. Gottstein acknowledges that in the later Tanhuma literature, several paraphrases expand the meaning of *zelem* to include eternal life, divine glory, and righteous behavior. None of these expansions overrides the older understanding of *zelem* as body but rather are derived from it (Gottstein, "Body as Image of God," 174 n. 9). See also Stroumsa, "Form(s) of God," 269–88, esp. 277–79; and G. Scholem, *Jewish Gnosticism, Merkabah Mysticism, and Talmudic Tradition,* 2nd ed. (New York: Jewish Theological Seminary, 1965), 36–42; Scholem, *On the Mystical Shape of the Godhead* (New York: Schocken Books, 1991), 21–55; and more generally on the topic of corporeality in Jewish mysticism, Wolfson, *Through a Speculum That Shines.* For an introduction to and English translation of the *Shi'ur Qomah,* see Pieter W. van der Horst, "The Measurement of the Body, A Chapter in the History of Ancient Jewish Mysticism," in *Essays on the Jewish World of Early Christianity* (Göttingen: Vandenhoeck & Ruprecht, 1990), 125–31. See also Griffin and Paulsen, "Augustine and the Corporeality of God," 100 n. 17.

The rabbinic interpretation of the image of God as referring to the body is clearly shown in the following representative selection, a story about Rabbi Hillel:

> His disciples asked him: "Master, whither are you bound?" He answered them: "To perform a religious duty." "What," they asked, "is this religious duty?" He said to them: "To wash in the bath-house." Said they: "Is this a religious duty?" "Yes," he replied, "if the statues of kings, which are erected in theatres and circuses, are scoured and washed by the man who is appointed to look after them, and who thereby obtains his maintenance through them—nay more, he is exalted in the company of the great of the kingdom—how much more I, who have been created in the Image and Likeness."[31]

Rabbinic anthropomorphism so strikingly contrasts with later (third century on) Christian immaterialism and so closely parallels Joseph Smith's understanding of God that it will be helpful to summarize Gottstein's account of the rabbinic concepts in some detail.

First, Gottstein shows that rabbinic anthropomorphism was not a crude notion in which God's body (or even Adam's body created in its image) was seen as identical or very similar to our present fallen human bodies.[32] For example, one rabbinic account describes Adam's body as one of great beauty and light.

> Resh Lakish, in the name of R. Simeon the son of Menasya, said: The apple of Adam's heel outshone the globe of the sun; how much more so the brightness of his face! Nor need you wonder. In the ordinary way if a person makes salvers [servants], one for himself and one for his household, whose will he make more beautiful? Not his own? Similarly, Adam

---

31. *Midrash Rabbah* Leviticus 34:3, in *Midrash Rabbah*, trans. H. Freedman and Maurice Simon (London: Soncino, 1983), 4:428.

32. Gottstein, "Body as Image of God," 183–86.

was created for the service of the Holy One, blessed be He, and the globe of the sun for the service of mankind.[33]

Thus Adam's original body was more radiant than the sun, but God's body, in whose image Adam's was made, is still more brilliant and beautiful;[34] though God's body resembles the human body in form, it differs from it in function. Gottstein quotes a passage from Peter in the Jewish-Christian Pseudo-Clementine Homilies that parallels notions found in Sefer Yezira:

He has the most beautiful Form for the sake of man, in order that the pure in heart shall be able to see Him [cf. Matt. 5:8], that they shall rejoice on account of whatever they have endured. For He has stamped man as it were with the greatest seal, with His own Form, in order that he shall rule and be lord over all things, and that all things shall serve him. For this reason, he who having judged that He is the All and

---

33. *Midrash Rabbah* Leviticus 20:2, in *Midrash Rabbah,* 4:252. Other texts corroborate Adam's possessing a body of light: *Midrash Rabbah* Genesis 12:6, in *Midrash Rabbah,* 1:91; *Midrash Rabbah* Ecclesiastes 8:1–2, in *Midrash Rabbah,* 8:213; and *Midrash Rabbah* Deuteronomy 11:3, in *Midrash Rabbah,* 7:173.

34. Compare Joseph Smith's description of the brilliance of God's body. In his 1838 account of the first vision, he told of a light "above the brightness of the sun" and attempted to describe the Father and the Son "whose brightness and glory defy all description" (Joseph Smith—History 1:16–17). Compare also the language that Zebedee Coltrin (Joseph's LDS contemporary) used to describe God (for example, "surrounded as with a flame of fire," "consuming fire of great brightness," and "flame of fire, which was so brilliant") with the rabbinic descriptions of the divine body. Statement of Zebedee Coltrin, 3 October 1883, *Salt Lake School of the Prophets: Minute Book 1883* (Palm Desert, CA: ULC, 1981), 38

man His image (*eikōn*)—He being invisible and His image, man, visible—will honour the image, which is man.[35]

Next, Gottstein proposes a model for reconciling apparently contradictory rabbinic passages pertaining to the issue of whether man, as the result of sin, lost the image of God.

> As we have seen, Adam's *zelem* is his luminous body. In other sources, such as the story of Hillel washing his body, the *zelem* referred to the physical body. *Zelem* can thus refer to various levels, or aspects, all of which bear a resemblance to the physical body. I would propose that these various levels, or various bodies, reflect one another. The physical body is a reflection of the body of light. . . . [A] kind of graded devolutionary process . . . may be a model for two ways of talking about *zelem*. The *zelem* in its original form may be lost, but the dimmer reflection of this form is extant in the physical body, which may still be spoken of as *zelem*.[36]

Finally, Gottstein ventures a partial explanation of why the rabbinic interpretation of image is exclusively bodily compared with the subsequent nonbodily interpretations given by Christian immaterialists. Rabbinic anthropology did not consider the soul to be immaterial or radically distinct from the body, as Platonists held it to be. He elaborates:

---

35. This passage is from a section of the homilies recently translated and discussed by Shlomo Pines in "Points of Similarity between the Exposition of the Doctrine of the Sefirot in the Sefer Yezira and a Text of the Pseudo-Clementine Homilies: The Implications of this Resemblance," *Proceedings of the Israel Academy of Sciences and Humanities* 7/3 (1989): 64–65. "Pines . . . considers this sentence a later gloss, for it contradicts the possibility of seeing the divine form." Gottstein, however, conjectures that "'invisible' may refer to the ordinary state, and not to the exceptional condition that the pure-hearted ones attain." Gottstein, "Body as Image of God," 173 n. 5.

36. Gottstein, "Body as Image of God," 188, emphasis in original.

Rabbinic anthropology differs . . . from Hellenistic and later Christian anthropology. The distinction between spirit and matter is not known in rabbinic literature.[37] . . . Metaphysically soul and body form a whole, rather than a polarity. Crudely put, the soul is like the battery that operates an electronic gadget. It may be different and originally external to the gadget, but the difference is not one of essence. . . . More significantly, the gadget and its power source ultimately belong together, rather than apart. Thus, the soul is the vitalizing agent, whose proper place is in the body, not out of it.[38]

Consistently, then, in rabbinic eschatology "the future life takes the form of resurrection of the dead, rather than the eternal life of the soul."[39]

---

37. Compare D&C 131:7–8: "There is no such thing as immaterial matter. All spirit is matter, but it is more fine or pure, and can only be discerned by purer eyes; We cannot see it; but when our bodies are purified we shall see that it is all matter."

38. Gottstein, "Body as Image of God," 176–77. Compare D&C 93:33: "For man is spirit. The elements are eternal, and spirit and element, inseparably connected, receive a fulness of joy." Joseph further explained his beliefs about spirit: "In tracing the thing to the foundation, and looking at it philosophically, we shall find a very material difference between the body and the spirit; the body is supposed to be organized matter, and the spirit, by many, is thought to be immaterial, without substance. With this latter statement we should beg leave to differ, and state the spirit is a substance; that it is material, but that it is more pure, elastic and refined matter than the body; that it existed before the body, can exist in the body; and will exist separate from the body, when the body will be mouldering in the dust; and will in the resurrection, be again united with it." *Teachings of the Prophet Joseph Smith*, 207.

39. Gottstein, "Body as Image of God," 177.

Even in first-century Alexandria, where Hellenistic ideas were already firmly entrenched, Jewish incorporealism was a minority position. For example, Harry Austryn Wolfson, author of the standard biography of Philo, tells us that in his writings Philo often opposed a traditional school of Alexandrian Judaism that interpreted the scriptures literally. In Wolfson's words, these traditionalists "display a self-confidence and self-contentment which flow from . . . a faith in the loyalty of their adherents among the great masses of the Alexandrian Jews."[40] He adds:

> The great mass of believers who will not have felt the impact of the foreign philosophy will see no need of any reconciliation between them. This great mass of believers will either remain indifferent to the innovations of the philosophic reconcilers, or will superciliously look upon them as mere triflers, or, if given provocation, will militantly oppose them as disturbers of the religious peace.[41]

In the end, Wolfson admits that despite Philo's effort to synthesize Jewish belief and Greek thought, "Alexandrian Judaism at the time of Philo was of the same stock as Pharisaic Judaism, which flourished in Palestine at that time."[42] Thus apparently in the first century the Jews in Alexandria, as well as in Palestine, almost universally believed in an embodied God.[43] And, as Kelly

---

40. Harry Austryn Wolfson, *Philo: Foundations of Religious Philosophy in Judaism, Christianity, and Islam* (Cambridge: Harvard University Press, 1948), 1:64.

41. Wolfson, *Philo*, 1:72.

42. Wolfson, *Philo*, 1:56.

43. It is interesting that Wolfson asserts "[t]he Jewish God indeed is incorporeal and free of emotions as is the God of the philosophers," despite his implication that "the great masses of Alexandrian Jews" believed otherwise. Wolfson, *Philo*, 1:26.

has reminded us, first-century Jewish thought was the mold in which primitive Christian theology took shape.[44]

Though data pertaining to Christian belief during the earliest period of Christian history is meager, it strongly supports the thesis that the earliest Christians generally believed God to be embodied. Thus the claim that the doctrine of divine embodiment was a restoration of primitive Christian understanding seems well corroborated.

Second-and Third-Century Belief in an Embodied God

Immaterialism was introduced into Christian theology at least as early as the mid-to-late second century, with Clement of Alexandria (about AD 150–213) being perhaps the first to unequivocally refer to God as immaterial.[45] Immaterialists ultimately triumphed, but not without a three-century-long struggle with Christians who held tenaciously to the primitive doctrine of divine embodiment.

Origen as Witness

The writings of Origen (about AD 185–253) provide substantial evidence that Christians in the second and third centuries generally continued to believe in God's embodiment—despite the efforts of Platonists both within and without the church to persuade them otherwise. Origen adopted the Platonistic metaphysics of his culture. He then devoted his life to the exegesis

---

44. Kelly, "Early Christian Doctrines," 6.

45. See Robert P. Casey, "Clement of Alexandria and the Beginnings of Christian Platonism," *Harvard Theological Review* 18 (1925): 79. For a brief summary of Clement of Alexandria's immaterialistic views on God, see Robert M. Grant, *Gods and the One God* (Philadelphia: Westminster, 1986), 90–91.

of biblical texts in an effort to construct and clarify Christian doctrine to fit his incorporealistic concept of God.[46] Origen's devotion to this task adds great evidentiary weight to his reluctant admissions, explicit and tacit, that his Christian contemporaries generally believed in an embodied God. Origen's writings support this conclusion in at least six ways.

1. In his most important theological work, *De Principiis* (*On First Principles*), Origen enumerated the doctrines that he claims were delivered to the church by the apostles. Significantly, he did not include the doctrine of divine incorporeality on the list.[47]

2. Origen explicitly acknowledged that when he wrote (around the middle of the third century AD), the issue of divine embodiment had yet to be settled in the church: "How God himself is to be understood,—whether as corporeal, and formed according to some shape, or of a different nature from bodies—[is] a point which is not clearly indicated in our teaching." He thus proposed to make the issue a matter of rational and scriptural investigation with a view to formulating a coherent body of doctrine "by means of illustrations and arguments,—either those . . . discovered in holy Scripture, or . . . deduced by closely tracing out the consequences and following a correct method."[48]

---

46. According to a recent biographer, Joseph Wilson Trigg, Origen did "more than anyone else to relate the Bible to Greek philosophy." Trigg, *Origen: The Bible and Philosophy in the Third-Century Church* (Atlanta: John Knox, 1983), 3. For a clear presentation of Origen's Platonism and its formative influences, see chapter 3 (52–75). See also Richard A. Norris, *God and World in Early Christian Theology* (London: Adam & Charles Black, 1966), 106–29; and Grant, *Gods and the One God,* 91–92.

47. Origen, *De Principiis,* in *The Ante-Nicene Fathers,* ed. Alexander Roberts and James Donaldson (1885; reprint, Grand Rapids, MI: Eerdmans, 1951), 4:239–41 (hereafter *ANF*).

48. Origen, *De Principiis* 1.9, 1.10 (*ANF* 4:241).

3. Origen discussed first- and second-century word usages dealing with divine corporeality, ignorance of which had contributed to misunderstanding of some biblical and other early texts. For example, he pointed out that nowhere in the Bible is God explicitly described as incorporeal; the Greek term for incorporeal, *asomatos*, does not appear there. Even where that term does appear in early nonscriptural Christian writings, Origen claimed that it does not have the same meaning that the Greek and Gentile philosophers assigned to it (i.e., having no material body). Rather, he asserted, Christian writers simply used the term to refer to a material body that is much finer and less palpable than those that can be perceived through the senses.

For example, he explained that in the treatise, *The Doctrine of Peter,* where the resurrected Jesus is quoted as saying to his disciples, "I am not an incorporeal demon," this statement

> must be understood to mean that He had not such a body as demons have, which is naturally fine, and thin as if formed of air (and for this reason is either considered or called by many incorporeal), but that He had a solid and palpable body. Now, according to human custom, everything which is not of that nature is called by the simple or ignorant incorporeal; as if one were to say that the air which we breathe was incorporeal, because it is not a body of such a nature as can be grasped and held, or can offer resistance to pressure.[49]

Among the early Christian writers who described God as *asomatos*, Origen was the first (with the possible exception of Clement of Alexandria) to consistently use the term in its technical Platonist sense. In doing so, Origen followed the lead of second-century non-Christian middle-Platonists such as Albinus.[50]

---

49. Origen, *De Principiis* preface, verse 8 (*ANF* 4:241).

50. See Gedaliahu Stroumsa, "The Incorporeality of God: Context and Implications of Origen's Position," *Religion* 13 (1983): 345–58.

More unexpectedly, Origen informs us that the New Testament passage "God is a Spirit" (John 4:24)—the proof text now cited most frequently in support of the doctrine of incorporeality—was initially understood as evidence against it.

> I know that some will attempt to say that, even according to the declarations of our own Scriptures, God is a body, because . . . they find it said . . . in the Gospel according to John, that "God is a Spirit, and they who worship Him must worship Him in spirit and in truth." . . . Spirit, according to them, [is] to be regarded as nothing else than a body.[51]

This surprising statement is easily explained. *Pneuma* (translated "spirit") literally means " air" or "breath," implying that spirit is composed of a material substance, one of the four basic elements. Furthermore, since Christian Stoics believed that existence was confined to material bodies, God (being spirit) was the purest of all bodies.[52]

4. Origen engaged in sustained polemics against those who affirmed God's humanlike embodiment. His argument has two parts. First, he tried to show that corporeality is logically incompatible with philosophical (Platonist) conceptions of the divine nature. Second, by means of painstaking exegesis and allegorical interpretation, he labored to convince his fellow Christians that the scriptures, notwithstanding their literal import, do not disprove divine incorporeality. It is instructive to consider some instances of the latter argument because they

---

51. Origen, *De Principiis* 1.1 (*ANF* 4:242). For an instance of this, see point 1 of the section "Tertullian as Witness" in this paper. Wolfson admits that "in Scripture . . . there is no indication that by spirit and soul were meant any such principles as form or immateriality." Wolfson, *Philo,* 2:95.

52. See Stroumsa, "Incorporeality of God," 345–47. See also Jantzen, "Theological Tradition and Divine Incorporeality," 22–23.

indicate the popular Christian understanding of the scriptures that Origen inveighed against.[53]

Origen argued that if scriptural passages that describe God as spirit, light, fire, and so forth were literally understood, they would erroneously suggest that God is corporeal. Consequently, he advocated a metaphorical interpretation.[54] For example, Origen argued that Genesis 1:26, properly interpreted, does not show God to be corporeal.

> We do not understand, however, this man indeed whom Scripture says was made "according to the image of God" to be corporeal. For the form of the body does not contain the image of God, nor is the corporeal man said to be "made," but "formed," as is written in the words that follow. For the text says: "And God formed man," that is fashioned, "from the slime of the earth."
>
> But it is our inner man, invisible, incorporeal, incorruptible, and immortal which is made "according to the image of God." For it is in such qualities as these that the image of God is more correctly understood. But if anyone suppose that this man who is made "according to the image and likeness of God" is made of flesh, he will appear to represent God himself as made of flesh and in human form. It is most clearly impious to think this about God.[55]

---

53. For an excellent analysis of the centrality of the doctrine of divine incorporeality to Origen's theology and his sustained polemics against anthropomorphic conceptions of God, see Stroumsa, "Incorporeality of God," 345–58. Though Origen does not explicitly identify his opponents, Stroumsa says, "they are, obviously, Christians" (p. 346).

54. Origen, *De Principiis* 1.1 (*ANF* 4:242–45).

55. Origen, *Homilies on Genesis* 1.13 in *Homilies on Genesis and Exodus,* trans. Ronald E. Heine (Washington, DC: Catholic University of America Press, 1981), 63.

Origen also made light of an anthropomorphic interpretation of Genesis 1:26 by showing the absurdity that results from interpreting other passages the same way.

> In brief, those carnal men who have no understanding of the meaning of divinity suppose, if they read anywhere in the Scriptures of God that "heaven is my throne, and the earth my footstool," that God has so large a body that they think he sits in heaven and stretches out his feet to the earth.[56]

Origen acknowledged that "the Jews indeed, but also some of our people, supposed that God should be understood as a man, that is, adorned with human members and human appearance," because in many scriptural passages God is described as speaking to men. But since, as Origen maintained, "the philosophers despise these stories as fabulous and formed in the likeness of poetic fictions," he attempted to show how God can speak to men without the physical ability to perform the function of speaking.

> But in this manner God is said to have spoken to man: he either inspires the heart of each of the saints or causes the sound of a voice to reach his ears. So also when he makes known that what each one says or does is known to him the Scriptures says that he "has heard"; and when he makes known that we have done something unjust, it says that he "is angry"; when he censures us as ungrateful for his benefits, it says he "repents," making known indeed these things by these dispositions which are common to men, but not performing them by these members which belong to corporeal nature.[57]

---

56. Origen, *Homilies on Genesis* 1.13 in *Homilies*, 63–64. As a matter of fact, some believers of this period did conceive of God as having a body of such cosmic proportions. Stroumsa, "Form(s) of God," 269–88.

57. Origen, *Homilies on Genesis* 3.1–2 in *Homilies*, 90–91.

Origen's criticism of his fellow-Christians' belief in divine embodiment was no doubt connected with his Platonistic low estimation of matter and the body.[58] His choice, as a young man, to castrate himself testified of his contempt for the body, although it seems he later judged this action rash.[59] Origen believed that the body was a humiliation—a punishment for the fall from the presence of God. Nonetheless, it served as a means of training whereby we may return to God's presence.[60] Thus, in Origen's view, the body had an instrumental value, but the spiritual life after the body's death was much to be preferred:

> I think that they love God with all their soul who with a great desire to be in union with God withdraw and separate their soul not only from the earthly body but also from everything material. Such men accept the putting away of the body of humiliation without distress or emotion when the time come[s] for them to put off the body of death by what is commonly regarded as death.[61]

Since Origen saw even human embodiment as a humiliation, he vigorously contested divine embodiment.

---

58. See Griffin and Paulsen, "Augustine and the Corporeality of God," 97–118. Platonists believed, unlike the Stoics, that there were intellectual principles that existed independently from matter. In the hierarchy of being these "ideas" were superior to their material instances, and above them all was the One, or God, who was necessarily incorporeal and as their source beyond intellect and matter. See also Ulrich Mauser's study, *Gottesbild und Menschwerdung: Eine Untersuchung zur Einheit des Alten und Neuen Testaments* (Tübingen: Mohr, 1971).

59. Trigg, *Origen*, 53–54.

60. Trigg, *Origen*, 106.

61. Origen, *Exhortation to Martyrdom* 1.3, in *Alexandrian Christianity*, trans. John E. L. Oulton and Henry Chadwick (Philadelphia: Westminister, 1954), 394.

5. Origen specifically included Melito as among the prominent second-century Christians who taught that God is embodied. Not much is known about Melito's life. Neither his date and place of birth nor his date of death are known, although he was probably dead by AD 197. He was active during the imperial reigns of Antoninus Pius (AD 138–161) and Marcus Aurelius (AD 161–180). Though he apparently spent some of his earlier life in Syria, he was made bishop of Sardis in Lydia in about 168 or 169. As bishop, he was polemically engaged as a Quartodeciman "in the controversy concerning Easter."[62] The only complete text that remains from Melito, *Peri Pascha* (On Easter), dealt with this controversy.

Melito was a prolific writer, authoring some eighteen to twenty works. Of these, only five or six have been definitely identified, and these are mostly in fragments.[63] Although the extant fragments provide no affirmation of divine corporeality, Origen's testimony, recorded about fifty years after Melito's death, explicitly identified Melito as among the Christians who taught that God has a humanlike body.[64]

---

62. Richard C. White, *Melito of Sardis: Sermon "On the Passover"* (Lexington, KY: Lexington Theological Seminary Library, 1976), 4–6. A Quartodeciman is "one of a group in the early church esp. in Asia Minor who during the 2d century and until the Nicene council in 325 observed Easter on the 14th of Nisan when the Jews slaughtered the Passover lamb no matter on what day of the week that date occurred." *Webster's New International Dictionary*, 3rd ed., s.v. "quartodeciman."

63. Stuart George Hall, ed., *Melito of Sardis: On Pascha and Fragments* (Oxford: Clarendon, 1979).

64. *Et Dixit Deus: Faciamus hominem ad imaginem nostram et similtudinem.* Prius discutiendum est ubi consistat illud, *ad imaginem,* in corpore, an in anima. Et in primis videamus, quibus utantur qui prius asserunt; e quorum numero est Melito, qui scripta reliquit,

Some have suggested that Origen was mistaken in attributing a corporealist view to Melito. They claim that Origen had no basis for this attribution other than a very weak inference from the title of a treatise, *On the Corporeality of God,*[65] which Eusebius included in his enumeration of Melito's works. Because the title of this work could also be translated as *On God Incarnate,* one commentator, while admitting that "it is not at all impossible that a writer as orthodox as Melito . . . held the opinions which Origen imputes to him," nonetheless questions Origen's claim:

> Here occurs the doubt: Had Origen himself read the treatise of Melito, or did he know nothing but the title, and rashly jump to the conclusion that Melito held views akin to those

---

quibus asserit Deum corporeum esse ["And God said, 'Let us make man in our image and likeness.' We must determine beforehand where the 'image' resides, whether in the body or in the soul. And let us first see what evidences the first writers on the subject used; among these was Melito, who has left treatises asserting the corporeality of God." Daniel W. Graham, trans., Department of Philosophy, Brigham Young University]. Origen, *Selections on Genesis* 2.5, in *Patrologia Graeca,* ed. J.-P. Migne (Paris: Geuthner, 1857–), 12:94 (hereafter cited as PG). See also Origen, *Commentary on the Epistle of Paul to the Romans* 476.16 (PG 14:870–71), where he continues his polemics against Christian anthropomorphites: "qui in Ecclesia positi imaginem corpoream hominis, Dei esse imaginem dicunt" ["those members of the Church who say that the corporeal form of man is the image of God." Origen, *Contra Celsum,* trans. Henry Chadwick (Cambridge: Cambridge University Press, 1965), 416 n. 3]. Unless otherwise indicated, I find the cited translations precise enough for present purposes.

65. See Eusebius, *Ecclesiastical History* 4.26.2, in *The Ecclesiastical History and the Martyrs of Palestine,* trans. Hugh J. Lawlor and John E. L. Oulton (London: SPCK, 1954), 1:132.

which he was at the moment combating? If Melito be the author of the Syriac apology no fault can be found with the spirituality of his conceptions of God. It does not seem possible now absolutely to determine the question. We are ourselves inclined to believe that Origen made a mistake, and that the subject of Melito's treatise was the Incarnation.[66]

Such speculation appears unwarranted. Given Origen's vigorous efforts to persuade his fellow Christians to give up their corporealism, it seems totally incongruous that he, without having read Melito's book and without any further evidence, would have attributed this view to a respected bishop of the Church. Moreover, Origen's testimony is further corroborated by Gennadius who, writing in about AD 425, affirmed that Melito was responsible for a sect of Christians who followed him in the belief that the body of man is made in the image of God.[67] Furthermore, since the doctrine of divine incorporeality eventually became Christian orthodoxy, the fact that Melito taught God's corporeality could help explain the otherwise mysterious disappearance of this work and other writings.[68]

6. Finally, it was Origen who preserved the testimony of Celsus, a second-century Middle-Platonist and non-Christian who wrote a comprehensive critique of Christianity (about AD 178) entitled *Alethes Logos* (*True Doctrine*), which was later

---

66. *A Dictionary of Christian Biography, Literature, Sects and Doctrines,* ed. William Smith and Henry Wace (London: Murray, 1882), s.v. "Melito."

67. Gennadius, *Liber ecclesiasticorum dogmatum,* 24.2, in Cuthbert H. Turner, "The *Liber Ecclesiasticorum Dogmatum* Attributed to Gennadius," *Journal of Theological Studies* 7 (1906): 90.

68. Stroumsa claims that the affirmation of Melito's anthropomorphism is unfounded, citing Othmar Perler, trans. and ed., *Méliton: Sur la pâque* (Paris: Cerf, 1966), 13 n. 1. Referenced in Stroumsa, "Form(s) of God," 270 n. 6.

suppressed or destroyed. It is known only through quotations in Origen's work, *Contra Celsum,* composed seventy years later. Celsus attempted to demonstrate the inadequacy of Christian doctrine, especially the doctrine of God, on the basis of assumptions drawn from Platonist philosophical theology.[69]

According to Origen, Celsus argued "at length" against what he understood to be the Christian belief that God "is corporeal by nature and has a body like the human form." To give the idea of divine corporeality as little attention as possible, Origen did not spell out Celsus's sustained anticorporeality arguments, explaining that if Celsus "invents out of his own head ideas which he heard from nobody, or, to grant that he heard them from somebody, notions which he derived from some simple and naïve folk who do not know the meaning of the Bible, there is no need for us to concern ourselves with unnecessary argument."[70]

---

69. See the introduction to Origen, *Contra Celsum,* trans. Chadwick, ix–xxxii. For an attempted reconstruction of Celsus's work from the quotations in Origen's *Contra Celsum,* see Celsus, *On the True Doctrine: A Discourse Against the Christians,* trans. R. Joseph Hoffmann (New York: Oxford University Press, 1987). Though by his own admission, Origen has omitted Celsus's sustained anticorporeality arguments, Hoffmann claims to have reconstructed several pages of these arguments (103–15).

70. Origen, *Contra Celsum,* trans. Chadwick, 416. This passage continues: "The Bible clearly says that God is incorporeal. That is why 'No man has seen God at any time' [John 1:18], and 'the first-born of all creation' is said to be an 'image of the invisible God' [Colossians 1:15]—using 'invisible' in the sense of 'incorporeal'" Origen, *Contra Celsum,* (trans. Chadwick, 416). Colossians 1:15 is one of four places where Paul uses the Greek word *aoratos,* which is usually translated "invisible." However, Origen's claim that Paul meant *incorporeal* here when he wrote "invisible" is dubious. In

Interestingly, in responding to Celsus—a fellow Platonist whose objections to divine corporeality he shared—Origen feigned ignorance of any Christians actually teaching the doctrine. But as already shown above, Origen elsewhere reckoned the learned bishop Melito among the Christian teachers of the doctrine, and throughout his writings he engaged in sustained polemics against his fellow Christians who believed the doctrine. Thus, it seems clear from the evidence in Origen's own writings that Celsus was neither misinformed nor did he

---

their translation of and commentary on Colossians, Markus Barth and Helmut Blanke suggest that Origen's interpretation is not the proper way to understand *aoratos*. "*Aoratos* is usually translated as 'invisible.' But the verbal adjective in the biblical Greek not only designates a possibility or impossibility, but is also used in a factual and pragmatic sense: the *agnostos theos* in Acts 17:23 is the 'unknown God,' not the 'unrecognizable' one; as also the *aniptoi cheires* (Matt 15:20) are the 'unwashed hands,' not the 'unwashable' ones. It is recommendable in Col 1:15 to translate *aoratos* in this pragmatic sense. This corresponds to the OT usage because there is no Hebrew equivalent of *aoratos* with the meaning of 'invisible.' According to the proclamation of the OT, God is not invi*sible*; it is simply not within the capacity of human beings to see Yahweh. . . . It is unlikely that Paul fostered different notions and cannot be demonstrated. In 1 Cor 13:12, he speaks of a 'time' when we will no longer look as though through a mirror, but rather 'from face to face.' Obviously, he does not presuppose an 'invisible God.'" Markus Barth and Helmut Blanke, *Colossians: A New Translation with Introduction and Commentary*, trans. Astrid B. Beck (New York: Doubleday, 1994), 195–96. Paul was then not suggesting that God is inherently unseeable, but only that he is presently unseen. Whether humans can see or have seen God is a separate issue because even if no man had ever seen God the Father, this fact in no way entails that God is incorporeal.

misrepresent second-century Christians' belief. They did, indeed, believe that God is embodied. And from Origen's testimony, it appears that this belief continued to be generally held in the third century as well.

Tertullian as Witness

Origen's implication that contemporary Christians who believed God to be embodied were confined to simple and naive folk is contradicted by one of the most cultured of all his Christian contemporaries—Quintus Septimius Florens Tertullianus (about AD 150–220). Tertullian stoutly maintained his belief that God is embodied and passionately resisted attempts by immaterialists to Platonize Christian doctrine. Tertullian not only personally believed in an embodied God, he claimed this to be the teaching of the Christian churches of his day, which they, in turn, derived from the original apostolic churches. He articulated in rich detail a unified corporealist understanding of their understanding of God.

Tertullian's genius with language allowed him to craft brilliant polemical theological treatises, which contributed profoundly to the clarification of Christian doctrine on topics such as the Incarnation, the Trinity, and the Sacraments.[71] As far as is known, Tertullian was the first to coin the Latin *trinitas*.[72]

Tertullian was active in a Christian movement known at the time as the New Prophecy.[73] This movement attempted to

---

71. For a fuller account of Tertullian's significance in relation to contemporary theology, see James Morgan, *The Importance of Tertullian in the Development of Christian Doctrine* (London: Kegan Paul, 1928), 148–65.

72. Morgan, *Importance of Tertullian*, 103.

73. Clear signs of Tertullian's involvement appear in his writings starting ca. 206–7. Timothy David Barnes, *Tertullian: A Historical and Literary Study* (Oxford: Clarendon, 1921), 46–47. Much later,

recover the prophetic revelation and spiritual gifts characteristic of the apostolic age, to preserve pristine Christian doctrine against philosophical intrusions, and to prepare a people for Christ's second coming, which was believed to be imminent. The movement apparently began about AD 170 in Mysia, a remote village in Phrygia, when a man named Montanus began to prophesy, claiming revelation through the Paraclete (or Holy Ghost). Soon after, he was joined by two prophetesses, Prisca (or Priscillia) and Maximillia.

> All three spoke as the mouthpieces of God himself: their possession was truly divine, not the doing of a mere angel or messenger from heaven. In them God spoke, the Almighty, the Father, the Son and the Holy Spirit. The prophets played a consciously passive role as God's instruments: they were the lyre which the Spirit plucked like a plectrum. Through them God spoke directly to the world, and especially to the humble, in order to give them the courage to die as martyrs. The end of the world was approaching, and the New Jerusalem (Rev. 21. 1 ff.) would descend on Pepuza in Phrygia. In a word, Montanism was a millenarian movement.[74]

Some Asian churches declared Montanus's prophecies "to be inspired by the Devil, and the Montanists were excommunicated, then vilified in slanderous pamphlets."[75] Despite this opposition, the movement spread rapidly to Rome, Alexandria, and even Gaul. It achieved its greatest success in Carthage, where Tertullian became a partisan, as Timothy Barnes explains:

---

adherents of the New Prophecy were called Montanists after the name of the movement's founder, Montanus. They were most often called Cataphrygians by their opponents, the title indicating their geographical origin. See Ronald E. Heine, *The Montanist Oracles and Testimonia* (Macon, GA: Mercer University Press, 1989), ix.

74. Barnes, *Tertullian*, 131.
75. Barnes, *Tertullian*, 131.

Since Christianity was a revealed religion, [Tertullian] was unwilling to believe that revelation had ceased in the Apostolic age. Inexorably, therefore, he was led on to espouse the Montanist cause. The issues were simple in his eyes. Recognition of the Paraclete, whom God has promised to send (Jn. 14. 16), severed him from the 'psychici'. The Paraclete, the 'deductor omnis veritatis' (Jn. 16. 13), gave necessary counsel to every Christian. Its promptings preserved doctrinal orthodoxy from the assaults of heresy.[76]

Tertullian himself sought to preserve original Christian doctrine, as founded on revelation, against the encroachments of Platonistic immaterialism. His understanding of Christianity included at least six points that support divine embodiment. He argued that (1) God, like all that is, is embodied, (2) beings of spirit may take on more solid bodily form, (3) Christ in the Incarnation specifically took on flesh that was unqualifiedly human, (4) human flesh is a sacred and glorious substance, (5) the same fleshy body that falls in human death rises in the resurrection, and (6) Christ's resurrected body is an everlasting and crucial attribute of the Godhead.[77] These complementary points form part of Tertullian's unified explication of his corporealist Christian faith.

1. Tertullian believed that God is and has always been a material body.[78] He believed that anything that exists is ma-

---

76. Barnes, *Tertullian*, 131–32. Although the Montanists were called heretical by later Christians, their differences from their contemporaries were in matters of practice, not theology. Barnes, *Tertullian*, 42. Likewise Tertullian's "orthodoxy in matters of doctrine remained impeccable" during his Montanist years, as before.

77. For a summary of Tertullian's views on God, see Norris, *Early Christian Theology*, 81–105.

78. Tertullian did not use the phrase "material body" to describe God, but simply "body" (Latin *corpore*). In fact, Tertullian used the

terial,[79] though not all material is the rough stuff we interact with in daily life. In an apologetic work addressed to pagans hostile to Christianity, Tertullian expressed approval of Zeno's

Latin *materia,* cognate to the English "matter," to refer specifically to the matter of the world in contradistinction to God's eternal substance. Tertullian, *Against Hermogenes* (*ANF* 3:477–502). (In addition to referring to the chapter and book [if any] of Tertullian's works, I cite the page number from Alexander Roberts and James Donaldson, eds., *Latin Christianity: Its Founder, Tertullian* (*ANF* 3.) He also specifically distinguished God and matter as "two words (and) two things." Tertullian, *Ad Nationes* 2.4 (*ANF* 3:133). Likewise, he said that the human soul is formed "by the breathing of God, and not out of [non-divine] matter," clearly distinguishing God from the matter of the world. Tertullian, *A Treatise on the Soul,* 1.3 (*ANF* 3:184). Although Tertullian did not apply the term "material" to God, the properties that he ascribed to God are what we now consider to be the defining properties of matter: spatial location, extension, shape, and "even a certain tangibility." Morgan, *Importance of Tertullian,* 182. Hence I describe Tertullian's conception of the soul and of God as materialistic. It is nevertheless important to remember that Tertullian distinguished between created, perishable, sensible matter and the uncreated, imperishable, insensible substance (matter) of God. Tertullian, *Ad Nationes* 2.4 (*ANF* 3:132).

79. Morgan, *Importance of Tertullian,* 15. This notion appears explicitly in Tertullian, *Treatise on the Soul* 1.7 (*ANF* 3:187); and implicitly in Tertullian, *Against Praxeas* 1.7 (*ANF* 3:602). Although Tertullian closely agreed with the Stoics on this and many other beliefs and methods, we should not thereby conclude that Stoicism was the source of his belief. See Morgan, *Importance of Tertullian,* 10–16. While Tertullian employed Stoic explanations, arguments, and beliefs, he exercised discrimination in doing so. For example, Tertullian used arguments of Stoic and other philosophers to support his belief in the corporeality of the soul, particularly agreeing with the Stoics' description of the soul "almost in our own terms." Tertullian, *Treatise*

model, which "separates the matter of world from God . . . [in which] the latter has percolated through the former, like honey through the comb."[80] Addressing heretics who taught that the Word was immaterial (AD 210),[81] Tertullian defined God's materiality as a more fluid or subtle mode of matter than that which comprises the world. He is also "a body, although 'God is a Spirit,'" for Spirit "has a bodily substance of its own kind."[82]

---

on the Soul 1.5 (*ANF* 3:184). Yet elsewhere, Tertullian pointed out that the Stoics do not believe in the restoration of the body, condemned them as the source of Marcion's and Hermogenes' heresies, and denounced broadly the teaching of Zeno as making the matter of the world equal with God. Tertullian, *The Prescription against Heretics* 1.7 (*ANF* 3:246); and Tertullian, *Against Hermogenes* 1.1 (*ANF* 3:477). On this last point, Tertullian criticized precisely the Stoic materialism that some say was the basis of his own belief. Morgan, *Importance of Tertullian*, 182. While Tertullian acknowledged that his beliefs sometimes coincided with those of this or that philosopher, he used philosophical authority strictly as a supplement to the ultimate authority of biblical and continuing revelation. He held that "all questions" should be referred "to God's inspired standard." Tertullian, *Treatise on the Soul* 1.2 (*ANF* 3:183). The discrimination Tertullian showed in regard to philosophical doctrine precludes a simple explaining away of Tertullian's materialism as due to inability to transcend Stoic prejudices (although Morgan suggests this explanation in *Importance of Tertullian*, 16). For further discussion of Tertullian's relationship to pagan philosophy, see R. Braun, "Tertullien et la philosophie païenne: Essai de mise au point," *Bulletin de L'Association Guillaume Budé* 2 (June 1971): 231–51.

80. Tertullian, *Ad Nationes* 2.4 (*ANF* 3:133).

81. To date Tertullian's writing, I rely on Barnes's chronology. Barnes, *Tertullian*, 55.

82. Tertullian, *Against Praxeas* 1.7 (*ANF* 3:602). This interpretation of John 4:25 was noted by Origen. See point 3 of the section "Origen as Witness" in this paper.

To support his claim that the creator of the material earth must be a body, Tertullian presented an argument reminiscent of modern versions of the so-called mind-body problem.

> How could it be, that He Himself is nothing, without whom nothing was made? How could He who is empty have made things which are solid, and He who is void have made things which are full, and He who is incorporeal have made things which have body? For although a thing may sometimes be made different from him by whom it is made, yet nothing can be made by that which is a void and empty thing. [83]

This argument attempts to show that the Word, by whom the worlds were made (Hebrews 1:2), must be a material body. The same argument applies to the Father, thus supporting Tertullian's understanding of the Father as Spirit and therefore materially embodied, although in the original text, Tertullian presented the Father's corporeality as needless of argumentative support; he gave the Father's corporeality as another reason to believe in the Son's corporeality.[84]

Tertullian's notion of material Spirit included attributes of location, extension, shape, texture, rarity, and density. In arguing against Hermogenes and others misled by Plato and the Stoics (in AD 206),[85] he described how God's breath, which is a portion of his Spirit,[86] condensed and became Adam's soul:

---

83. Tertullian, *Against Praxeas* 1.7 (*ANF* 3:602).

84. While some may find this argument persuasive, my point in presenting it is to illustrate Tertullian's understanding of God, not to suggest that this understanding is demonstrated by this reasoning. Tertullian, *Against Praxeas* 1.7 (*ANF* 3:602).

85. See Barnes, *Tertullian*, 123.

86. Tertullian cited Isaiah 24:5 as teaching that man's soul is a condensation of the Spirit or breath of God: "My Spirit went forth from me, and I made the breath of each. And the breath of my Spirit

> After God hath breathed upon the face of man the breath of
> life, and man had consequently become a living soul, surely
> that breath must have passed through the face at once into
> the interior structure, and have spread itself throughout all
> the spaces of the body; and as soon as by the divine inspira-
> tion it had become condensed, it must have impressed itself
> on each internal feature, which the condensation had filled
> in, and so have been, as it were, congealed in shape, (or
> stereotyped). Hence, by this densifying process, there arose
> a fixing of the soul's corporeity; and by the impression its
> figure was formed and molded. This is the inner man, dif-
> ferent from the outer, but yet one in the twofold condition.
> It, too, has eyes and ears of its own.[87]

Thus, according to Tertullian, before its impression in the
body, the Spirit of God apparently has no fixed shape, but it
has extension and position so that it can pass through Adam's
face and flow through his body before condensing and transforming into soul.

---

became soul." Tertullian, *Treatise on the Soul* 1.11 (*ANF* 3:191).
Hence man's soul was once a part of God. This concept is especially
significant because Tertullian expressly asserted elsewhere that the
matter out of which God formed the world had a beginning when
God created the world out of nothing. Tertullian, *Against Hermogenes* 1.33 (*ANF* 3:496). In this book, he contrasted creation out
of nothing with creation out of God's own substance. Tertullian,
Against Hermogenes 1.2 (*ANF* 3:477–78). Hence, Tertullian made
the human soul of eternal, uncreated, divine substance in contrast
with created and perishable matter.

87. Tertullian, *Treatise on the Soul* 1.9 (*ANF* 3:189). Although he
says "the face of man," Tertullian clearly alludes to Genesis 2:7 in
this passage, which he quotes as referring to Adam. Tertullian, *Treatise on the Soul* 1.3 (*ANF* 3:184).

Even in his earliest writings (between AD 198 and 203), Tertullian represented the Spirit of God explicitly as "subtlety" material, having location and form, although its shape may not be fixed. He described the Spirit of God as corporeal, although not human in form.

> The Spirit of God, who since the beginning was borne upon the waters, would as baptizer abide upon waters. A holy thing in fact was carried upon a holy thing—or rather, that which carried acquired holiness from that which was carried upon it. Any matter placed beneath another is bound to take to itself the quality of that which is suspended over it: and especially must corporal matter take up spiritual quality, which because of the subtlety of the substance it belongs to finds it easy to penetrate and inhere.[88]

2. Tertullian did not think it strange that a being of subtle spirit should take more solid bodily form. He considered the human spirit to be one of the inseparable faculties of the human soul,[89] which has the same form as the body of flesh it inhabits. He used reason, religious experience, and biblical revelation to support this belief.

Criticizing Plato, Tertullian argued rationally that the soul must be corporeal in order to (1) sympathize and interact with the body, (2) move the body, and (3) be described as departing the body at the time of death.[90] Then he reasoned that since the soul is corporeal,

> We shall not be at all inconsistent if we declare that the more usual characteristics of a body, such as invariably accrue to

---

88. Ernest Evans, trans., *Tertullian's Homily on Baptism* (Cambridge, England: University Printing House, 1964), 9, 11. See also a slightly different translation in Tertullian, *On Baptism* 4 (*ANF* 3:670).

89. Tertullian, *Treatise on the Soul* 1.10 (*ANF* 3:190).

90. Tertullian, *Treatise on the Soul* 1.5–6 (*ANF* 3:185).

the corporeal condition, belong also to the soul—such as form and limitation; and that triad of dimensions. . . . What now remains but for us to give the soul a figure [*effigiem*]?[91]

To his rational argument that a soul must have humanlike form, Tertullian added evidence drawn from the religious experiences of a contemporary Christian woman associated with New Prophecy. She claimed:

> "There has been shown to me a soul in bodily shape, and a spirit has been in the habit of appearing to me; not, however, a void and empty illusion, but such as would offer itself to be even grasped by the hand, soft and transparent and of an etherial colour, and in form resembling that of a human being in every respect."[92]

Finally, he rounded out his case for the humanlike form of the soul by an appeal to biblical authority. For instance, he relied on the New Testament account of Lazarus and the rich man in hell (Luke 16:23–24): "[The soul], too, has eyes and ears of its own . . . ; it has, moreover all the other members of the body. . . . Thus it happens that the rich man in hell has a tongue and poor (Lazarus) a finger and Abraham a bosom."[93]

Tertullian believed that angels, though beings of spirit, appear in temporary solid bodies. Furthermore, addressing heretics who claimed Christ's corporeality was illusory (about AD 206), Tertullian even attributed to the Holy Spirit the power to take literal bodily form.

---

91. Tertullian, *Treatise on the Soul* 1.9 (*ANF* 3:188). The word that Tertullian uses for figure is cognate with the English "effigy," which roughly means a copy of something.

92. Tertullian, *Treatise on the Soul* 1.9 (*ANF* 3:188).

93. Tertullian, *Treatise on the Soul* 1.9 (*ANF* 3:189). In this passage, Tertullian also refers to Paul hearing and seeing the Lord (2 Corinthians 12:2–4). For other arguments based on scripture, see Tertullian, *Treatise on the Soul* 1.7 (*ANF* 3:187).

The Gospel of John . . . declares that the Spirit descended in the body of a dove, and sat upon the Lord. When the said Spirit was in this condition, He was as truly a dove as He was also a spirit; nor did He destroy His own proper substance by the assumption of an extraneous substance. But you ask what becomes of the dove's body, after the return of the Spirit back to heaven, and similarly in the case of the angels. Their withdrawal was effected in the same manner as their appearance had been. . . . Still there was solidity in their bodily substance, whatever may have been the force by which the body became visible.[94]

3. Tertullian believed that the Word took on human flesh when he was born as the Son of God. Tertullian wrote an entire book, *On the Flesh of Christ,* to argue that Christ's flesh was very much human flesh; that the soul, which gave that flesh life, was of the same sort that inhabits other human bodies; and that Christ's humanity was essential to the purpose of his life and work on earth. He affirmed that Christ's was a flesh "suffused with blood, built up with bones, interwoven with nerves, entwined with veins, *a flesh* which knew how to be born, and how to die, human without doubt, as born of a human being." Such a flesh was necessary so that Christ could suffer and die to redeem mankind. While fully divine in spirit, Christ was fully human in body: "The powers of the Spirit, proved Him to be God, His sufferings attested the flesh of man. If His powers were not without the Spirit in like manner, were not His sufferings without the flesh."[95]

4. In no way did Tertullian consider it degrading for God to take bodily or even human form. As part of his multifaceted argument that Christ really dwelt in human flesh, Tertullian argued vehemently for the worthiness of human flesh. To those

---

94. Tertullian, *On the Flesh of Christ* 1.5 (*ANF* 3:523).

95. Tertullian, *On the Flesh of Christ* 1.5 (*ANF* 3:525); emphasis in original.

who considered the flesh a shameful thing, Tertullian said of
the condition of being clothed in flesh:

> And are *you* for turning these conditions into occasions
> of blushing to the very creature whom He has redeemed,
> (censuring them), too, us unworthy of Him who certainly
> would not have redeemed them had He not loved them?
> Our birth He reforms from death by a second birth from
> heaven; our flesh He restores from every harassing malady;
> when leprous, He cleanses it of the stain; when blind, He re-
> kindles its light; when palsied, He renews its strength; when
> possessed with devils, He exorcises it; when dead, He reani-
> mates it,—then shall *we* blush to own it?[96]

Far from an embarrassment, Tertullian considered the
body and its process of generation to be sacred, calling it a
"reverend course of nature."[97] Elsewhere he reiterated that "nature should be to us an object of reverence, not of blushes."[98]
Tertullian also denied that the flesh is the source of sin.

> [The soul] suffuses even the flesh (by reason of their con-
> junction) with its own shame. Now although the flesh is
> sinful, . . . yet the flesh has not such ignominy on its own
> account. For it is not of itself that it thinks anything or
> feels anything for the purpose of advising or commanding
> sin. . . . It is only a ministering thing.[99]

Thus Tertullian held that the soul is the origin of sinful im-
pulses and that the flesh is sinful only as an abettor in the commission of the sins the soul initiates.[100]

---

96. Tertullian, *On the Flesh of Christ* 1.4 (*ANF* 3:524); emphasis
in original.

97. Tertullian, *On the Flesh of Christ* 1.4 (*ANF* 3:524).

98. Tertullian, *Treatise on the Soul* 1.27 (*ANF* 3:208).

99. Tertullian, *Treatise on the Soul* 1.40 (*ANF* 3:220).

100. Tertullian, *Treatise on the Soul* 1.40 (*ANF* 3:220).

Far from being a degrading substance, Tertullian maintained that earthly flesh is a glorified substance, since God created it.

> You have both the clay made glorious by the hand of God, and the flesh more glorious still by His breathing upon it, by virtue of which the flesh not only laid aside its clayey rudiments, but also took on itself the ornaments of the soul.[101]

He further compared the flesh to splendid gold, which similarly derives from the refining of earth.[102]

5. Tertullian believed that the resurrected rise in a body of flesh. Arguing against those led by philosophy to deny bodily resurrection, Tertullian points to Christ's fleshly resurrection as paradigmatic of our own; stated of Christ:

> For the very same body which fell in death, and which lay in the sepulchre, did also rise again; (and it was) not so much Christ in the flesh, as the flesh in Christ. If, therefore, we are to rise again after the example of Christ, who rose in the flesh, we shall certainly not rise according to that example, unless we also shall ourselves rise again in the flesh.[103]

To clarify Paul's teaching regarding the resurrection—"It is sown a natural body; it is raised a spiritual body" (1 Corinthians 15:44)—Tertullian explained the difference between natural and spiritual bodies: "As therefore the flesh was at first an animate (or natural) body on receiving the soul, so at last will it become a spiritual body when invested with the spirit [of God]."[104] Thus Tertullian believed that resurrected flesh is flesh similar to mortal flesh, but the spiritual body of the resurrection is a fleshy body that has been purified by accepting God's Spirit.

---

101. Tertullian, *On the Resurrection of the Flesh* 1.7 (*ANF* 3:550).

102. Tertullian, *On the Resurrection of the Flesh* 1.18 (*ANF* 3:557–58); 1.6 (*ANF* 3:549–50).

103. Tertullian, *On the Resurrection of the Flesh* 1.48 (*ANF* 3:581).

104. Tertullian, *On the Resurrection of the Flesh* 1.53 (*ANF* 3:587).

In a similar manner, Tertullian claimed, our (fleshy) bodies may become spiritual even in mortality.

> First of all there comes the (natural) soul, that is to say, the breath, to the people that are on the earth,—in other words, to those who act carnally in the flesh; then afterwards comes the Spirit to those who walk thereon,—that is, who subdue the works of the flesh; because the apostle also says, that "that is not first which is spiritual, but that which is natural, (or in possession of the natural soul,) and afterward that which is spiritual." [105]

The fact that a person's body can become a spiritual one while it is still mortal further clarifies that the spiritual body is material. Clearly, for Tertullian, the spiritual body of the Resurrection is a body of flesh, purified by the Spirit of God.

6. Tertullian believed that the Word not only took on human flesh when he was born as the son of God, but that he also will retain that flesh forever in its resurrected, glorified state.

> He who suffered "will come again from heaven," [Acts 1:2], and by all shall He be seen, who rose again from the dead. They too who crucified Him shall see and acknowledge Him; that is to say, His very flesh, against which they spent their fury, and without which it would be impossible for Himself either to exist or to be seen; so that they must blush with shame who affirm that His flesh sits in heaven void of sensation, like a sheath only, Christ being withdrawn from it; as well as those who (maintain) that His flesh and soul are just the same thing, or else that His soul is all that exists, but that His flesh no longer lives. [106]

Without his body, Christ could not have accomplished his mission on earth, and deprived of it, he would not be Christ.

---

105. Tertullian, *Treatise on the Soul* 1.11 (ANF 3:191).
106. Tertullian, *On the Flesh of Christ* 1.24 (ANF 3:542).

Insofar as Christ and his mission contribute to the glory of the Godhead, so contributes the flesh. Tertullian's belief clearly contrasts with later interpretations of the Resurrection that deny Christ's eternal embodiment.

Tertullian's defense of God as materially embodied, of the Resurrection of the flesh, and of the soul as humanlike in form is part of a larger effort to preserve what he understood to be pristine Christian doctrine and to defend it against attempts by late second-century and early third-century Christian Platonists to recast it within an immaterialistic, metaphysical framework.[107] Since Christianity is a revealed religion, Tertullian insisted that discussants must refer "all questions to God's inspired standard." This standard included the Old Testament, the words of the apostles, and the tradition of the churches that the apostles established. Tertullian cited all three in support of his doctrines.

While combating heresy, Tertullian maintained that the apostolic tradition had been well preserved. The "many" and "great" Christian churches that continue in "one and the same faith" evidence that the tradition is strong.[108] Moreover, his own doctrine "has its origin in the tradition of the apostles" and the churches they organized, being "in no respect different from theirs."[109] Tertullian thus implied that from the

---

107. See Tertullian, *Treatise on the Soul* 1.23 (*ANF* 3:203). For a fuller discussion of Tertullian's resistance to Platonism, see Robert E. Roberts, *The Theology of Tertullian* (London: Epworth, 1924), 63–78.

108. Tertullian, *On Prescription against Heretics* 1.28 (*ANF* 3:256).

109. Tertullian, *On Prescription against Heretics* 1.21 (*ANF* 3:252–53). Although this work stands on its own as a general statement on heresy and orthodoxy, it also serves as a preface to a series of Tertullian's works addressed to particular heresies, including *A Treatise on the Soul, Against Praxeas, On the Flesh of Christ, On the Resurrection*

beginnings of Christianity to his day, there had been a unified body of Christians who, faithful to the apostolic tradition, affirmed that God is embodied.[110]

As an educated Christian, Tertullian was in a position to resist philosophical intrusions into Christian doctrine in a way that unlearned Christians could not. After his conversion, Tertullian devoted all his efforts to the defense of Christianity.[111] He asserted that philosophy is the parent of heresy and posed the trenchant questions that have continued to haunt conventional Christian theologians through the centuries:

> What indeed has Athens to do with Jerusalem? What concord is there between the Academy and the Church? what between heretics and Christians? Our instruction comes from "the porch of Solomon," who had himself taught that "the Lord should be sought in simplicity of heart." Away with all attempts to produce a mottled Christianity of Stoic, Platonic, and dialectic composition![112]

---

of the Flesh, Against Hermogenes, and *The Five Books against Marcion.* Note also the many places where Tertullian refers to his appeal to apostolic authority as a criterion for distinguishing orthodox Christian doctrines: *The Prescription against Heretics* 1.31, 1.34 (*ANF* 3:258, 259–60); *Against Marcion* 5.1 (*ANF* 3:429); and *Against Hermogenes* 1 (*ANF* 3:477).

110. Tertullian, *On Prescription against Heretics* 1.20, 1.28 (*ANF* 3:252, 256). See also numerous instances where Tertullian speaks as "we" and of his doctrines as those of "ourselves," as in Tertullian, *Treatise on the Soul* 1.2 (*ANF* 3:182).

111. As a new convert, Tertullian devoted himself to the obvious threats to Christianity outside the Christian community. His earliest writings defended Christianity against pagans and Jews. However, as he became more deeply involved in the issues threatening Christianity, Tertullian turned to internal threats, which he saw as the most significant dangers.

112. Tertullian, *On Prescription against Heretics* 1.7 (*ANF* 3:246).

Fourth- and Fifth-Century
Christian Belief in an Embodied God

Tertullian's vigorous attempt to preserve within Christianity the understanding that God is embodied would, of course, ultimately fail. But the triumph of immaterialism came about only gradually. Indeed, significant pockets of Christians resisted Hellenistic influences and continued to believe in an embodied deity as late as the fourth and fifth centuries. This is clearly shown in the writings of Augustine (AD 354–430) who, ironically, was himself an uncompromising advocate of incorporealism.

Augustine was born at Thagaste in North Africa in 354. His mother, Monica, was a Christian. During his youth and early adulthood, Augustine apparently understood that Christians believed God to be embodied; by his own admission, it was this very doctrine that for many years constituted an insurmountable stumbling block to his acceptance of the Christian faith. He said that as a youth, he was much embarrassed by the doctrine and thus succumbed to the logic of those who maligned it.

> My own specious reasoning induced me to give in to the sly arguments of fools who asked me . . . whether God was confined to the limits of a bodily shape, whether he had hair and nails. . . . My ignorance was so great that these questions troubled me, and while I thought I was approaching the truth, I was only departing the further from it. . . . How could I see this when with the sight of my eyes I saw no more than material things and with the sight of my mind no more than their images? I did not know that God is a spirit, a being without bulk and without limbs defined in length and breadth. . . . Nor had I the least notion . . . what the Scriptures mean when they say that we are made in God's image.[113]

---

113. Augustine, *Confessions* 3.7, in R. S. Pine-Coffin, trans., *Confessions* (Middlesex, England: Penguin, 1961), 62–63.

At first unable to accept Christianity because of its doctrine that God is embodied in humanlike form, Augustine was much attracted to the Manichaean sect, which endorsed a nonanthropomorphic, though still material, deity. Augustine wrote:

> I had lost hope of being able to find the truth in your Church, O Lord. . . . The Manichees had turned me away from it: at the same time I thought it outrageous to believe that you had the shape of a human body and were limited within the dimensions of limbs like our own. . . .
>
> For when I tried to fall back upon the Catholic faith, my mind recoiled because the Catholic faith was not what I supposed it to be. . . . but, O my God . . . I thought that this was a more pious belief than to suppose that you were limited, in each and every way, by the outlines of a human body.[114]

Eventually, Augustine's career as a teacher of rhetoric took him from his native Africa to Italy, first to Rome and then to Milan. There, under the influence of Bishop Ambrose, he became acquainted with Latin translations of Platonist writings and with the possibility of God's being a "purely spiritual being" in the sense of being totally immaterial, invisible, and incorporeal.[115] This view of God dissolved his long-standing aversion to Christian doctrine and was a major factor in his conversion in 386. The following year, at age thirty-two, he was finally baptized a Christian. In his newly found Platonic understanding of God, he exulted:

> I learned that your spiritual children . . . do not understand the words *God made man in his own image* to mean that you are limited by the shape of a human body, . . . nevertheless I was glad that all this time I had been howling my complaints not against the Catholic faith. . . .

---

114. Augustine, *Confessions* 5.10 (104–5).
115. Stroumsa, "Incorporeality of God," 352.

O God, you who are so high above us and yet so close, hidden and yet always present, you have not parts, some greater and some smaller. You are everywhere, and everywhere you are entire. Nowhere are you limited by space. You have not the shape of a body like ours. . . . Your Catholic Church . . . I had learnt [*sic*] . . . did not teach the doctrines which I so sternly denounced. This bewildered me, but I was on the road to conversion and I was glad. . . . [I] had no liking for childish absurdities and there was nothing in the sound doctrine which she taught to show that you, the Creator of all things, were confined within a measure of space which, however high, however wide it might be, was yet strictly determined by the form of a human body.[116]

---

116. Augustine, *Confessions* 6.3–4 (114–15); emphasis in original. Paulsen and Griffin further write: "At times scholars have read this and similar passages rather naively, expressing surprise at how Augustine, schooled in and so otherwise perceptive of Christian teaching from his youth, could have been ignorant of such fundamental doctrines as the incorporeality of God and the soul." (Footnote 41: See So Maurice Testard, *Saint Augustin et Cicéron*, [Paris: *Études augustiniennes*, 1958], 1:110, "though he is certain Augustine *must* have been taught it" ['nul doute cependant qu'il les reçut'].") "Simply put, in the West they were not fundamental doctrines before Augustine, although they became fundamental largely because of him." (Footnote 42: "We here follow and are indebted in many particulars to the studies of Ronald J. Teske, especially, 'The Aim of Augustine's Proof That God Truly Is,' *International Philosophical Quarterly* 26 [1986] 253–68, and 'Divine Immutability in Saint Augustine,' *The Modern Schoolman* 63 [1986] 233–49. See also Goulven Madec, 'Deus,' in *Augustinus-Lexikon* [ed. Cornelius Mayer; vol. 2; Basel: Schwabe, 1996, 323–26.]") See Griffin and Paulsen, "Augustine and the Corporeality of God," 105. This footnoted text includes the footnotes accompanying the quoted text from that same article.

From these passages, it is evident that in his youth and probably until his early thirties, Augustine understood Christians to believe that God is embodied.[117]

In two ways, Kim Paffenroth has recently challenged this view of Augustine's arguments. He claims that young Augustine's references to Christian belief in an embodied deity are either merely allusions to the Incarnation or misunderstandings caused

---

117. Griffin and Paulsen, "Augustine and the Corporeality of God," 104. Augustine says that at the time of his conversion to Manichaeism, "'I had not realized that God is a Spirit, not a figure whose limbs have length and breadth and who has a mass' (Conf. 3.12.12). The Manichaeans conceived of God as a being of light, corporeal in the Stoic sense, but not a 'figure' with 'limbs.' On Manichaean doctrine, see Samuel N. C. Lieu, *Manichaeism in the Later Roman Empire and Medieval China: A Historical Survey* (2d ed.; Tübingen: Mohr, 1992), and François Decret, *L'Afrique manichéenne, IVe–Ve siècles: étude historique et doctrinale* (2 vols.; Paris: Études augustiennes, 1978)" Griffin and Paulsen, "Augustine and the Corporeality of God," 104 n. 39. Paulsen and Griffin further write: "While in other works he argues explicitly against Manichaean corporealism, here Augustine assigns no real antagonist to the opposing view (Evodius is obviously a rhetorical fiction). Supposing there is an antagonist external to himself and the source of his own error, one is led to ask if he is addressing, not simply (non-Christian) Stoic or Manichaean corporealism, but that Christian corporealism of which we have made mention. Tertullian had said, 'Nothing is incorporeal except that which is nothing,' and this very belief was for the young Augustine 'the principal and almost sole cause of my error.' It may be that Tertullian's views on corporeality were prevalent among African Christians. If Teske and others are correct, they were prevalent not just among Africans but Western Christians in general, for 'there simply was no spiritual concept of God or of the soul in the Western Church' at this time outside of a small group of *platonici*." Griffin and Paulsen, "Augustine and the Corporeality of God," 106–7.

by Manichaeans who, intent on discrediting Christian beliefs, misrepresented them.[118] However, the fact that young Augustine understood that Christians believed that God was embodied—and not merely as the incarnate Son—seems beyond dispute, for according to Augustine's own account, the scriptural warrant for Christian belief in divine embodiment was largely found in the Old Testament and, hence, was not based on the Incarnation alone. For instance, he disclosed that it was only after he met Ambrose in Milan that he learned that God's "spiritual children . . . do not understand the words *God made man in his own image* to mean that [God is] limited by the shape of a human body."[119]

Moreover, that Augustine, as a result of Manichaean misrepresentations, for many years simply misunderstood what Christians of his acquaintance believed seems incredible. How could he be so radically mistaken when his own mother was a Christian, when he grew up among Christians, and when he even studied Christian catechism? But quite apart from inference, Augustine provided considerable evidence of Christian belief in an embodied deity.

Augustine discussed "the carnal and weak of our faith, who, when they hear the members of the body used figuratively, as, when God's eyes or ears are spoken of, are accustomed, in the license of fancy, to picture God to themselves in a human form." Though Augustine found laughable these Christians' belief that God has "a human form which is the most excellent of its kind," he nonetheless found their belief more "allowable" and "respectable" than the Manichaean alternative. Moreover, unlike the Manichaeans, Augustine said that these "carnal" Christians are

---

118. Kim Paffenroth, "Paulsen on Augustine: An Incorporeal or Nonanthropomorphic God?" *Harvard Theological Review* 86 (1993): 233–35.

119. Augustine, *Confessions* 6.3 (114); emphasis in original.

teachable and, with proper instruction in the Church, may gradually come "to understand spiritually the figures and parables of the Scriptures."[120]

Furthermore, Augustine provided a catalogue of heretical Christian communities or sects.[121] He identified two Christian communities, contemporary with himself, that explicitly taught that God is embodied in humanlike form. Members of the first community were called Audiani (sometimes Vadiani). They were followers of a Christian deacon, Audius of Edessa, and were located primarily in Syria and Mesopotamia. Members of the second community were called the Anthropomorphites and were located in Egypt. John Cassian, a Christian monk who spent about fifteen years (about AD 385–400) in the Egyptian monastic communities, corroborated Augustine's testimony with respect to Egyptian anthropomorphism. Although Cassian was an Origenist and an incorporealist, he nonetheless made it clear that for late fourth-century Christian monks in Egypt, anthropomorphism was the long-established norm and incorporealism was the innovation.[122]

---

120. Augustine, "Against the Epistle of Manichaeus Called Fundamental," 23.25, in The Nicene and Post-Nicene Fathers, Series 1 (hereafter *NPNF*), ed. Philip Schaff (reprint, Grand Rapids, MI: Eerdmans, 1956), 4:139.

121. See Liguori G. Müller, *The De Haeresibus of Saint Augustine: A Translation with an Introduction and Commentary* (Washington, DC: Catholic University of America Press, 1956). Müller writes, "It becomes evident immediately in the *De Haeresibus* that Augustine envisioned a heresy as a concrete sect, not a heretical proposition, since he speaks of the individual members of the sect rather than of the tenets they hold" (50).

122. Otto F. A. Meinardus concludes that "anthropomorphists appear to have outnumbered the liberal party [the Origenists who preferred allegorical interpretations of the Scriptures] by at least

Cassian records that Theophilus, Bishop of Alexandria, sent a letter in 399 to the Egyptian churches to set the dates of Lent and Easter. In that letter, Theophilus included a condemnation of anthropomorphism, which,

> was received very bitterly by almost every sort of monk throughout all Egypt. . . . Indeed, the majority of the older men among the brethren asserted that in fact the bishop was to be condemned as someone corrupted by the most serious heresy, someone opposing the ideas of holy Scripture, someone who denied that almighty God was of human shape—and this despite the clear scriptural evidence that Adam was created in His image.[123]

Even the monks in Scete, "who were far ahead of all the Egyptian monks in perfection and knowledge,"[124] and all the priests except Paphnutius—an Origenist in charge of Cassian's church—denounced the bishop's letter. Those in charge of the three other churches in the desert refused to allow the letter to be read or publicly presented at their assemblies.

Cassian chronicled the particular struggles of one monk, Serapion, in accepting the view that God is not embodied. According to Cassian, Serapion had long lived a life of austerity and monastic discipline that, coupled with his age, had brought him into the front ranks of the monks. Despite the persistent efforts of Paphnutis to dissuade him, Serapion had held fast to his belief that God is embodied. The concept of a non-embodied God seemed newfangled to him. It was something unknown to his predecessors and not taught by them.

---

three to one." *Monks and Monasteries of the Egyptian Deserts,* rev. ed. (Cairo: American University in Cairo Press, 1989), 53.

123. Colm Luibheid, trans., *John Cassian: Conferences* (New York: Paulist, 1985), 125–26.

124. Luibheid, *Cassian: Conferences,* 126.

By chance, a well-versed anticorporealist deacon named Photinus visited Cassian's community in Scete. In order to support the condemnation of anthropomorphism contained in the bishop's letter, Paphnutis brought Photinus into a gathering of all the brethren and asked him how the Catholic churches of the East interpreted the words in Genesis, "Let us make man in our image, after our likeness" (Genesis 1:26).

Photinus explained that all the leaders of the churches were unanimous in teaching that the image and likeness of God should be understood not in an earthly, literal sense but spiritually. In a lengthy discourse, Photinus attempted to demonstrate to Serapion the truth of this teaching.

> At last the old man was moved by the many very powerful arguments of this extremely learned man. . . . We stood up to bless the Lord and to pour out our prayers of thanks to Him. And then amid these prayers the old man became confused, for he sensed that the human image of God which he used to draw before him as he prayed was now gone from his heart. Suddenly he gave way to the bitterest, most abundant tears and sobs. He threw himself on the ground and . . . cried out: "Ah the misfortune! They've taken my God away from me. I have no one to hold on to, and I don't know whom to adore or to address."[125]

According to Owen Chadwick, Cassian's description of Serapion's capitulation greatly understated the resoluteness of Egyptian resistance to Theophilus's decree proscribing anthropomorphism. Chadwick writes:

> Were Cassian the sole authority, the impression would be left that, despite the fierce opposition of great numbers, the decrees of Theophilus were ultimately accepted by the Egyptians. We hear nothing in Cassian of the riots in Alexandria, of the bishop's submission, of the expulsion of Origenism.

---

125. Luibheid, *Cassian: Conferences*, 126–27.

Except in Cassian's community in Scete, where Paphnutius succeeded in bringing round his congregation to the Origenist viewpoint, a violent agitation arose. A band of monks repaired to Alexandria and caused riots. Theophilus had courage. He went out to meet the approaching band, and, as soon as he could make himself heard, "When I see you," he said, "I see the face of God". "Then," said the leaders, "if you really believe that, condemn the works of Origen." Theophilus, whom Palladius nicknamed "Mr. Facing-both-ways", consented on the spot to condemn the Origenists. . . . He sent letters to his suffragans ordering the expulsion of the Origenist monks from the monasteries and the desert. There appear from this moment a drift out of Egypt by some members of the now condemned Origenist party.[126]

Finally, Augustine provided evidence that fourth- and fifth-century Christian anthropomorphism was not confined to priests, monks, and laity. For instance, in "A Letter of Instruction to the Holy Brother, Fortunatianus (Epistle 148)," written in AD 413, Augustine discussed an unnamed brother bishop who was teaching that we are able, or at least will be able after the Resurrection, to see God with the eyes of our bodies. In a prior letter, without mentioning the bishop by name, Augustine had

---

126. Owen Chadwick, *John Cassian*, 2nd ed. (Cambridge: Cambridge University Press, 1968), 28–29. On the causes of the controversy and the subsequent expulsion of Origenists, see Elizabeth A. Clark, *The Origenist Controversy: The Cultural Construction of an Early Christian Debate* (Princeton: Princeton University Press, 1992). Chapter 2 focuses on anthropomorphism. For a tentative questioning of the generally accepted view that the Egyptian monks believed in an embodied God, see Graham Gould, "The Image of God and the Anthropomorphite Controversy in Fourth Century Monasticism," in *Origeniana Quinta*, ed. Robert J. Daly (Leuven, Belgium: Leuven University Press, 1992), 549–57.

sharply rebuked those who held this view, and the bishop had been offended. Augustine asked Fortunatianus's intercession on his behalf in seeking the bishop's forgiveness and in effecting reconciliation. Nonetheless, Augustine said he had no regrets about having written the letter, for his intent was to

> prevent men from believing that God Himself is corporeal and visible, as occupying a place determined by size and by distance from us (for the eye of this body can see nothing except under these conditions), and to prevent men from understanding the expression "face to face" as if God were limited within the members of a body.[127]

Thereupon, Augustine argued at length against the bishop's view.

On the basis of the evidence detailed above, it seems clear that Christians, from the very inception of the faith up until at least the early part of the fifth century, commonly believed God to be an embodied being. This belief continued despite the fact that it was challenged by both Christian and non-Christian Platonists from at least the time of the second century. As Platonism became entrenched as the dominant Christian worldview, the idea of an embodied God gradually faded into obscurity.

Conclusion

Precisely what happened to disrupt the primitive Christian belief in an embodied God has not received exhaustive treatment here but is dealt with elsewhere in this volume. My concern was simply to establish that, contrary to contemporary

---

127. Augustine, *Letters of St. Augustine* 148.1.1 (*NPNF* 1:498). Note also that the bishop's basis for his belief was apparently Old Testament, not incarnational, passages about God.

misunderstanding, the belief in divine embodiment did in fact exist and persist among the faithful followers of Christ from Christianity's earliest beginnings into the fifth century AD. Such a belief was not only *not* heretical, but apparently was the widely held understanding of God within both formative Judaism and Christianity for the greater part of the first three centuries. This understanding was gradually abandoned as Neo-Platonism became the dominant worldview of Christian thinkers. Far from being a departure, then, from the faith once delivered to the saints, Joseph Smith's declaration of divine embodiment is a sign of the "times of refreshing . . . the times of restitution of all things" (Acts 3:19, 21). It is the return to, even the restoration of, the primitive Christian knowledge of "the only true God" (John 17:3).

Substantial portions of this paper were drawn from the following writings by this same author: "Must God Be Incorporeal?" *Faith and Philosophy* 6/1 (1989): 76–87; "Early Christian Belief in a Corporeal Deity: Origen and Augustine as Reluctant Witnesses," *Harvard Theological Review* 83 (1990): 105–16; "Reply to Kim Paffenroth's Comment," *Harvard Theological Review* 86 (1993): 235–39; "The Doctrine of Divine Embodiment: Restoration, Judeo-Christian, and Philosophical Perspectives," *BYU Studies* 35/4 (1996): 6–94; "Augustine and the Corporeality of God," *Harvard Theological Review* 95 (2002): 97–118 (with Carl Griffin), reprinted by permission. Student assistants Marc-Charles Ingerson, Matthew Fisher, Spencer Noorlander, and David Vanderbeek have each contributed to the preparation of this paper. Laura Rawlins, Manager of Faculty Editing for the College of Humanities, assisted with final polishing and editing.

The Decline of Covenant in Early Christian Thought

Noel B. Reynolds

In the late fourth century John Chrysostom (347–407) described Christian baptismal rituals in which the converts would stand and face west while renouncing Satan, and then turn east to declare their belief in the Father, Son, and Holy Ghost. This verbal act was referred to as the candidate's "contract" (*suntheke*)—a term which is repeated more than twenty times in Chrysostom's *Baptismal Instructions*.[1] This ancient Christian ritual of renouncing the devil was associated with convert baptism in several sources through much of Christian history, which illustrates dramatically how ritual forms can persist long after their original meanings have been lost.

Nor was the ritual a late invention. Writing almost two centuries earlier, Tertullian (155–225) describes the same pre-baptismal ceremony: "When we are going to enter the water, but a little before, in the presence of the congregation and under the hand of the president, we solemnly profess that we disown the

---

1. Hugh M. Riley, *Christian Initiation* (Washington, DC: Catholic University of America Press, 1974), 92.

devil, and his pomp, and his angels. Hereupon we are thrice immersed."[2] Tertullian admits there is no scriptural basis for the ritual but justifies it as an ancient practice, "confirmed" by tradition. The writings of other third and fourth century writers support his claims. Hippolytus uses the standard language when he writes that through the ritual of confession and baptism, one "renounces the devil, and joins himself to Christ . . . puts off the bondage, and puts on the adoption."[3] Cyril of Jerusalem (d. 387) discusses the ritual in some detail, calling it a breaking of the covenant with Satan, with the clear suggestion that it was to be replaced by a covenant with Christ.[4] Basil (329–379) also makes reference to the rite of renunciation and profession. In his condemnation of those who deny the spirit, Basil points back to the confession and renunciation made before baptism and accuses the transgressors of "having violated the covenant of their salvation."[5]

Though not commonly known, this kind of ritual makes perfect sense to Latter-day Saints who understand their relationship with the divine in terms of personal covenants they have made with God. Further, they understand these covenants to be equivalent or even identical to the covenants made by Adam and the saints of God in every dispensation of the gospel since Adam's time. God's plan of salvation was set forth before this world was and has always been the same,

---

2. Tertullian, *De Corona (The Chaplet)*, in *The Ante-Nicene Fathers* (hereafter *ANF*), ed. Alexander Roberts and James Donaldson (Peabody, MA: Hendrickson, 1995), 3:94.

3. Hippolytus, *The Discourse on the Holy Theophany*, *ANF* 5:237.

4. Cyril of Jerusalem, *Catechetical Lectures XIX*, in *Nicene and Post-Nicene Fathers* (hereafter *NPNF*), ed. Philip Schaff (Peabody, MA: Hendrickson, 1995), 7:144–46.

5. *Basil, NPNF* 8:17.

however much the particular experience of successive dispensations might have differed. But, as will be demonstrated,
this prebaptismal ritual apparently lasted as a Christian practice far beyond the time when baptism was understood to be
linked to a fundamental covenant undertaken by repentant
converts. By the time any of the writers quoted above were
involved, baptism and the other ordinances had all been
transformed theologically into sacraments, none of which
were understood to be based in covenants. So when we look
closely at the writings of the earliest Christians, we might
naturally ask, "Where have all the covenants gone?" Though
the writings of this period occasionally allude to covenants
and even occasionally feature them, there is nowhere evidence that the concept of ordinances based in covenants is
either central or pervasive.

While the defining treatment of the Christian apostasy in
the Book of Mormon predicts that the covenants will be removed or lost (see 1 Nephi 13:26), this key element has never
been systematically explored in Latter-day-Saint thought. I
will show that the covenantal understandings of ordinances
were lost or de-emphasized very early, and that this change
made the later accommodation of Greek philosophy much
easier for the third- and fourth-century Christians. But that
only exacerbated the problem. As Christian thinkers turned
increasingly to Greek philosophy after the mid-second century, they naturally shifted from the traditional Hebrew focus
on history, including the covenants made at specific times and
places, as a source of truth and obligation, to the Hellenistic
contemplation of nature as a source of universal truth. And
this shift solidified the attenuation of covenants in Christian
thought and practice for the centuries that would follow.

The Absence of Covenant in Early Christianity

The Latter-day Saint concept of the sacred ordinances links them fundamentally to covenants. Baptism is "a witness and a testimony before God, and unto the people" (3 Nephi 7:25), that the candidate has repented and covenanted to obey the commandments of God and to take the name of Christ upon him (Mosiah 18:10). Confirmation publicly fulfills the eternal covenant of the Father—given to his spirit children before this world was—by which he promised to all who will repent and be baptized that he will bless them with his Spirit. The sacrament is a frequently repeated ordinance which enables the faithful to explicitly renew the covenant by witnessing again to the same things they first witnessed at their baptisms. Ordination to the priesthood establishes publicly that the recipient has entered into a special covenant to obey the Lord and labor in his service in love (D&C 84:39–41). And marriage explicitly stands on a covenant made between the husband and wife, individually and collectively with their Father in heaven, with great blessings promised by him for their future faithfulness in keeping that covenant. To lose the essential connection of each of these ordinances to these basic covenants would be to transform fundamentally the way in which the faithful would understand their relationship to their God.

Yet that seems to be exactly what happened in the first Christian century. The earliest Christian writings on the ordinances, including the *Didache,* Ignatius (d. ca. 110), Justin Martyr (d. ca. 163), and Irenaeus (ca. 115–202) barely hint at a covenantal understanding of the ordinances. For the most part, the explicit covenantal language Latter-day Saints would expect is almost completely absent. Across the centuries, there were sufficient echoes of the covenantal concept of ordinances to support LDS expectations that it must have been present originally.

In the second century, Justin Martyr mentions "promises" to live up to God's expectations that were associated with baptism. And in the fourth century John Chrysostom explicitly discusses repentance and baptism as a contract with Jesus and describes an elaborate ceremony depicting this to be conducted at the time of a convert's baptism. Basil, also in the fourth century, even referred briefly to the "covenant of baptism."[6] The short-lived resurgence of the rite in the fourth century, as evidenced in the writings of Chrysostom, Cyril, and Ambrose (339–397), may explain the contemporary spike in covenant language in the writings of Chrysostom, Gregory of Nanzianzus (329–390), and Basil. In the Protestant Reformation a millennium later, Zwingli (1484–1531) and his successor Bullinger (1504–1575) clearly promoted the concept that baptism was the public affirmation of a private covenant made by the individual Christian convert.[7] But their effort made little significant impact on the larger Christian world, which seemed to have excised the notion of personal covenants from its understanding of ordinances and of Christian life generally.

The scarcity of covenant language in Christian discussions of the ordinances may explain why Tertullian's introduction of the word *sacraments* to refer to the ordinances was so quickly adopted. Because *sacramentum* was the term Roman armies used for the oath of loyalty that soldiers made to their commanders, it might well have signaled to Christians an earlier covenantal context for their ordinances. All of the original Christian ordinances were transformed into noncovenantal

---

6. *Basil, NPNF* 8:21–23.

7. For a detailed report and analysis of these sources, see Bryson L. Bachman and Noel B. Reynolds, "Traditional Christian Sacraments and Covenants," in *Prelude to the Restoration: From Apostasy to the Restored Church* (Salt Lake City: Deseret Book, 2004).

sacraments before the third century. Instead of communicating new covenants, or even fealty relationships, sacraments were understood to be the means by which infusions of divine grace could be transmitted to the recipient through the mediation of a priest. The recipient made no commitments, but only needed to request the sacrament. And in the case of infant baptism and last rites, someone else could make this request or decision for the recipient. The balance of theological authority over the centuries insisted that these sacraments would be effective for any recipients who did not actively create obstacles to their reception.[8]

If the results of this preliminary study hold up in more detailed analyses, the third-century hellenization of Christianity will prove to be an anticlimax for covenant theology. The crucial covenantal understandings of the Christian ordinances did not survive even into the second century, thus severing the intensely personal links each individual might have with divine history and changing the structure of Christian teaching in a fundamental way. With truth and right no longer derived from these personal covenantal events, the Christian world was in far greater need of new, independent, and stable sources of truth than we have heretofore realized.

Truth in History and in Covenants Made with God

The ultimate dependence of truth and right on historical events and witnesses of those events is clear in both Jewish and Christian scriptures. The Hebrew scriptures record, and the Christian scriptures confirm, that God has repeatedly offered covenants to his people by which he bound himself to bless them and them to obey him. Some scholars believe there is evidence

---

8. Bachman and Reynolds, "Traditional Christian Sacraments and Covenants."

for an original "cosmic covenant" given to all men from the time of the creation.[9] More clear in the biblical tradition are the covenants given to Noah, Abraham, Moses, and David. The Jews in Jesus's day traced their genesis as a nation to the events at Sinai, in which they bound themselves by covenant with the Lord that he should be their God and they should be his people (Exodus 24:10, 27; Deuteronomy 4–5). The Book of Mormon features this same theme, referring repeatedly to "the covenant people of the Lord" (2 Nephi 30:2; Mormon 3:21; 8:15, 21).

This notion of covenant is central both to Old Testament theology and to Israel's self-conception as a nation. It was this historical event that united as a single entity the separate tribes that had fled Egypt.[10] Biblical accounts of the covenant at Sinai (and especially the extended treatment of it in the book of Deuteronomy) and its renewal under Joshua at Shechem (Joshua 24) are cast in the form of the ancient Hittite suzerainty treaties, by which a vassal king joined himself to a more powerful suzerain king.[11] A major element of these covenants is the recitation of the history of the parties involved and the provisions they

---

9. Robert Murray, *The Cosmic Covenant: Biblical Themes of Justice, Peace and the Integrity of Creation* (London: Sheed & Ward, 1992), xx–xxi.

10. The group certainly was not naturally homogenous. In addition to identifying themselves into twelve (or thirteen, if Ephraim and Manasseh are counted separately) distinct families, "whole groups of the population of Palestine must have entered *en bloc* into the Israelite federation." George F. Mendenhall, *Law and Covenant in Israel and the Ancient Near East* (Pittsburgh, PA: Biblical Colloquium, 1955), 36; see also 42. Newcomers were adopted by covenant into one of the tribes.

11. Because large numbers of treaties have survived only from the Hittite empire, Hittite treaties are our primary nonbiblical comparison source for ancient covenants. See Mendenhall, *Law,* 27–28.

both accept for the perpetuation of the covenant. A copy of the covenant is then placed in the temple and read periodically to the people, perhaps along with a ritual re-enactment. Thus the covenant itself is situated historically, looking both backward and forward; and those bound together by the covenant understand their relationship in terms of its history.

Biblical scholars generally believe that the original texts of the Pentateuch underwent significant revisions and rewritings, so it is difficult for them to determine whether the covenants originally exhibited the form of suzerainty treaties, or whether this form was later imposed on the text of Israel's sacred covenants. But whatever their form, for the ancient Israelites themselves the covenants were very real and tangible. Circumcision became a sign of the Abrahamic covenant, a reminder to the people of their covenantal obligations. The Sinai covenant was witnessed originally and renewed periodically by the shedding of animal blood. There was no place in this system for philosophizing about nature in pursuit of moral knowledge. God had revealed his commandments, and men had chosen to bind themselves to God—to keep those commandments. This choice was dated to a specific time and place, and involved both specific practice and periodic ritual renewal.

Another aspect of the secular covenants that seems to be in the content (not merely the form) of Israel's covenants with Jehovah is the curse formula. Jehovah's side of the covenant is everlasting, but Israel may break the covenant and incur the wrath of God. Many of the prophets warned Israel that she was breaking (or had broken) the covenant. Jeremiah taught that Israel's utter rejection of the covenant would leave Jehovah no choice but to reject her and establish a new covenant. This new covenant would not be written on stone, but would be written "in their hearts" (Jeremiah 31:33). Early Christians saw their movement as the fulfillment of this new covenant foretold by Jeremiah. Mark quotes Christ as saying, at the last supper, "This is my blood of the new covenant" (Mark 14:24).[12] Christ here repeats the rituals that formed Israel's acceptance of the Sinai covenant—shedding of blood and ritual meal: "And Moses took the blood, and sprinkled *it* on the people, and said, Behold the blood of the covenant, which the Lord hath made with you.... And they saw the God of Israel: ... and did eat and drink" (Exodus 24:8–11). Paul quotes Christ as saying, "This cup is the new testament in my blood: this do ye, as oft as ye drink *it,* in remembrance of me" (1 Corinthians 11:25). The Sacrament of the Lord's Supper is thus the primary means of renewal of the new covenant. It is ritual memory, serving the same purpose as the sacrifices under the Mosaic law.

Through the middle of the second century, leading Christian spokesmen appealed consistently to the theological priority of those events for the Christian faith. The great martyr Ignatius, while en route to his own execution at Rome, wrote repeatedly enjoining Christians in many places to stand firm against the false wisdom of those debaters who boasted of their own intelligence—by remembering the historical facts on which the Christian message was grounded. "Jesus the Christ was conceived by Mary according to God's plan." Further, he was born and baptized that by his suffering he might cleanse the water (of baptism) so that men could be freed from sin. He died, and he "appeared in human form to bring the newness of eternal life."[13] Writing to the Magnesians, Ignatius again emphasized the historical and physical reality of Christ's birth, suffering,

---

12. The King James Version has "new testament"; the word translated "testament" is *diatheke,* the word used in the Septuagint to translate Hebrew *berit,* "covenant."

13. "The Letter of Ignatius Bishop of Antioch to the Ephesians," in *The Apostolic Fathers,* trans. J. B. Lightfoot and J. R. Harmer, ed. and rev. Michael W. Holmes (Grand Rapids, MI: Baker, 1989), 92.

and resurrection.[14] To the Trallians he insisted that Jesus Christ was a descendant of David and son of Mary, "who really was born, who both ate and drank; who really was persecuted . . . , who really was crucified and died . . . , who, moreover, really was raised from the dead."[15] To the Smyrneans he clarified further: "For I know and believe that he was in the flesh even after the resurrection." Not only did Christ prove this to Peter and others by inviting them to touch and handle his hands and body, but "he ate and drank with them" after his resurrection.[16]

Ignatius thus exemplifies the early Christian practice of witnessing and confessing to the teaching of the church, through which he "expresses a commitment and an obligation, a bond and a claim."[17] As Otto Michel goes on to explain, these proclamatory statements "all find their starting point in an event of history vouched for by a specific tradition. They interpret this event and prevent its evaporation into myth and theory. In the confession of the community is a new and genuine historicity far surpassing all false traditionalism and intellectualism, all the non-obligatoriness of mere opinion and all mythology."[18] These physical and historical realities in the life of Christ were linked through his gospel and his atonement to the baptisms of his adherents, who at some point in time and space made that commitment to God and began their new lives as his disciples, giving Christianity a continuing reality in the historical present.

---

14. "Letter of Ignatius," 96.

15. "Letter of Ignatius," 100.

16. "Letter of Ignatius," 111.

17. Otto Michel, "ὁμολογέω, etc.," in *Theological Dictionary of the New Testament*, ed. Gerhard Kittel and Gerhard Friedrich, trans. Geoffry W. Bromiley (Grand Rapids, MI: Eerdmans, 1999), 5:212.

18. Michel, "ὁμολογέω, etc.," 5:212.

The Fading Covenants of the Early Christian Era

Mendenhall agrees that "the early Christians did regard themselves as a community bound together by covenant."[19] However, he concludes that cultural forces worked to shift the Christian basis away from covenant after the first century. The term *covenant* itself was charged with political significance: "The covenant for Judaism meant the Mosaic law, and for the Roman Empire a covenant meant an illegal secret society."[20] As a result, "the old covenant patterns [soon became] not really useful as a means of communication, and may have been dangerous in view of the Roman prohibition of secret societies."[21] The temple ceremonies were changed or abandoned;[22] the meaning of the sacrament was altered; and the notion of covenant was abandoned.

Daniel Elazar speculated further that in establishing orthodoxy and unity, the concept of covenant may have "presented a number of practical and theological problems" for Christians. The church, he said, "de-emphasized covenant especially after it believed that it had successfully superseded the Mosaic covenant and transferred the authority of the Davidic covenant to

---

19. George F. Mendenhall, "Covenant" in *The Interpreter's Dictionary of the Bible* (New York: Abingdon, 1962), 722. Because of its formal differences with the Hittite treaties, Mendenhall and his followers are wary of referring to the Christian mode of relationship to God as "covenant."

20. Mendenhall, "Covenant," 722

21. Mendenhall, "Covenant," 723.

22. Margaret Barker has argued convincingly that the earliest Christians were restoring the true temple tradition. See her *Temple Theology: An Introduction* (London: SPCK, 2004), 10. She points to Christian conflation of rituals and teachings that preserve the earliest temple teachings in one form or another.

Jesus. After Augustine (354–430), the Church paid little attention to covenant and, even though the Eucharist remained central to the Christian liturgy, it ceased to be a truly common meal and its covenantal dimension was overshadowed by other features and meanings attributed to the Last Supper."[23]

In spite of this early waning of the idea of covenant in Christianity, some third- and fourth-century writings evidence the persistence of covenant notions, however attenuated, within early Christianity. In particular, the rite of renunciation and profession included covenant undertones. The recurring verbal formula for the renunciation, which occurred before baptism, includes disowning "the devil, and his pomp, and his angels."[24] This renunciation is described by Tertullian,[25] who in one account adds that after the profession of disowning the devil, the baptismal candidate is immersed in water and makes a "pledge."[26] Supporting references by Hippolytus, Basil, and Cyril of Jerusalem are quoted in the opening paragraphs of this paper. John Chrysostom's (347–407) detailed description of the ritual made explicit the idea of a contract with Christ that baptismal candidates made before entering the waters of baptism. He tells how candidates would first face west to renounce Satan, and then east to declare their belief in the Father, Son, and Holy Ghost as well as in baptism. Hugh Riley concluded that for Chrysostom, "the notion of a contract is the central vehicle whereby he interprets the act of renunciation and profession. The term 'the contract (*suntheke*),' which

---

23. Daniel Elazar, *Covenant and Commonwealth: From Christian Separation Through the Protestant Reformation* (New Brunswick, NJ: Transaction, 1996), 2:32.

24. Tertullian, *De Corona, ANF* 3:94.

25. Tertullian, *De Spectaculis (The Shows), ANF* 3:79–91.

26. Tertullian, *De Corona, ANF* 3:94.

occurs more than twenty times in the *Baptismal Instructions* of Chrysostom, is used to interpret several aspects of the rite of renunciation and profession. The verbal act by which the candidate expresses his turning away from Satan and turning toward Christ is called by Chrysostom his 'contract.'"[27]

Interestingly, this ritual has in some form or another continued over time. Apparently referring to the same customary ceremony, Aquinas called it a vow.[28] The "renunciation of the devil" persists today in various attenuated forms as part of the baptismal ritual in many Christian traditions, including Anglican, Armenian, Eastern Orthodox, Jacobite, Coptic, and Ethiopic, but was repressed by Lutherans for fear it would perpetuate superstitious beliefs in the devil. Even the contractual nature of the rite persists in modern language as godfathers and godmothers take the vow on behalf of the infant being baptized.[29] The lack of a scriptural foundation for the ritual was addressed by Tertullian through appeal to widely accepted tradition,[30] and by other early writers through appeal to 1 Timothy 6:12: "thou hast professed a good profession before many witnesses."[31] But even this persistence of covenantal language has not prevented the ordinance of baptism from being redefined and understood as a sacrament. Within the theological system that had emerged by the fourth century,

---

27. Riley, *Christian Initiation*, 92.

28. Thomas Aquinas, *Summa Theologica* (New York: McGraw Hill, 1964), 39:159–201, esp. 163 (Question 88).

29. W. Gilmore and W. Caspari, "Renunciation of the Devil in the Baptismal Rite," in *The New Schaff-Herzog Encyclopedia of Religious Knowledge*, ed. Samuel M. Jackson (Grand Rapids, MI: Baker, 1977), 9:488–89.

30. Tertullian, *De Corona*, ANF 3:95.

31. Gilmore and Caspari, "Renunciation," see esp. 488.

Greek philosophical ideas left little room for personal covenants made with God.

Transition and Hellenization: Christian History in the Absence of Covenant

When he first forged the pattern followed later by hellenized Jews and Christians, Philo recounted the stories of both Abraham and Moses without any mention of their famous covenants.[32] Though the Jews in Diaspora produced some early sympathizers to this philosophical approach, the Palestinian Christians who arose in the first century did not appear to pay much attention, since they found adequate grounding for their beliefs and practices in the nonphilosophical positions of the Hebrew prophets as these were articulated and affirmed across many centuries. From the time of their Mosaic origins, Israelites were taught the dangers of religious syncretism and accommodation to the worship of other gods. Further, for them there was no doubt of Jehovah's moral authority or worthiness. And their ancient covenant with him provided a sure and adequate guide for conduct and moral relations with one another.

The New Testament provides ample evidence that it was the fervor of their commitment to that ancient covenant that prevented the majority of Jews from accepting Jesus Christ, who reaffirmed this tradition, yet reformed it to make the covenant individual and personal. Every Christian convert could point to the time and place where he or she had determined to forsake the ways of the world and had undertaken a new covenant with God (signaled publicly through baptism) to follow Jesus and obey his commandments. Not only was the world

---

32. See *The Works of Philo*, trans. C. D. Yonge (Peabody, MA: Hendrickson, 1993): "On Abraham," 418–19; "The Decalogue," 518, and "On the Life of Moses II," 496–97.

ordered by the covenant at Sinai, but now each Christian was linked to God by an individual covenant that similarly gave structure and grounding to all other understandings and expectations. Because Jesus was the son of God, this new approach was not thought to conflict with the old, but only to make it more elevated and feasible. By trusting and following him and the apostles and prophets he had provided for their instruction and direction, men and women could transcend the vagaries and imperfections of this life and be prepared for a future life with God.

Here is the crux of the matter. Platonists, Stoics, and other Greeks sought to transcend the uncertainties and instabilities of the world and human life as we actually experience it by positing a higher and governing reality that does not change. Once the focus on history and covenant was lost, this stability was exactly what both Jews and Christians needed in their theologies. Such a nature is not the creation of the gods, but sets the limits of all possibilities, including the divine. While that nature may not be readily experienced by mere mortals in its full reality, philosophical reason was thought to provide a means by which the wise can access its higher truths. And so it was that philosophy (and later science) gained favor as a means of overthrowing uncertainty and relativism. According to that perspective, history becomes less important. Because history is only past human experience, it might be characterized by the same types of imperfections seen in our present experience, and we escape or transcend its defects most effectively through the appeal to nature and reason. Many philosophers thought it doubtful whether a god was even needed in this system, or whether one could even exist. The hellenizers in both Judaism and Christianity followed the more theistically inclined philosophers and assumed a place for an absolute god in such a model. As Christian thought became hellenized, the concept of natural law gained predominance, and no significant role was left within Christian theology for the notion of covenants in history. The morality based on and understood in relation to covenants had been replaced by a morality that was supposed to be "naturally" defined and naturally discovered through reason. This Hellenistic approach was eventually completely and explicitly adopted in the work of Thomas Aquinas.[33] And it was not until the Protestant Reformation and the attempts to return to original pre-Hellenistic Christianity that the notion of covenant made even a modest comeback in Christian theologies—though in a novel form.

As nearly as I can determine, no one has yet attempted to construct a developed account of the connection between the early Christian revision or even abandonment of the notion of covenant, which was so central to ancient Israelite and early Christian understanding and theology, and this later process of hellenization. Hatch built his case against hellenized Christianity on its philosophizing of the concept of God and its incorporation of foreign rituals.[34] Adolf Harnack, in his attempt to recover the presuppositions of original Christianity and to contrast them with the philosophical doctrines that replaced them, focused on personal faith and spiritual experience as the common glue of the community, at the expense of any notion of covenant.[35] While my efforts might be seen

---

33. Aquinas, *Summa Theologica*, 40:3–9 (Question 92); 40:19–35 (Question 94); 40:37–69 (Question 95).

34. Edwin Hatch, *The Influence of Greek Ideas on Christianity* (New York: Harper, 1957), is the most readily available edition of the 1888 Hibbert lectures.

35. Adolf Harnack, *History of Dogma* (Eugene, OR: Wipf and Stock, 1997), 1:41–149.

as an extension of this same genre, I do not rely on these earlier approaches as I explore the unstated epistemological assumptions of the covenant framework of the Bible to show why these could be more easily exchanged for the rationalistic assumptions of a Platonized Stoicism once the focus on historical covenants had evaporated, leaving the Christians with a real need for new and stable standards of truth and virtue. Further, the studies demonstrating an earlier hellenization of Judaism, which probably contributed considerably to the eventual hellenization of Christianity by its Jewish converts, have paid little attention to the idea of covenants specifically.[36]

Traditional Christianity Turned to Hellenistic Thought in a Desperate Quest for Certainty and Stability

As traditional Christianity entered its third millennium, its theologians and historians had achieved rather general peace and reconciliation on one of the most contentious issues in its long tradition of self-interpretation. Tertullian first attacked the pride, vainglory, money-seeking, and theological wrangling in the early third-century church as the consequence of its budding romance with Greek philosophy and asked, "What indeed has Athens to do with Jerusalem?"[37] Since that time, Christian thinkers have repeatedly raised radical questions about the validity of a biblical tradition that has so extensively incorporated elements of the Greek philosophical tradition into its core theology. The early twentieth century saw these issues sharpened and strengthened in the works of

---

36. For a recent study of the Hellenism of Judaism and its effect on Christianity that brings together earlier scholarship on the subject, see Oskar Skarsaune, *In the Shadow of the Temple: Jewish Influences on Early Christianity* (Downers Grove, IL: InterVarsity, 2002).

37. Tertullian, *On Prescription Against Heretics*, ANF 3:246.

Edwin Hatch[38] and Adolf Harnack,[39] as well as many others, who have now been superseded by a tradition that finds more to celebrate than to criticize in what is without controversy regarded as Hellenistic Christianity.

The surprisingly irenic state of affairs that prevails among a broad spectrum of Christian writers in the early twenty-first century is a testament to the ability of Protestant thinkers particularly to broaden their view and find in the hellenization of Christianity after the third century the salvation of an orphaned and splintering Christian movement—and not its corruption. A recent history of Christian theology written from an evangelical perspective explains that had not the Christian apologists introduced philosophical categories into the defense and articulation of Christian teaching and practice, the church would have dwindled into a folk religion—languishing in cultic warfare and the ridicule of the intellectual and social elites of the Roman Empire.[40] As will be shown below, church fathers as early as Clement were embracing Greek philosophy as a parallel, divinely inspired movement. In their view, it was only through the union and integration of the two that Christianity could reach its highest and divinely intended form. It is less often noticed that these same apologists "had little to say about the historical Jesus."[41] This paper argues that the third- and fourth-century adoption of Greek philosophy as the language of Christian theology was only possible after the fundamental historical claims and understandings of the

---

38. Hatch, *Influence of Greek Ideas.*

39. Harnack, *History of Dogma.*

40. Roger E. Olson, *The Story of Christian Theology: Twenty Centuries of Tradition and Reform* (Downers Grove, IL: InterVarsity, 1999).

41. Olson, *Christian Theology,* 66.

first Christians, including their focus on covenant-based ordinances, had attenuated.

On all sides there is clear recognition of the basic facts. Before Clement of Alexandria, and during the first century and a half of Christianity, references to contemporary schools of philosophy by Christians served principally rhetorical functions in dealing with outsiders. Following a tradition going back to Paul (Acts 17:18–23), missionaries could cite beliefs of contemporary philosophers that were similar to the beliefs and practices of Christians as a means of introducing their own message. This was an attractive strategy because the philosophical community shared with the Christians a seriousness about living a good life and avoiding the vulgar excesses of pagan worship practices and the silliness of pagan mythologies. Second-century Christian apologists, such as Justin Martyr, found the philosophical beliefs of the Roman elites a most useful ground on which to defend their own religious beliefs and practices. In so doing, they paved the way for Clement of Alexandria, his student Origen, and their successors among third-century theologians to incorporate prevailing philosophical assumptions and methods into their understanding of Christianity.[42]

In the early second century, things were not going well for the increasingly divided Christians. The return of Christ was delayed. The generation of apostles and other eyewitnesses died. Then the disciples of that first generation died. No one had clear authority to speak for God. Christians in many areas experienced various forms of discrimination and even violent

---

42. One of the best accounts of these developments is to be found in Jaroslav Pelikan, *The Christian Tradition: A History of the Development of Doctrine*, Volume 1, *The Emergence of the Catholic Tradition (100—600)* (Chicago: University of Chicago Press, 1971), 25–41.

opposition or persecution. Entrepreneurial opportunists lured segments of the Christian community away to novel doctrines and practices. In the hope of persuading Roman elites to treat them with greater tolerance, Christian apologists wrote epistles and treatises arguing that the Platonized Stoicism of the times was not significantly different from the essential beliefs and practices of Christians. By the end of the second century, a few Christian thinkers were already turning to philosophy and adopting its rationalist strategy to stabilize and clarify their own tradition. And by the early fourth century, the marriage of Greek philosophy and Christianity was irreversible.

The twentieth-century reconciliation of Protestant and Catholic interpretations of hellenized Christianity would seem to vindicate the then-radical step taken by Clement of Alexandria near the end of the second century when he consciously adopted the rational methods of philosophy as the appropriate tools for Christians in pursuit of the truth. While this philosophical gambit was never uncontroversial, it spread rapidly throughout the Christian community and was both officially and firmly established by the time of the fourth-century councils as is especially clear in the creeds they produced. It is worth noting that Clement was consciously following the example of Philo, the Jewish philosopher and fellow Alexandrian from the early first century, who had allegorized the Old Testament systematically in his prolific writings to make it accord with contemporary forms of Greek philosophy.

Lacking faithful witnesses of the founding events of Christianity, Christians were left without authoritative voices to clarify scriptural ambiguities or to give divine direction in the resolution of new challenges for the community. Like his contemporaries, Clement recognized that "the prophets and apostles knew not the arts by which the exercises of philosophy are exhibited."[43] Rather, he explained, the prophets and disciples were of the Spirit and knew these things infallibly by faith. But this is not possible for others, says Clement, disagreeing with some of his own contemporaries who insisted on avoiding contact with philosophy, logic, or natural science, "demanding faith alone."[44] Clement saw their approach as both sterile and ignorant. He urged instead the cultivation of the vine (Christ)—watering, pruning, and tending it that it might bring forth good fruit. So by bringing all disciplines to bear on the truth (geometry, music, grammar, and philosophy itself), "he guards the faith against assault." Only one educated in these things "can distinguish sophistry from philosophy" or the varieties of philosophical teaching "from the truth itself." From this he concluded it is necessary "for him who desires to be partaker of the power of God, to treat of intellectual subjects by philosophizing."[45]

Clement quite explicitly claimed that Greek philosophy was divinely provided for Christianity in his times. He called Hellenistic culture "preparatory" and argued that "philosophy itself . . . (had) come down from God to men."[46] This preparatory movement was illustrated for all Israel in the case of Abraham, who attained wisdom by "passing from the contemplation of heavenly things to the faith and righteousness which are according to God." So also Hagar (the young and fruitful maiden) was given to Abraham that, by allegorical interpretation, he should "embrace secular culture as youthful, and a handmaid."[47] "Philosophy is characterized by investigation

---

43. Clement, *The Stromata, or Miscellanies,* ANF 2:310.
44. Clement, *Miscellanies,* ANF 2:309.
45. Clement, *Miscellanies,* ANF 2:310.
46. Clement, *Miscellanies,* ANF 2:308.
47. Clement, *Miscellanies,* ANF 2:306.

into the truth and the nature of things (this is the truth of which the Lord Himself said, 'I am the truth'); and that, again, the preparatory training for rest in Christ exercises the mind, rouses the intelligence, and begets an inquiring shrewdness, by means of the true philosophy, which the initiated possess, having found it, or rather received it, from the truth itself."[48] Hence the Christian view of philosophy as the (fruitful) handmaiden to theology.

Clement claimed not to be promoting any particular philosophical school of his day (Stoic, Platonic, Epicurean, or Aristotelian), but identified philosophy (the love of wisdom) with "whatever has been well said by each of those sects, which teach righteousness along with a science pervaded by piety,— this eclectic whole I call philosophy."[49] So rather than follow a particular non-Christian school, he strives to be "conversant with all kinds of wisdom" and bring "again together the separate fragments, and makes them one" in order that he might without peril "contemplate the perfect Word, the truth."[50] And so it was that Christianity—bereft of its eyewitnesses or even witnesses of its eyewitnesses—incorporated philosophy as an additional and much-needed source of truth and doctrinal stability.

Nature's Appeal as a Universal Standard

In seeking to understand why Christianity turned to Greek philosophy, it is helpful to consider what it was that the Greek philosophies had to offer a faltering Christianity. One of the most fundamental and perennially attractive contributions of early Greek thinkers was the concept of nature—the idea that behind all the variety and vagaries of human experience

---

48. Clement, *Miscellanies, ANF* 2:307.
49. Clement, *Miscellanies, ANF* 2:308.
50. Clement, *Miscellanies, ANF* 2:313.

there might be a solid, regular, and permanent reality. Nor did they limit this insight to the physical and material world, but rather they also glimpsed (or diligently sought) the possibility of finding ultimate truth in matters pertaining to human morality and the good. This was an important quest in a Greek world where the gods (whether Olympian or of the family hearth) served better as examples of human weakness than as models of moral aspiration—and where the popular intellectuals of the day were exploring the implications of the surging relativism that arose from growing intellectual independence from traditional thought and the explosion in awareness of the varieties of belief and values among the cultures of their rapidly expanding world.

Though he did not develop the potential connection, Jaroslav Pelikan did notice how hellenized Christianity no longer needed the covenantal perspective of Judaism.

> In Judaism it was possible simultaneously to ascribe change of purpose to God and to declare that God did not change, without resolving the paradox; for the immutability of God was seen as the trustworthiness of his covenanted relation to his people in the concrete history of his judgment and mercy, rather than as a primarily ontological category. But in the development of the Christian doctrine of God, immutability assumed the status of an axiomatic presupposition for the discussion of other doctrines.[51]

In 1888, Edwin Hatch launched the twentieth century debate over hellenized Christianity and argued that by the third Christian century a philosophical blend of views derived from Plato, Aristotle, Stoics, and Epicureans had attained the status

---

51. Pelikan, *Emergence of the Catholic Tradition,* 22.

of dogma among the educated classes of the Roman Empire and was widely regarded as possessed of universal validity. The "subjective and temporary convictions" of the original philosophers "were thus elevated to the rank of objective and eternal truths." Further,

> It came also to be assumed that the processes of reason so closely followed the order of nature, that a system of ideas constructed in strict accordance with the laws of reasoning corresponded exactly with the realities of things. The unity of such a system reflected, it was thought, the unity of the world of objective fact. It followed that the truth or untruth of a given proposition was thought to be determined by its logical consistency or inconsistency with the sum of previous inferences.[52]

Though now outdated in some respects, Thorleif Boman's widely regarded investigation of the differences between Greek and Hebrew ways of understanding the world still makes some valid points for our inquiry. Boman noticed the respective emphases on nature and history and agreed with Reinhold Niebuhr's observation that "the classical culture, elaborated by Plato, Aristotle and the Stoics, is a western and intellectual version of a universal type of ahistorical spirituality."[53] Boman identifies through linguistic analysis a fundamental contrast between these two cultures in that the Greek focus on *vision* and seeing leads to the association of truth with the unveiling of nature, of ideas and intellectual insight, while the Hebrew

---

52. Hatch, *Influence of Greek Ideas,* 121.

53. Thorleif Boman, *Hebrew Thought Compared with Greek,* trans. Jules L. Moreau (New York: Norton, 1960), 168–70. The Niebuhr quote is from *Faith and History: A Comparison of Christian and Modern Views of History* (New York: Scribner's, 1949), 16.

focus on *hearing* associates truth with subjective certainty, which is achieved by being steady and faithful.[54] What Boman did not notice was the Hebrew reliance on covenant as a means of establishing stable expectations in a changing world.

This new system of ideas proved irresistible to the Christians who were fighting heresy on every side—when they were not fending off persecution. The appeal to nature as a universal and immoveable standard and to reason as an objective mode of access to nature could free Christians from their awkward dependence on an increasingly remote and unproveable history of God's direct contacts and interventions with or revelations to his people.

The Book of Mormon Illuminates the Christian Covenant and Its Demise

The God of Hebrew and Christian scripture is portrayed as Lord of both nature and history and human beings—whom he regards as his children. He created the world specifically to provide these children with the experience of uncertainty and instability at the level of human experience. The only way for them to transcend the conditions of mortality was to turn to God and to entrust themselves fully into his care. God is both loving and powerful and provides guidance and protection from evil by means of the covenants which he offers to mankind. Through these covenants, God provides his earthly children with commandments and writes his law upon their hearts by his Spirit (Jeremiah 31: 33, as interpreted in Hebrews

---

54. Boman, *Hebrew Thought*, 200–204. Unlike Hatch and Harnack of an earlier generation, Boman chose not to see these as conflicting but as complementary ways of seeing the same underlying truth, as our five senses give us different access to the same world in which we live, p. 207.

8:10–11 and 10:15–17) as a means of countering their inevitable ignorance of what is right, or of what will lead to good in specific life situations.

Unfortunately, the nature and function of the covenant idea in biblical traditions has become more rather than less confused and controversial as scholars have worked on it over the years. There is as yet no clear agreement even as to the etymology or meaning of the Hebrew term for covenant (*berit*). And scholars widely believe that the covenant with Abraham was unilateral, not imposing an obligation of obedience on him or his descendants. Furthermore, theologians and scholars have not generally seen any connection or unity between the covenants of God with Adam, Noah, Abraham, and Israel at Sinai—or between any of these and Christian baptism. And while it is true that many Christians saw baptism as a replacement for circumcision, this view could not last long when baptism itself lost its covenantal basis. Some Reformation theologians such as Heinrich Bullinger attempted to recover the early concept of Christian covenanting, but their work never dominated mainstream Christian thought and was largely forgotten.[55] Small wonder that Nephi, in speaking of the scriptures as maintained by Christians after the apostasy, would emphasize that "they have taken away from the gospel of the Lamb *many parts which are plain and most precious*; and also *many covenants* of the Lord have they taken away" (1 Nephi 13:26).

The situation which Nephi reports is largely responsible for the continuing confusions and disagreements among scholars on these basic issues regarding the nature and role of covenant in the Christian and Jewish traditions. It is helpful at this point to turn to the Book of Mormon treatment of the covenant idea

---

55. See generally, Bachman and Reynolds, "Traditional Christian Sacraments and Covenants."

to get a clear notion of what, in fact, must have been taken away from the Bible. Nephi radicalizes the traditional notions of Israel's covenant with God by extending the covenant invitation to all peoples and making it an individual choice for each person: "For behold, I say unto you that as many of the Gentiles as will repent are the covenant people of the Lord; and as many of the Jews as will not repent shall be cast off; for the Lord covenanteth with none save it be with them that repent and believe in his Son, who is the Holy One of Israel" (2 Nephi 30:2) "[For] the covenant people of the Lord . . . are they who wait for him" (2 Nephi 6:13). Here we have a clear focus on repentance, a clearly reciprocal action, as the principal identifying feature of covenant establishment. The covenant people of the Lord are all those, and only those, who have turned away (repented) from their worldly ways by making a covenant with God to obey him and take his name upon them. This then is the covenant that Christians witness to publicly when they enter into the waters of baptism. As Alma explained at the waters of Mormon, "what have you against being baptized in the name of the Lord, as a witness before him that ye have entered into a covenant with him, that ye will serve him and keep his commandments?" (2 Nephi 6:13). And as was recorded by a later Nephi, the repentant "should be baptized with water, and this as a witness and a testimony before God, and unto the people, that they had repented and received a remission of their sins" (Mosiah 18:10). The prayers used by the Nephites in "administering the flesh and blood of Christ" unto the church, clearly constitute a renewal of this covenant as participants witness again "that they are willing to take upon them the name of thy Son, and always remember him, and keep his commandments which he hath given them" (3 Nephi 7:25).

This consistent Book of Mormon characterization of the ordinance of baptism as the public witnessing of an internal covenant made at the moment when an individual repents, relies directly on the plan of salvation. It assumes that the Father of all men has extended to each individual an open invitation to repent and come unto him. Further, he has promised, through the power of the atonement of Christ, to forgive all who repent and are baptized and to sanctify them through the cleansing power of the Holy Ghost—that all who endure through faith on his name to the end will receive eternal life. So the gospel of Jesus Christ articulates the terms of this covenant, as it applies to men.[56] The covenant is clearly bilateral since it requires a response from any who will become "the covenant people of the Lord." And Nephi clearly explains that it has been the same for all men in all times and places.

This is the core of what is rejected or lost when men rebel against the Lord, falling into apostasy—and clearly what was lost from Christianity by the second century. In the absence of true covenants, theologians still focused much of their religious discourse on the sacraments or ordinances of the church, but the emphasis was now on Christ's grace, the importance of the clergy, and the primacy of the church—and not on the covenantal relationship of the individual to God. While Christianity certainly still included a strong moralistic element, the basis of this morality was transferred from personal covenants to the commands of the church. This situation helps account for the fact that, with the exception of the rite of renunciation described above, no clear description of

---

56. See the analysis of the three Book of Mormon passages in which the Savior himself articulates this gospel or doctrine in Noel B. Reynolds, "The Gospel of Jesus Christ as Taught by the Nephite Prophets," *BYU Studies* 31/3 (1991): 31–50.

the Christian covenant survives in any New Testament text or in the teachings of the early Christian writers. With the Book of Mormon teaching in mind, we can see allusions to this idea of covenant throughout early Christian writing. But the allusions were insufficient to preserve the clear teaching, which has presumably been "taken away" (1 Nephi 13:26). The personal relationship element of the gospel was overshadowed and, in the centuries that followed, theological discourse would not include a prominent place for individual covenants with God.

The essence of covenantal relationships is that they are historical. They are artifacts of human and divine action at particular times and places. The principal New Testament term for covenant (*diatheke*) refers to the human activity of disposing of or arranging things by choice and by will.[57] The Israelites annually celebrated and re-enacted the covenant they had received at Sinai. Covenant renewal ceremonies emphasized the historicity of the originals they celebrated. Christians could tell you the date and place of their baptisms and, no doubt, the name of the particular authorized individual who had administered the ordinance in their behalf (1 Corinthians 1:12–16). Yet it was the commitment made to God that constituted these covenants—and not transcendent nature—that structured their moral universe. Grounding one's moral universe in historical events and human actions sounds like the sure road to relativism. But the Christians did not see this as a relativistic position. God's love, power, and goodness were all the security his children would need. Dependence on him, through the covenant relationship, is what provided their escape from the otherwise inescapable relativism and uncertainty that characterize life in this world. The combination of God's constant love

---

57. Gottfried Quell and Johannes Behm, "διατίθημι, διαθήκμ," in *Theological Dictionary of the New Testament*, 2:104–34.

and his children's consistent obedience was their answer to the dangers of a relativistic and morally uncertain world. Any attempt to validate the content of these covenants by appeals to reason or nature could be seen as an indication of weak faith or a failure to grasp the radical dependence on God and one's own commitment to him that the world of covenant required.

Conclusion

We have seen that the insight that late second- and early third-century theologians rearticulated Christian teaching in the language and categories of Greek philosophy is no longer controversial, and not even evangelical Protestant historians regret this development today. Rather, it is seen by a growing variety of Christians as a divinely enabled move that completed and preserved an endangered Christian movement, bringing it to its full glory as God's work. This paper assumes this historical hellenization of traditional Christianity and goes on to show that this development also replaced the earlier Christian and Jewish emphasis on history as the ground of truth and faith with a focus on nature and reason. The centrality of the Christian's covenant to repent of sin and obey God's commands had already been marginalized, and the traditional ordinances had lost their covenantal basis, being redefined as sacraments by which God's grace could be transmitted to a recipient through the mediation of a priest. The subsequent shift to a theology that found truth in nature through reason ensured that the original covenantal understandings of the Christian's relationship to the Father could never be recovered, though their echoes would reverberate hauntingly down through the ages, leading many dissatisfied Christians to long for a restoration of original Christianity.

Appendix A

Guide to Important Christian Documents and Writers from the Early Church to the Reformation[1]

Barry R. Bickmore

The purpose of this appendix is to provide a few basic background facts about Christian writers and documents that readers might find mentioned in this book, or other discussions of the great apostasy. Document titles are given in italics.

The Acts of Paul (ca. AD 185–195) According to Tertullian, this document was written by a presbyter in Asia Minor, who was expelled from his church for the forgery. The document itself contains nothing that would have been considered overtly heretical, except one passage where a female heroine, Thecla, baptized herself.[2]

---

1. Many of the entries are expanded from those found in the appendix of Barry R. Bickmore, *Restoring the Ancient Church: Joseph Smith and Early Christianity* (Ben Lomond, CA: Foundation for Apologetic Information and Research, 1999).
2. Willis Barnstone, ed. *The Other Bible* (San Francisco: Harper & Row, 1984), 445–47.

Ambrose of Milan (AD 339–397) Bishop of Milan, Ambrose
was elected when he was only a catechumen (one preparing to be baptized) because, as a political official, he was
instrumental in negotiating peace between the Arian and
Catholic Christians in the city. Ambrose was not an especially innovative theologian, but was instrumental in the
conversion of Augustine. His extant works include a number of sermons and treatises against Arianism, on church
ordinances, the Bible, and ministerial practice.[3]

Anselm of Canterbury (AD 1033–1109) A forerunner of Scho-
lasticism, Anselm was born in Italy and became a monk
in Normandy in 1060. In 1093 he became Archbishop of
Canterbury. He is most famous for his "ontological proof"
of the existence of God, first propounded in his *Proslogion*.
In brief, he argued that humans are thinking of God when
they conceive of "that than which no greater thing can be
thought." If so, and if this being is not real, then an existing being would be greater than "that which no greater
thing can be thought." Since this situation is absurd, God
(defined in this way) must exist.[4]

The Apocalypse of Abraham (ca. first century AD) A Jewish or
Jewish-Christian apocalypse preserved only in the Slavonic
language, *The Apocalypse of Abraham was* first published
in 1863. It is an account of some events in the patriarch

---

3. Henry Bettenson, ed. and trans., *The Later Christian Fathers: A
Selection from the Writings of the Fathers from St. Cyril of Jerusalem to
St. Leo the Great* (Oxford: Oxford University Press, 1970), 20–22.

4. Anne Fremantle, *The Age of Belief: The Medieval Philosophers*
(New York: Penguin Books, 1954), 88–97; Justo L. González, *The
Story of Christianity,* vol. 1, *The Early Church to the Dawn of the* Ref-
ormation (San Francisco: Harper & Row, 1984), 311–14.

Abraham's life, including various revelations. In one scene, Abraham has a vision of the pre-existent spirits of mankind.[5]

The Apostolic Constitutions (fourth century AD) This compilation of Christian teachings and practices includes canon law. The material included is of varying age, and some of it may be based on earlier source documents, such as the *Didache,* going back as early as the first century.[6]

Aquinas, Thomas (AD 1224–1274) A Dominican monk and professor of theology at the university in Paris, Aquinas is regarded, along with Augustine, as the greatest Catholic theologian of all time. His great accomplishment was to harmonize Aristotelian philosophy (which was becoming popular in Europe) with Catholic dogma. His literary production was enormous, but his most famous work is the *Summa Theologica.* This work, however, was never finished, because he stopped writing after he experienced things that made all he had written seem to be made "of straw."[7]

Arius (ca. AD 320) A presbyter (elder) of the church in Alexandria, his opposition to Bishop Alexander on the doctrine of the Trinity sparked the doctrinal controversy leading to the Council of Nicea in AD 325 and thirteen subsequent councils, culminating with the Council of Constantinople in AD 381. Arius took the traditional teachings that Jesus is subordinate to the Father, that God is an indivisible,

---

5. H.F.D. Sparks, ed., *The Apocryphal Old Testament* (Oxford: Clarendon, 1984,) 363–67.

6. Alexander Roberts and James Donaldson, eds. *The Ante-Nicene Fathers*, 10 vols. (Buffalo: The Christian Literature Publishing Company, 1885–1896), 7:387–88.

7. Fremantle, *The Age of Belief,* 144–79.

eternally unchanging substance, and that God created everything outside of himself from nothing to their logical conclusion—Jesus cannot be God in the strict sense and must have been created from nothing. Followers of this doctrine were called "Arians," and were the dominant Christian sect in parts of Europe for centuries.[8]

The Ascension of Isaiah (ca. first or early second century AD) This early Jewish-Christian apocryphal work was probably written in the first and second centuries AD. The first section, which deals with the martyrdom of Isaiah, is probably of Jewish origin and was written at least as early as the first century. The second section deals with Isaiah's vision and journey into the heavens. This probably had its origin in early second century Christianity.[9] Its Jewish-Christian provenance can be discerned by various details such as an anthropomorphic description of God.

Athanasius of Alexandria (ca. AD 300–373) Bishop of Alexandria from AD 328 to 373, Athanasius led the fight against the Arians at the Council of Nicea (AD 325) while a deacon under Bishop Alexander. Active in this controversy till the end of his life, Athanasius was exiled and readmitted as bishop several times during his career as the political winds changed to favor the Arians or Nicenes.[10] Some of his more important extant works include *Orations against the Arians* (*Orationes Contra Arianos*) and *On the Incarnation* (*De Incarnatione*).

---

8. Everett Fergusen, ed., *Encyclopedia of Early Christianity* (New York: Garland, 1990), 92–93.

9. Barnstone, ed., *The Other Bible*, 517–19.

10. Fergusen, ed., *Encyclopedia of Early Christianity*, 110–11.

Augustine of Hippo (AD 354–430) Augustine was bishop of Hippo in North Africa. Although his mother was a Christian, he did not convert until he was over thirty, after having been a Manichean and a Neoplatonist. One of the most prolific writers of early Christianity, Augustine was also one of its most important theologians.[11] His life's work was essentially to put Christian theology on what he saw as the solid foundation of Platonic philosophy.[12] Extant works are too numerous to list here, but prominent are *On the City of God* (*De Civitate Dei*) and *On the Trinity* (*De Trinitate*).

Basil of Caesarea (AD 330–379) Bishop of Caesarea from AD 360 to his death, Basil is considered an important theologian and monastic, especially in the Eastern Orthodox churches.[13] Surviving works are too numerous to list here, but include many sermons, letters, and treatises on theological and practical subjects, as well as two sets of rules for the monastic life.

Benedict (b. ca. AD 480) A Christian monk who founded the Benedictine order, his *Rule* was written as a model of life for his monastic community.

Book of the Secrets of Enoch: see "Enoch Literature."

Calvin, John (AD 1509–1564) Born in Noyon, France as Jean Chauvin, Calvin was the founder of the Calvinist system of theology prevalent in various Protestant sects. Calvin was the first great systematizer of Protestant theology. His most

---

11. Fergusen, ed., *Encyclopedia of Early Christianity*, 121–26.

12. Etienne Gilson, *Reason and Revelation in the Middle Ages* (New York: Scribner's, 1938), 16–24.

13. Fergusen, ed., *Encyclopedia of Early Christianity*, 139–40.

famous work, the *Institutes of the Christian Religion*, was first published in 1536 as a small book of six chapters. Over the years, Calvin added to subsequent editions, until the final 1559 edition consisting of four books with eighty chapters.[14]

1 Clement: see "Clement of Rome."

2 Clement (ca. AD 150) Second Clement is the oldest complete Christian sermon now extant. Although the author is unknown (and it certainly was not Clement of Rome), this document came to be associated with *1 Clement* by the fourth century.[15]

Clementine Homilies: see "*Pseudo-Clementines*."

Clementine Recognitions: see " *Pseudo-Clementines*."

Clement of Alexandria (AD 160–215) Clement was the head of the Christian catechetical school in Alexandria; one of his pupils was Origen. Clement tried to present the gospel in a manner that would be acceptable to the Greek mind, and to combat Gnosticism by presenting what he saw as the authentic secret knowledge in a somewhat veiled form. His work had a significant impact on later theologians.[16] Extant works include *The Instructor* (*Paedagogus*), *Miscellanies* (*Stromateis*), *Who is the Rich Man who is Saved?* (*Quis Dives Salvetur?*), *Exhortation to the Heathen* (*Protrepticus*), and a number of fragments.

Clement of Rome (Pope ca. AD 88–97) Second or third bishop of Rome, Clement reportedly knew Peter and had significant

---

14. González, *The Story of Christianity*, vol. 2, *The Reformation to the Present Day* (San Francisco: Harper & Row, 1984), 61–69.

15. Fergusen, ed., *Encyclopedia of Early Christianity*, 217.

16. Fergusen, ed., *Encyclopedia of Early Christianity*, 214–16.

influence even outside his own See. *First Clement*, which was written to exhort the Corinthian saints to resist certain factions that had arisen in opposition to the leadership of the Corinthian Church, has traditionally been attributed to Clement, although the author is not specifically identified. Its composition is usually dated to ca. AD 96.[17]

Cyprian (ca. AD 200–258) Elected bishop of Carthage in AD 248 or 249, Cyprian was involved in various schisms, persuading the various factions to preserve unity.[18] Surviving texts include several treatises such as *On the Unity of the Catholic Church* (*De Catholicae Ecclesiae Unitate*), *On the Lapsed* (*De Lapsis*), *To Donatus* (*Ad Donatum*), and a large number of letters.

Cyril of Jerusalem (d. AD 387) Elected bishop of Jerusalem ca. AD 349, his *Catechetical Lectures* (*catecheses*) were designed to explain the faith to catechumens (those who were studying to join the church) and to explain the sacraments (mysteries) of baptism and the eucharist to those who had just participated in them for the first time.[19]

Didache (late first or early second century AD) This document, whose full title translates as *The Teaching of the Lord through the Twelve Apostles to the Nations*, includes moral teachings and instructions for church practice. It was probably written in Syria or Egypt by Jewish Christians.[20]

---

17. Fergusen, ed., *Encyclopedia of Early Christianity*, 216–17.

18. Fergusen, ed., *Encyclopedia of Early Christianity*, 246–48.

19. Fergusen, ed., *Encyclopedia of Early Christianity*, 250–51.

20. J. W. C. Wand, *A History of the Early Church to AD 500* (London: Methuen, 1937), 24–25; Fergusen, ed., *Encyclopedia of Early Christianity*, 262; Ray R. Noll, *Christian Ministerial Priesthood: A Search for its Beginnings in the Primary Documents of the Apostolic Fathers* (San Francisco: Catholic Scholars Press, 1993), 34.

An early date is assigned to this work in part because it includes instructions for what to do when traveling prophets visit a local church.

1 Enoch: see "Enoch Literature."

2 Enoch: see "Enoch Literature."

Enoch Literature: Manuscripts of a body of literature based on the life and revelations of the biblical prophet Enoch have lately come to light, revealing that he was a favorite hero in Jewish apocalyptic literature. It has also become clear that many early Christian documents, including those in the New Testament, relied heavily on the language and teachings of these texts. The most well-known examples of this genre are *1 Enoch* and *2 Enoch (Secrets of Enoch)*; both documents are thought to have been written in the first two centuries before Christ, but parts of *1 Enoch* may be much older.[21] *1 Enoch* in particular was very respected in the early church. Not only did Jude quote from it in the New Testament, but it was considered canonical by many early Christians, including the author of *Barnabas*, Clement of Alexandria, Irenaeus, and Tertullian.[22]

The Epistle of Barnabas (late first or early second century AD) is an early letter by an unknown author attacking Judaism. It was traditionally attributed to Barnabas, the companion

---

21. See Margaret Barker, *The Lost Prophet: The Book of Enoch and Its Influence on Christianity* (London: SPCK, 1988).

22. Norman R. Cohn, *Cosmos, Chaos and the World to Come: The Ancient Roots of Apocalyptic Faith* (New Haven, CT: Yale University Press, 1993), 176; Barnstone, ed., *The Other Bible*, 485, 495; Rutherford H. Platt Jr., ed., *The Forgotten Books of Eden* (New York: Random House, 1980), 81.

of Paul, but this is unlikely.[23] The work has a definite Jewish-Christian outlook, which may help explain its overt antagonism to Judaism.

The Epistle of the Apostles (ca. AD 150) is an apocryphal work purporting to record a post-resurrection dialogue between Jesus and his Apostles. This was a literary form used extensively in Gnostic writings, but apparently the author of this work used it as a vehicle to propagate strongly anti-Gnostic views. For example, the work argues for the full humanity of Christ, the resurrection of the flesh, and the necessity of literal water baptism.[24]

Epistula Apostolorum: see "*The Epistle of the Apostles.*"

Erasmus, Desiderius of Rotterdam (AD 1466–1536) Erasmus was one of the leaders of the "humanist" movement that sought to revive classical learning and reform Christianity by a return to the New Testament and Patristic sources. When the Reformation broke out, both sides sought Erasmus as an ally, but while he sympathized with the Lutherans, he felt he could not follow them all the way. During his life, therefore, he was attacked by both Protestants and Catholics, but later it was recognized on both sides that Erasmus had something to teach them. One of his most famous works was *Handbook of the Christian Soldier* (*Enchiridion*

---

23. John G. Davies, *The Early Christian Church* (New York: Anchor Books, 1965,) 80; Wand, *A History of the Early Church to AD 500*, 40.; Richard Hanson, "The Achievement of Orthodoxy in the Fourth Century AD," in *The Making of Orthodoxy: Essays in Honour of Henry Chadwick*. ed. Rowan Williams (New York: Cambridge University Press, 1989,) 143–44.

24. Fergusen, ed., *Encyclopedia of Early Christianity*, 309.

Militis Christiani—Dagger), in which he used military met-
aphors to explain what he saw as the ideal Christian life.[25]
In 1516, Erasmus published a new Greek edition of the New
Testament that included information from recently discovered manuscripts, annotations, and a Latin translation. This
was the most scholarly study of the New Testament manuscripts produced up to that time, and it was later used by the
translators of the King James Version of the Bible. In 1517,
he wrote his best-known work, *In Praise of Folly*, which is a
satirical essay on the dominant religious beliefs of the day.[26]

Erigina, John Scotus (fl. AD 840–877) Born in Ireland, and exposed to the knowledge of antiquity that had been preserved
in the Irish monasteries, Erigina was one of the most erudite
and original thinkers of the medieval period. In AD 840, he
began teaching at the palace school of the Frankish king,
Charles the Bald. His greatest work, *The Division of Nature*,
has been said to be the synthesis of fifteen centuries of Western philosophical thought, and it is generally recognized
that it is more Neoplatonic than Christian.[27]

Eusebius of Caesarea (ca. AD 260–339) Bishop of Caesarea, his
most famous work was his *Ecclesiastical History*, and, indeed, he was the first major historian of Christianity. Many
fragments of early writings that are otherwise lost can be

---

25. Gonzalez, *Story of Christianity*, 2:10–13.

26. For more complete background information on Erasmus,
see Erika Rummel, *Erasmus* (New York: Continuum, 2004); and
C. Augustijn, *Erasmus: His Life, Works, and Influence*, trans. J. C.
Grayson (Toronto: University of Toronto Press, 1995).

27. Fremantle, *The Age of Belief*, 72–87; González, *Story of Christianity*, 1:269–70.

found in Eusebius's writings.[28] Other extant works include a glowing history of Emperor Constantine, *The Proof of the Gospel*, and *Preparation for the Gospel*. The latter has many valuable quotations of Greek philosophical works that are otherwise lost.

The Gospel of Philip (third century AD) This is a collection of statements concerning ordinances and ethics which probably originated with the Valentinian Gnostics in Syria and was most likely used to prepare investigators for initiation rites.[29] Some of the rites referred to evidently included something similar to the Latter-day Saint endowment and marriage ceremony in a mirrored bridal chamber.

The Gospel of Thomas (late first century AD) Many scholars feel that this collection of sayings of Jesus is closely related to the hypothetical source of the gospel narratives in the New Testament. Many of the parables and sayings of Jesus found in the Gospels appear in the Gospel of Thomas as well but in an apparently more primitive form. It was probably written in the second half of the first century AD, but the version available today may not be original. Clearly some Gnostic influence has been exerted on the text, but the extent of this influence is not clear.[30]

Gregory of Nazianzus (ca. AD 329–390) Bishop of Constantinople, Gregory was instrumental, along with Hilary of Poitiers, Basil of Caesarea, and Gregory of Nyssa, in

---

28. Fergusen, ed., *Encyclopedia of Early Christianity*, 325–27.

29. Barnstone, ed., *The Other Bible*, 87–88.

30. Barnstone, ed., *The Other Bible*, 299–300; Bart D. Ehrman, *Lost Christianities: The Battles for Scripture and the Faiths We Never Knew* (Oxford: Oxford University Press, 2003), 55–65.

negotiating the final Trinitarian position and related issues.[31] His extant works include 245 letters, 45 orations or sermons, and a number of poems.

Gregory of Nyssa (ca. AD 331–395) Elected bishop of Nyssa in AD 372, Gregory was an extremely influential theologian, heavily involved in the fight against extreme forms of Arianism. He was very acquainted with the Greek philosophy of the day, especially Middle Platonism and Neoplatonism, and he put this education to use in his theological speculations. His major theological accomplishment was to elaborate on the concept of the fundamental distinction between God and created beings and to exclude from mainstream Christian belief any concept of subordinationism. His brother, Basil of Caesarea, was also a noted theologian.[32] His extant writings are too numerous to list here, but include important treatises such as *That There Are Not Three Gods* (*quod non sint tres dii*) and a number of sermons.

Gregory the Great (Pope, AD 590–604) Bishop of Rome (Pope Gregory I) amid a very troubled political scene, he is remembered as a champion of Catholic orthodoxy and for strong leadership when the political structure of Rome was dissolving. He also strengthened the Papacy and promoted monasticism. His writings are too numerous to list here.[33]

Hermas (fl. early second century AD) Herman was the brother of an early bishop of Rome and author of the document known as the *Shepherd of Hermas* or the *Pastor of Hermas*. This

---

31. Fergusen, ed., *Encyclopedia of Early Christianity*, 397–400.

32. Fergusen, ed., *Encyclopedia of Early Christianity*, 400–402.

33. J. N. D. Kelly, *The Oxford Dictionary of Popes* (Oxford: Oxford University Press, 1986), 65–68.

work describes a series of visions given to Hermas in which an angel sometimes appeared as a shepherd. The *Shepherd* was considered canonical by many Christians for centuries.[34] The fact that this document, which did not claim authorship by the apostles or their associates, was considered canonical shows that many early Christians were open to the idea of continuing revelation.

Hippolytus (ca. AD 170–236) A presbyter (elder) at Rome who led a schism against the bishop of Rome, becoming the first "anti-Pope," his most important work, *The Refutation of All Heresies*, describes a large number of heretical groups.

Ignatius of Antioch (d. ca. AD 110) During the reign of Trajan, while bishop of Antioch, Ignatius was arrested and martyred. On the journey to Rome, Ignatius wrote seven letters that have been preserved. One purpose of the letters seems to have been to establish the authority of the bishops.[35]

Irenaeus of Lyons (ca. AD 115–202) Bishop of Lyons and a student of Polycarp, Iraenaeus's most famous work is *Against all Heresies* in which his major concern was to stop the spread of Gnosticism in Christianity.[36] Another important work is *Proof of the Apostolic Preaching.*

Jerome (ca. AD 345–420) One of the most famous early Christian scholars, Jerome is best known for his Latin translation of the Bible, known as the Vulgate.

---

34. Davies, *Early Christian Church*, 81; Fergusen, ed., *Encyclopedia of Early Christianity*, 421.
35. Fergusen, ed., *Encyclopedia of Early Christianity*, 451–52.
36. Fergusen, ed., *Encyclopedia of Early Christianity*, 471–73.

Jeu, Two Books of: An early third-century Egyptian Gnostic work, the *Books of Jeu* claim to be a record of some conversations between Jesus and his disciples after his resurrection. A Coptic manuscript was discovered in 1769, and published in 1891.[37]

John Chrysostom (ca. AD 347–407) Chrysostom was bishop of Constantinople from 398 till shortly before his death. Chrysostom means "golden-mouthed," and refers to John's reputation as the greatest preacher in early Christianity. John took some uncompromising moral stances and even criticized the empress for the opulent life of the court.[38]

Justin Martyr (d. ca. AD 163) A second-century Christian apologist and theologian, Justin established a Christian school in Rome. He had been educated in philosophy before his conversion and afterward continued to wear his philosopher's cloak. His works show a tendency to harmonize Middle Platonic philosophy with Christian doctrine, but also retain many archaic elements. Justin was condemned, scourged, and beheaded by the Romans when he would not deny his faith and sacrifice to the pagan gods.[39] His best-known extant works include the *Dialogue with Trypho, a Jew*, which argues that Christianity is the fulfillment of the Old Testament, the *First Apology*, and the *Second Apology*, which were written to the Roman Emperors in defense of Christianity.

---

37. Wilhelm Schneemelcher, ed., *New Testament Apocrypha*, trans. A. J. B. Higgins and others (Philadelphia: Westminster, 1963), 1:259–61.

38. Fergusen, ed., *Encyclopedia of Early Christianity*, 495–97.

39. Wand, *A History of the Early Church to AD 500*, 54; Fergusen, ed., *Encyclopedia of Early Christianity*, 514–16.

Leo the Great (Pope AD 440–461) Bishop of Rome (Pope Leo I), he is remembered for strengthening the position of the papacy, strong opposition to heretical movements, personal courage, and for settling the controversy over whether Christ has one or two natures. Leo's *Tome* was written to Flavian of Constantinople to explain the doctrine of the two natures. The *Tome* was read at the Council of Ephesus in AD 449, where Leo's point of view was rejected, and the Council of Chalcedon in AD 451, where the decision at Ephesus was reversed.[40]

Luther, Martin (AD 1483–1546) Founder of the Lutheran churches, Luther was a Roman Catholic monk who sought the reformation of Catholicism. Luther ended up leading a schism that began the Protestant Reformation. While teaching at the University of Wittenberg, Luther became convinced of the need to reform the church, especially its teachings about grace, works, and salvation. He composed a set of ninety-seven theses designed to stir up academic debate on such issues, but there was little response. Later, Luther wrote another set of ninety-five theses in 1517 that unleashed a firestorm of debate, mainly because the sale of indulgences was included as an issue. The publication of the *95 Thesen* is generally considered the beginning of the Reformation. Luther's works are too numerous to mention here, but include a German translation of the Bible, various commentaries, voluminous correspondence, and theological treatises.[41]

---

40. Kelly, *Oxford Dictionary of Popes*, 43–45.
41. González, *Story of Christianity*, 2:6–45.

Melito of Sardis (ca. AD 170) Bishop of Sardis, Melito was one of the most voluminous writers of the second century, but only fragments of his works survive.[42]

Novatian (ca. AD 200–258) A presbyter (elder) in Rome, Novatian believed the holiness of the church was threatened by the readmission of apostates. He led a schism and was ordained counter-bishop (anti-Pope) by three other Italian bishops. He had a formidable reputation as a theologian, and his treatise on the Trinity is considered the greatest Christian theological treatise from the West before 350.[43] The movement he started spread widely, persisting into the fifth century. The Novatianists were orthodox in doctrine, except for their teaching that there could be no forgiveness for serious sins after baptism.

The Odes of Solomon (first century) are a collection of beautiful songs or poems dedicated to Christ. One of the most plausible explanations of their origin is that they were written by newly baptized Christians in the first century.[44]

Origen of Alexandria (ca. AD 185–251) Origen was one of the most important theologians of the early church and produced some 2000 works, including commentaries on almost every book in the Bible. He was born of Christian parents in Alexandria. He eventually succeeded Clement as the head of the catechetical school there. Origen was an incurable speculator at a time when orthodoxy was not

---

42. Robert M. Grant, *Second-Century Christianity* (London: Society for Promoting Christian Knowledge, 1946), 69.

43. Fergusen, ed., *Encyclopedia of Early Christianity*, 654.

44. Platt, ed., *Forgotten Books of Eden*, 120; Grant, *Second-Century Christianity*, 11.

strictly defined, and later councils judged some of his doctrines heretical.[45] On the other hand, Edwin Hatch calls Origen's *On First Principles* (*De Principiis*) the first complete system of dogma in Christianity, and recommends the study of it because "of the strange fact that the features of it which are in strongest contrast to later dogmatics are in fact its most archaic and conservative elements."[46] Some of Origen's other important works include *Against Celsus* (*Contra Celsum*), a treatise against a second-century pagan critic of Christianity, *On Prayer* (*De Oratione*), and a number of scriptural commentaries and homilies.

The Pastor of Hermas: see "Hermas."

Papias (ca. AD 70–155) Bishop of Hierapolis, Papias wrote a series of five books about the gospel, of which only fragments have been preserved. He made a special effort to collect items of doctrine preserved orally by those who had actually heard the apostles speak.[47]

The Pistis Sophia is a group of Gnostic documents composed at various times during the third century in Egypt. Included in this work is a supposed conversation between Jesus and his disciples after his resurrection.

Polycarp (d. ca. AD 156) Bishop of Smyrna, Irenaeus claimed that he had been appointed to that post by the apostles themselves and was taught by the Apostle John. Polycarp

---

45. Wand, *A History of the Early Church to AD 500*, 72–76; Fergusen, ed., *Encyclopedia of Early Christianity*, 667–69.

46. Edwin Hatch, *The Influence of Greek Ideas and Usages Upon the Christian Church* (London: Williams and Norgate, 1914,) 323.

47. Fergusen, ed., *Encyclopedia of Early Christianity*, 686.

apparently wrote several letters to neighboring congregations, but only his letter to the Philippians remains. An early account of his martyrdom is also preserved, which describes various miracles accompanying that event.[48]

Pseudo-Clementines (second through fourth centuries) A collection of early Jewish-Christian documents, especially the *Clementine Homilies* and the *Clementine Recognitions*, pseudonymously attributed to Clement of Rome. Apparently, these works derive from a common second-century source document, adapted for various purposes over the next one or two centuries. They describe various travels of Clement, his conversion, and conversations with the apostle Peter. They were originally written in Greek, but the only extant version of the *Recognitions* is a Latin translation by Rufinus of Aquileia, who apparently made some emendations to the text. A number of conservative and Jewish elements are evident, as well as a distinct anti-Pauline bias, and many scholars consider them to be a product of a widespread branch of Jewish-Christianity of which we have no other witness.[49]

Secrets of Enoch: see "Enoch Literature."

The Secret Gospel of Mark (early third century?) In 1941, Morton Smith was looking through the library at an Orthodox

---

48. Fergusen, ed., *Encyclopedia of Early Christianity*, 742.

49. Fergusen, ed., *Encyclopedia of Early Christianity*, 768–69; Roberts and Donaldson, eds., *The Ante-Nicene Fathers*, 8:69–76.

50. For a popular treatment, see Morton Smith, *The Secret Gospel: The Discovery and Interpretation of the Secret Gospel according to Mark* (New York: Harper & Row, 1973). For a more scholarly treatment, see Morton Smith, *Clement of Alexandria and a Secret Gospel of Mark* (Cambridge, MA: Harvard University Press, 1973).

monastery in Mar Saba, near Jerusalem, when he found a document claiming to be a copy of a letter of Clement of Alexandria to Theodoret, a local church leader. Clement wrote that a document called the *Secret Gospel of Mark*, an expanded version of Mark's canonical gospel written by Mark after Peter's death, was in the possession of the church at Alexandria. However, the Carpocratian Gnostics had corrupted it to suit their agenda. Clement quoted an intriguing passage from the work and claimed that it was composed for those who were being initiated into the "great mysteries."[50] However, a number of scholars have expressed some suspicion that Smith forged the document. In fact, although Smith published photographs of the manuscript, it has been subsequently lost. However, Guy Stroumsa (a Jewish scholar at Hebrew University) claims to have seen the original in the monastery and that the librarian had told him that the manuscript had been removed for safe-keeping, and subsequently was lost.[51]

The Shepherd of Hermas: see "Hermas."

Tertullian of Carthage (ca. AD 155–225) Born to heathen parents in Carthage, Tertullian was trained to become a lawyer. When he became a Christian, he used his training to write tracts in defense of the church. Tertullian was an ordained a presbyter (elder), but eventually defected to the Montanist camp and wrote several bitter attacks against the Catholics.[52] Important works include *Against Praxeas* (*Adversis Praxean*), which is a treatise against Modalism (the idea that

---

51. For a summary of the details of the controversy, see Ehrman, *Lost Christianities*, 70–84.

52. Wand, *A History of the Early Church to AD 500*, 79.

the Father, Son, and Holy Spirit are one person who appears in three different modes), *On the Soul* (*De Anima*), *On Baptism* (*De Baptismo*), and *A Demurrer to the Heretics' Plea* (*De Praescriptione Haereticorum*), as well as many others.

Wycliffe, John (AD 1328–1384) English churchman, scholar, and diplomat, Wycliffe criticized the Papacy for being self-serving rather than serving others. This message was at first received well by the English court, which was constantly wrangling with the Papacy over its rights regarding taxation and temporal authority in general. However, Wycliffe soon began criticizing the civil authorities on the same grounds and fell out of favor. He taught Augustine's doctrine of predestination and argued against the dogma of transubstantiation. He is most famous for his English translation of the Bible.[53]

Zwingli, Ulrich (AD 1484–1531) Zwingli was a priest whose lectures on the New Testament in 1519 launched the Swiss Reformation movement.

---

53. González, *Story of Christianity*, 1:346–48.

Appendix B

Christian Councils

Barry R. Bickmore and Adam W. Bentley

During most of the Christian centuries, doctrinal and ecclesiastical disputes have been settled via councils of bishops and other ecclesiastical officers. Latter-day Saints have typically charged that these councils, and the creeds they produced, substituted worldly wisdom for the guidance of revelation. However, it is clear from our own history that Latter-day Saint leaders have sometimes preached contradictory opinions on issues of doctrine and practice, so the simple fact that Christians have sometimes been misled by the wisdom of the world cannot, in itself, be a foolproof indicator of apostasy. It is probably fair to say that all human beings have, to some extent, been limited by the wisdom of their times. Why, then, did God tell Joseph Smith that the Christian creeds "were an abomination" (Joseph Smith—History 1:19)? Joseph Smith said that, although the creeds of the different denominations all have some truth, "I want to come up into the presence of God, and learn all things; but the creeds set up stakes, and say, 'Hitherto shalt thou come, and no further'; which I cannot subscribe to."[1]

---

1. *Teachings of the Prophet Joseph Smith.* sel. Joseph Fielding Smith (Salt Lake City: Deseret Book, 1976,) 327.

In this appendix, a number of important councils are briefly described to give the reader a sense of the major issues that have confronted Christianity over the centuries, and the decisions regarding these issues that have been set in stone via the creeds. For a complete list of Christian councils and creeds and analysis of their contributions from an LDS perspective, see John W. Welch, "'All Their Creeds Were an Abomination': A Brief Look at the Creeds as Part of the Apostasy," in Prelude to the Restoration *(Salt Lake City: Deseret Book, 2004), 228–49.*

The First Council of Nicea (AD 325)

The First Council of Nicea was called by Emperor Constantine in an attempt to unify the church and resolve certain disagreements that had arisen in the church. Most importantly, a theologian named Arius, who had gained a large following, asserted that Christ as the Son was of a different essence than God the Father. Because the Son is a creation of the Father, he "had a beginning of existence; and from this it is evident, that there was a time when the Son was not. It therefore necessarily follows, that he had his subsistence from nothing."[2] At this time, nearly all Christian intellectuals assumed that God was a unique, eternally self-existent, spiritual being, completely distinct from all other entities, which were created from nothing. The orthodox response to Arianism was that the church had always believed that Jesus was truly God, and there cannot be more than one unique divine essence.[3] To resolve this problem, Constantine called the council, inviting 318 bishops, as well as priests, deacons, and other members of clergy. They

---

2. Howard A. Slaatte, *The Seven Ecumenical Councils* (Lanham, Maryland: University Press of America, 1980), 9.

3. Slaatte, *Seven Ecumenical Councils,* 10.

represented the majority of the regions where Christianity was established. Those attending consisted of three primary groups:[4] (1) the Nicenes, including Athanasius, who believed that the Father and Son were separate persons coexisting in the same being (2) the Arians and (3) a group J. N. D. Kelly called the "the great conservative 'middle party,'" who taught that there were three divine persons, "separate in rank and glory but united in harmony of will."[5] The council eventually rejected the Arian view and concluded that the Son and Father are "of one essence" and that the Son "came down from heaven and was incarnate" in order to redeem man.[6] Since the wording of the creed was acceptable to both the Nicenes and the middle party, the entire council accepted the creed, except Arius and two other bishops. They were consequently exiled to Illyria. In addition to addressing the debate over the doctrine of the Godhead, the council also issued a letter to all regions represented at the council proclaiming the Nicene Creed and a number of ecclesiastical canons. These canons outlined the jurisdiction of various bishops in provinces such as Rome, Alexandria, and Ephesus, and addressed the execution of priesthood and clerical duties that were passed at the council.

The First Council of Constantinople (AD 381)

Despite the conclusions made by the Council of Nicea, the church failed to unite the way that Constantine hoped. The East

---

4. Slaatte, *Seven Ecumenical Councils* 11.

5. J. N. D. Kelly, *Early Christian Doctrines*, 5th rev. ed. (San Francisco: HarperCollins, 1978), 247–48.

6. Slaatte, *Seven Ecumenical Councils*, 13, quoting *The Seven Ecumenical Councils*, in *A Select Library of Nicene and Post-Nicene Fathers of the Christian Church* (hereafter *NPNF*), series 1, ed. Philip Schaff and Henry Wace (New York: Christian Literature Co., 1890) 14:3.

did not accept the Nicene Creed as readily as the West, and Constantine himself, and some of his successors, leaned toward Arianism.[7] Theodosius the Great called the first Council of Constantinople to resolve the disagreements. The nature of this council was not as combative as the Council of Nicea, and its purpose was to expand upon some points of the Nicene Creed. The council added several clauses, expressing that Christ is incarnate "by the Holy Ghost of the Virgin Mary," and that after being crucified and buried, Christ "sitteth at the right hand of the Father."[8] The new creed also included a clause regarding the status of the Holy Ghost. "And (we believe) in the Holy Ghost . . . who proceedeth from the Father, who with the Father and the Son together is worshipped and glorified, who spake by the prophets."[9] Thus, in contrast to the Nicene Creed, the Creed of Constantinople includes the divinity of the Holy Ghost and acknowledges Christ's birth from the Virgin Mary. The canons passed at this council ratified the Nicene Creed, addressed jurisdictional issues, and placed Constantinople as second to Rome in ecclesiastical authority.[10]

The Council of Ephesus (AD 431)

The Council of Ephesus was called by the Co-Emperors, Theodosius II and Valentinian III, in response to a request by Pope Celestine. Celestine received a letter from Bishop Cyril of Alexandria asking him to condemn the teaching of Nestorius. Nestorius, the bishop of Constantinople, taught that in order for

---

7. Slaatte, *Seven Ecumenical Councils,* 15.

8. Slaatte, *Seven Ecumenical Councils,* 17, quoting the Constantinopolitan Creed, in *NPNF* 14:163.

9. Slaatte, *Seven Ecumenical Councils,* 17, quoting the Constantinopolitan Creed, in *NPNF* 14:163.

10. Slaatte, *Seven Ecumenical Councils,* 18–19.

Christ to be perfectly human and also perfectly divine, his parentage must be part human and part divine. Nestorius would not refer to the Virgin Mary as the "Mother of God," for her nature was human. Thus, in Christ's body God's nature coupled with human nature. Nestorius states, "We will separate the natures and unite the honor; we will acknowledge a *double* person and worship it as one."[11] It is not entirely clear what Nestorius meant by this, because the terms *person* and *nature* had more than one meaning.[12] However, Cyril considered this heresy, for, "if our Lord is God, and if he was born of the Virgin then the Virgin was certainly the . . . 'bringer-forth of God.'"[13] The council, having reviewed the Nicene Creed, affirmed the "one person" view of Christ and concluded that the Virgin Mary ought to be called the "Mother of God."[14] The council found Nestorius's position incommensurable with the Nicene Creed and condemned him. He died eight years later in exile.[15] The controversy at the Council of Ephesus illustrates how the church had to grapple with problems associated with the adoption of the view that the divine nature is completely distinct from human nature, and yet, Christ is both fully human and fully divine.

The Council of Chalcedon (AD 451)

Due to Cyril's victory at Ephesus, the influence of the Eastern Church grew considerably. After deposing Nestorius, the

---

11. Slaatte, *Seven Ecumenical Councils*, 20, quoting William P. Dubose, *The Ecumenical Councils*, 3rd ed. (New York: Scribner and Sons, 1900), xlix.

12. Justo L. González, *The Story of Christianity*, vol. 1, *The Early Church to the Dawn of the Reformation* (San Francisco: Harper & Row, 1984), 254.

13. Slaatte, *Seven Ecumenical Councils*, 20.

14. Slaatte, *Seven Ecumenical Councils*, 20.

15. Slaatte, *Seven Ecumenical Councils*, 21.

Eastern Church swung heavily toward the view that Christ, the incarnate Son, had only one nature, instead of two. In other words, the divine nature of God "absorbed" the human nature, leaving Christ clothed in a deified body.[16] Thus, after the incarnation, God and God's body were one, divine nature.[17] This doctrine, called *Monophysitism,* was condemned around AD 448 by Flavian, bishop of Constantinople, because it seemed to imply that Christ was not really human. (This may have been the case for some Monophysitists, but for most, their concern was simply that the divine and human natures in Christ might be so separated as to render the Incarnation meaningless).[18] In response to Flavian, Dioscorus, the patriarch of Alexandria, pressured Emperor Theodosius II to convoke a new council. The council convened again at Ephesus in 449, but Dioscorus took over the proceedings with his bands of Egyptian monks and terrorized the bishops present. Even though Pope Leo I sent a letter to Flavian dogmatically rejecting Monophysitism and was represented by legates, Dioscorus prevailed. Flavian was killed, the Papal legates were denied an audience, and the Pope's letter to Flavian was never read. But this victory was short-lived, for Pope Leo, hearing the news, called the council a "Robber Synod," and appealed to the emperor to convene another council.[19] This request was granted when Theodosius II died, and Emperor Marcian came to power in 451. Marcian changed the council's location to Chalcedon and regulated the council's security with imperial forces. Although the Western Church was only represented by four bishops (two of which were the Pope's

---

16. Francis Dvornik, *The Ecumenical Councils* (New York: Hawthorn Books, 1961), 25.

17. Dvornik, *Ecumenical Councils,* 25.

18. González, *The Story of Christianity,* 1:257.

19. Dvornik, *Ecumenical Councils,* 25.

legates) and the East had over 500 bishops present, the council ultimately condemned the acts of the Robber Synod. They read Pope Leo's letter attacking Monophysitism and concluded: "'We all confess unanimously one and the same Christ, Son, Lord, Only-begotten, made known in two natures [which are] without confusion, change, separation or division and which both meet in one person.'"[20] The bishops at this council began the practice of formally acclaiming the emperor. "'To Marcian, the new Constantine, the new Paul, the new David . . . you have the faith of the apostles . . . You are the light of the orthodox faith . . . Lord, protect the light of peace. . . . Many years to the priest-emperor. You . . . have set the Churches right, . . . doctor of the faith . . . Be your empire eternal.'"[21]

The Second Council of Constantinople (AD 553)

Nearly a century after the fourth ecumenical council, Emperor Justinian I called a council, without Pope Vigilius's consent, in order to win the support of the Monophysitists in the East. To do so, he proposed to condemn the "Three Chapters," which were the writings of three anti-Monophysitist theologians in Antioch.[22] While the council did condemn these writings, it stopped short of reversing the decision made at Chalcedon.

The Third Council of Constantinople (AD 680)

The decision that Christ is one person with two natures brought up another problem. That is, if Christ has two natures, does he also have two wills? Sergius, Patriarch of Constantinople, argued that a single person can have but one will, so the divine

---

20. Dvornik, *Ecumenical Councils*, 27.
21. Dvornik, *Ecumenical Councils*, 27–28.
22. Dvornik, *Ecumenical Councils*, 32.

will must have taken the place of the human will in Christ. (This view is called *Monothelitism*.) Others argued that a person without a human will is not fully human. The Third Council of Constantinople was called by Emperor Constantine Progonatus to discuss the issue of Monothelitism.[23] The council condemned Monothelitism, as well as Pope Honorius for accepting this view. The council concluded that "in him (Jesus Christ) *are two natural wills* . . . we say that his *two natures* shone forth in his *one* subsistence."[24]

The Second Council of Nicea (AD 787)

After the Empire became Christian, concern developed that the use of images in worship would lead converted pagans back into idolatry. The Second Council of Nicea was called by Emperor Constantine VI and Empress Irene to address the issue. Several edicts forbidding any kind of image worship or pictorial representations of Christ were issued by Byzantine emperors in the eighth century,[25] but the council decided to allow the veneration of images as long as the personages represented by the images, not the images themselves, were honored. The Fathers strictly distinguished between veneration of images and worship of idols and anathematized any who refused to salute the venerable images or anyone who called the images gods. The pope confirmed the Acts of the Seventh Council, and the East accepted them, although it took at least sixty years for this acceptance to become nearly universal.[26]

---

23. Dvornik, *Ecumenical Councils*, 33.

24. Slaatte, *Seven Ecumenical Councils*, 26–27, quoting *The Definition of Faith*, III Constantinople, in *NPNF*, 14:344ff (emphasis in original).

25. Slaatte, *Seven Ecumenical Councils*, 28.

26. Dvornik, *Ecumenical Councils*, 40.

The Council of Trent (AD 1545–1563)

The Council of Trent, which lasted for 18 years, was convened in response to the crisis caused by the Protestant Reformation. In the face of Protestant attacks against Catholic traditions and sacraments, the Roman Catholic Church formally discussed and defined every major item the Reformation had brought into question. For example, the council affirmed the authority of tradition and of the Vulgate (the Latin translation of the Bible prepared by Jerome in the late fourth century), defined the seven sacraments (i.e., ordinances) and the nature of the Mass as a true sacrifice, affirmed the necessity of good works in addition to grace, and defined the doctrine of purgatory. A number of badly needed reforms were also enacted. For example, the veneration of saints, relics, and images, and the granting of indulgences, were regulated. In addition, bishops were no longer allowed to reside outside their jurisdictions, it was forbidden that anyone should hold multiple ecclesiastical posts, the obligations of the clergy were defined, and requirements were set for acceptance into the ministry.[27]

The First Vatican Council (AD 1869–1870)

Faced with radical new philosophies in the fields of natural science and politics, the Roman Catholic Church found it necessary to formally define the doctrine of Papal Infallibility to head off trends that led some to call for the reformation of previously defined doctrines.[28] The doctrine of Papal Infallibility states that the Pope, when speaking in the discharge of his

---

27. Philip Hughes, *The Church in Crisis: A History of the General Councils 325–1870* (Garden City, NY: Hanover House, 1961), 322–23: González, *The Story of Christianity*, vol. 2, *The Reformation to the Present Day* (San Francisco: Harper & Row, 1984), 119–21.

28. Dvornik, *Ecumenical Councils*, 95.

office, cannot err when defining doctrine regarding faith or morals, and that such decrees are irreformable.

The Second Vatican Council (AD 1962–1965)

The Second Vatican Council, convoked by Pope John XXIII on 11 October 1962, addressed many concerns of Roman Catholics around the world about how to adapt the life of the church to the modern world. Against the objections of conservatives, progressive delegates won sweeping reforms that allowed the use of native languages and other local adaptations to the liturgy, promoted religious freedom (which had generally been rejected as an ideal by the popes of the nineteenth century), paved the way for increased ecumenism, and emphasized the need to address the plight of the poor. Pope Paul VI concluded the council in 1965 and initiated programs to ensure implementation of the council's directives. However, Paul VI was more conservative than his predecessor and took steps to make sure the reforming zeal fostered by Vatican II did not go too far. For example, a papal commission recommended that some forms of artificial birth control be allowed, but in 1968 the Pope issued the encyclical, *Humanae vitae*, in which all such methods were banned.[29]

---

29. González, *Story of Christianity*, 2:350–55.

Appendix C

New Testament Evidences and Prophecies of Apostasy in the First-Century Church

Noel B. Reynolds

It is usually assumed in discussions of a Christian apostasy that the early Christian church was able to hold on to its original teachings, behavioral standards, ordinances, authority, and organization well into the second or third century. Although problems are mentioned in many of the epistles, the usual assumption is that they were duly resolved, and that the church continued to grow and progress on the path which Jesus had established.

However, a careful reading of the New Testament text raises questions about this assumption. The text repeatedly reports serious divisions and only rarely reports resolutions (e.g. 2 Corinthians 7:9). Further, numerous passages indicate rather clearly that Paul, like Jesus before him, knew by prophecy that there would be a "falling away." Could this have occurred in the early decades after the death of Christ?

As I have collected these statements and worked on this problem over the last several years, I have had a growing realization that the New Testament seems to document a process of disintegration that was virtually irreversible. In city after city where Paul and other missionaries had established branches of the church, fast-talking, self-appointed men began to take over and to exploit the faith of Paul's converts for their own material and even lascivious benefit. The pattern appears to be common in the letters that Paul and others write to those members they see as being faithful. Further, the faithful often seem no longer to be in control of the local situation. The writings of Peter, James, Jude, and John all describe the same kinds of problems that Paul was addressing. We get a very consistent picture from all five witnesses of the decline of the church in their own lifetimes.

As we reflect on the administrative problems the early church faced, we have to be impressed with the impossibility of their task. No branch of the church had the benefit of experienced, second-generation leadership. Paul and the other apostles were themselves converts, with no established tradition or well of practical wisdom to draw on. Their writings make clear that the early leaders were not always on the same page themselves regarding major policy or administrative issues. And it is abundantly clear that they could only occasionally actually visit the scattered branches personally. Some letters show clearly that different social structures emerged, and there was nothing that anyone could do about it. Paul's emissaries were often ignored or demeaned. Even Paul's own authority is challenged repeatedly, and he finds it necessary to defend his claims to authority against the competition that has taken over locally.

The early church had no monthly reporting system and no instant communication. The mail system was slow, ad hoc, and unreliable. News was usually seriously out of date. Crises came and went on the local level without any intervention or guidance from the general authorities of the church. Travel was slow, dangerous, and difficult. The organizational and logistical systems that have contributed so dramatically to the unity of the modern church did not exist. Small wonder that the Christian world was in disarray by the second century, and that third-century Christians turned in desperation to Greek philosophy to bring back the "unity of the faith," that had been lost, probably even before the demise of the apostles. Small wonder that no writings have survived from that dark period in church history. The trials of faithful and humble Christians must have been excruciating as they witnessed the demise of Christ's church at the hands of self-promoting and entrepreneurial fellow members who strove with one another for dominance and fashioned new doctrines and interpretations to justify their presumed authority.

Following is a selection of scriptural references divided into two groups and summarized for what they say about this question. The first group lists prophecies of apostasy, and the second group reports examples of apostasy among the followers of Christ and his apostles. While different readers will choose different passages, I have settled on nine passages that seem to me to rather clearly demonstrate foreknowledge of the impending demise of the church. The list below features thirty-four passages where the writer is describing significant and troubling examples of apostasy in the New Testament period. There are many others which might have been included, but these thirty-four seem to be the most obvious and require little interpretation to make the point. And thirty-four is more than adequate to make the point that these local apostasies are common and pervasive. There are hardly any passages commenting on the successful repression of such apostasies. For me, this all adds up to a convincing case that there was widespread apostasy in the church even before the deaths of the

apostles, and that this provides the most convincing and readily available explanation for the dark period at the end of the
first century—almost no textual evidence remains from that
period that would explain how the church had become so dis-
united and confused by the early second century—it would
also explain why the apostles were not able to perpetuate themselves as a continuing organization of general authorities. This
left the church to devolve into a weakly associated world of cit-
ies with bishops and elders as local leaders without any higher
authority to coordinate them until the emergence of councils
and later the bishop of Rome and other regional leaders in the
east and in Egypt.

New Testament Prophecies
of the Demise of Christ's Church

Matthew 13:24–30

In the parable of the wheat and tares, Jesus describes the
kingdom of God being filled with tares sown by his enemy,
which are then allowed to grow until the harvest.

Matthew 24:5, 24

Jesus prophesies to his disciples that before his time comes,
many false prophets and false Christs or messiahs will arise,
deceiving many.

Acts 20:29–30

Luke records that Paul had called together the elders of
the church in Ephesus to hear his farewell. He pled with them
to take heed, for he knew that "grievous wolves" should come
among them "not sparing the flock" (v. 29), and that even

some of the elders themselves would "arise, speaking perverse things, to draw away disciples after them" (v. 30).

Romans 11:19–21

Paul warns the Roman saints that just as apostate Israel had been cut off, so would the Christians should they fail to "continue in goodness" (v. 22).

2 Thessalonians 2:3–4

Paul prophesies that Christ would not return before the "falling away" (v. 3)—the apostasy—and the son of perdition be exposed.

1 Timothy 4:1–3

Paul prophesies of future times when Christians will leave the faith and give "heed to seducing spirits and doctrines of devils; speaking lies in hypocrisy; . . . forbidding to marry, and commanding to abstain from meats."

2 Timothy 3:1–9, 12; 4:3–4

Paul speaks of a coming "perilous" (3:1) time when men, apparently affiliated with the church, will be wicked in so many ways, loving pleasures more than God. These "traitors" (3:4) will have "a form of godliness" (3:5), but they will deny the power that makes godliness possible in men. All that will live godly lives in Christ will suffer persecution (3:12). Apparently speaking again of these same traitors, Paul prophesies that in that future time, "they will not endure sound doctrine" (4:3), but will "turn away" (4:4) from the truth unto fables. And they will find teachers who will justify the indulgence of their lusts.

2 Peter 2:1–3

Peter prophesies not only that false teachers will come among the Christians, but also that many will follow "their pernicious ways" (v. 2).

Revelation 13:7

John is shown in his vision that the beast will "make war with the saints, and . . . overcome them."

Evidences of First-Century Apostasy from the New Testament

John 6:66

Many of Jesus's disciples left him because of his teachings.

Romans 1:8–32

Paul congratulates the Roman faithful and contrasts their case with that of those Christians "who hold the truth in unrighteousness" (v. 18), but who by their sins of idolatry, murder, homosexuality, and fornication have changed the truth of God into a lie and will receive severe judgment.

Romans 2:17–24

Paul confutes the Judaizers in the church who exalt themselves as circumcised Jews and defenders of the law, while they hypocritically commit all kinds of grievous sin and blaspheme the name of God among the Gentiles by their bad examples.

Romans 16:17–18

Paul recognizes that there are already some Roman Christians who "cause divisions and offenses contrary to the doctrine" (v. 17). These appear to be smooth speakers who deceive the simple believers with their "good words and fair speeches"

(v. 18), but not in the service of Christ, but rather to make a living for themselves.

1 Corinthians 1:11–12; 3:4

Paul describes the splintering of churches as church members begin to proclaim allegiance to different leaders, such as Apollos and Paul, rather than Christ.

1 Corinthians 4:18

Pride in the church at Corinth causes some to reject the words of the apostle Paul.

1 Corinthians 5:1, 6

Fornication and incest are named as sins committed by, or perhaps between, church members.

1 Corinthians 10:14

Some Corinthian saints begin to engage in idolatry.

1 Corinthians 11:18–22, 29–30, 34

There are divisions and heresies among the Christians at Corinth.

The Corinthians desecrate the sacrament by substituting for it pagan feasts.

Because they take the sacrament unworthily, they eat and drink damnation to themselves, and many have been made weak and sickly or have even died for it.

There are also other offenses which Paul hopes to straighten out when he comes.

1 Corinthians 14:1–37

There is confusion in the Corinthian church. Many are claiming to prophesy and to speak in tongues by inspiration. And the women, who should be silent, have joined in the fray.

Paul pleads for good order and peace, which would be an indication that they were guided by God's inspiration.

2 Corinthians 3:1; 7:2

Members begin to reject legitimate authority, and Paul's credentials appear to be questioned.

2 Corinthians 6:14–17

Paul pleads with the Corinthians to separate themselves from the heathens with whom they seem to be joined in their lives. Specifically they appear to be participating in idol worship at heathen temples

2 Corinthians 11:3–4, 12–15.

Paul argues to the Corinthian church that they should follow him rather than those who come preaching another Jesus, or another spirit or gospel. Paul recognizes his own weaknesses, but these others "are false apostles, deceitful workers, transforming themselves into the apostles of Christ" (v. 13). But if Satan himself can be "transformed into an angel of light" (v. 14), it is not to be unexpected that his ministers should "be transformed as the ministers of righteousness" (v. 15).

Galatians 1:6–9; 3:1

Local leaders and false teachers are changing the gospel of Christ and are preaching "another gospel" (v. 6) as the truth. Paul marvels that the Christians there are "so soon removed from him" (v. 6) to these teachers of other gospels, and he curses all who are preaching their own gospels.

Galatians 4:8–11; 5:7, 15–22

Paul bemoans the retrogression of the church membership for their disobedience, their backbiting among church members, and their observation of pagan and Jewish holidays. He calls on them to stand fast in their Christian liberty gained through the atonement of Christ and not to let themselves get entangled again with the works of the flesh—"adultery, fornication, uncleanness, lasciviousness, idolatry, witchcraft, hatred, variance, emulations, wrath, strife, seditions, heresies, envyings, murders, drunkenness, revellings, and such like" (5:21)—of which he has warned them before. The sense is clearly that some significant part of the Galatian members have returned to their sinful ways.

Ephesians 4:1–5:21

Paul describes for the Christians in Ephesus the kinds of lives, the unity, and spiritual consistency that they can enjoy, if they would live according to "the vocation wherewith [they] are called" (4:1). If they will heed his call, they can come to a "unity of the faith . . . unto the measure of the stature of the fulness of Christ . . . [and] be no more children, tossed to and fro, and carried about with every wind of doctrine, by the sleight of men, and cunning craftiness, whereby they lie in wait to deceive" (4:13–14). In the process he names a long list of sinful acts which are preventing them from leaving the world of the Gentiles and establishing a community of perfected saints. Paul calls them to stop walking "as other Gentiles walk, in the vanity of their mind" (4:17), with their "understanding darkened being alienated from God . . . because of the blindness of their heart" (4:18). As converts to Christ they are taught to put off works of greediness and lasciviousness. They must put away lying, anger, stealing, bitterness, evil speaking. He pleads with them to become "followers of God . . . walk[ing] in love" (5:1–2) If they would do this and be proper saints, such sins as fornication, uncleanness, covetousness, filthiness, foolish talk and jesting would never need to be named among them. But whatever the vain men among them might say, "no whoremonger, nor unclean person, nor covetous man, who is an idolater, hath any inheritance in the kingdom of Christ" (5:5–6). But all things which are shameful even to speak of, that are being done in secret, shall be "made manifest by the light" (5:13). Again he pleads with them that they be "not unwise . . . [and] drunk with wine" (5:17–18), but that they be filled with the Spirit.

Colossians 2:8–9, 18

Paul writes to the faithful brethren at Colosse and encourages them to stand fast in the gospel of Christ that he taught them and not to heed the beguiling men who seek to spoil them through philosophy and vain deceit, after the traditions of men.

2 Thessalonians 2:7–9

Paul calls upon the Christians of Thessaly to withstand the strong delusions and lying wonders of their times. If they can stand fast, they will obtain the love and glory of Christ.

2 Thessalonians 3:6

Paul further notes that the Thessalonians are supporting disorderly busybodies who do not accept Paul's epistles. He calls on local believers to separate themselves from such, and not to support their leadership.

1 Timothy 1:3–4, 6–7, 19–20

Paul explains why he left Timothy at Ephesus to call upon those Christians who were teaching false doctrines, "fables and endless genealogies" (v. 4), which only raise questions without edifying. These teachings have caused some to swerve and turn aside "unto vain jangling; desiring to be teachers of the law" (vv. 6–7) but without understanding. While among his own disciples, Timothy has been faithful, Hymenaeus and Alexander have blasphemed and "made shipwreck" (v. 19) of their faith, and Paul has delivered them to the buffetings of Satan.

1 Timothy 5:15

Paul advises Timothy about how to address growing domestic apostasies in the Church and acknowledges that through these problems, members have "already turned aside after Satan."

1 Timothy 6:1–10

Paul instructs Timothy on how to distinguish in the church between faithful teachers of godliness and those who are seeking the praise and riches of this world. The teaching of the latter group is marked by envy, strife, and "perverse disputings" (v. 5) that are destitute of truth. Those who love money rather than godliness "fall into temptation and a snare, and into many foolish and hurtful lusts" (v. 9).

1 Timothy 6:20–21

Timothy is further warned to beware those Christians who profess the faith, but who are engaged in "profane and vain babblings, and oppositions of science, falsely so called" (v. 20).

2 Timothy 1:8–18; 2:16–18; 4:14–17

Paul writes Timothy to encourage him not to be ashamed of his testimony of Jesus or of his affiliation with Paul. He cites two prominent Christians by name as examples and complains "that all they which are in Asia be turned away from me" (1:15). He excepts "the house of Onesiphorus" of Ephesus who "refreshed" Paul and was "not ashamed of [Paul's] chain" (1:16). Timothy is warned specifically to avoid "profane and vain babblings" (2:16); for they will increase unto more ungodliness, as in the cases of Hymenaeus and Philetus, who are teaching a false understanding of the resurrection. Further, Paul recites the specific case of a coppersmith who did Paul "much evil," for he "greatly withstood our words" (4:14–15). And no one of the congregation would stand with Paul against him.

Titus 1:10–14

Paul left Titus in Crete specifically "to set in order the things that are wanting" (v. 5). He is warned to be careful who he selects to be elders or bishops because "there are many unruly and vain talkers and deceivers . . . who subvert whole houses, teaching things which they ought not, for filthy lucre's sake" (vv. 10–11). Paul hopes that sharp rebukes may return them to soundness of faith, so that they will no longer give "heed to Jewish fables, and commandments of men, that turn from the truth" (v. 14).

Titus 2:1–15

Paul exhorts Titus to set the church in order, as all age groups from both sexes need to be raised from inappropriate behavior, that Christ might "redeem [them] from all iniquity and purify unto himself a peculiar people, zealous of good works" (v. 14).

Titus 3:9–11

Paul goes on to enumerate other failings of the members, which he seems to think can be corrected by Titus's teaching. But he also recognizes the serious dangers of those who are focused on "foolish questions, and genealogies, and contentions, and strivings about the law" (v. 9). If a man maintains his heretical position after being admonished a second time, Titus is to reject him as a sinner and subverter of others.

James 1–2

James recognizes that all are tempted and that the members of the church must not only speak the truth, but their lives must reflect comparable good works. Otherwise their religion is vain. In addition to other sins, he emphasizes the practice of despising the poor and ignoring the teaching of Christ to love their neighbor. For until their works meet these expectations of Christ, their faith is dead.

James 4:1–8

James describes "wars and fightings" (v. 1) among the Christians which arise from their own lusts. Calling them adulterers and enemies to God, he urges them to be humble and resist the devil, that God may cleanse their hands and purify their double-minded hearts.

2 Peter 2:1–22; 3:16–18

Peter warns the members against those of their own number who engage in all kinds of sins, including "damnable heresies" (2:1), covetousness, walking "after the flesh in the lust of uncleanness" (2:10), evil speaking, "having eyes full of adultery" (2:14). These have all gone astray. For having once escaped the world "through the knowledge of the Lord" (2:20), and becoming again entangled therein, and overcome, the latter end is worse with them than the beginning. They exemplify the proverbs of the dog that is turned to his own vomit and the washed sow that returns to wallowing in the mire (2:22). After discussing false teachings by scoffers in the church, he warns the members again not to wrest the scriptures or to be led away by the errors of the wicked, but to remain steadfast and grow in grace and in the knowledge of the Lord (3:16–18).

1 John 2:9–27; 4:1

John warns the members that any who hate their brothers are in darkness. He warns them not to love the world, the lusts of the flesh or the pride of the eyes, as these things are "not of the Father" (2:16). For "even now are there many antichrists" (2:18), that arose from within the church. But now they deny the Father and the Son. But the anointing which the members have received can protect them from these seducers. Further, because there are many false prophets, James teaches those who would be faithful how to distinguish the true from the false.

3 John 1:9–10

A prideful and apostate local leader, presumably an elder or a bishop, rejects apostolic authority and even excommunicates those who stand up for the apostles.

Jude 1:3–19

Jude writes to the faithful who he fears have been taken in by ungodly men who have crept in unawares, denying Christ and turning his grace into lasciviousness. Jude invokes Old Testament and other writings as examples and prophecies of this kind of thing and calls the ungodly among them "murmurers, complainers, walking after their own lusts; and their mouth speaketh great swelling words, having men's persons in admiration because of advantage" (v. 16).

Revelation 2–3

John sees the Son of Man, who commands him to write to the seven churches. Ephesus has done many good things, is now fallen and must repent, having left the Lord (2:5–6). The church in Pergamos has held fast against Satan, but harbors proponents of the doctrine of Balaam that eat meat sacrificed to idols and commit fornication. There are also Christians there who hold the doctrine of the Nicolaitans—which the Lord hates (2:12–16). In spite of many good works, the church at Thyatira permits Jezebel to pass herself off as a prophetess while seducing the Lord's servants to fornicate and to eat things sacrificed unto idols (2:18–20). There appear to be only a few members in Sardis who "have not defiled their garments" and who are worthy to walk with the Lord (3:1–6). Laodiceans focused on wealth, are comfortable and do not recognize their need for the Lord's aid. They are neither cold nor hot, and the Lord will spew them out (3:16–17).

Appendix D

Bibliographical Note on
Latter-day Saint Writings
on the Apostasy

Ryan G. Christensen

The idea that Christ's church no longer existed was central to Joseph Smith's prophetic claims, and as such was among the earliest of the doctrines established in this dispensation. Joseph quotes Christ as telling him during the first vision that he "must join none of [the sects], for they were all wrong; . . . that all their creeds were an abomination in his sight; that those professors were all corrupt; that: 'they draw near to me with their lips, but their hearts are far from me, they teach for doctrines the commandments of men, having a form of godliness but deny the power thereof'" (Joseph Smith—History 1:19). While there may be some debate about the specifics (which creeds and which professors),[1] the overall message is clear: there has been a universal apostasy; the true church of Christ is no longer on the earth.

---

1. See John W. Welch, "'All Their Creeds Were an Abomination': A Brief Look at Creeds as Part of the Apostasy," in *Prelude to the Restoration: From Apostasy to the Restored Church* (Salt Lake City: Deseret Book, 2004), 228–49.

It has been claimed that Joseph only later came to this understanding. His earliest account of the first vision, it is said, focuses not on this quest to find the true church but on a personal odyssey for forgiveness. But even this account states clearly that he had come to know that mankind "did not come unto the Lord but that they had apostatized from the true and living faith and there was no society or denomination that built upon the Gospel of Jesus Christ."[2] It may be true that he did not immediately understand this as a prophetic call, as were the theophanies of Moses, Lehi, and Isaiah (among many others); indeed, his initial reaction to his vision related only locally, if unequivocally, to the apostasy, in that he had "learned for [him]self that Presbyterianism [was] not true" (JS—H 1:20)

Later, the understanding of this concept was deepened to include a cosmic history, including the universal history of the earth as a cycle of dispensations and apostasies. Joseph understood himself as standing at the head of a chosen generation, a climax in this drama; following the greatest apostasy the world has ever seen comes the greatest dispensation the world has ever seen, the one in which all things would be restored, the one which would not end in apostasy, the one which would truly spread to all the world to prepare it for the great and dreadful day of the Lord. In a sense, this became the central teaching of Mormonism, what some scholars refer to as a "myth"; like the story of the fall and the atonement, for the followers of Joseph Smith the story of the apostasy and restoration came to define the world and their place in it.

Parley P. Pratt, for example, was quite emphatic that Mormonism is more ancient than traditional Christianity: Though

---

2. Milton V. Backman Jr., *Joseph Smith's First Vision: The First Vision in its Historical Context* (Salt Lake City: Bookcraft, 1971), 156.

many refer to the beliefs of the church as Mormonism, "they might as well have called them, *Abrahamism, Enochism,* or *Isaiahism*; because the ancient Prophets, Patriarchs, and Apostles, held to the same truths . . . according to the particular circumstances that surrounded them."[3] He goes on to say, speaking specifically about the doctrine of angels, "It is astonishing then, to me, that the modern Christian world consider this a new doctrine, an innovation—a trespass on Christianity. No! it is as old as the world, and as common among the true people of God, as His every day dealings with man. We will leave that point, and say, it is the Christian world, and not the Latter-day Saints, that have a new doctrine, provided they discard that principle."[4]

Many during the nineteenth century saw in the apostasy an illuminating precursor of contemporary apostasies. Just before he catalogues nineteenth-century apostates and their reasons for disaffection, George A. Smith speaks of the restoration: "When the Lord commenced his work, he . . . passed over the learned institutions of the day, and went into a field and laid his hand on the head of Joseph Smith, a ploughboy . . . whom he inspired, appointing him to translate the Book of Mormon, and authorizing him to proclaim the Gospel and administer the plan of salvation."[5] The apostasy was seen almost typologically, the great apostasy foreshadowing contemporary individual apostasies.

By the end of the nineteenth century, as part of the project to merge secular learning with spiritual truth, several attempts were made to historicize the doctrine of apostasy. Typically, the

---

3. *Journal of Discourses,* 1:298 (emphasis in original).

4. *Journal of Discourses,* 1:299–300.

5. *Journal of Discourses,* 7:111.

revealed doctrine of the apostasy was lined up with the available knowledge of history to explain or prove the apostasy within the conventions of secular scholarship. The first such attempts were by the great member of the Seventy and apologist B. H. Roberts, whose contributions to Mormon scholarship are arguably unparalleled. In addition to his *Comprehensive History of the Church*, he wrote several works on theology (*Seventy's Course in Theology, The Mormon Doctrine of Deity*, and his masterwork *The Truth, The Way, The Life*), history (*Outlines of Ecclesiastical History, The Falling Away*), and defense of the Book of Mormon (*New Witnesses for God*, as well as several manuscripts not meant for publication outlining his research program). His histories of the apostasy occur principally in his *Outlines of Ecclesiastical History* and his radio addresses collected and published under the title *The Falling Away*. Though not a professional historian, Roberts read widely and brought a wealth of self-taught learning to the topic of the apostasy. He described the controversies surrounding the death of the apostles and the subsequent changes in hierarchy, doctrine, and practice; he explained the corruption of the church through the Middle Ages as evidence of the falling away from the church of Christ; he outlined the secular and ecclesiastical changes that took place to allow a farm boy to start a new church. While Roberts's work was not, from a scholastic point of view, groundbreaking (he depended heavily on Protestant historians who were equally committed to proving the apostasy and corruption of the Catholic Church), his studies were seminal among Mormon letters.

Perhaps more visible to most Mormons is the work of Roberts's contemporary, the noted scholar and apostle James E. Talmage. Talmage's *Great Apostasy* is still, perhaps, the most widely read book on the topic. Talmage's approach to the apostasy is very similar to Roberts's, and he largely uses the same sources. Also dependent on Roberts's vision is Joseph Fielding Smith, who wrote on the apostasy in his capacity as church historian.

Following these early historicizing works, the apostasy was frequently the topic of instruction for priesthood quorums in the mid-twentieth century, with manuals being published in 1951–1956 and 1960. The basis of most of this work was the research of James L. Barker, a linguist and amateur historian. His three-volume *The Divine Church: Down through Change, Apostasy Reform, and Restoration* was studied from 1952 to 1954 and formed the basis of his posthumous 1958 work *Apostasy from the Divine Church*. The editor of this latter volume, T. Edgar Lyon, wrote the much briefer *Apostasy to Restoration*, which was used as the priesthood manual in 1960, and was based on the ideas in Barker's work.

In these works, the main focus is to identify causes or influences of the apostasy. Lyon lists the church's struggle for political power, changes in theology, a shift in the locus of salvation (from individual responsibility to a central church), and loss of priesthood authority.[6] Welker, in his 1955–56 priesthood manual *The Divine Church Restored*, has a similar list,[7] as do Barker and Milton Backman. It is during this period that serious scholarship begins on the historical apostasy, examining ancient sources and scholarly histories. The works of this period have been an important influence on later work.

Perhaps the greatest apologist since B. H. Roberts is Hugh W. Nibley, who has brought a stunning array of findings from many fields to his work of understanding the Book of Mormon, the Book of Abraham, the temple, and the apostasy. Three of his

---

6. T. Edgar Lyon, *Apostasy to Restoration* (Salt Lake City: Deseret Book, 1960), 4–9.

7. Roy A. Welker, *The Divine Church Restored* (Salt Lake City: Church of Jesus Christ of Latter-day Saints, 1955), 4:17–21.

papers written on the apostasy, originally published in non-LDS scholarly journals, have recently been collected in the FARMS publication *When the Lights Went Out.*[8] These three articles take three different approaches to show that the early church did not survive, and that historical Christianity lost some essential components of first-generation Christianity.

In his "Evangelium Quadraginta Dierum: The Forty-day Mission of Christ—The Forgotten Heritage," Nibley discusses the tradition of what happened during the forty days between Christ's resurrection and ascension, the time during which Christ was seen by the apostles and spoke "of the things pertaining to the kingdom of God" (Acts 1:3). Nibley first argues (against some who doubt it) that this did in fact take place—something happened, after all, to transform the zealous but insecure apostles at the time of the crucifixion into the pillars of the church described in the book of Acts. Then Nibley turns to examining what this means for the historical church. A favorite theme of apocryphal literature is the teaching of Christ during these forty days, many of the various groups in early Christianity attempting to assert legitimacy by claiming to have preserved the teachings or practice revealed during this time. Implicit in these claims is that something has been lost from mainstream Christianity, and the success of the various groups reveals that many recognized this fact. Nibley sees the loss of any teaching from the forty days as striking evidence that something fundamental is missing in the Christian tradition.

Much of the teaching that Nibley finds in the forty-day apocrypha concerns the temple, a theme he would elaborate in his "Christian Envy of the Temple." In this article he traces

---

8. Hugh W. Nibley, *When the Lights Went Out* (Provo, UT: FARMS, 2001).

various Christian views of the loss of the Jewish temple, finding ambivalence in these attitudes. On the one hand, Christians were embarrassed by the vestiges of paganism implied by a temple, but also envied the unity of the temple and were forced to result to rhetoric of a universal, intellectual, spiritual temple. They interpreted the temple's destruction in AD 70 to signify the triumph of Christianity over Judaism, but their excessive prohibitions against the Jews betrayed their fear that the temple ever should return. Through all this, Nibley discerns in the Christian writers a certain (often subconscious) envy, a feeling that God's church should have temples.

The piece in which Nibley argues most directly for his thesis that the early church did not survive is positioned first in the book, "The Passing of the Primitive Church: Forty Variations on an Unpopular Theme." In this paper, Nibley examines the practices of the early church and finds them strange if the early saints expected their church to survive, but perfectly natural if they expected it not to outlast them. For example, many essential matters of doctrine and policy were not published, the missionary program was not systematic (and the missionaries expected to be rejected and killed), and the church owned no property. Summing up, Nibley says, "The sensational change from the first to the second generation of the church was not, as it is usually depicted, a normal and necessary step in a long steady process of evolution. It was radical and abrupt."[9] Nibley also garners an impressive bundle of biblical and noncanonical writings in which he finds evidence that the early apostles did not expect the church to outlast them.

Nibley's lush assortment of proof texts has attracted criticism. Many of the passages he cites do not seem to prove his points; many of them seem to be taken out of context or even

---

9. Nibley, *When the Lights Went Out,* 18.

to be irrelevant to his thesis. For example, Nibley says, "As soon as the Lord departs there comes 'the lord of this world, and hath nothing in me'; in the very act of casting out the Lord of the vineyard the usurpers seize it for themselves, to remain in possession until his return;"[10] as support for this claim he lists four scriptures: John 14:30; Matthew 21:38; Mark 12:7; and Luke 20:14.[11] These scriptures are prophecies of Christ's coming death; if Nibley really intends for them to support his thesis that the church did not survive, he would have to date the apostasy at the death of Christ, something he probably does not want to do. In short, the criticism is that the New Testament does not provide evidence for the apostasy.

This criticism arises from the very nature of the New Testament itself. Unlike the Book of Mormon, in which a prophet outlasts the general apostasy of his day and chronicles the decline of the church, the New Testament was compiled and edited centuries after the texts were written by men who were committed to the thesis that the church had survived. While the Book of Mormon was written specifically for the benefit of saints of the distant future, the writings which became the New Testament were written for contemporary saints. Whatever the apostles may have written about the approaching apostasy or the eventual restoration would not have survived the textual controversies of those first few centuries. Rather, as contemporary scholars have argued, the texts that were selected and edited for the early Christian canon were shaped to support an emerging theological orthodoxy.[12] But as the appendix on "New

---

10. Nibley, *When the Lights Went Out,* 4

11. Nibley, *When the Lights Went Out,* 30, n. 18.

12. See Bart D. Ehrman, *The Orthodox Corruption of Scripture: The Effect of Early Christological Controversies on the Text of the New Testament* (New York: Oxford University Press, 1993).

Testament Evidences" demonstrates, a careful reading of the New Testament as it stands today provides a surprising quantity of often-overlooked evidence for disunity and corruption in the church within the first century after Christ. And the growing volumes of early writings that were not selected for the canon make this picture even more convincing.

In spite of the recurring criticisms, Nibley's work provided a cosmic scope that has proved to be a watershed in Mormon studies. Many later works revisit ground Nibley has covered before, attempting to chart in more specific detail the landmarks Nibley first noticed decades ago. S. Kent Brown and Wilfred Griggs, for example, have jointly authored papers on the forty-day ministry and the perspectives on Christ portrayed in apocryphal works.[13] Truman G. Madsen edited a volume containing Nibley's essays on the ancient temple, one of his perennial topics.[14] In many respects, FARMS itself is one of Nibley's offspring, as it has pursued many of the lines of research that Nibley pioneered.

Other writers have been less influenced by Nibley and seem to fall into a more traditional cast. Joseph F. McConkie's book *Sons and Daughters of God* explains in detail what amounted to a smaller section of the mid-century books, focusing on the loss of the doctrine of the literal fatherhood of God. He discusses

---

13. S. Kent Brown "Whither the Early Church?" *Ensign,* October 1988, 6–10; Brown, "The Postresurrection Ministry," in *Studies in Scripture, Volume Six: Acts to Revelation,* ed. Robert L. Millet (Salt Lake City: Deseret Book, 1987), 12–23 (in collaboration with C.W. Griggs); Brown, "Whither the Early Church?" in *Studies in Scripture, Volume Six: Acts to Revelation,* ed. Millet, 276–84.

14. Hugh W. Nibley, *Nibley on the Timely and the Timeless,* ed. Truman G. Madsen and Gary Gillum, 2nd ed. (Provo, UT: BYU Religious Studies Center, 2004).

different translations of the Bible from the Greek Old Testament (Septuagint) to contemporary versions, showing how the wording obscures—and in some cases has been purposely changed to eliminate—what the translators saw as embarrassingly primitive conceptions of God. Kent P. Jackson also published *From Apostasy to Restoration*, in which he traces the causes and consequences of the apostasy. He is sharply critical of the internal divisions and intellectualism of the early church, saying that false beliefs played a more prominent role than apostate practices in the New Testament period, and that the apostasy was caused not by persecution, but by internal intellectualism.[15] In a chapter in his comprehensive *Principles and Practices of the Restored Gospel*, Victor Ludlow treats the dispensation cycle, emphasizing the great apostasy and the restoration. Ludlow does not examine the causes of the apostasy, as other writers do, but he does propose a reason: Satan is trying to delay the second coming by keeping mankind in spiritual darkness. He also traces seven steps to apostasy and seven corresponding steps to restoration.[16]

Working independently of these traditions, Richard Bushman has critiqued many of the earlier approaches to investigation of the apostasy. He perceived that the approach of Roberts and Talmage was dependent on Protestant histories, themselves committed to demonstrating the falsity of the Catholic Church. "It would be interesting to know," he wonders parenthetically, if Roberts and Talmage "added anything to the findings of Protestant scholars."[17] Against Nibley he has

---

15. Kent P. Jackson, *From Apostasy to Restoration* (Salt Lake City: Deseret Book, 1996), 2–13, 21.

16. Victor L. Ludlow, *Principles and Practices of the Restored Gospel* (Salt Lake City: Deseret Book, 1992), 511–17.

17. Richard L. Bushman, "Faithful History," *Dialogue: A Journal of Mormon Thought* 4/4 (1969): 19.

a different criticism. Though he is impressed with Nibley's accomplishments and regards him as a watershed in Mormon scholarship, he has reservations about the charity of his approach as history. Seeing in the Mass of the medieval church a remnant of the temple ceremonies may accurately delineate its genealogy, but does not explain what it meant to those involved—they did not see it as a corrupted fragment, but as a living sacrament. Bushman's criticism of all the mid-century writers is similar: "Standard procedure thus far has been to list the doctrines of primitive Christianity and note departures as they occurred."[18] This comes in a review of Milton Backman's book, but applies just as well to Barker, and to Nibley, Talmage, and Roberts. Early in Christian history there is some concern about apostasy and the tension between revealed truth and philosophy, but these concerns soon disappear. It is unfair to them to impose on them our own framework for understanding their times, and thus "impose on them motives and tensions they never felt."[19]

Though he does not consider himself a student of the apostasy, Bushman has sketched an approach to the apostasy, seeing it as an expression of the fall. Mankind feels its fallen nature and so strives to recover its unity with God, and so long as revelation is forthcoming, that longing is fulfilled through the priesthood and the temple. Once revelation is severed, man seeks God in new ways, though originally the forms are the same. As time progresses, the content has changed so much it is only with difficulty that the forms can be recognizable as related to our own. But whatever the details, Bushman sees that much of the work

---

18. Richard L. Bushman, review of *American Religions and the Rise of Mormonism,* by Milton V. Backman, *BYU Studies* 7/2 (1966): 164.

19. Bushman, review of *American Religions,* 164.

done has only been a partial view of the apostasy, that the scholars who have contributed thus far have been pioneers, paving the way for new views and new understanding.[20]

The response of a range of LDS scholars to Bushman's call to new work on the apostasy, including the studies published in this volume, has been fueled by the impressive growth of new findings in early Christian history and related fields. In recent years, Latter-day Saint readers have seen a number of new works, more or less independent of the earlier traditions on the apostasy. In one example, Stephen Robinson wrote a paper challenging the usual reading of Nephi's vision of the apostasy in 1 Nephi 13–14, relying to some extent on New Testament apocrypha, and arguing against a facile equivalence of the "great and abominable church" with any specific group.[21] The 2004 Sidney B. Sperry Symposium at Brigham Young University provided a forum for several new studies that explored elements of the historical apostasy in new and informative ways.[22] Most recently, Alexander B. Morrison, an emeritus General Authority, has written a volume on the apostasy that is directed at the general membership of the church.[23] It draws on current scholarship, including a number of the papers now published in this volume, and early Christian writings to produce an updated and deeper LDS understanding of the great apostasy. It corrects many common misperceptions

---

20. See Bushman, review of *American Religions,* 161–64.

21. See Stephen E. Robinson, "Early Christianity and 1 Nephi 13–14," in *1 Nephi: The Doctrinal Foundation,* ed Monte S. Nyman and Charles D. Tate Jr. (Provo, UT: BYU Religious Studies Center, 1988), 177–91.

22. *Prelude to the Restoration.*

23. Alexander B. Morrison, *Turning from Truth: A New Look at the Great Apostasy* (Salt Lake City: Deseret Book, 2005).

while promoting greater appreciation for the contributions of faithful Christians across the centuries.

Annotated Bibliography

The following bibliography lists items that have been widely available or have had significant influence on the thinking of Latter-day Saints regarding the apostasy. It does not include a number of articles or manuscripts that are available in libraries or journals.

Backman, Milton V., Jr. *American Religions and the Rise of Mormonism*. Salt Lake City: Deseret Book, 1965. Backman analyzes the causes of the apostasy and discusses the religious scene in America at the time of the restoration.

Barker, James L. *Apostasy from the Divine Church*. Salt Lake: Bookcraft, 1960. T. Edgar Lyon produced this slightly reworked edition of *The Divine Church*. It marks a milestone in apostasy scholarship. This represents the first effort at reading and analyzing the primary texts.

———. *The Divine Church: Down through Change, Apostasy therefrom, and Restoration*. Salt Lake City: The Church of Jesus Christ of Latter-day Saints, 1952–56. This compilation of sources served as the basis for Barker's *Apostasy from the Divine Church*.

Chase, Daryl. *Christianity Through the Ages*. Salt Lake City: Department of Education of the Church of Jesus Christ of Latter-day Saints, 1944. The first half is a typical account of the apostasy—describing the beliefs and practices of the primitive church and outlining the history of changes to those beliefs and practices. The second half is a comparison of major Christian denominations, including the Latter-day Saints.

Clark, J. Reuben. *On the Way to Immortality and Eternal Life.* Salt Lake City: Deseret Book, 1949. These transcripts from radio addresses emphasize the apostasy.

Jackson, Kent P. *From Apostasy to Restoration.* Salt Lake City: Deseret Book, 1996. This is an overview of the apostasy and restoration for general audiences.

Lyon, T. Edgar. *Apostasy to Restoration.* Salt Lake: Deseret Book, 1960. This Melchizedek Priesthood textbook was based on Barker's *Apostasy from the Divine Church.*

McConkie, Joseph F. *Sons and Daughters of God.* Salt Lake City: Bookcraft, 1994. This book discusses the doctrine of God's physical body and literal fatherhood and how this doctrine was lost from mainstream Christianity.

Morrison, Alexander B. *Turning from Truth: A New Look at the Great Apostasy.* Salt Lake City: Deseret Book, 2005. This synthesis of emerging LDS perspectives on the apostasy is both readable and up-to-date.

Nibley, Hugh. *When the Lights Went Out: Three Studies on the Ancient Apostasy.* Provo: FARMS, 2001. Three reprints of articles published in non-Mormon scholarly journals which inspired a new generation of LDS scholars and brought the growing corpus of noncanonical texts from the earliest Christian centuries into center stage.

Roberts, B. H. *Outlines of Ecclesiastical History.* Salt Lake: Deseret Book, 1902. This was the first LDS attempt at historicizing the doctrine of the apostasy and borrowed heavily from Protestant histories. This book provides the content for Roberts's *The Falling Away* and, largely, for Talmage's *The Great Apostasy.*

———. *The "Falling Away": Or the Loss of the Christian Religion and Church.* Salt Lake City: Deseret Book, 1929. These transcripts of a radio lecture series have largely the same content as the earlier *Outlines*.

Sjödahl, Janne M. *The Reign of Antichrist, or the "Falling Away."* Salt Lake City: Deseret News, 1913. This derivative account of the atrocities carried out by agents of the Catholic Church identifies the period of apostasy with the reign of the antichrist foretold in the book of Revelation.

Talmage, James E. *The Great Apostasy: Considered in the Light of Scriptural and Secular History.* Salt Lake City: Deseret Book, 1909. For Latter-day Saints, this has long been the standard work on the apostasy.

Ward, J. H. *The Hand of Providence: As Shown in the History of Nations and Individuals, from the Great Apostasy to the Restoration of the Gospel.* Salt Lake: Juvenile Instructor Office, 1883. A universal history, beginning with the fall of Jerusalem, continuing through the rise of Islam and the Middle Ages, and ending with Joseph Smith.

Welker, Roy A, *The Divine Church Restored.* Salt Lake City: The Church of Jesus Christ of Latter-day Saints, 1955–56. This Melchizedek Priesthood textbook for the two years following Barker's *The Divine Church* focuses mainly on the restoration, but includes a brief overview analyzing the causes of the apostasy.

Young, W. Ernest. *Proof of the Apostasy.* Salt Lake: Deseret Book, 1960. This volume presents quotations from the Spanish Catholic bible, both scriptures and footnotes (with very sparse commentary), in English and Spanish on facing pages, and claims to demonstrate differences between biblical religion and Catholicism.

CITATION INDEX

INDEX

About FARMS

Brigham Young University's Foundation for Ancient Research and Mormon Studies (FARMS) encourages and supports scholarly work on Latter-day Saint scriptures and on selected subjects dealing with various aspects of the ancient Middle East and Mesoamerica. It publishes periodicals and books dealing with these topics, geared for a Latter-day Saint readership, while also working with scholars to get the results of their research published by various university presses aimed at academic audiences.

FARMS views the Bible and the Book of Mormon, as well as other scripture such as the Book of Abraham and the Book of Moses, as authentic, historical texts. Scholars whose work on these ancient writings and related subjects is supported by FARMS approach their topics using a number of disciplines ranging from history, linguistics, and literary and cultural studies, to geography, anthropology, archaeology, and legal studies. Such work that is done from a faithful perspective and that is grounded in solid research and is well thought-out and written, can shed light on the various ancient contexts from which these sacred writings emerged, can further scholarship in several related areas of study, and can significantly contribute to a better understanding of and appreciation for our LDS scriptural heritage.

Established as a private research organization in 1979, FARMS became part of BYU in 1997. At the time, Gordon B. Hinckley, president of the Church of Jesus Christ of Latter-day Saints and chairman of the BYU Board of Trustees, observed that, "FARMS represents the efforts of sincere and dedicated scholars. I wish to express my strong congratulations and appreciation for those who started this effort and who have shepherded it to this point." He concluded by noting that he sees, "a bright future for this effort now through the university."

The quality work supported by FARMS that is subsequently published either by FARMS or by other academic publishers, conforms to established canons of scholarship, is peer reviewed, and reflects solely the views of individual authors and editors. It represents an important contribution to the broad field of Mormon studies.

For more information:

FARMS
P.O. Box 7113
Provo, Utah 84602
800-327-6715
http://farms.byu.edu

To order publications:

BYU Bookstore
Provo, Utah 84602
800-253-2578
http://byubookstore.com